AF632328

Private Sector Participation in Public Services

Education

Private Sector Participation in Public Services

Education

Edited by

K.B. Saxena

AAKAR

Private Sector Participation in Public Services: Education
Edited by K.B. Saxena

© Council for Social Development, New Delhi

First Published 2022

ISBN 978-93-5002-762-2

All rights reserved. No part of this book may be reproduced or transmitted, in any form or by any means, without the prior permission of the Publisher.

Published by
AAKAR BOOKS
28 E Pocket IV, Mayur Vihar Phase I
Delhi 110 091 India
www.aakarbooks.com

Laser Typeset at
Sakshi Computers, Delhi

Printed at
Sapra Brothers, Noida

Contents

Preface 7
Foreword by Muchkund Dubey 11
Introduction 17

GENERAL

1. Public Provisioning of Services in the Context of Democracy 61
—*Prabhat Patnaik*

2. Experience of PPPs as Observed from Field Visits 64
—*Syeda Hameed*

3. Changing Perspectives: Neo-liberal Policy Reform in Education and Health in India 66
—*Kuldeep Mathur*

EDUCATION—PRIMARY

4. Private Schools, Religion and Commerce: Blurred Boundaries and Opaque Governance in India 85
—*Jyotsna Jha*

5. Public versus Private Provisioning of Elementary Education in India: A Trend in Privatization 102
—*Ashok Pankaj and Poornima M.*

6. Low-Fee Private Schools: A Global and Indian Perspective 127
—*Anjela Taneja*

7. Learning Crisis in School Education in India and Telangana: A Brief Analysis 153
—*D. Narasimha Reddy*

8. Public versus Private Provision of Elementary Education: Challenges Facing the Right to Education in India 178
—Kiran Bhatty

9. Enhancing Quality of Education Through Partnership: A Case Study of Vodafone Idea CSR Initiative in Education 199
—Nilay Ranjan

10. Privatization of Teacher Education in India: Virtual Capture of the 'Public' 214
—Poonam Batra

EDUCATION—SECONDARY

11. Education in Public and Private Schools in Telangana 243
—L. Reddeppa

EDUCATION—HIGHER

12. Private Higher Education in India 267
—Jandhyala B.G. Tilak

13. Public-Private Partnerships in Higher Education: An Interrogation of the Role of Private Sector Participation in the Context of India 283
—Saumen Chattopadhyay

14. Welfarism to Neoliberalism: State of Higher Education in India 303
—G. Haragopal and G. Sudarshanam

15. Privatization *is* Capitalism: Making Sense of the Educational Disaster in India 321
—Ravi Kumar

Contributors 345

Preface

India made a paradigm shift from a welfare to a market economy in the early 1990s as a result of the structural adjustment programme adopted by it at the behest of IMF. This entailed injecting substantial privatisation in both production and distribution of marketable goods and services which were hitherto undertaken in the public sector and dismantling controls to enable growth of the private sector. This shift also witnessed the Government's retreat from universal provision of necessary public goods and services to its citizens which are considered essential for leading dignified lives and transferring this responsibility in part or full to the private sector. This move was justified on the grounds that it would bring in additional investment for expansion of access to these services, improve the quality of their delivery, achieve financial and operational efficiency in their management and reduce corruption as a result of enhanced competition. This privatisation has been pursued through various structural forms, the most widely advocated and used of which is the public-private partnership. This withdrawal of state supply of public services, however, impinges on fulfilment of basic principles of constitutional responsibility, particularly equality, non-discrimination, ensuring life of respect and basic human rights for all citizens of the country and their democratic right to hold service providers accountable.

The working of the privatised model of provisioning of public services over the past more than two decades has resulted in adverse consequences for the poor and the marginalised groups. It was, therefore, considered desirable in the public interest to assess its rationale in terms of realisation of the claimed advantages of efficiency of investment, availability, access, cost and affordability to the users, coverage of difficult areas and disadvantaged groups and effectiveness of regulatory mechanisms in respect of pricing of services and their quality as also accountability of service providers to the service users. The issues to be covered also included how alternatives to privatisation practised in some states compare with both public and private production and distribution of services. This exercise was undertaken with evidence based papers invited for the purpose in a National Seminar organised by the Council for Social Development on March 28-30, 2016 at the India International Centre, New Delhi. The seminar dealt with six sectors of social development—Health, Education, Drinking Water, Sanitation and Waste Management, Urban Development and Housing and Electricity. The papers presented in the seminar along with a few which were specially sought to present a holistic picture of the subject are now being published. Originally intended as a single volume covering all six sectors, the publication has now been split into three independent books due to a larger number of papers in the health and education sectors as also considering the utility of the books to the users interested in a specific sector(s). This is the second book which covers exclusively the Education sector along with a few papers touching on the conceptual aspects and field experience. First book in the series covered the Health sector. The remaining sectors will be covered in the third book. Each book also carries a detailed introduction which besides discussing structural forms of privatisation in Public Services in India, also refers to the global debate on Public-Private Partnership. It follows up with tracing the evolution of private sector involvement in policy design on the provisioning of services in India in each of the sectors covered.

The publication of this series has been enormously delayed due to several unavoidable reasons the most important of which related to the Covid-19 Pandemic. This, however, has not diminished its relevance for researchers, policy makers and social activists working in these sectors. It is hoped that they would find it a useful source of reference for advocating alternatives to privatisation to mitigate its adverse consequences particularly for the poor and the weaker sections and underserved areas.

I am grateful to Prof. Muchkund Dubey, Chairperson, Council for Social Development for making this effort possible by providing financial assistance for the seminar and also writing the Foreword to this volume. It is also necessary to mention that the idea to discuss this important subject originated with Prof Imrana Qadeer, Distinguished Professor, Council for Social Development who persuaded me to organise the seminar and also helped in crystallising the issues to be discussed. The late Anita Kaul, the then Director, Council for Social Development provided the needed logistics support. I also thank all the scholars who have contributed their papers to this volume and have persevered with the delay in publication. Jayalakshmi Nair, senior research associate, cannot be thanked enough for attending to all the operational aspects of this effort right from the stage of correspondence with contributors for getting the papers for the seminar to the publication of this volume. The patience with which Dev Dutt, computer assistant, ungrudgingly typed out the introduction with its several revisions and Gurmeet Kaur who readily met the demand for library support is acknowledged with appreciation. Thanks are also due to Aakar Books for retaining interest in the publication of this series despite setbacks caused by the Covid-19 Pandemic.

K.B. Saxena

Foreword

A central feature of the Indian Constitution is that in its Chapters on Fundamental Rights and Directive Principles of State Policy, it contains a social contract between the state and the citizens of the country, to provide to the latter minimum necessary goods and services essential for leading a decent life and realising, to the maximum extent possible, their full potential. These goods and services are in the nature of public goods which the state alone is capable of and is, in fact, obliged to provide. It is also a fact that the poor people of India cannot afford to purchase these goods and services from the market, assuming that they are available there in sufficient quantities and in good quality. Let us for example, take the case of education. The private sector is in no position to ensure universalisation of quality school education within a finite period of time. The atomistic agents in the market place, each motivated by the urge of profit maximisation, cannot together come to an agreement, let alone take action, for the universalisation of school education from early childhood to the higher secondary level. That is the reason why the provision in Article 45 in the Directive Principles of State Policy of the Constitution, to provide free and compulsory education for all children in India till they complete the age of 14 years, could not be implemented. That is also the main reason why the policy measure adopted by successive governments after the expiry of this stipulated period of 10 years did not result in universalisation of early childhood and primary education.

The prospect for realising this vision appeared near reach only with the enactment in 2009 of the Right of Children to Free and Compulsory Education Act.

But this prospect was marred by the provision in the same Act for reliance not only on public schools but on a hierarchy of schools, including various categories of private schools. The significance of the Act was further diluted because of the exclusion from its mandate, of early childhood and secondary education. Later, for secondary education, the government announced its intention to establish one model school in each district of India in the Public-Private-Partnership (PPP) mode. This mode has recently emerged as a new form of privatisation not only in India but also in other countries of the world. This is one of the most pernicious forms of privatisation because it involves almost the complete blurring of the accountability of the private sector. And it has proved more difficult to implement in social sectors than in other sectors. In India, privatisation of school education has assumed other forms like closing down of public schools and merger of these schools, thereby opening avenues for the entry of private operators in the space vacated by the closed down public schools.

The same is the case with the provision of primary health services to the citizens of India. The main difference here is that privatisation in the health sector has gone much further than that in the field of school education. The private sector has emerged as the main health service provider, far outstripping the public sector. The private operators have never been interested in reinvigorating, expanding and improving the quality of primary healthcare services which are likely to benefit mostly the poor people who cannot afford to buy such services from five-star hospitals. In any case, such hospitals are located primarily in the urban centres whereas the primary health centres are needed most in the rural areas. What is true of health and education is true of the other goods and services designed to serve the interest of the poor, like food, nutrition and shelter.

In India, which carried a huge backlog of massive poverty from the colonial era, it was necessary to enter into the social contract of the type mentioned above. This was necessary to ensure the survival of the poor at the minimum level of necessity, and provide them minimum security and individual dignity. The supply of public goods to the citizens of the country is required also for serving such wider purposes as facilitating development, setting an example for the rest of the economy, as a guarantee against market failures which these days tend to be quite spectacular, engulfing the entire economy, and to provide a minimum guaranteed income and safety net. That is the reason why a large part of the GDP and budgetary resources of developed countries are devoted to providing good health and education services. In some of these countries, the state assumes the responsibility of providing even university education almost free of cost to its students.

Unfortunately, in India more than 60 years of development effort has not resulted in the elimination of poverty which in absolute numbers is still massive. That is why the state is still called upon to guarantee to its citizens the availability of minimum necessary goods and services.

The process of privatisation on a large scale was launched in the Indian economy as a part of the policy of full-fledged liberalisation adopted by the Government of India in the early 1990s. At that time, several advantages were claimed for it. For example, it was stated that it would provide greater access to goods and services to consumers in the country. It was also argued that it would give incentives for the establishment of new and additional industrial units and those for providing services. It was also argued that introduction of enhanced competition by way of removal of constraints would result in a reduction in the prices and fees for goods and services. Finally, it was claimed that privatisation would reduce corruption which had become endemic to the Indian economy, particularly in the public sector. Thus, privatisation was touted as a significant reform of governance.

Subsequent events belied all these claims and expectations. Instead of opening the door for new entry of firms, the privatisation process pushed out of the market small self-employed suppliers of goods and services. Those who stepped in to occupy the space vacated by the public sector enterprises, were the big business houses of India, and foreign multinational corporations with which these Indian enterprises were linked through financial dependence and management control. The big businesses raised the prices for the supply of services like water and electricity which were outsourced to them. Privatisation no doubt eliminated the cases of petty corruption indulged in by government functionaries at the lower level. However, in its place it introduced large-scale corruption indulged in by senior officials and political leaders in the process of negotiating the terms and conditions of outsourcing or issuing contracts. The earnings from these cases of corruption were used for financing elections and for lining the pockets of the high and mighty.

As regards the claim for introducing market stability, there have been far more numerous cases of market failures since ushering in the policy of liberalisation than during the decades preceding it. And these market failures have more often than not, engulfed the whole economy, and at times the global economy. The last mentioned phenomenon has occurred mainly in advanced industrial countries, particularly the United States and Europe, but has hit the developing countries also very hard.

This led the state in developed countries to intervene on a very large scale in their respective economies. They have incurred public expenditure on a massive scale to rescue failed or failing manufacturing companies and banks. They have also injected a vast amount of resources into their economies to bolster investments in social sectors like health, education, old age pensions and guarantee of minimum income for those most adversely affected by the consequences of market failure. Today it has become difficult to make a distinction between these market economies and those still largely under state control, as in the case of Russia and China. It is also equally difficult to make out whether in the current global situation, nations are liberalising or conferring back new roles and responsibilities on the public sector.

In spite of these global trends, several emerging economies, like that of India, are continuing to neglect their public sector, provide incentives for the operation on a much larger scale of the private sector and remove the remaining regulatory restrictions on their operation. A direct result of this policy has been further impoverishment of the poor, and greater marginalisation of the marginalised. These sections of the population were primarily dependent on public provisioning, at a very low cost or minimum cost, of services like health, education and housing. The state had earlier assumed the role of the primary supplier of these public goods. The withdrawal of the state from the provisioning of these services has made it difficult for the poor to obtain these services at a price which they can afford. The alternative of tapping the private sources for the supply of these services is too expensive for them and, often, is not of a good quality. Thus the overall trend of privatisation has deepened the crisis facing the Indian economy.

It is in view of these far-reaching adverse consequences for the poor, of the withdrawal of the state from the provision of public goods that the CSD organised a seminar on the subject in 2016. The idea behind the seminar was to discuss on the basis of technical papers, the experience with privatisation in the social sectors, assess its rationale and consequences and suggest measures for reversing or countering its adverse effects. The areas covered for discussion in the seminar were health, education, drinking water, sanitation, municipal waste management, urban development, housing and electricity. The papers prepared for the seminar and some received thereafter, are intended to be published in a series of three books—one on Health, another on Education and the third one on the remaining areas.

These three books in the series will constitute a unique contribution to the study of the phenomenon of privatisation in social sectors. The chapters in these books are based both on analytical studies of data drawn from secondary sources as well as primary data gathered through field visits. I strongly commend this series to researchers, policymakers and activists working in the relevant social sectors covered in these books. They are likely to find it a very useful source of reference as well as a basis of advocacy for reversing the trend of privatisation of social sectors and putting in place an effective regulatory system to mitigate its adverse consequence.

I cannot conclude this Foreword without expressing my deep sense of gratitude to Prof. K.B. Saxena for his remarkable introduction to the volume and stupendous effort made by him in obtaining chapters from prospective writers, for inclusion in these volumes.

Muchkund Dubey

New Delhi
December 17, 2021

Introduction

Private Sector Participation in Public Services

An Overview of the Social Sector

The hallmark of a democratic polity lies in a morally binding social contract between government and citizens manifested in the former's political commitment to pursue social goals which are widely accepted as essential human rights. The core of this contract is the universal provision of public services that satisfy human needs and creation of essential conditions for individuals to lead dignified lives and realize their human potential (Bayliss and Kessler, 2006). In India, the essentials of this social contract were built into the Constitution itself which put pressure on the state to make these services available to all its citizens. The government chose to discharge this responsibility by making these services available through state-directed, state-driven and publicly financed production (facilities creation) and distribution of these services. This mode of provisioning of these services emerged naturally from and integrated well with the political economy of the time which subscribed to the state control over key sectors of the economy and regulation of the private sector therein so as to fit into the larger framework of planned development. These public services/utilities were seen as public goods to be available to all citizens free of cost and without discrimination. The state, therefore, created infrastructure for production of these services and also undertook to distribute them to individual households. These services which included drinking water, sanitation, electricity (with user charges), education, health and supply of foodgrains, were delivered within the limits of its financial capacity with varying degree of efficiency, adequacy, and access to them by different social groups, and user satisfaction.

Improvements were made in policy design and execution of these services on the basis of feedback gathered from their delivery from time to time. This continued by and large, till the 1980s. Several of these sectors despite the policies of equitable distribution showed evidence of distortions and inefficiencies and failure of access to them. However, instead of addressing these deficiencies, a fundamental shift took place in the economy as a result of Structural Adjustment programme adopted by the country. Injecting substantial privatization in both production and distribution of marketable goods and services and dismantling controls which acted as barriers to entry and growth of the private sector were proposed to be the only way out of the morass. This was expected to help the government reduce fiscal deficit, attract private, particularly foreign investment, improve productivity and efficiency in various economic activities.

This shift also extended to the state's role in production and distribution of public goods and services by transferring this responsibility in part or full to the private sector. The directional change was also rationalized as an economic solution to investment constraints and fiscal deficit and an institutional solution to governance weaknesses in state-delivered services. It was also advocated as a poverty reduction measure which would enable expansion of access to these services in the absence of state provisioning (Bayliss and Kessler, 2006). This reform towards privatization and commercialization entailed recovery of most or all its cost from the users to enable a fair return on investment. While this shift is increasingly penetrating the Indian economy including the social sector due to international donors' pressure, persuasion and loan conditionalities (Hall, 2015) as also the influence exerted by the private sector and economists of neoliberal thinking within the country, it has essentially undermined the social contract between citizens and the state (Bayliss and Kessler, 2006). This is an account of gradual withdrawal of state's commitment to provisioning of services and shifting its focus to overseeing the process of privatization. The reforms converted the citizens into users and eroded their role of holding the service providers accountable through the democratic process (Ibid); (Starr, 1987). This model of economic reforms has provided distinct advantages for the participating private agency (Hall, 2015). It enables the private sector participants to determine/influence, the design, financing, construction, operation, maintainance and distribution of public services and utilities and optimize its profits.

In the Indian economy, this private sector participation has taken various forms. These include financing of public services with recovery of cost and forcing public providers of services to partially generate their resources so as to reduce public expenditure, outsourcing of functions by public sector agencies to private suppliers, reimbursement from public funds of services rendered by private service providers, exposing public sector producers to compete with the private sector, incremental withdrawal of public services and thereby forcing users to access privately funded services, transfer of management of public funded service provider institutions to private sector agencies, sharing responsibility of implementation of public funded programmes with the private sector, permitting establishment of private sector funded facilities in the premises of public institutions with a view to improving productivity and efficiency. It's most crystallized and widely advocated and used form is the Public-Private Partnership.

'A Public-Private Partnership is a contract between the government and a private company under which the latter finances/builds/operates or undertakes all three or some elements of public service and gets paid over a number of years, either through charges paid by users or payments from public authority or a combination of both' (Hall, 2015) and non-monetary subsidies such as concessions relating to land, developed infrastructure, trained personnel, provision of public space for setting up services and transfer of established public institutions to be run privately. The contract envisages selection of a service provider through competitive bidding and negotiation, mechanism of payment by public agency to private service provider, risk and revenue sharing between the two, monitoring and evaluation by the public sector agency. This partnership has taken varied forms such as:

- Public funding with private service delivery and private management.
- Public as well as private funding with private delivery and private management.
- Private funding with private service delivery and private management.
- Public as well as private funding with public/private/joint management.

Though PPPs have come into use since the 1990s, but concessions to a private agency by the government existed earlier too for development of water and energy resources and transport the cost of which was paid by the consumers or the government. This arrangement provides an attractive business opportunity to private/corporate agencies as it assures a long-term flow of income guaranteed by the government itself (Hall, 2015). In India, various forms of private sector involvement in public services indicated above are loosely termed as public-private partnership. This partnership also includes partnering with the voluntary/NGO sector, (Van Dijk, 2008) which are labelled as private sector for no profit. In social development, this structural collaboration has been used in education, health, poverty alleviation, urban development and housing, drinking water, sanitation and waste management, (Planning Commission 2004) electricity. However, PPP's more extensive usage is in infrastructure projects.

Private-public partnerships are widely claimed by the governments as a win-win situation for both parties, private and public (Van Dijk, 2008), which in effect they are not. This institutional arrangement has come in for strong criticism across the countries, developed as well as developing, including India. The key issues raised in their evaluation for assessing their performance in terms of stated objectives include (Hall, 2015):

- Cost of capital
- Cost of construction
- Efficiency of execution
- Transaction cost
- Uncertainties created by incomplete contracts
- Impact on public policy, public services and different social groups

In their enthusiasm for PPPs, the governments usually refrain from comparison with public sector production and distribution of goods and services in terms of value for money and opt for them irrespective of the cost they involve (Hall, 2015). This 'value for money' objective is crucial because public services have multiple public interest objectives (Hall, 2015; Starr, 1987). On the distribution side, these objectives include availability, cost and quality of services, coverage of difficult areas and access of the poor, and particularly disadvantaged/vulnerable groups, users' capacity to pay, etc. On the production side, the objective of achieving economic efficiency is paramount which can be assessed from multiple parameters such as cost of capital, extent of profit, cost of production/construction, degree of competition (cartelization), transaction cost, timely delivery, environmental impact, operational flexibility and element of risk. International evidence has shown that in terms of all these parameters, public investment alternative of production, development and distribution of public services (and even of infrastructure creation) is a superior one as it gives several advantages (Hall, 2015; Bayliss and Kessler, 2006). Public agencies can raise cheaper capital, have greater flexibilities, control and comparative efficiency due to reduced transaction cost and uncertainty of execution, and achieve efficiency gains due to democratic accountability. This alternative also avoids fiscal instability and provides protection against risks (Hall, 2015).

The other consideration against the PPPs is that government agencies have been found to have poor capacity to draft, regulate and enforce contracts which is exacerbated by asymmetry of information available with the government and the private agency (Baru and Nandy, 2011; WSP, 2011; Bayliss and Kessler, 2006). They lack bargaining power and negotiating experience leading to renegotiation, to the advantage of the private party. After winning the contract, the private agency uses control over information to seek major changes and create conditions which make cancellation of the contract difficult (Bayliss and Kessler, 2006). Regulatory agencies to address these issues are ineffective particularly in evaluating pricing of service and assessing productivity and quality due to supply of inadequate and distorted information by the private agency which results in higher pricing and low quality of delivery (Ibid.). PPPs also induce the state to cut back its expenditure (reduced budget provision) on these services, resort to contractual nature and insecure jobs which demotivates service providers in public provided services. These impact the quality of services, erode state capacity to meet the needs of citizens and lack of public trust in it (Ibid.). Long-term concession with assured revenue backing enhances corrupt practices. UN Survey findings point to the roads and power sector which are hot beds of corruption in India (Hall, 2015). Even the much touted injection of private capital to overcome resource constraints turns out to be illusory as the bulk of private investment comes from tax payers or end users in the form of Public Finance and | or guarantees from governments and development banks (Arral, 2009; Hall, 2015; Bayliss and Kessler, 2006). Besides, the high cost of privately financed services forces people to divert funds for meeting essential needs like food with its negative consequences (Bayliss and Kessler, 2006).

Private Sector Participation in Public Services/Utilities in general has also come in for strong criticism for other reasons. PPPs fail to bring in extra money/additional capital, or transfer risk to the private entity, underestimate costs of investment and exaggerate demand for services leading to higher prices for services. They also distort policy priorities, damage environment and crowd out space for spending on other services and erode the status of workers, their security and their organization (Hall, 2015). The private sector is disinterested in services used primarily by the poor and in areas predominantly inhabited by them (Bayliss and Kessler, 2006). It, therefore, resorts to cherry picking, i.e., concentrating on services used by the more affluent sections and areas inhabited by them (NFED, 2006). Private sector insurers are known to do cream skimming of clients. Private entity is risk averse and seeks guarantees for profitability. The state therefore, bears the risk which disincentives competition (Ibid.). The services are overpriced and there is no guarantee of quality. The social composition of beneficiaries narrows. Equity objective (access of the poor) is hit hard as the sections which need the services most get excluded (Ibid.). It also leads to differentiation in quality of services among different sections of population depending upon capacity to pay. The richer sections opt out of the public system which reduces pressure on the public system to improve (Ibid.). This arrangement also promotes greater influence of private entities in public decision-making and weakens their public scrutiny and accountability. Regulation of the private sector becomes ineffective due to resistance, under supply of information and high cost of monitoring. Persistent propaganda against public sector production and distribution of services erodes public trust in publicly provided services and undermines the legitimacy of the state and its responsibility (Bayliss and Kessler, 2006).

This is not to ignore the weaknesses in state-produced and delivered services particularly to the low income households, which essentially emerge from inadequate provision of funds, poor governance and social exclusion and need to be addressed (Ibid.). Resource constraints can only be addressed by expanding taxation and not by user fees. Governance weaknesses can be overcome by a transparent, fair and farsighted human resource management and an effective mechanism of accountability of service providers to service users/citizens. The latter needs to be pursued with input of technology, organization of users, vigorous involvement of civil society organizations and strengthening local level democratic structures. (PRIs in the Indian context). Social exclusion could be neutralized through a participatory evaluation mechanism to assess whether benefits have reached the vulnerable groups, public funding of basic services and strong political commitment to equitable allocation of resources towards vulnerable groups and their effective involvement in designing and implementation of programmes (Ibid.).

Despite the negative dimensions of private sector involvement in production and/or delivery of public services, the push towards privatization is being more aggressively pursued in the current dispensation and is also accompanied by fiscal consolidation with reduced expenditure on the social sector which adversely impacts human capital formation and poverty alleviation. The planning process has been abolished. Five Year Plans have been replaced by a 15-year plan. The distinction between plan and non-plan expenditure has been removed. Some of the critical social sector schemes have been transferred to the states with reduced share of central funding which is justified on the ground of increased devolution of taxable resources to states by the Fourteenth Finance Commission. Direct cash benefit transfer and insurance are being increasingly resorted to as the preferred mode of supply of services. These developments have further aggravated existing unequal access to and quality of public services.

Although PPP has emerged as the most preferred form for development of infrastructure, particularly physical such as roads, transport, ports, buildings with India ranking second in developing countries as per Private Participation in Infrastructure Database of the UN, both by number of PPP projects as well as associated investments (as on January 2014) these PPP projects are floundering (Pratap, 2014) as there is a high rate of project failure and cancellation particularly in water and sewerage projects (Pratap, 2016) as a result of which there is a clamour for reversal and putting public agencies back in position. Operational and financial efficiency is projected as the strongest argument in favour of private sector delivery while the reverse is considered characteristic of public provisioning of services. This hype in favour of the private sector has unravelled due to its opportunistic behaviour. Over the years, many private sector projects have sought relief for 'unforeseen events' as well as 'renegotiation' of contracts. Many other projects are stalled and stressed. This has undermined sanctity of contracts (Pratap, 2014).

Regulatory mechanisms which are the bedrock of impartial enforcement of laws and protection of consumer interests as well as environmental health have failed to inspire confidence in their intellectual integrity, transparent functioning and consistent objectivity (Delhi High Court cited in Pratap, 2014). This has created regulatory uncertainty which undermined their credibility. These bodies are afflicted with pliable appointments, lack of autonomy and accountability. Also, economic regulation is privileged over environmental and consumer protection (Ibid.). This is compounded by lack of strong accountability to support contract oversight and performance evaluation (WU, 2016; NFED, 2016).

PPPs have also been assessed as governance failure. There is marked tilt in favour of private party against public agency and 'Value for Money' has been grossly disregarded (Hall, 2015). In fact, VFM is not even a requirement for PPP projects in India which is a serious lacuna and has brought marginal returns for the government (Pratap, 2014). There is a shift towards separation of construction from operation and maintenance of PPP projects relating to infrastructure which is a major driver for value for money. Lack of due diligence is observed in designing and monitoring contracts.

PPPs have been pushed by governments and funding agencies and are backed by huge information offensive against public provisioning and management of public services in various spaces of public discourse. This negative rhetoric of public service bashing is integral to the neo-liberal political objective (McDonald and Ruiters, 2012). As against this, counter information in favour of the public sector is not as 'vigorous, voluminous, consistent, sophisticated or sufficient' (Ibid., p. 497) as that of favouring the private sector. While reclaiming public service provisioning there is also a need to recognize the poorly run public sector services and to make them 'more participatory, more democratic, more equitable, more transparent, more environmentally sound (Ibid., p. 6) and cost reducing and cost effective. It is also necessary to take care of the concerns raised in the debate on reforms and particularly in respect of access of marginalized sections, SCs/STs, women, children, minorities and disabled persons to services.

In the context of this overview of privatization of public services, as emerging from academic writings and empirical evidence across the world, we will examine the experience of privatization and PPP projects in the social sector in India with a view to assessing their utility and rationale. This has been attempted in a series of three books which map out critically the status of private sector involvement in areas of health, education, drinking water, sanitation, municipal waste management, urban development, urban housing and electricity and conclude with an overall assessment of this significant structural shift in political economy and governance and its social impact. This book covers the major area of educational services besides a small section on general assessment of privatization in essential public services. Another book in the series covers the health services and the third with the remaining other services. The following pages attempt to trace the growth of private sector participation in the educational services and discuss critical issues relating to it.

Education

Primary Education

Private initiative in education has a long history in India. In its earliest form, it was a part of religious obligation carried out by religious organizations, makhtabs, gurukuls and pathshalas which covered both secular and religious aspects of it. The state had no role in or control over it though royal grants were given to some institutions for this purpose. It took a more developed form with a wider ambit of learning and advanced to higher levels during the Buddhist period. Colonial interventions in education came from two sources, Government and Christian missionaries, but with different objectives. Government initiative was focused on promoting the English language so as to produce lower level bureaucracy for administration and interpreters between government and the people while the Christian missionaries were motivated to spread their religion. While government initiative concentrated on higher education for the upper classes and established colleges and universities, missionaries provided school education which had both secular and religious content. Many caste/religious organizations also established schools and colleges to promote education. But both these efforts remained confined to upper and middle classes and mass education was neglected. This deficiency was met with Lord Curzon's 1904 educational policy following which, besides expansion of school education, content of learning was also diversified. Still, literacy at the time of independence was only 15 per cent and 84 per cent of boys and 92.1 per cent of girls had no schooling. (Kaur, 2008) Private sector participation by religious bodies, charitable trusts and philanthropists continued but it was not for profit but for service to society or specific group/ groups within it.

Post-Independence, as with most public services, provision of school education was the primary responsibility of the government. In the federal set up, this responsibility lay with the State government and therefore government or government aided schools provided these services. However, in 1976 education was transferred to the concurrent list. Though universalization of education up to 14 years of age within a period of 10 years was included in the Directive Principles of State Policy, it did not receive the priority and resources it deserved. Even so, there was a very substantial expansion of the education sector at all levels - schools, colleges, universities and technical and scientific institutions in the public sector, though the private sector not for profit also continued in a limited way to supplement these facilities. Till the early 1980s this expansion continued though the sector faced inadequate resources for it compared to the needs of the people. The situation changed with ascendancy of neo-liberal thinking worldwide which had its impact on India too. This ideology got firmly embedded in economic policies subsequent to the acceptance of the IMF-driven Structural Advancement Programme resulting from the fiscal crisis faced by the country. The goal of providing education was restricted to extension of literacy, i.e. of learning three R's implying that children should be provided with necessary knowledge to fit them for participation in the market economy. Also, the budget allocation for public sector education began to decline which progressively affected its quality. With the onset of globalization of economy, there has been a perceptible withdrawal of the state from the provisioning of education which is manifested in reduction of budgetary support for expanding school infrastructure and improving quality of education imparted. This was compounded by worsening of state finances, reduced devolution of funds from the centre to states and constraints in increasing public expenditure imposed by the Fiscal Responsibility and Budget Management Act. The Private sector quickly filled the vacuum with ill-equipped private schools with English medium mainly targeting low income groups—an area in which big capital also foresaw lucrative profits. Besides resource deficit, quality of public school education was also affected by teacher absenteeism, shortage of teachers, unsatisfactory level of teaching imparted and poor level of learning outcomes which also contributed to the rapid growth of private sector schools and people's attraction to them. This has the disturbing effect of creating sharp inequalities with affluent parents sending children to high fee charging private schools while the poor and the marginalized groups are left to access government schools or low cost private schools. Its worst victims have been children from families of deprived and vulnerable sections.

Along with increasing presence of private schools, informalization has also set into the public sector school education resulting from pressure on the centre and states to compress development expenditure and to contain the public sector wage bill. This led to the introduction of para teachers and teachers recruited on contract basis whose recruitment procedures, remuneration and service conditions are different from those of the regular teachers. This category covers a wide range which includes those hired in formal schools to those employed in a variety of part-time and ad hoc educational programmes like non-formal education and alternative schooling centres. Para teachers in regular primary schools/ secondary schools were initiated with the launch of the World Bank supported programme in the 1990s. This practice of employment of part-time teachers, however, got entrenched in almost every state of the country and was justified in financial terms as three to five para teachers could be engaged within the salary of one regular teacher and rationalized as having helped in expanding access to education. There is evidence that apart from creating differentiation within the public educational system, this has severely damaged the quality of education imparted by such teachers due to their sense of job insecurity, low level of motivation and constant search for better alternative jobs. Although RTE (Right to Education) invalidated this practice, in reality it still continues.

The push for the private sector in school education has come from transnational advocacy networks and their national pro-market organizations. It has passed through three phases (Nambisson, 2012 a & b). During the first phase till around 2008, they pressed for parental choice and the voucher system with the objective of influencing public opinion and creating a congenial policy environment for legitimizing unregulated schools and to channelize government funds to budget schools through vouchers. The second phase started when corporate players sensing profit in low budget schools went ahead with setting up school chains and adopted a market strategy to build brands and to generate demand for them. Not getting much response from the local communities, in the third phase, they have shifted to setting up affordable schools for the upper segment so as to yield greater profit along with providing a range of services such as improved teaching methods, teachers training/workshops, curriculum management, etc.

The first variant of privatization, i.e., the voucher scheme has not really taken off. Only two minor initiatives were taken, one in Delhi, where in 2007, school vouchers worth up to Rs. 3,600 per year were awarded to 408 students in 68 wards. Another was PAHAL in Uttarakhand in 2007 that provided vouchers worth Rs. 3,000 per student per year who belong to the most vulnerable groups like rag pickers, scavengers, etc. in three cities covering 651 children (6-14 years) (Shah and Miranda 2012). Nothing has been heard about the success, continuation/expansion of these schemes. However with regard to the impact of school vouchers on performance of students who were attending public schools but shifted to private schools, a research study has suggested that private school enrolment provides no value addition to learning outcomes as compared to government schools (Karopaty, 2014 cited in Taneja, in this volume). The more serious form of privatization is the low budget unregulated private schools which have been projected as a cost effective and an equitable solution to the education of the poor and enables the state to expand availability and coverage of education. The resulting competition between different types of schools, it was argued, would generate greater accountability to parents and students. It was claimed that the poor families preferred private schools to cost-free public schools even though they had to pay fees. Some research studies have come out with findings which support these claims though critics have commented that these studies were funded by the advocacy network. The debate continues (Brinkman, 2012).

The research findings in favour of low budget schools have come under considerable scrutiny. The superiority of such private budget schools for the poor in these studies is based on two grounds 1. Private schools are more cost efficient in terms of per student expenditure (Jain and Dholakia, 2009; Kingdon, 2008 and Murlidharan, 2006) 2. They also perform better than public schools in terms of quality judged by student attendance (different from enrolment), teaching activity, accountability of teachers (Goel and Pandey, 2009; Mehta, 2005; Murlidharan and Kremer, 2006). Children in private schools have higher reading and arithmetic skills than in government schools after controlling family income-related factors (Desai, 2008). Further, these schools offer parents/students the option to choose and therefore enable equality of opportunity (Shah and Miranda, 2012). The reason for lower cost of private schools lies in much lower salaries (one-fifth to one-tenth) being paid to the teachers than what is paid in the government schools. There is no significant difference in infrastructure between public and private schools. This allows private schools to recruit a larger number of teachers within the salary of a single teacher in government schools, reduce multi-grade teaching and have a lower pupil-teacher ratio. This results in better performance of private schools besides English teaching at an early age and more teaching activity. Private schools are also prompt in taking disciplinary action against shirking teachers. Also, students' attendance rates are also substantially higher in private schools.

Both the grounds of cost efficiency and better quality of teaching in private schools are strongly contested by scholars (Sarangpani, 2009; Ramachandran, 2009; Nambisson, 2012a, 2012b). As for cost, the comparison of the two school systems is conceptually and methodologically flawed because parameters of cost calculation and environment and organizational framework within which the two operate are different (Bhatty et al., 2015). Per student expenditure in government schools is based on total government expenditure on elementary schools divided by the number of children enrolled. Total government expenditure includes expenditure on government schools, grants given to aided schools, teachers' training, examination system and curricular development and administration. This increases per capita spending in government schools. Besides, a teacher in a government school is required to have prescribed qualifications and is recruited through a competitive examination. Their pay scales are governed by terms and conditions of service and range in pay hierarchy. Government teachers also perform additional duties besides teaching. This increases the per teacher cost in government schools. In private schools, the cost per student is calculated on the basis of household expenditure as per NSSO. The method of recruitment, eligibility conditions of recruitment and pay scale, are not governed by any system and norms. (except in reputed schools for children from richer families). Cutting down costs in low fee private schools is at the expense of teachers which has detrimental effects on their morale and is reflective of democratic and ethical deficit (Basu, 2012). Also, accountability cannot be enforced by reducing salaries nor can it ever be instrumental in improving the quality of teaching. Besides, cost efficiency and effectiveness cannot be delinked from the equity dimension in availability of, access to and quality of education. Private schools certainly do not expand educational access to the poorest due to the fee component as also requirement of expenditure such as uniforms and other charges while public schools are free. Accessing private schools by the poor represents a huge burden in many cases which constrains the choice available and is unaffordable to the poorest households (James and Woodhead, 2014). Government schools do not choose children that study there nor do they turn them out for poor performance. They provide access to difficult to reach children. They also provide midday meals. Private schools are usually set up in urban areas and rarely if ever in remote and underserved areas where there is no capacity of parents to pay. Therefore, these schools do not expand availability of schooling. Public schools, on the other hand, deliver a public good and are not governed by profit motive. As for quality of teaching, most teachers in low budget private schools lack professional qualifications and have no training. They have, therefore, no capacity to deliver quality education 'Para skilling of teachers and breakdown of curricular and pedagogic processes into simple routine standard tasks' is resorted to enable under qualified teachers to handle the tasks assigned to them. (Basu, 2012). Ipads are given to them with a fixed lesson plan guiding the teachers with no autonomy to chart out their own methods. Worse, the private sector is offering qualitatively better schools for children coming from richer families and thus creating a class divide between the type of education imparted to the poor and wealthy. Besides, if teaching in private schools is superior, why do the children going to them have to take tuition as well (Banerjee and Wadhwa, 2012). Private schools, therefore, can never contribute to equitable and universal education.

Regarding the superior performance of private schools, learning outcomes in both public and private schools are differentiated by the social background of the students. When socio-economic and parental background of students is taken into consideration, it has been found that there is hardly any difference between the learning outcomes of those who go to public schools and those who go to private schools (Taneja, in this volume). Similar narrow level differentiation in performance is between children going to government schools taking tuition and those going to private schools taking it (Banerjee and Wadha, 2012). As for the social environment within which the two school systems operate, government schools function within the public school system which is subjected to intense public scrutiny while private schools work as individual units in an environment controlled by the management which has no public accountability. They also resist regulation and have been found to misuse government concessions granted to them (Tanjea, in this volume). For children from poorer families, private schools neither provide better learning nor are costs low. There is no large and consistently positive private schools effect and they are not clearly an adequate solution (Singh, 2015, Taneja, in this volume). In any case, after the enactment of Right of a Child to Free and Compulsory Education, 2009 all private schools have come under a formal registration and recognition system which would imply adherence to norms laid down by it. Therefore, continuing poorly equipped private schools is a violation of these norms and a failure of enforcement. That many government schools too do not comply with these norms (Basu, 2012) cannot be a ground for its acquiescence in private schools. This is because of the huge number of government schools and the quantum of resources required to comply with these norms. There is however, a legal commitment to fulfil the RTE norms and a continuing public pressure on government to do so. This is not to deny that poor learning levels of children in the age group 6-14 in rural areas as revealed by ASER data is a serious problem and has to be tackled on priority. There is also a need for greater accountability of public school teachers to ensure that students are learning since public schools continue to remain the only option for children from socially and economically disadvantaged grounds, particularly girls. In this effort, teachers' beliefs and attitudes will need to be given critical importance in teachers' training (Singh and Sarkar, 2015). Poor quality of teachers training is a significant factor that contributes to it. The low level of teachers' training is on account of the huge gap between the number of seats available for pre-service teachers training in the teachers training institutions approved by NCTE compared to what is needed. This has led to mushrooming of substandard teachers training institutes to fill the unmet demand of more than 3/4th of elementary school teachers (Batra, 2012). This neglect has accumulated over a long time due to lack of expansion of training institutes and lack of efforts in strengthening and rejuvenating the existing ones in the public sector. The problems have increased, more so after the shift to the neo-liberal economy and coming into effect of RTE.

Ironically, privatization in the form of Public-Private Partnership has received a boost from RTE Section 12 of which requires unaided private schools to reserve 25 per cent of seats in the entry level (nursery level or Class 1) for socially advantaged and economic weaker sections, though the provision is intended to plug the equity gap. The government is committed to provide such private schools with reimbursement, equal to their fees or per student cost in government schools whichever is lower. The scheme has been termed as the largest school voucher programme (Shah and Miranda, 2012). It is also an affirmative action programme. The provision was upheld by the Supreme Court when challenged by associations of private schools. However, the scheme is facing multiple challenges. Transparency in the selection process, definition and identification of qualified candidates, verification of the qualified candidates and mechanism to check its abuse, timely payment of reimbursement and satisfactory basis of its quantum, the manner in which inclusiveness and integration of EWS students with other students would be achieved are only some of them. No detailed studies are yet available on how it has worked out at the ground level, what happens after such children are admitted. Do they feel alienated? How do teachers and other students treat them? What behavioral changes occur in them, etc? It is therefore, difficult to comment on its success or failure. But resistance of high fee paying schools in some form or another to this move continues to be reported in the media.

There are three other types of private schools not-for-profit, run by NGOs which usually provide service to the poor and disadvantaged children run by volunteers and charge minimal fees and promote strong community links in curriculum and teaching and community participation in school management. The best example of this category of schools is Bharat Gyan Vigyan Samiti in Kerala. The other variant is 'alternative' schools also run by NGOs, philanthropists or concerned individual activists on very low budgets and adopt an activity-based learning approach which focus 'on experimenting with progressive philosophies of education' and usually target marginalized children. Rishi Valley Education Centre (AP) is cited as an example of this category of schools. The third category of such schools is NGO run non-formal education (NFE) targeting deprived children, school dropouts, working children etc. who are enabled after reaching Class V to move to formal schools. SSA (Sarva Shiksha Abhiyan) strongly encouraged such schools. MV Foundation in AP and Gyan Shalas in Ahmedabad are examples of these schools. These NGOs get government funding under SSA (Sarva Shiksha Abhiyan). These schools have been criticized for providing below standard quality of teaching to underprivileged children and not getting these children absorbed in formal schools (Brinkman, 2012) though contested by their promoters. None of these experiments fulfill RTE norms and are therefore, 'illegal' but they do meet a critical gap in reaching children left out by mainstream schools and provide a service with no profit motive. They cannot therefore be equated with low budget for profit schools and should be appropriately integrated with the RTE framework with financial help to progressively upgrade their facilities and quality of teachers.

The policy environment which pushes private sector expansion in the primary school system is also reducing budgetary support to the public schools for implementation of RTE which slows down the process of compliance of its norms. As a result, only 25.50 per cent of elementary schools are compliant with 10 RTE indicators (UDISE, 2019-20), 11.70 per cent teachers' posts remain vacant, 12.70 per cent of teachers are still on contractual arrangement and 18.5 per cent teachers do not possess prescribed academic qualifications (UDISE, 2017-18). Inequalities are also getting institutionalized within the public schools system by special category schools such as Kendriya/ Navodya Vidyalays, etc. with differential norms of expenditure relative to general schools. Worse, measures have been taken to dilute some of the progressive provisions of the RTE Act which undermine legal entitlements. No detention policy has been brought back in practice and completion of teachers training within the stipulated time period has not been fulfilled. Examinations continue to be held and continuous and comprehensive evaluation has not been introduced. What is more disquieting is that private sector ethos is creeping into the public school system. This is exemplified by defining a 'minimalist' vision of education for the poor which is limited to achieving basic numeral and literacy skills and quality of education is being equated with outcomes measured through marks and realized through standard achievement tests. Far more disconcerting is the move of the Delhi government to introduce the technocratic model of streaming students based on their abilities tested through 15 simple questions, segregate children as soon as they come out of Standard 9, with a view to pushing out those who do not qualify to the vocational education stream for earning a livelihood which reinforces the class divide. The Delhi government has even removed parity between teachers in government schools and teachers in private schools. Some states have handed over a few government schools to business houses, closed down schools in large numbers ostensibly on the ground that there were insufficient number of students attending them (without investigating why this happened) to achieve efficiency of investment (Rampal, 2019). They have also merged some of the existing schools with others leaving the children's population in the areas served by them with no alternative public school to attend and already enrolled students in them to dropout due to their inability to attend the school with which their existing school was merged owing to distance. This brings private sector culture in Public schools, distorts the core values of the latter and blurs the boundaries between public and private. The Delhi government is even introducing CCTV cameras in classrooms and intending to monitor teachers through biometric attendance and children's entry and exit from school promises. The stress is on surveillance where a watch is kept on what teachers are doing and parents are given feedback on children's behaviour (Ibid.). To combat policing of teachers and students and segregation of children in provision of schooling and opportunity for acquiring education on the basis of their performance and social background is a far more serious challenge to tackle in the public school system than even resource deficit for achieving the desired vision of school education and RTE norms.

Secondary Education

The secondary education is the weakest link and the most stressed space in the educational ladder where the demand is rapidly increasing due to high returns from it but GER is 45.8 per cent and dropout rates are quite high, particularly among girls (Basu, 2012). Non-availability and distance are serious barriers to access besides caste and gender and quality aspects are more demanding. Expanding access and effecting equity constitutes the first steps towards addressing the complexity of the problem in this sector.

The institutional environment in secondary education differs from that in primary education. The private sector is far more present in secondary schools while in primary education it is still very small. Private sector share in secondary schools is already very large with 63 per cent of secondary schools being privately managed. Also, there are various models of school governance (Linden, 2012). Private Sector secondary schools are of three categories: aided, recognized unaided and unrecognized unaided. Aided schools are a form of public-private partnership. Unaided schools are entirely run on fees charged from students. Unrecognized private schools are illegal and vary between 10-15 per cent of all schools. In the aided schools, salaries and some other costs are paid by state governments while capital cost and other investments are borne by the management. As the government does not provide non-salary recurring cost, a separate fee in different forms is charged (Linden, 2012). In the recognized and unaided category, schools receive no funds from the government. Around one-fourth of the total children study in unaided schools and a slightly larger percentage in aided schools. (WB, 2011) The share of two types of private schools differ from state to state West Bengal, Maharashtra, Goa and Gujarat account for more than 60 per cent of private aided schools while AP, Bihar, HP, Chhattisgarh, Jharkhand, Karnataka and Punjab have a majority of government schools. Private aided schools are managed by individuals, trusts, societies or corporate bodies and account for 30 per cent of enrolment. There is no clear pattern in the performance either in government managed schools or private aided schools, or even private unaided schools across states. Secondary schools also face problems of quality due to shortage of teachers in core subjects. As per the World Bank Report (2012), only 30 per cent of schools (public and private) have a sufficient number of teachers. Professional development of secondary education teachers' training is a far more complex issue both in public and private schools. Government schools also lack institutional structures of support. Secondary schools also lack reliable systems of assessment, testing and examination. There is no comprehensive and continuous evaluation (CCE) compared to primary education. Technical quality of state board examinations for assessment of students is also inadequate (Basu, 2012). In terms of cost per student, government schools fare better but overall when cost is linked to achievement of students the evidence is ambiguous and inconclusive. The proportion of state governments' aid allocated to secondary schools also differs from state to state but bears no relationship with the proportion of enrolment in them. Grants are not linked to performance of students or accountability nor to number of students' attendance and teachers (West Bengal, 2011; Basu, 2012; Linden, 2012).

As the demand-supply gap in secondary schools is very large, the PPP mode is being adopted to expand access to secondary education. Six different types of PPPs operate in India 1. Private sector philanthropic initiative 2. Private management of public schools 3. Purchase of educational services from private schools 4. School Voucher Programme 5. Capacity building of schools 6. Provision of Infrastructure. Satya Bharti School programme is an example of the first form which delivers free quality education to under privileged children across rural India and operates 263 schools of which 187 have been constructed by it while the remaining are public schools adopted by it. It has plans to set up 508 primary and 50 senior secondary schools. Punjab's Adarsh Schools Scheme is an example of second category of PPP under which Edu Camps, a private entity, has established and is running five senior secondary schools where land is provided free of cost and capital cost and recurring expenditure is shared between the Government and Edu Camp. Gyan Shala, an education service organization in Gujarat is an example of the third type of PPP which provides elementary education to out-of-school children in slums from Class I to III in Ahmedabad and is funded up to 70 per cent by the Gujarat government. ARK's Ensure Access to Better Learning Experiences Project in Delhi is an example of the Voucher model of PPP and is the fourth model of PPP. The fifth variant of PPP, i.e. capacity building operates in Gujarat where a private entity improves the level of learning across schools and the State government enters into agreement with it for this purpose and the cost of providing services is paid by it. The sixth category of PPP is focused on infrastructure in which the private party builds, owns and operates the infrastructure facilities and ownership of assets may be either be transferred to the government or owned by it (WB, 2012). There is yet another category of PPPs somewhat akin to the first category where the corporates or NGOs or both are involved in improving the quality of government schools. It is actually a model of philanthropic activity, a variant of corporate social responsibility. An example of this model is to be found in the Karnataka government's school adoption programme under which several foundations belonging to corporates/NGOs have adopted 120 schools and are providing teaching aids, library books, extra materials, assessments and scholarships. Similar efforts by corporates have been initiated in partnership with the government in some other states (Nilayranjan's paper in this volume) (Brinkman, 2012).

The cost effectiveness of private sector secondary schools and their superiority over publicly managed schools needs to be assessed on grounds of infrastructure, pupil-teacher ratios, quality of teaching, training of teachers, regional spread and learning outcomes. Sufficient material based on empirical investigations in respect of these parameters is not available to make a judgment. But the limited evidence available does not support the claim made by UNICEF India (1999) that most private schools are better in respect of infrastructure, PTRs, quality of teaching and training of teachers (WB, 2012). On the quality aspects whether in private or public schools, there is no uniformity in curriculum and standards between state boards which results in widely varying outcomes of state board level examinations affecting their reliability. There is no national level assessment of performance. However, studies reveal that the dismal performance is shared both by private and public schools and there is no particular merit in choosing private schools. Better performance wherever in private schools is on account of the family status and home environment (Basu, 2012). Private aided schools despite having management autonomy have not shown any sign to improve performance by guiding teachers' professional development, materials and methodology of teaching, bridge the gap significantly between students coming from different socio-economic backgrounds and reduce reliance of students on private tuitions, particularly in English, Mathematics and Science (Ibid.). The secondary school education also faces problems of recruitment of competent teachers due to insufficient objectivity in selection process, difficulty in getting qualified candidates from reserved categories and high frequencies of court cases questioning the selection process (WB, 2009).

As the performance of schools crucially depends upon the quality of teaching, there is an acute need for teachers' training institutions of good quality. The situation in this regard is quite alarming. The institutional capacity to train teachers suffers from acute shortage. Of the available

7,300 training institutions (in 2007) and their potential seats for pre-service training, 51 per cent institutions and 64 per cent of the available seats are assigned to train secondary school teachers and 43 per cent of institutions and 34 per cent of seats to train elementary school teachers. However, they are able to cater to only 27 per cent of students at the secondary level and 73 of students at the primary level (Batra, 2012). Implementing RTE would require 65 million additional teachers over and above the existing level of 0.5 million. The huge gap in the available number of approved training institutes in states and number of seats they offer compared to the requirement is being filled by substandard teaching institutes in the private sector which have arisen during the past 15-20 years. However, even those who have been fortunate to get training in public institutes, the training is inadequate and curricula and pedagogic approaches are outdated. Private teaching institutes are not only of poor quality but also unregulated. These institutions suffer from inadequate faculty specialization, outdated curriculum and reliance on sub-standard guidebooks. An official report in Maharashtra found 86 per cent of private institutes unfit to carry out such training (Ibid.). The spread of private training institutes has also an urban bias which disadvantages candidates in rural areas, particularly of the marginalized groups. There is no escape from the government coming out in a big way to meet this shortage by expanding teachers' training institutes, particularly in rural areas, strengthening existing ones not only with infrastructure but also modernization of curricula and pedagogic approaches (Ibid.) and putting in place a robust regulatory arrangement to govern the quality aspect of private teachers' training institutes.

There is, however, a consensus that whether it is outright private management or a PPP, a strong regulatory framework is required and quality assurance is fundamental (WB, 2012). On both these counts, evidence available does not create confidence about the suggested superiority of the privately managed schools. Some privately managed schools have bypassed the requirement that trusts and societies running private schools should plough back surplus generated for its development by creating a dual structure—a trust that runs schools and a company that owns assets. What the management has done in the cited evidence is to transfer surplus generated to the company rather than to the school and then distribute it to shareholders as dividend (Jayshanker, 2010; Madhavan and Sanyal, 2012). Governance deficit is particularly marked in grant of recognition to the private sector schools and the rules are diluted or bent to favour the private sector. Lack of adequate enforcement machinery is responsible for undeserving private schools obtaining recognition which seriously constrains efforts to ensure minimum level of quality in private schools and for parents to decide the desirability of admitting their children. Teachers in aided schools despite having the same entitlement in terms of salaries as in government managed schools are paid less. Reduction in grants to them leads to salary cuts and employment of contractual teachers. Governance failure also lies in non-observance of norms set by the National Council of Teacher Education in non-elite private schools. In unaided schools, salaries are as low as Rs. 2,000-3,500 for 24 days of work. This leads to their taking up secondary jobs which affect their quality and effort in teaching (World Bank, 2009).

RMSA (Rashtriya Madhyamik Shiksha Abhiyan) launched in 2009 is designed to address the problem of quality along with those of access and equity. The access is to be improved by achieving an enrolment rate of 75 per cent from 52.26 per cent (2005-06) within 5 years by providing a secondary school within a reasonable distance from the habitation (Linden, 2012). Both central and state governments are expanding availability and access by adopting a PPP approach. On the quality front it aims at making schools conform to prescribed norms of physical infrastructure, PTR, qualification of teachers, curriculum, focus on science subjects, teachers' training and ICT. But these inputs are not sufficient to improve learning achievements which would require a strong evaluation and assessment mechanism and also to align state assessment mechanisms with the national level uniformity in standards across States (Basu, 2012).

In addition to RMSA, the Government of India launched in 2008-09 a model schools scheme to provide quality education to talented rural children through setting up 6,000 model schools as benchmark of excellence at block level @ one school per block. The scheme is being implemented from 2009-10. The objectives of the schemes are (1) to have at least one good quality senior secondary school in every block, (2) to have a pace setting role (3) to try out innovative curriculum and pedagogy (4) to have model infrastructure, etc. The scheme has two modes of implementation viz 1. 3,500 model schools are to be setup in educationally backward blocks under state/UT governments and 2. the remaining 2,500 schools are to be set up under public—private partnership (PPP) mode in the blocks which are not educationally backward. Presently, only the component for setting up of 3,500 modal schools in educationally backward blocks under state/UT governments is operational. As regards remaining 2,500 schools under PPP mode, there is no information if any such schools have been established. State governments have also come up with their model of PPPs which have different norms of tasks and cost sharing between government and the private party. Residential schools in AP and Adarsh schools in Punjab and Rajasthan are examples of such PPP under state schemes. But these are very few in numbers.

There is no comprehensive policy framework for such PPPs with measurable and quantifiable key performance indicators spelt out in the agreement with the private party (Basu, 2012). As non-availability and distance are greater barriers in access, besides caste and gender, this scheme may not be sufficient to address them. More important, setting up a few better quality schools tends to increase differentiation in access and quality and exacerbates existing inequalities in opportunities.

Higher Education

Privatization in higher education originated in the colonial period, with the establishment of three universities in Calcutta, Bombay and Madras and subsequent setting up of colleges (some even preceding universities) by Christian missionaries and some philanthropists and other religious organizations to promote English education and western learning to supply lower level bureaucracy to government establishments. The colonial government had thus established a pattern of public universities and private managed and affiliated colleges, some by government or aided by it. This pattern was replicated and expanded manifold post-independence as the state assigned priority to higher education recognizing its importance as a supplier of qualified and trained manpower for planned development and nation building (Basu, 2012). Public universities and even colleges became a dominant model and even some private institutions were nationalized. Private colleges and financially supported private aided colleges also continued to be encouraged. But this 'private' was not for profit. This model changed since the 1980s with the ascendancy of market economy worldwide and more pronouncedly in the 1990s with introduction of economic reforms and curtailment of public expenditure on higher education, and priority being given to primary education in government policy. Unmet demand for access to higher education also contributed to it.

Thereafter, the private higher educational institutions emerged both as private universities and non-university institutions offering professional training courses, the former awarding degrees while the latter awarding certificates and diplomas. But privatization implying market principle of cost recovery in public institutions had already begun in the 1970s and 1980s in the form of self-financing courses (Verghees, 2012). The higher education sub-sector has thus witnessed huge expansion from 28 universities and 578 colleges in 1950-51 to more than 1960 universities (including 130 deemed universities) and 33,000 colleges the bulk of which are in the private sector and concentrated in four professional fields of engineering, medicine management and ICTs (Basu, 2012) leaving government funded institutions far behind. As a result, privatization of higher education in India exceeds even the developed countries and private unaided self-financing institutions one of the largest in the world (Tilak, 2014).

Privatization of higher education is not merely manifested in setting up self-financing institutions but also financial privatization of public institutions resulting from pressure for mobilization of finances from students in the form of higher fees or donations from individuals, industry and business. The third mode of privatization of higher education, particularly technical, is by way of loans from banks which have replaced scholarships even to needy students. The ultimate objective is to progressively reduce if not altogether eliminate government responsibility to finance higher education. The fourth mode of privatization is to encourage government-funded higher educational institutions to introduce self-financing courses so that the demand of public institutions for fund support from the government can be at least partially met from revenue generated. This introduces the culture of the private sector in public institutions and further erodes their 'public' character (Tilak, 2014). The fifth mode of financial privatization of higher education can be derived from the latest government policy of creating a corpus for meeting the needs of public institutions for expansion, improvement of infrastructure etc. Public institutions needing such resources would have to take a loan from this fund managed by a body proposed to be constituted for this purpose under the new law. The institution taking such a loan would have to pay back from resources to be generated by it. Higher Education has now virtually become a private good which has to be purchased. Investment in higher education has become a lucrative business with minimal risk and quick and high returns. Philanthropy-based institutions have virtually disappeared from the scene. This has serious equity implications as privatization of higher education has shut out not only the poor and vulnerable sections from access to it but even the lower middle class students from pursuing higher education due to very high fees. This deprivation of access not only widens inequalities but also blocks prospects of higher mobility. No private institution geared to generate ever higher profit would promote access to weaker sections with liberal scholarships. Interventions by the government to provide fee reimbursement, interest subsidy on loans or provide quota in admission to address this situation are unlikely as fee reimbursement involves too heavy a financial commitment with too few beneficiaries. Students from weaker sections would fail to get loans as they have no collateral to offer and there is no certainty of getting high salary jobs. Quota in the private sector would be stiffly opposed by institutions and challenged in the Court (Ibid.).

The promotion of private sector in higher education is justified on grounds that it would expand coverage, access, improve quality, promote equity and efficiency. It has undoubtedly expanded availability but this expansion neither serves the objective of equitable regional spread nor provides educational facilities across disciplines (Rao et al., 2011). The establishment of private higher educational institutions is concentrated in South India and Maharashtra. The choice of location is better off states with developed infrastructure rather than rural and underserved areas, and caters to the needs of urban population. These institutions impart education in disciplines of engineering, management medicine and ICTS, and commerce while ignoring social sciences, humanities and basic sciences. Their focus is on saleable short-term courses based on market demand which students prefer for access to jobs. As for access, it is limited to affluent sections who can afford to pay the high fees which further aggravates the class divide. The absence of government funding in its provisioning would fail to mitigate this barrier in access (Chattopadhya, 2012). Thus, far from promoting equity, privatization in higher education severely undermines it. As for quality, the picture is extremely dismal. Even according to the National Accreditation and Assessment Council, these private institutions suffer from over capacity, uneven regional distribution, faculty shortage, poor curriculum and quality of pedagogy, inadequate infrastructure and under equipped laboratories and ill equipped libraries. Commercialization is rampant while capitation fees are common (Nandi and Chattopadhery, 2012), They recruit under qualified teachers who are underpaid and inadequate in strength to cover the courses. Poor quality of teaching imparted in them are unlikely to fetch the students pursuing various courses in them a well-paid job even after paying high fees. The values inculcated by them promote single minded focus on earning money with total indifference to social concerns (Tilak, 2014).

In the field of medical education, besides faculty shortage (Ananthkrishnan, 2007), inadequate infrastructure (Rao et al., 2011), ill-equipped libraries and laboratories, lack adequately equipped hospitals with very few patients provide highly inadequate theoretical learning and very little exposure to practical learning (Diwate, 2019; Rao et al., 2011). In medical education, uneven distribution of medical colleges has caused severe imbalances across states in production and availability of doctors (Choudhary, 2016). They also promote high-tech urban-centric, hospital-based education with orientation towards specialization in lucrative segments and neglect of preventive care. The worst aspect is that this education changes the value system of doctors whose guiding motive is to make money rather than render service (Antia, 1990). The poor qualities of doctors produced by private medical colleges are a risk in dispensing healthcare.

This unchecked and poorly governed growth of private higher educational institutions has now thrown up an acute crisis of demand particularly in engineering and management courses with empty seats, ghost campuses on the one hand, and rising fees and loans for students and decreasing salaries for teachers on the other hand (Verghese, 2012). It has done nothing to bring about improvement in curriculum, teaching methodology, research and development and learning outcomes (Sudarshan and Subramaniam, 2012). The Bulk of Institutions produce graduates of poor quality, an assessment confirmed particularly in engineering and management courses in respect of deemed universities by a review committee set up by MHRD in respect of deemed universities (Ibid.). This is despite the plethora of regulations that deal with the functioning of higher education institutions, with the underlying premise that they ensure quality (Goswami, Amlanjyoti, 2012). In fact, higher education has been described by the National Knowledge Commission as 'over regulated and under governed' Existing governance architecture is characterized by multiple regulatory agencies with overlap of functions and mandates, tight governance and excessive controls laying down norms for every conceivable aspect and yet corruption continues along with connivance in it by regulators. (Sudarshan and Subramaniam) The basic requirement of law is that higher education institutions have to be established as a trust or society on a non-profit basis. But dishonest persons have defeated this requirement and even taken tax exemption in setting up of such institutions. In medical education, at the time of inspection by the Medical Council of India preceding recognition, private medical colleges fill up empty hospital wards with patients after paying them money, hiring doctors by showing them as recruited and even borrowing instruments from other colleges, putting up lists of non-existing staff, showing false records, false faculty, etc. (Chattopadhyay, 2008; Diwate, 2019). There has been a lot of public criticism against the very high fees, corrupt and unfair practices, unregulated expansion and production of low quality graduates. There have also been cases in the Supreme Court to check profit making in such institutions and levy of capitation fee is already an offence. But charging capitation fee continues in different ways (Madhavan and Sanyal, 2012). The government is attempting to address these issues through new regulatory measures replacing existing regulatory bodies. The Higher Education Commission of India Bill placed in the Parliament in 2018 recommends a single regulator of higher education to set standard and norms for maintenance of academic standards and an overarching control over accreditation agencies. National education policy 2020 proposes a more elaborate structure under such a commission. What shape regulatory arrangements finally take has not yet emerged. But the track record of enforcement does not inspire confidence that new regulations would fare any better in holding private players more accountable and effect better governance than the older ones because of the nexus between political and business interests in policy making. Despite this experience with privatization, the government continues to encourage public-private partnerships in government-funded institutions such as industry and higher educational institution linkages on the grounds that it cannot meet the increasing demand for resources from the government-funded institutions and this linkage would bring in additional resources and improve the efficiency of their management. As for resources, industry linkage would not provide resources for strengthening infrastructure and expansion but only for specific courses which suits its requirement. The efficiency concept is 'weak, irrelevant and misleading' in the educational field (Chattopadhyaya, 2012). Education is not an economic activity geared to making money but a social activity oriented to human development and cannot be measured by norms of business and industry. Experience has shown that such models of privatization do not succeed in achieving intended objectives due to the differing ethos of the two systems. Rather, they end up transforming the 'public' in public institutions. Such partnerships lead to increase in revenue-generating activities in the institution, cost-centric concern affecting every activity, irreversible damage in the academic culture of institutions, subordination of equity considerations and change in the value system of faculty and staff. Research projects undertaken in the PPP mode distort research agenda and findings of research and damage the core academic values of the institution. Besides, such partnerships end up by transferring public resources to the private sector party. When the government faces a resource crunch to fund higher education, such a transfer is even more disturbing and only helps the private sector grow at the cost of the public sector. Considering that higher education in India at present covers a narrow base with only 10.6 per cent of the population above 15 years having completed a graduate degree as per All India Survey 2017-18, of which only 5.7 per cent is in rural areas and 8.3% are women and pressure for seeking avenues of higher education grows particularly after expansion of school education, when higher education is relegated to market forces it results in elitisalion of basic need and deprives access to it for lakhs of underprivileged students (Anand, 2020). This clearly signals a disowning of state responsibility in the sector which would undermine its goal of achieving inclusive growth. Only equitable expansion of government-funded institutions and adequate resource allocation to their can address exclusion and achieve equity in availability of and access to higher education and contribute to ensuring its quality.

This then is the broad picture of the penetration of private sector in respect of educational facilities. The papers in the volume that follow discuss some of the issues raised above, among others. Of the fifteen papers covered in it, three are general in nature dealing with assessment of privatization in essential public services carried from the first volume, and twelve relate to education. The following is the summary of these papers.

Summary of Papers

Jyotsna Jha's paper traces the history and evolution of private schooling in India to understand its motivations and implications for both the educational processes in schools and for the regulation governance by the state. From this narrative it has emerged that religion has played a major role in emergence of private schools in India throughout history. Commerce is also an important motivation and currently these two motivations are coming together though traditionally they were not necessarily united. But unlike the colonial and even pre-colonial phases, the place for reason and dialogue tradition has shrunk gradually and widely in education-related discourse in the contemporary phase as a result of, among other reasons, a lack of focus on comprehensive definition of quality. Mere mugged knowledge became important for success and it coincided with internalization of values and thoughts without questioning becoming the norm in schools. While public schools have not necessarily been overly religious, they also lack power and wherewithal to become secular and resilient spaces for knowledge creation. The central and state governments have also shown a woefully negligent approach in developing clear and transparent regulatory mechanisms for either public or private schooling systems that enables understanding and growth of secular spaces for learning. And now private commercial interests entering the public through public-private partnerships and majoritarian singular ideology entering educational institutions that guide the curricula, textbooks, and teachers training education, India is perhaps going to be even more influenced by religion and commerce bereft of any focus on reason and dialogue in years to come.

Government and private schools have existed since the commencement of modern education in India. **Ashok Pankaj** and **Poornima M.** in their papers argue that the nature of involvement of the private sector in providing school education has however been changing. A major shift has taken place in the decade of the 1990s. The government through its various policy documents has indicated its intention to withdraw from the social sector and has shown greater dependence on the private sector to provide public services. This shift is reflected in school education and paradoxically continues notwithstanding the constitutional amendment declaring Right to Education as a fundamental right and enactment of law on Right to Education. As a result, the share of government schools in total elementary schools has declined and that of the private sector has increased. The social profile of children attending government schools and private schools points to a distinct class division. More SCs/STs, girls, poor and rural children attend government schools. As a result, government schools are heading towards ghettoization. This has its social costs. A large number of children from these groups are likely to be deprived of education amidst increasing privatization leading to closure of government schools. Providing their children education in private schools has opportunity cost for many parents. They would have used the money, they are forced to spend on private education, on other necessities of life and savings and investment for their economic uplift. Many poor households have to sell their economic assets, mortgage their properties and borrow money for meeting the cost of private school education with long-term adverse consequences for them.

Anjela Taneja's paper examines some of the claims about private education and especially low fee private schools, to assess whether such schools provide higher quality of education, provide more efficient and accountable service delivery, expand access to the poorest, and respond best to parental demand. She also examines the evidence on private education and specifically low-fee private schools on whether expansion of and investment in such schools is an effective route to universal, equitable and non-discriminatory education of high quality. This is done by citing studies from India while global evidence provides the background to this analysis. The conclusion that emerges from this exercise is that privatization and commercialization of education is producing a negative impact and growth of private involvement in education risks a decline in quality and equity. Referring to the 2015 Global Education Monitoring Report, the author contends that there is a push back against privatization in many countries due to severe stratification of the educational system it created. It is not going to be any different in India which is already highly stratified. Besides, private schools have also not adhered to existing regulatory frameworks and have been found to misuse government concessions granted to them. This has happened even after RTE has come into force as indicated by continued evasion of private schools of their obligation to fill 25 per cent of seats with students from poor and marginalized families. Admitting that there are failings in India's public education system, the author concludes that public schools continue to be the major provider of education worldwide and the best and the only hope for universal and good quality education for all and promoting values of equality, social mobility, stability and democracy.

D. Narasimha Reddy's paper deals with dysfunctional policies in respect of school education at the national and state level. At the national level, this is manifested in learning crisis which shows that overall performance in school education both at Class 5 and at Class 10 is distressingly low in government schools, and slightly less so in the low budget private schools, resulting in poor foundation capabilities. This crisis intensified with the shift to a market economy, resistance to increase budgetary resources for education, and encouragement to private provision of public goods leading to unregulated expansion of private schools. As a result, government schools have become a ghettoized option for students from poorest and marginalized sections of society and some of them facing closure while the poor shifting to low budget schools end up learning hardly anything. This problem can only be addressed by strengthening of the public school system with provision of better human and infrastructural resources and higher investment. But government expenditure continues to stagnate around 3 per cent of

GDP. The learning situation at the state level is no better as shown by the author in respect of Telangana. In the Niti Ayog's school education quality index, Telangana among southern states has the lowest score just above the bottom in overall performance in terms of 'outcomes', 'governance', 'infrastructure' and 'equity'. The performance gradually declines as students move to higher classes. Social group differences are more pronounced in respect of lower caste categories. Growing privatization and poor availability of budgetary resources are among the reasons responsible for this situation. With profound technological transformation taking place globally and India also adapting to it slowly, lack of good fundamental school education has resulted in lack of access to jobs and uncertain future for entrants to the labour market. The government's response to provide skill development would fail to address this crisis as building skills for the changed working environment requires human capital foundation. But India ranks very low in human capital index due to low investment in education and health.

Kiran Bhatty in her paper laments that RTE (Right to Education) has not had the desired impact in terms of intended improvements in the quality of public schools due to lack of universal compliance of the norms mandated in it. But private schools have equally failed to comply with the mandatory provision imposed on them. She argues that RTE has been remiss in addressing issues of privatization adequately, especially in the transfer of obligations from public to private sector and implications of this transfer for accountability. This is particularly problematic in cases of PPPs. Without clarifying the conditions under which a fundamental right can be delivered by private institutions, the Act and the Supreme Court have left the possibilities of interpreting the law and allowing the private institutions to escape its radar. The exclusion of privately run minority institutions from the ambit of RTE has kept the minorities away from enjoying their fundamental right to education. Further, despite adopting the rights framework, the state continues to reproduce inequalities through a hierarchical education that it legitimizes within the public education system. The paper also shows that the state has failed to put into place adequate enforcement structures that would enable it to fulfil its obligations under the law. Loopholes in enforcement mechanisms for RTE in both public and private schools have led to gross violations of rights of children with its adverse impact on disadvantaged children getting magnified. Lack of punitive measures on public school violations defeat the purpose of improving quality in public schools to the benefit of the disadvantaged. To realize the intent of the Act, the focus of action should be on the public sector and not on the private sector. However, since private provisioning is on the rise, better regulatory mechanisms will have to be considered to ensure that the rights of the child within private schools are also protected.

School education suffers from a learning crisis manifested in poor learning outcomes leading to learning poverty. Government intervention has focused on increasing enrolment of students and provision of schools but neglected addition of teaching staff and teachers' training. Technology-based digital education can address this inadequacy through provision of ICT skills to teachers on use of digital mode of contents in the classroom. Lately, corporates have partnered with government under the corporate social responsibility in improving the school education system. One such partnership of government is with the company, Vodafone. **Nilay Ranjan** in his paper describes the broad range of activities of this company which cover entire aspects of school education—creative content for primary level students, teachers' capacity building, developing e-learning platform for teachers and students and building capacity of school teachers and educators to develop digital content. One of their projects has been development of digital content for Classes 1 to 8 for science and mathematics in a phase-wise manner. Phase 1 is taking education directly to learners. Phase 2 focuses on enhancing problem-solving abilities of learning. Phase 3 covers activity-based learning. Phase 4 initiative deals with development of an online learning platform for teachers called Gurushala which covers their professional, social and psychological needs. A robust monitoring mechanism has been put in place to ensure that these initiatives are sustained and continue to be useful. An external impact assessment was undertaken in 2019 which received an extremely positive response from teachers. Emphasis in future would be on transition of Gurushala to be a public platform by teachers, for teachers and of teachers.

Unprepared teachers and stagnant teacher education sector characterized the landscape of school education when elementary education was declared a fundamental right. Many teacher vacancies and the sizable presence of professionally unqualified teachers posed critical challenges to the task of universalizing quality education. The Justice Verma Commission noted that over 90 per cent of teachers were being trained in private teachers' educational institutions (TEIs) while 80 per cent of school children were enrolled in state schools. There has been a 13 per cent rise in private TEIs since then. **Poonam Batra** in her paper argues that privatization of teacher education is largely an outcome of policy inaction characterized by gross neglect of the need for institutional capacity development and the professional development of serving school teachers. Teacher education suffered for years of intellectual isolation as a result of rigid and unimaginative regulatory norms and the proliferation of substandard private TEIs that were separated from the universities. The gross neglect by the state of institutional capacity building left many gaps in the preparation of teacher educators as well; the most critical was the normalization of a culture of uncritical engagement with questions of educational theory and practice. As a result of state inability to address the complexity of diverse classrooms and teachers' unpreparedness, policy debates shifted to learning outcomes that narrowed the policy discourse on learning achievement scores and teachers' accountability. Meanwhile, the virtual business takeover of teacher education has happened via contracts between governments and private providers that focus on providing digital solutions to enhance learning outcomes. The capture of school teachers by private interests, the paper concludes, has led to subversion of the commitment to the Constitution-based policy frame of equity and justice and the institutionalized nexus between an entrenched private sector in teacher education and a compromised state system that shapes education policy.

Though the private sector schools are unaffordable for most students, particularly of the poor and marginalized households, there is gradual abandonment of government schools by students in favour of private schools. This is attributed to deficiencies of the public school system. **L. Reddeppa's** paper investigates this issue in respect of secondary schools, public and private in Telangana with reference to four parameters—enrolment, attendance, and infrastructure—toilets, clean environment, computers, electricity and playground, and pedagogy and quality and finds that in respect of all these private sector schools score over public schools. Within the public schools, there is a high degree of diffentiation. The position is better in respect of the special category of schools such as Kendriya Vidyalyas whose performance is far better than the general category of public schools and is comparable to good private schools. Performance of private schools in respect of basic learning skills of students is better due to higher degree of control exercised by management over teachers. What is worse is that, in public schools, one-fifth of teachers are not regular in attending schools and engage in their private business activities and another one-fifth have poor teaching skills. But private schools promote enrolment to their institutions through market strategies. The paper concludes that fulfilment of goals of RTE (Right to Education) and SDGs (Sustainable Development Goals) is possible only through public schools as three-fourth of the students are enrolled there. The need is to reform the public schools through better funding, infrastructure improvement and efficient management.

An important feature of the very high rate of growth of higher education experienced in India, particularly since the 1990s is the alarming growth of private higher education. This has stemmed from the conviction of the state that privatization would promote access, quality and equity in higher education and is an effective solution to most of the ills plaguing the higher educational system. This represents a shift from welfare orientation to the market approach in higher education. As a result, the size of the private sector is about twice that of the public sector in terms of the number of institutions and students' enrolment to the extent that the higher education system in India is more privatized than in market economies of developed countries. This has several consequences which include concentration on saleable courses of study which generate higher surplus such as engineering, management and commerce, preference for short-term to long-term programmes, under qualified and under paid teachers, very high fees—fifty to eighty per cent higher than those in public institutions, poor quality of education imparted and severe compromise on equity and inculcation of values which revolve around selfishness and a lack of concern for social issues. Despite all this, the government has shown inability to enforce the regulation it has put in place. Refuting the claim that private education is good in itself and will improve efficiency, quality and access, **Jandhyala B.G. Tilak** in his paper expresses grave concern that the state is gradually abdicating its responsibility towards higher education policy making and transferring the funding and delivery of higher education to the private sector. The author suggests that while philanthropy-based private education should be encouraged, only a strong, vibrant, high quality of public higher education system, accessible to all is the solution to the problems of the education system.

Policy making in India has been advocating public-private partnership as a major policy initiative and part of ongoing reforms in both school education and higher education. **Saumen Chattopadhyay's** paper examines the possible ramifications of different models proposed by the government to implement PPP for education and saving of public resources and highlights the tradeoff involved in most of them. Though private sector engagement in public sector education may lead to efficiency gains and improvement in quality, the reduced government grant can lead to compromise with equity and access issues. Besides, the concepts of efficiency gains and improvements in quality remain contestable because of the specific nature of education and an educational institution. The choice of PPP models should therefore be examined closely and should not be guided by pragmatism and acceptance of offer by the private sector but by the realization of basic objectives of public education. The author argues that stated positives of PPP like efficiency gains and delivery of quality of education are really not tenable in the context of education in particular. Even if there is gain in efficiency, it can come at a high cost. A corporate style governance reform can curb academic freedom, lead to shrinkage of liberal space within the university though it may increase research output. But the nature of research and knowledge generation would change, and in the process, it would lead to weakening of the linkage between university and society though possibly strengthening the university and the economy relationship albeit from a narrow perspective.

The shift from state managed and financed higher education to market-driven and privately managed system in line with changes in political economy has transformed the culture and value system of education, content of knowledge imparted and restricted access to it. This is reflected in the drastic changes in the educational vision and direction emerging from the Kothari Commission to the New Education Policy 1985 and then to the Knowledge Commission headed by Sam Pitroda. The constitution of the Birla-Ambani Committee 2000 conveyed total subordination of higher education to market forces. A significant dimension of this shift is large-scale market-friendly reforms in educational governance pushed by the government in line with the global pattern with particular emphasis on creating space and environment for entry of foreign universities to set up campuses here. This privatisation and globalisation of higher education has been justified on the grounds that the government does not have enough resources to strengthen and expand higher education and the private sector would not only fill the resource gap but would also lead to greater efficiency, initiative and dynamism in the educational system. **Haragopal and Sudarshanam** in their paper have questioned these assumptions and have argued that private sector financing and management of higher education would gravely restrict the content of education to profitable and skill-driven courses to suit the needs of the market, increase its cost enormously and severely limit access to those who can afford it. The crisis in higher education is also due to its phenomenal expansion to meet political exigencies and the resultant loss of autonomy of universities due to increasing political control for which Vice-Chancellors are also responsible in no small measure. With the erosion of autonomy, it becomes easier for the state to promote privatisation and commercialisation of higher education. The gradual withdrawal of the state from the field of higher education has resulted in declining resources allocation to existing public universities and institutes leading to huge deficits and forcing them to raise loans and donations and start self-financing courses. This thrust on privatisation of higher education and entry of foreign universities has been reinforced by the New Education Policy 2020 which totally ignores social justice concerns. The authors point to the grave danger of religious organisations setting up private universities which may contribute to growing authoritarianism and fascist culture. However, resistance to privatisation has also emerged and is slowly increasing.

Ravi Kumar's paper makes a strong plea for understanding privatization as capitalism. Under the neo-liberal economy, capital not only transforms economy and all aspects of state activities but also thought, behaviour and individual's way of life in society. The field of education, therefore, cannot remain untouched by it. This can be seen in state-run institutions being handed over to private players whether wholly or in parts such as outsourcing service delivery in different forms, expansion of low-fee private schools, mandating institutions of higher education to undertake resource mobilization through increase in fees and taking up courses in partnership with industry and business though paucity of state resources is cited as the reason for it. This privatization implies not only limiting access to higher education to a few who can afford it but also changing the nature of education imparted which inhibits critical thinking and alternative imagination. Private entities in school education existed even earlier but were primarily philanthropic. The present privatization is the unabashed pursuit of profiteering and building its own pedagogic and curricular structures. Educational training is reduced to moulding teachers and students to suit the requirements of capital. Privatization's deeper impact is to change the minds of people, turning them sectarian, homophobic and inegalitarian. Unemployment is an innate characteristic of capitalist economy which thrives on creating precarity to optimize profit for the capital. Development agencies' financial support for improving education is not geared to strengthening the public education system but outsourcing it to non-state entities, increasing use of technology and creating a market for the private sector. The state is collaborating with them in this privatization process through capacity building such as STARs as well as its defence of appointment of contractual low paid teachers and building a segmented schooling system along lines of segmented labour market. The author concludes that privatization in education has therefore to be contested with this understanding rather than by opposing outsourcing of certain activities in it.

References

Arral, Eduardo (2019). "The Failure of Water utilities Privatization: Synthesis of Evidence, Analysis and Implications", *Policy and Society* 27:3, 221-228 DOI 10- 1016 I polsoc, 2008, 10.006.

Baru, R.V. and M. Nandi (2008). "Blurring Boundaries: Public-Private Partnerships in Health Services", *Economic and Political Weekly* 43, No. 4, January 26, pp. 62-71.

Bayliss, Kate and Tim Kessler (2006). "Can Privatization and Commercialization Help Achieve MDGs?" International Poverty Centre, UNDP, Working Paper No. 22, July 2006.

Hall, David (2015). *Why Public-Private Partnerships Do Not Work: The Many Advantages of Public Alternative.* Public Services International Research Unit, University of Greenwich, UK, www.world-psi.org.

McDonald, David A. and Greg Ruiters (eds.) (2012). *Alternatives to Privatization: Public Options for Essential Services in Global South*, Introduction: In Search of Alternatives and Conclusion: Way Forward for Alternatives to Health, Water and Electricity, Routledge.

Planning Commission (2004). *Report of the PPP Sub-Group on Social Sector*, Government of India, November 2004.

Pratap, Kumar V. (2014). "Floundering Public-Private Partnerships: Some Suggestions", *Economic and Political Weekly*, Vol. XLIX, No. 15, April 12.

Pratap, Kumar V (2016). "The increasing Incidence of PPP Project Cancellations in India", *Economic and Political Weekly*, Vol. LI, No. 39, September 24.

Starr, Paul (1987). The Limits of Privatization, Economic Policy Institute, Washington, DC cited in John B. Goodman and Gary W. Loveman 'Does Privatisation Serve Public Interest?', *Harvard Business Review*, November-December, 1991.

The Norwegian Forum for Environment and Development (2006). Privatization of Water, Public-Private Partnerships: Do They Deliver to the Poor? April 2006.

Van Dijk Meine Pieter (2008). "Public-Private Partnerships in Basic Service Delivery: Impact on the Poor, Examples from Water Sector in India", *International Journal of Water*, UNESCO-IHE Institute for Water Education, The Netherlands.

Water and Sanitation Programme (2011). "Trends in Private Sector Participation in the Indian Water Sector: A Critical Review". wsp@worldbank.org. WSP.

Wu, Xun (2016). "Public Private Partnerships (PPPs) in Water and Sanitation in India: Lessous from China" *Water Policy*, 18(51), 153-176 (December 2016).

Primary Education

Banerji, Rukmini and Wilima Wadhwa (2012). "Every Child in School and Learning Well in India: Investigating the Implications of School Provision and Supplemental Help", *India Infrastructure Report 2012*, IDFC, New Delhi and Routledge.

Basu, Sambit (2012). "Private Sector in Education: An Overview, *India Infrastructure Report 2012*, IDFC, New Delhi and Routledge.

Bhatty, Kiran, Anuradha De and Rathin Roy (2015). "The Public Education System and What the Costs Imply", *Economic and Political Weekly*, Vol. L, No. 31, August 1.

Brinkmann, Suzana Andrade, "Thinking Outside the Government Box: The Role of the Nongovernment Sector in Achieving Quality Education for All," *India Infrastructure Report 2012*, IDFC, New Delhi and Routledge.

Desai, Sonalde, Amaresh Dubey, Reeve Vanneman and Rukmini Banerji (2008). "Private Schooling in India: A New Educational Landscape." Working Paper No. 11, India Human Development Survey.

Goyal, Sangeeta and Priyanka Pandey (2009). "How do Government and Private Schools Differ? Findings from Two Large Indian States," Report No. 30, South Asia Human Development, World Bank.

Jain, Pankaj and Ravindra Dholakia (2009). "Feasibility of Implementation of Right to Education Act," *Economic and Political Weekly* 44(25): 38-43.

Kaur, Harpreet (2008). *Development of Education in India*, Commonwealth Publishers, New Delhi.

Kingdon, Geeta G. (2008). "School Sector Effects on Student Achievement in India," in Rajshri Chakrabarti and Paul E. Peterson (eds.), *School Choice International: Exploring Public-Private Partnerships,* MIT Press, Cambridge.

Mehta, A.C. (2005). "Elementary Education in Unrecognised Schools in India, A Study of Punjab Based on DISE 2005", National Institute of Educational Planning and Administration, New Delhi.

Muralidharan, Karthik and Michael Kremer (2006). *Public and Private Schools in Rural India*, Department of Economics, Harvard University.

Muralidharan, Karthik (2006). "Public-Private Partnerships for Quality/ Education in India," *Seminar* 565.

Nambissan, Geetha B. (2012)[a]. "Private Schools for the Poor Business as Usual", *Economic and Political Weekly,* October 13, Vol. XLVII, No. 41.

Nambissan, Geetha B. (2012)[b]. "Low-Cost Private Schools for the Poor in India: Some Reflections," *India Infrastructure Report 2012*, IDFC, New Delhi and Routledge.

Ramachandran, Vimala (2009). "Right to Education Act: A Comment," *Economic and Political Weekly*, 44 (28): 155-57.

Rampal, Anita, (2019). "National Seminar on Private Sector Participation in Public Services March 28-30, 2016: A Report", Council for Social Development, New Delhi.

Sarangapani, Padma, (2009). "Quality, Feasibility and Desirability of Low-Cost Private Schooling," *Economic and Political Weekly*, 44(43): 67-69.

Shah, Parth J. and Miranda Luis (2012). "Private Initiative in India's Education Miracle," *India Infrastructure Report 2012*, IDFC, New Delhi and Routledge.

Singh, Abhijit (2015). "Private School Effects in Urban and Rural India" Panel Estimates at Primary and Secondary School Ages," *Journal of Development Economics* 113 (2015) 16-32.

Singh, Renu and Sudipa Sarkar (2015). "Does Teaching Quality Matter? Students Learning Outcome Related to Teaching Quality in Public and Private Primary Schools in India", *International Journal of Educational Development* 41 (2015), 153-163.

Unified District Information on School Education (UDISE) 2019-18, Ministry of Education, Government of India, New Delhi.

United District Information on School Education (UDISE) 2019-20 cited in reply to Unstarred Question No. 1170 on July 29, 2021 in Rajya Sabha.

Zoe, James and Martin Woodhead (2014). "Choosing and Changing Schools in India's Private and Government Sectors: Young Lives; Evidence from Andhra Pradesh," *Oxford Review of Education*, Vol. 40, No. 1, http://dx.doi.org/10.1080/03054985.2013.873527.

Secondary Education

Basu, Sambit (2012). “Private Sector in Education: An Overview”, *India Infrastructure Report 2012*, IDFC, New Delhi and Routledge.

Batra, Poonam “Positioning Teachers in the Emerging Education Landscape of Contemporary India,” *India Infrastructure Report 2012*, IDFC, New Delhi and Routledge.

Brinkmann, Suzana Andrade “Thinking Outside the Government Box: The Role of the Nongovernment Sector in Achieving Quality Education for All,” *India Infrastructure Report 2012*, IDFC, New Delhi and Routledge.

Jayshankar, Mitu (2010). “The Business Schools”, *Forbes India*, April 8 cited in Linden, Toby “Secondary Education,” *India Infrastructure Report 2012*, IDFC, New Delhi and Routledge.

Madhavan, M.R. and Kaushiki Sanyal (2012). “Regulations in the Education Sector,” in *India Infrastructure Report 2012, Private Sector in Education*, IDFC New Delhi and Routledge.

World Bank (2011). *Public Private Partnerships in Secondary School Education in India*, World Bank, Washington, DC.

World Bank (2012). “Secondary Education Project”, Project Appraise Document, Education Unit, Human Development Department, South Asia Region.

World Bank Study (2009). *Quality and Efficiency of Secondary Education in India, 2007.*

Higher Education

Anand, Ishan (2020). “After... Education Skill Out of Reach for Indians,” Sunday, *Hindustan Times*, New Delhi, January 12.

Ananthakrishan, N. (2007). “Acute Shortage of Teachers in Medical Colleges: Existing Problems and Possible, Solutions”, *The National Medical Journal of India*, 20 No. 1 (January-February).

Antia, N.H. (1990). “Medical Education: In Need of Cure,” *Economic and Political Weekly*, July 21.

Basu, Sambit (2012). “Private Sector in Education: An Overview”, in *India Infrastructure Report: Role of Private Sector*, IDFC, New Delhi and Routledge.

Chattopadhyay, Saumen (2012). “The Emerging Market for Higher Education: Rationalising Regulation to Address Equity and Quality Concern,” *India Infrastructure Report 2012*, IDFC, New Delhi and Routledge.

Choudhury, P. (2016). "Role of Private Sector in Medical Education and Human Resource Development for Health in India", *Economic and Political Weekly*, 51(3): 71-79, January 16.

Diwate, Archna (2019). "Growth of Private Medical Colleges in Maharashtra and its Implication or Universal Healthcare," in Imrana Qadeer, K.B. Saxena and P.M. Aarthi (eds.) (2019) *Universalization Healthcare in India: Care to Coverage*, Aakar, Delhi.

Goswami, Amlanijyoti (2012). "Higher Education Law and Privately-Funded University Education in India" in *India Infrastructure Report 2012, Private Sector in Education*, IDFC, New Delhi and Routledge.

Madhavan, M.R. and Kaushiki Sanyal (2012). "Regulation in the Education Sector," in *India Infrastructure Report 2012, Role of Private Sectors in Education*, IDFC, New Delhi and Routledge.

Rao, Mohan, Krishna D. Rao, A.K. Shiva Kumar, Mirai Chatterjee and Thiagarajan Sundararaman (2011). "India: Towards Universal Health Coverage 5" www.thelancet.com Vol. 377, February 12.

Sudarshan, Anand and Sandhya Subramanian (2012). "Private Sector's Role in Indian Higher Education", *India Infrastructure Report 2012*, IDFC, New Delhi and Routledge.

Tilak, J.B.G. (2014). "The Privatisation of Higher Education", *Economic and Political Weekly*, Vol. XLIX, No. 40.

Varghese, N.V. (2012). "Private Higher Education: The Global Surge and Indian Concerns," *India Infrastructure Report 2012*, IDFC, New Delhi and Routledge.

General

1

Public Provisioning of Services in the Context of Democracy

Prabhat Patnaik

The 'Public' and 'Private' in provisioning of public services can be problematized in terms of following four different conceptual issues:

1. In a democratic polity, people are not "subjects" but citizens who exist on the footing of equality, shape their own destiny and collectively contribute to the realization of the social goals of the polity. The provisioning of public goods and services is not for the experts to decide on behalf of citizens. The experts may advise citizens but should not encroach upon people's power to decide. To understand and use their powers, citizens need a minimum bundle of goods and services such as education, food and health. Individualization, fragmentation and social differentiation in the provisioning of these goods and services among citizens are barriers to democratic functioning and constrain the realization of people's freedom. These barriers isolate citizens rather than bring them together. It is the responsibility of the State to provide this bundle of goods and services in a manner that overcomes fragmentation, isolation and social differentiation among citizens. Further, the quality of services to citizens must not be compromised.
2. This minimum bundle of goods and services should not be in the form of commodity production, i.e. these should be provided not as commodities but as direct public provisioning without any discrimination, as this constitutes an essential condition of citizenship. This is particularly true in a society like ours, where the

concept of citizenship goes contrary to the long history of social inequalities that we have inherited. The very idea of a fraternity of equal citizens is something which is fundamentally antithetical to the caste system which believes in institutionalized inequalities. The rights of citizens both in terms of their getting access to a minimum bundle of goods and avoiding social differentiation by not having these bundle of goods delivered in the form of commodities have to be maintained. If this is not insisted upon, then the existing social differentials would continue to be exacerbated over time instead of being overcome as a democracy requires. This is because the poor do not have sufficient resources to purchase the minimum bundle of goods and services. When the cost of a service increases, it leads to a reduction of expenditure on other items like food, clothes, etc. in the budget of a poor household. Due to low purchasing power, the poorer segment of citizens cannot access this minimum bundle of services. This leads to deprivation.

3. The public provisioning of goods and services and their private production results in a certain incompatibility because such services would then have to be purchased by the government. This is problematic because the private producer keeps increasing the price of these services when it is known that the government is the purchaser; for the same reason if these services are provided through the insurance mode and the government pays for then premia, then the government budget gets increasingly drained, while the private producer flourishes by appropriating larger public resources. Therefore, public provisioning must be associated with public production to make it sustainable. In India, services are publicly provided but not publicly produced in their entirety. This situation is tailor-made for the private producers of these services to go on charging more and more to the state for providing these services. Therefore this system is not sustainable. If there is a mix of both public and private sectors producing these services but universal public provisioning, then over a period of time the government sector would atrophy since the private sector would be taking more and more for producing these services. The private sector would eventually replace the public sector as the former starts to appropriate public resources for its own purposes.

The provisioning of public goods and services in India occurs within a universe that is individualistic and fragmented. Whether it is education or health, their supply to citizens is marked by a significant differentiation in availability, access and quality. This is on account of increasing commoditization which militates against equal citizenship. This mode of production and distribution of services does not make them available to all in a uniform or consistent manner. The commoditization of services undoubtedly gives users a choice. But it gives rise to differentiation as people with money can have better access to them both in terms of quantity and quality. Therefore, a minimum level of essential services should be made available to all in equal measure. Beyond this minimum level, if someone wants to seek a better alternative, he/she should be left free to do so. But this minimum should not be provided as a commodity but as a service directly by the government as a citizen's entitlement.

4. The resource constraint of the state is an untenable argument for not producing public services. The state is not a private individual. It has no constraint in raising resources through taxation or borrowing. India has a very low Tax-GDP ratio, among the lowest in the world. Since it is deliberately declining to augment its tax base on ideological considerations, it is thereby abdicating its responsibility to citizens. The resource constraint argument is embedded in neo-liberal thinking: it illicitly extends the logic of private rationality to the state. This logic compels an individual to spend within the limits of the resources available to him, lest he is trapped into insurmountable indebtedness. But applying this logic to the state is deeply flawed. The state cannot act as a private individual. It is supposed to be an embodiment of social rationality. However, there is a forcible curtailment of the powers by the state, enjoining upon it the logic of private rationality because of neoliberalism. The state under neoliberalism is integrated with the global financial order and the economy is open to globalized financial flows, as a result of which a nation-state's capacity to raise resources is constrained. But the state as an embodiment of social rationality should overcome this constraint and raise resources through taxes or borrowings. So a resource constraint of the state should be conceptually non-existent. India's Tax-GDP ratio is among the lowest in the world. There is hardly any capital gains tax or wealth tax. Hence, there is no shortage of resources, but the government does not borrow or tax because it is caught in the vortex of globalized financial flows. The objective should be to get out of this vortex.

2

Experience of PPPs as Observed from Field Visits

Syeda Hameed

With the change of government at the Centre, there have been major changes in governance from the period when the author was a member of the Planning Commission. The planning process has been abolished as there was no discussion on the Thirteenth Five Year Plan. The expertise of preparing Five Year Plans has been given up. Some unique features of the Twelfth Plan such as addressing the problems of new vulnerable groups ('Internally Displaced Persons' (IDPs), for example) had also been buried. Even the sub-plan arrangements for SCs and STs stand abolished. Looking at the overall situation, the future of planning looked very grim.

The experiment with PPPs as a new arrangement to deliver public services is a mixed bag. There were PPPs that were successful as well as those that were not so successful. Based on the experience of having looked into PPPs, there are the following examples of failed PPPs:

- Power loom weavers in Bhiwandi who were agitating as the private electricity companies were charging exorbitant rates.
- In Madhubani and Sitamarhi districts of Bihar, diagnostics were outsourced by the government to private providers and people were unable to pay for it.
- The Baran to Bundi road in Rajasthan had a heavy levy/toll on the road and people were unable to use the road.
- The Chiranjeevi scheme in Gujarat did excessive billings, performed a large number of hysterectomies and unnecessary caesarean sections.

- The Arogyashree scheme in Andhra Pradesh operated under PPP mode for delivering health services became unmanageable by the government.
- In Azamgarh district of Uttar Pradesh there was a partnership with ICICI Lombard for providing health services to 'bunkars' and weavers. The scheme failed miserably. The Ministry of Handloom and Handicrafts was asked not to renew the contract. Yet the contract was renewed.

The PPPs that were relatively successful were the following:

- In Arunachal Pradesh, a PPP scheme was undertaken with the NGO, Karuna Trust, which was running primary health centres and people seemed to be satisfied with the services provided.
- In Udaipur, there was a school health programme with the Nandi Foundation. It seemed to be cost-effective and children were cared for.
- 108 ambulance services were part of NRHM and ambulances were made available in remote areas and lives were saved due to timely intervention.
- In Sahariya village in Rajasthan, Akshaya Patra offered decent meals to the poorest of the poor tribal children with care and affection.

Wherever PPPs were carried out in collaboration with NGOs or non-profit foundations, the results were visibly more beneficial to the people. For partnership of government with other agencies to succeed, a '4 P' process, i.e. public private partnership with people's participation is suggested.

3

Changing Perspectives: Neoliberal Policy Reform in Education and Health in India

Kuldeep Mathur

During the last two decades we have faced the challenge of transforming the way we govern ourselves. It is widely accepted that the traditional system has not fulfilled the expectations of our development and are now looking for transforming or changing it to a system that can stand up to our aspirations. On the one hand, this involves dismantling an institutional structure that is entrenched and has deep roots in our society. On the other hand, it is choosing an institutional structure that can replace it.

It is easy to dismantle but the challenge lies in making choices of new institutions and determining their relationship with state and society. Several decision-makers in our country have turned to neoliberalism as the only framework in which these choices seem to lie. Globalization is a strong source of active influence in closing doors to all other alternatives. India has accepted the neoliberal strategy of development and is an active participant in the globalized world. It is therefore important to understand this framework and particularly explore its consequences in determining public policies in the education and health sector.

What I intend to do in my presentation is draw upon the institutional consequences of the neoliberal agenda and point to the direction of the kind of transformation that is taking place in these two sectors. I try to argue that neoliberalism has introduced new modes of institutional management in higher education and public health and these can be best understood by understanding its tenets of governance reform. The question is whether the issues that we face in these sectors can be resolved by these new institutional arrangements. There does not appear to be an easy answer to this question. As a matter of fact, contradictions and dilemmas are emerging which lead further to uncertainties

II

Broadly speaking, neoliberalism is a theory of political economic practices that proposes that human well-being can best be advanced by liberating the individual entrepreneur's freedoms and skills within an institutional framework characterized by strong property rights, free markets and free trade. The role of the state is to create and preserve an institutional framework appropriate to such practices. (see Harvey, 2007) The core concepts in this theory are of holding individuals responsible and accountable for their own actions and well-being. This principle extends to designing institutions in the realm of welfare, education and health so that the individual expresses his own choices for his own welfare and becomes responsible for them. Together with this is the concept of competition. Individuals bring out the best when they compete with others and this is true for institutions as for individuals. Competition is a way to improve performance and giving an opportunity to individuals and institutions to excel. Therefore the culture of competition is to be inculcated by the state and society. The role of the state, in this theorizing, is clearly demarcated. It is to provide an institutional framework for neoliberal practices to thrive.

The major concern that led to the adoption of the neoliberal strategy was frustration with the traditional system not being able to fulfil the promises held out. It was a reaction to the growth of inefficiencies in the role of the state and its inability to be effective in generating and implementing public policies. In the 1980s and 1990s, this quest for efficiency led to the movement for limiting the scope of state activity. Conventionally, education including higher education and health were included as public good and hence responsibility of the state. With financial and bureaucratic deficiencies the state did not seem to undertake its responsibilities fully. With wide acceptance of liberal ideas, the scope of state activities was redefined and both higher education and public health which were supposed to be in the sole domain of state responsibilities were claimed to be private goods too allowing for the participation of the private sector in state endeavours.

Governance, the term given to the provisioning of institutional framework in the neoliberal agenda, in which the role of the state was clearly defined, had two very important implications. One was that the pursuit of good governance became essentially a pursuit of establishing such institutions and processes that would facilitate the functioning of markets. The state began to be seen as a facilitator for non-state actors to operate and not an institution to intervene in society. Consequently, providing support for successful operation of business and civil society became the central theme of the state's role and activity. The second implication flowing from the first was that business assumed greater power and influence than other segments of society. Large corporate houses began to see themselves as partners of the state in development. Thus, good governance came to mean the development of governing styles in which boundaries between and within public and private sectors became blurred. (Stoker, 1998: 155) The new formulation underlined that political institutions no longer exercise a monopoly of the orchestration of governance. (Pierre, 2000: 4) The concept of governance indicated a shift away from well-established notions of the way government sought to resolve social issues through the top down approach.

In this formulation, the state itself was enjoined to generate public policies in conjunction with non-state actors. It was no more an independent entity intervening or guiding society. Thus, it must be emphasized that it gave up its perceived neutral role and was expected to work in collaboration with business and the non-governmental sector.

Thus the new conceptualization of governance was based on the idea of network relationships of three actors—the state, market and civil society. It is this concept of relationship that became the core thrust of the idea of governance. Governance is seen as an interactive process where institutions work together to achieve results. What is significant in this conceptualization is that the role of government is considerably diluted to give space to private sector and civil society actors. The idea that the public and private sectors are distinct is being subsumed by the idea of cooperation and working together.

In this new world view, the primary role of the government is not merely to direct the actions of the public through regulation and decree, nor is it merely to establish a set of rules and incentives through which people will be guided in the proper direction. Rather the government becomes another player in the process of moving society in one direction or the other. Where traditionally government response to needs has been 'yes, we can provide service' or 'no, we cannot', governance mode would be a response like saying 'yes, let us work together to figure out what we are going to do and then make it happen'.

Markets are relied upon for optimal solutions but markets need certain conditions to succeed. When these conditions do not prevail, markets fail. States could also fail in their obligations. Thus both failures of market and state can occur. Quest for establishing new institutions which could cope with challenges from both state and market failures thus began. Public Private Partnerships offered a new institutional arrangement that would mitigate the perverse effects of the state and market. In this normative formulation, PPPs are associated with desirable attributes of collaboration, trust, responsibility and participation. (Utting and Zammit, 2006: 3)

The emphasis on public-private partnerships changed the pattern of governance, as well as adaptations in management practices and in perceptions regarding the role and responsibilities of different development actors in the context of globalization and liberalization. This transformation has also been termed as a pragmatic turn in official development practice and as pointed out 'approaches to development interventions, and in particular the role of the private sector, are said to be driven by "what works" and less by ideology.' (Utting and Zammit, 2006: 2)

PPPs appeared even more as a pragmatic turn because of the context where the financial circumstances of both the government and private sector were changing. Governments were suffering from financial crisis and fiscal deficits in the 1980s while the corporate sector was doing well with good returns and technological advancement. The corporate sector was being lauded for its efficient management practices. Government sought to tap these private resources for public benefit. Across the world partnership among the three actors—state, market and civil society began to be promoted as a strategy of good governance. The partnerships promise to avoid duplication of efforts and are seen to draw on their complementary resources and capabilities to design a more effective problem-solving mechanisms. They promise to increase responsiveness of policies and create accountability by including other actors—market and civil society—into decision-making processes. They are also presumed to improve compliance with and implementation of political decisions.

The wide appeal of the PPP model was rooted in the political ideals of individual liberty and freedom long regarded sacrosanct and which were the banners of rebellion against the oppression of the state. These were as Harvey (2006:146) calls 'central values of civilization' that continue to resonate throughout the world of various shades of democracy. However, the social and economic policies generated by neoliberalism and its lofty ideals yielded mixed results. Increase in income inequalities and poverty became endemic features of development performance in many countries. The whole emphasis on market and downsizing of state institutions failed to give adequate impetus to growth and investment that would provide adequate protection to the poor.

III

Public Private Partnerships began with infrastructure projects as these demanded heavy investments which only the private sector could provide. Now they are being tried in the social sector. While the challenge that policy makers face in the infrastructure sector is that of creating a more favourable enabling state to attract greater private investment, the story of PPP projects in the social sector has an additional challenge. The concern is not only of creating physical infrastructure but also to provide access to it equitably. With these concerns in mind or ignoring them, the government is moving towards different forms of public-private partnerships at various education levels. There are frequent announcements that it is establishing more schools in this mode. Sometime ago, an erstwhile HRD Minister announced that the government was planning to set up over 2,500 model and 200 central schools on public-private partnership (PPP) basis in the country in the next two years. (*Indian Express*, August 29, 2009). He added that the schools would be set up in public-private partnership as part of our efforts to strengthen the human resource base and then went on to ask the corporate houses to invest in a big way in the education sector emphasizing that developing human resources is key to success of any nation.

Other institutions and researchers have also joined in stressing the need of introducing PPPs in the education sector for similar reasons and also for fulfilling the commitment of raising literacy levels. A World Bank study (Jagannathan, 2001), has explored the working of six NGOs that extend primary education to rural children in India. It is argued that these NGOs have demonstrated effective grassroots action to enhance the quality of basic education and have also influenced mainstreamed education through replication of their models and through policy dialogue with the government. While suggesting that NGOs are best suited for small projects and micro-level interventions, the study strongly advocates sustainable and enduring partnership with the voluntary sector that will strengthen the government's efforts to actualize the goal of universal elementary education. In their official documents both the World Bank as well as Asian Development have been advocating the policy of 'pppisation'.

The Centre for Civil Society launched a School Choice Campaign in 2007 arguing that what the poor need today 'is not just Right to Education, but the Right to Education of Choice.' It advocates public-private partnership through the use of the voucher system. At a recent Conference in 2009, the speakers included representatives of the World Bank and the private sector and stressed the need of quality education by providing choices to the poor. This scheme was called funding the students and not schools and giving choice to the students through a voucher system.

The Ambani-Birla Committee appointed by the Prime Minister's Council of Trade and Industry went on to recommend in its Report in the year 2000 that there needs to be greater association of the private sector in higher education. The Federation of Indian Chambers of Commerce and Industry has been holding summits in higher education from 2004. It has been organizing them as annual international events with the support of the Ministry Human Resources Development and the Planning Commission, Government of India. For some time now, Ernst and Young have joined FICCI to prepare the background paper at these meetings. In the paper prepared for the 2009 summit, titled 'Leveraging Partnerships in India in the Education Sector' the need for PPPs in the higher education sector is underlined. This is necessary to meet the financial constraints of the government and to meet the demand of skilled persons of the industry. It identifies various types of partnerships and also recommends collaboration with foreign universities for research and student exchange.

Thus, the international donor agencies, corporate houses and some civil society organizations are demanding greater public-private partnership in the education sector. Government having articulated its commitment to provide education for all through the enactment of the Right to Education into law is also becoming receptive to these ideas. For it is facing a resource crunch and lack of capacity to run a responsive and efficient educational system.

But the government having articulated its commitment to PPPs in education is still at the stage of experimentation. For one thing, the forms that partnerships can take place in education are diverse. Government aid to schools is a form of partnership that has existed for a long time but does not fit into the current mould. In this partnership, a private entrepreneur or trust provided the school buildings and infrastructure while the government paid for the salary of teachers and regulated the curriculum and quality of teaching. There are also alternatives where the government just provides the land and infrastructural facilities at varying rates of subsidy. There are now many other openings like financing of services like those of IT, underwriting midday meals or handing over of a school to the private sector to provide management services.

At the higher education level the forms it can take is in establishing research collaboration between government and industry, giving space to private entrepreneurs to enter the field and opening up for partnership with foreign universities. For quite some time, large business has been a big player in the field of higher education like engineering and medical education. These institutions were primarily colleges affiliated to universities which exercised control over their academic norms. These colleges were seen as response to the market need of more professionals as doctors and technologists. By the mid-1990s, promoters of private colleges saw the regulatory control of the affiliating university and state governments as cumbersome, impeding the full utilization of the colleges' market potential. Thus, they wanted university status to wriggle out of control of state governments and the affiliating universities. This resulted in the proliferation of private universities and private deemed universities. Earlier, the deemed university provision that empowered an institution to award its own degree was sparingly used to allow leading institutions to offer programmes at an advanced level in a particular field or specialization. The Indian Institute of Science in Bangalore and the Indian Agricultural Research Institute in Delhi were the first two institutions to be declared deemed universities in 1958. This number increased to 29 in 1990/91 and 38 in 1998 and now stands at 122 as of 2017. Most of the post-1998 deemed universities are private. (Agarwal, 2007) The current Minister of HRD is soliciting partnerships with Universities in USA and UK to enhance the quality of education in India.

Privatization in higher education went apace with greater adherence to the governance model laid out in the neoliberal framework. Colleges providing professional education in engineering and medicine and schools at secondary and higher secondary levels multiplied in the private sector. The private sector was hesitant in entering primary schooling for it perceived that it did not give adequate dividends. But even at the level of multiplication of private professionals it has not all been a success story. A recent announcement by the Chairperson of the All India Council of Technical Education says that 800 engineering colleges that have had a student enrolment of less than 30 per cent over five years will be shut down from the coming academic year. However, keeping up with the broader context of neoliberalism, an official from the same Council also says that there is no need for the AICTE to intervene and close down colleges. These colleges will eventually shut down when there is no market demand. (*The Hindu* September 2, 2017)

In the past four decades, the number of universities has grown more than six times. Out of 33,023 colleges, one-third was set up only during the past five years. The number of private institutions grew faster than public institutions. (Gupta, 2016: 360) Some of these institutions are now vigorously seeking alliance with foreign universities to enhance their credibility. The current government is actively encouraging this outreach for this provides the ladder to compete with international institutions and have a place in world rankings.

Privatization has also meant that these institutions are out of direct control of the government. For this reason they have been loosely regulated by it. In any case there are some regulatory bodies like the UGC and AICTE and some professional councils. Many professional institutions are directly under relevant ministries that finance and regulate them.

For-profit organizations, however, have entered for personal gain introducing unscrupulous practices that seem to exploit the students and the community. These practices are not only related to what is taught and how but to financial misdemeanours. There are now capitation fee colleges which demand high admission fees and the students are asked to bear the costs of services that may be advertised but not provided. There is now an increasing risk that financial costs and fees may be out reach of a vast number of students and may lead to restricting education to those who have the ability to pay. Economic deprivation may also result in educational deprivation.

Another equally important, if not more, is the fear that for-profit institutions and foreign collaborations may not fulfil India's quest of social equity. Broadening access may leave out the socially deprived segment of the population. Policies of affirmative action have been pursued in government institutions while private institutions are not mandated to do so. Such expansion in education may not fulfil social aspirations unless adequate steps are taken. Recent surveys and data alert us to what the future may hold.

For example, in Delhi the traditional mode of providing land and infrastructural facilities at subsidized rates has dominated the scene of school education to attract the private sector. But within this sector primary schools have not been so attractive to the private sector. Therefore, this responsibility lies with the municipality and Delhi administration. After the passage of the Right to Education Act, the Supreme Court has made it mandatory for private unaided schools to admit 25 per cent of its students from the economically weaker sections. The Delhi administration has begun enforcing this mandate but has not been very successful. This insistence has met with reluctance as well as some form of resistance from many private managements of schools.

The government has turned to establishing regulatory bodies that can play a more effective role in seeing that private institutions fulfil social goals and work in an ethical fashion. At the same time also allow them adequate autonomy to function well. But it is still struggling to develop an appropriate design. In 2010 the then government had introduced several bills in Parliament to regulate higher educational institutions. Most of them lapsed with the coming of the new government in 2014. These bills could not be passed owing to stiff resistance from the votaries of both public and private sectors. In the meanwhile, the government is going ahead attempting to open the education sector to privatization and international higher education institutions.

If 'partnerships' have to be equitable and accountable, they need an interventionist state which can or be willing to mediate and use its institutional, financial and regulatory resources to create a level playing field. However, if the state itself turns out to be the enabler of the market only, such an interventionist role is doubtful. Partnerships by their very nature mean equality of partners but over the years it has emerged that the corporate houses have used their financial and managerial strength to leverage greater advantages for themselves. Clearly the strength of the corporate sector lies in its ability to refuse to participate in a venture that is not profitable to it.

IV

Government strategy of reforming provisioning health services through public-private partnership bears a dismal record. But in spite of apparent failures it continues to rely on the strategy to improve people's access to health services. It is reported that even the two private parties who were part of NITI Aayog consultations for PPP in healthcare, the Confederation of India Industries and the private healthcare players federation called NATHEALTH were hardpressed to give examples of successful PPP in healthcare. (*Times of India*, August 4, 2017)

State governments in India, under whose jurisdiction the health sector falls, are experimenting with partnerships in many dimensions of the health sector. The scope of these initiatives span disease surveillance, purchase and distribution of drugs in bulk, contracting specialists for high risk pregnancies, national disease control programmes, social marketing, adoption and management of primary health centres, co-location of private facilities (blood banks, pharmacy), looking into subsidies and duty exemptions and joint ventures, contracting out medical education and training, engaging private sector consultants and pay clinics, etc. (Venkatraman and Bjorkman, 2009: 81) It is probably because of this complexity that PPP advocates claim their inability to find successful examples.

There is no single model of partnership in healthcare. What is referred to as the non-government sector, comprises several types of medical tradition that range from local therapies to traditional medicines. Then there is allopathy practised by individual doctors and practitioners of medicine in private clinics and nursing homes, as well as large general or superspeciality hospitals. In this complex space, government has sought partnerships with 'for profit' private sector that usually runs larger hospitals and technical services.

In the past few years, PPPs have multiplied and have entered more fields of healthcare. What is significant is that in most of these PPPs user charges have emerged for primary healthcare services in the urban areas particularly where collaboration is with the private sector. The assumption is that urbanites have the capacity to pay. Thus, entry of the private sector provides little assurance to the poor for adequate health service. This is in face of the well known fact that many such hospitalized patients have to borrow money or sell assets and several fall below the poverty line to cover expenses. Thus the dilemma is that while the public sector does not provide adequate health services, demanding services from the private sector is so expensive that it leaves them further impoverished.

Taking into account the provision of poor health services in the country, the Government of India announced a New Health Policy 2017. The policy continues to advocate a positive engagement with the private sector and pushes for financial and non-financial incentives for it to participate in the provision of health services. NITI Aayog has also out with a strong recommendation for increased private sector participation and has gone to the extent of proposing its participation in district hospitals in tier 2 and 3 cities. A former Union health secretary has gone public criticizing the proposal and arguing that it has adverse implications for the working of district hospitals which are a refuge for the poor. (*Indian Express*, August 11, 2017) The proposal is designed to allow the private sector in the infrastructure facilities to provide treatment for three diseases: cardiology, cancer and pulmonology while the government wing takes care of other diseases. She has called this hybrid model 'bizarre or hair-brained depending on which side of the equation one is on.'

Thus, PPP in health services is on an uncharted path of providing services to the middle and upper classes while depriving the vast majority of the poor of them. But even cases where PPP for establishing superspeciality hospitals with for profit private sector has not turned into a happy one. Costing and pricing of services continues to worry the patients and government faces challenges in regulating them. While there are many examples of relative successes of PPPs in infrastructure, evidence of success in the health sector is rather limited. A health ministry official is quoted as saying that 'we have to deal with a highly corrupt private healthcare sector looking to maximize profits and trying to get the most out of the PPP and a government that behaves like a demanding and suspicious husband in the partnership, making impractical demands with no real management structures.' (*Times of India*, August 4, 2017)

Resource deficiency is cited as the reason for the government to seek partnerships in providing healthcare. But it appears to be a weak alibi because the government does not increase its spending on health. The recent Economic Survey 2016-17 presented to the Parliament points out that the country's public spending on health is slightly over 1 per cent of GDP. It further adds that it was as low as 0.22 per cent of GDP in 1950-51 and does not not seem to have made significant progress since then. The New Health Policy 2017 claims to move towards a target of 2.5 per cent but that has been a moving target for years. It also mentions that capacity, delivery of essential services such as health and education which are predominantly the preserve of the state government remains 'impaired.' Again, poor management of government hospitals and health centres is a reflection of lack of concern and not merely lack of finances.

V

The significant feature of public-private partnerships, is their flexibility and being out of the direct loop of ministerial accountability. They also present the view that development is a technical process amenable only to expert decision-making. JNURM, water user committees, implementation of mid-day meal schemes in schools and running ambulances are recent examples. An equally important dimension of this feature is that issues that are declared technical are simultaneously rendered as non-political. This notion is widely espoused in the new governance style as disenchantment with politics grows. Both the government as well as corporate sources join to voice the need to insulate economic reforms from politics.

One serious implication of this kind of thinking is dilution of public accountability of these institutions. Governance institutions are based on customer accountability and of those who are stakeholders in the endeavour. The larger public or panchayat, for example, does not fall into this domain of accountability. Constitutionally, the Comptroller and Auditor General have the responsibility to certify the legal and financial basis of public expenditure. However, in the case of partnerships, the CAG continues to grapple with ambiguities of scope of audit of PPPs. The guidelines issued for audit of PPPs state that the purpose of audit is not to audit the private sector but to review the end results rather than the way they were achieved. The erstwhile Planning Commission insisted that only the public part of the PPP should be audited and not its component of the private sector. The CAG insists that every rupee spent out of the public exchequer is within its purview. Despite the hesitation of government, the CAG has gone ahead and has submitted audit reports on some PPP projects including those of the construction of international airports at Delhi and Bengaluru and substantiated many comments of misdemeanour that were already in public domain. These related to many decisions that favoured the private sector in face of public interest. Is PPP a public authority within the scope of public audit? Or is it a private institution?

The introduction of the Right to Information Act has further brought to the fore issues of transparency and accountability. It is a welcome move in democracy that recognizes transparency as a key to accountability. However, information on this count is given hesitatingly. The Chief Information Commissioner insists that PPP is a public authority. However, the erstwhile Planning Commission questioned this by saying how a private concessionaire, a private firm, performs its job is not relevant from the RTI point of view.

In both cases of audit and right to information, there is hesitation to make the operations of PPPs public. It must be realized that there appears to be a trend in which transparency and openness in decision-making is actively discouraged to the extent that violence against the information gatherers acts as a warning to dissuade others from seeking information. Parliament is another institution in our democracy that can seek information. But that is also not a success story. A recent survey of questions asked in Parliament showed that questions were few and rare and those that were, were in the form in which written replies were given. No debate has been raised. (For this see Mathur et al., 2013)

A consequence of this understanding is that a crisis of redressal of grievances is growing. As these new institutions exist on the basis of contracts, the legal basis has to be found to enforce the demands of the public. This comes out clearly in case of schools which have been contracting out services or have been enjoined to provide some in return of what the government has assured. For parents in Delhi, remedy lies in court action if certain proportion of seats for weaker sections have to be filled or midday meals schemes have to be more effective. As a matter of fact, in a partnership in which a hospital was supposed to provide a certain number of beds to the poor and the marginalized, it took the High Court to issue a notice to the hospital in response to a doctor's appeal. There are also a few evaluation studies that can assess the working of partnerships.

Regulatory agencies are being proposed as mechanisms to keep educational institutions on track. Past experience has not been particularly a happy one and establishing new ones are already facing problems in their embryonic stage.

Let me conclude by saying that the government's commitment to education has shifted to looking at the private sector in fulfilling its ambitions and goals of raising the stature of India in the world of education. The process generated in the neoliberal framework, represents education as an input-output model. Public-Private Partnerships or contracting out of services to private players rest on terms on what has to be achieved. A contract is signed in which objectives are clearly defined and quantitatively measured outputs are indicated. Much store is laid by, for example, on number of students passed, number of them recruited after graduation or expectation from faculty is on number of research papers published or seminars attended.

These measures of quantitative outputs are taken as indicators of excellence in institutions of higher learning. Much attention is paid on devising measuring indices that could rank these institutions and thus permit their evaluation. These rankings are seen as a source of encouragement of competitive spirit among institutions and a spur for a competitive spirit as valued in neoliberalism.

The whole concept of an institution of higher learning is being redefined in this input-output model. The opportunities of intellectual debate or quality of contribution to knowledge finds little space in this model. Notions of professional norms are not measurable and therefore not included in its evaluation. The traditional professional culture of open intellectual enquiry and debate has been replaced by institutional stress on performance as measured by measurable indicators. (see Olssen and Peters, 2010) The underlying ethos of higher education is a spirit of curiosity, a spirit of tolerance of differing views. What seems to be evolving in this framework is a narrowly instrumental educational system that closes horizons instead of broadening them. How do you produce an argumentative Indian?

Public healthcare is also facing similar challenges. Its problems are complex and assuming that for profit the private sector will provide easily accessible and cost-effective services may not always be valid. A contract is signed with a private entity, the government fulfils its obligation of providing financial and non-financial incentives and demands in return some services for its poorer citizens. This demand is not always fulfilled. Public accountability is weak and patients pay the price.

What I am trying to stress is that we are responding to the slow decline of public welfare institutions as if it just happened because there is a resource crunch without realizing that it is embedded in a coherent philosophy of neoliberalism. Its ideas have become so commonplace that we seldom recognize it as an ideology, a framework in which policies are determined. (Monibiot, 2016)

It appears that neoliberal solutions, privatization or partnerships may be creating more problems than one can foresee. In a country where backwardness is not defined by economic factors alone, the major goal of any public policy is equity and justice. This was recognized by our founders and incorporated into various dimensions of affirmative action. Goals of neoliberalism and governance hold individual incentives and market values of efficiency in high esteem but it is questionable if they can tread the path of equity and justice.

What is needed is a re-evaluation of the role of the state in education and public health and all other public services. The government needs to strengthen its own commitment. Outlays in the welfare sector have not kept pace with demand and have actually been falling in the last few years. But falling outlays is only one part of the problem and is magnified as the only problem. It is not the only culprit. Public welfare institutions are being allowed to decay due to mis-management and government's neglect of its responsibilities of taking timely action in appointments of teachers and heads of institutions, doctors and hospital administrators and release of already budgeted funds. One gets suspicious if there is a deliberate effort to allow public institutions to fail and thus create a policy context for privatization and partnership with the private sector. The state needs to rearrange its priorities, by strengthening its own public institutions and demonstrate that non-state actors only supplement state action and not replace it.

References

Agarwal, Pawan (2007). Higher Education in India: Growth Concerns and Change, *Higher Education Quarterly* 6(2):197-207.

Harvey, David (2007). *A Brief History of Neoliberalism*, Oxford University Press, Oxford.

Gupta, Asha (2016). Emerging Trends in Private Higher Education in India in *Indian Higher Education Report 2015*, eds. N.V. Varghese and Garima Malik, Routledge, London.

Jagannathan, S. (2001). *The Role of Non-Governmental Organizations in Primary Education in India: A Study of Six NGOs*, Policy Research Working Paper, The World Bank, Washington.

Mathur, Kuldeep et al. (2013). *Public-Private Partnership and Public Accountability An Exploration*, Centre for Democracy and Social Action, Delhi.

Monibiot, G. (2016). Neo-Liberalism—The Ideology at the Root of All Our Problems, *The Guardian*, April 16.

Olssen, Mark and Michael Peters (2010). Neo-Liberalism, Higher Education and the Knowledge Economy: From the Free Market to Knowledge Capitalism, *Journal of Education Quarterly* 20, 3:313-345.

Pierre, Jon, ed. (2000). *Debating Governance*, Oxford University Press, Oxford.

Stoker, Gerry (1998). Governance As Theory: Five Propositions, *International Social Science Journal* 50, 155: 17-28.

Utting, Peter and Anne Zammit (2006). *Beyond Pragmatism: Appraising UN Business Partnerships Markets, Business and Regulation Programme*, Paper No. 1, Geneva, United Nations Research Institute for Social Development.

Venkatraman, A. and Bjorkman W. James (2009). *Public-Private Partnerships in Healthcare Services in India: Lessons for Developing Countries*, Routledge, London.

Education—Primary

4

Private Schools, Religion and Commerce: Blurred Boundaries and Opaque Governance in India

Jyotsna Jha

A private school is often mentioned in India as a reference for high quality and usually an 'English medium' school. In the same vein, a public or government school is often referred to as the opposite of this: a poor quality and an Indian language-medium school. It is common to hear statements such as these: "He went to a government school and *still* did well in life' or 'despite poor circumstances, I am sending my children to a private school' usually referring to *his* skills and resilience despite a bad schooling rather than to the good quality of the public school, or a sense of commitment to one's children's education by managing to send them to a private school. Considering that the public schooling system has witnessed an exodus of the middle class in most Indian states, and despite variations, the quality of schooling in government schools largely remains poor, it is not surprising that this perception about the relative quality of public and private schooling is now deeply ingrained. This perception is backed by reality to an extent, especially if viewed from the lens of the high performance of the selected few. But, this is only a half reality.

The available evidence points to diverse realities indicating that the quality of private as well as public schools is varied, and perhaps the variation is higher for private than for public. However, since the 'toppers' are almost always from private schools, they get noticed for their 'quality'. As a society, in recent decades, we have been so deeply concerned about the 'falling quality of schooling' that these results in public examinations and some assessments of learning outcomes are taken as the only and most authentic sources for making a comment on the quality of schooling. Not only the larger goals of schooling both at individual and social levels, such as the ability to question and reason, and build an inclusive and cohesive society, are forgotten but even the instrumental objective of employability is seldom referred to in this debate of learning outcome, which often focuses only on narrow objectives tested through rigid and often decontexualized tools. In this process, we have rarely examined the very genesis and roots of private schooling, and their motivations to understand if that could have implications for the nature and quality of education, especially if the quality is understood beyond the narrow frame of learning outcomes alone.

This paper tries to trace the history and evolution of private schooling in India to understand their motivations and implications for both education processes in schools and for the regulation framework of the state. In a context of growing dependence on privatization of schooling at all stages, and the absence of transparent processes and procedures of both public and private institutions despite an expansion of legal rights and entitlements, it becomes imperative to have such as inquiry and analysis. Examining the relationship of education with religion and with commerce, the paper argues that these two have been the prime motivators of private education provisioning across space and time, and continue to be so in the contemporary periods. This has also influenced the public provisioning even though not necessarily acknowledged overtly. The paper further argues that this needs to be considered in the framing of education policy of a sovereign, socialist, secular and democratic India.

The paper should be read more as an idea to be explored further through deeper research into the subject rather than a result of any deep research into this area. It first examines the pre-colonial and colonial phases followed by an analysis of immediate post-colonial and contemporary phases, and argues that though many changes have occurred in the nature of private schools over a period of time, these two—religion or commerce, or both—have remained the primary motivation for private schooling notwithstanding any other shift. Although the focus here is on schools and not necessary on higher education, my conjecture is that the same is largely true there as well. It is also important to point out that the paper refers to schooling, i.e. institution-based education, when talking of education. The emphasis is on the contemporary, and therefore on colonial and post-colonial phases but I start with a reference to pre-colonial, which is essential to contextualize what we see in later phases. Although the paper does not go into great details, it is also important to understand how the role and interpretation of religion in education and schooling has also changed over time.

Pre-Colonial 'India'

India, as we know today, did not exist but the idea of India existed and covered large parts of the subcontinent. Religion was a prime mover of education in ancient India, of course giving space for intellectual inquiry and philosophical discussions in both Vedic and non-Vedic traditions. Education in ancient India was exclusive and consisted of the orally transmitted education for males belonging to the high caste Brahmin community with Vedic literature as the main source of teaching for Hindus. The emergence of Sanskrit as the language of the educated upper castes throughout the subcontinent isolated other castes for many centuries (Thapar, 1966, p. 48). With the emergence of Buddhism, educational institutions for higher education became prominent. The number of learners increased eventually, and the education system began to get institutionalized. At the same time, the desire for upward social mobility through education had begun to take roots. Buddhist temples and monasteries remained centres for education in the subcontinent including in the present day's Sri Lanka and Myanmar for centuries. With the advent of Islam, two parallel education structures began to emerge in what can be described as pre-colonial India, the *Pathshalas* (Sanskrit-based) for Hindus and the Madrassas (Persian and Arabic-based) for Muslims. While specialized teaching of Art and Music were highly recognized in certain areas, barring certain parts of modern Bengal, Bihar, Tamil Nadu and Kerala, mass education in the form of schools meant to impart literacy and numeracy to young children were absent in pre-colonial India (Kumar, 1991).

Three aspects of education in pre-colonial India are notable: (i) the question of knowledge and its exploration was essentially linked with religion but available evidence does not point to commerce playing any major role in this endeavour, (ii) the institutionalized form was exclusive, especially in the case of Hindu traditions, and (iii) the emphasis on argumentation and dialogic tradition was high, and the heterodoxy of traditions was an important feature of the ancient Indian traditions (Sen, 2005). The question arises how could reason, which is intrinsic to a dialogic tradition, could survive with exclusion on the basis of caste, class and gender. Sen (2005) argues that it was the argumentative tradition of knowledge creation that enabled women to participate in dialogues, and enabled many movements against the caste system questioning orthodoxy and questioning hierarchy (Sen, 2005, p. 10). However, the fact remains that despite strong heterodoxy of thoughts and traditions, provisioning of education was largely a private affair, it was deeply tied to religion, and remained largely the privilege of upper caste males in pre-colonial India.

Colonial India

In the colonial phase, motivated primarily by 'expansion of the faith and civilization of the masses', Christian missionaries became a very important entity. While the relationship between Christian missions and the East India Company or British empire has not necessarily been cordial and complementary throughout the history (Chancey, 1998), Christian missions influenced the Indian school education system significantly for years to come. Despite colonial rulers being cautious in allowing the Christian Missions to interfere with Indian religious beliefs, either Hindu and Muslim, the Mission schools viewed the use of Western education, which also included Christian morals, as a means for expansion of faith; and played a pivotal role in expansion of Western education in India (Bellenoit, 2007). Coming from diverse countries (Denmark, Portugal, UK, Germany and USA) and faith (Catholic, Protestant and other strands of Christianity) but united by their ultimate goal of proselytizing or conversion, they all established schools as a major instrument to establish themselves and to reach 'natives' (Venilla, 2018).

While they questioned exclusion of girls and untouchables, and therefore had a massive appeal as a 'modern' education institution, they also positioned themselves as superior schooling systems based on modern science and technology (Subrahmaniam, 1979). The upper caste Indians who already had exposure to Western liberal thoughts were attracted to English education for both their interest and its use for the higher level jobs in colonial India. While this gave the missionary-based schools an audience and acceptance, these people had the wherewithal to question the need for conversion (Subrahmaniam, 1979). Therefore, Bellenoit (2007) argues that:

> To a degree, Indians usurped the educational enterprise from within to contest the 'superiority' of both Western knowledge and Christianity. In doing so they located traditions of reason and logic in Indian thought. Rather than serving as a hegemonic colonial undertaking, mission schools were subject to Indian agency and contestation. Indians were alert to the advantages of Western educational institutions introduced under British

> rule and appropriated them to reproduce their own social and intellectual foundations. ...conversion, examination preparations and the reliance upon Hindus and Muslims to staff mission schools all ensured that the interaction between Indians and Europeans, in this case, was defined by complexity, contestation and interdependency (Bellenoit, 2007, pp. 393-94).

It was not only in India that Christian Missions played a role in promoting schooling. Christianity had close links with formal schooling both for private and public schooling in the West as well. For instance, Weiner (1991) argues that 'the conviction that every individual, starting at childhood, should be able to read the scriptures was a powerful element in the diffusion of mass education in Protestant countries, so powerful an idea that mass education became widespread even before state intervention' (Weiner, 1991, pp. 181-82). He also argues that religious institutions—Buddhist in Sri Lanka and Hindus in Travancore in Kerala played a key role in diffusion of mass education, even before the arrival of Christian missionaries. He goes on to argue that higher than average literacy rates in the Indian states Goa, Mizoram, Nagaland and Manipur, where the share of Christian population is much higher than the All-India average, 'can be related to the role of Christian missions and government reactions to their educational presence' (Ibid., p. 182).

During the nineteenth century, India also witnessed indigenous debates, discourses and initiatives in education that were linked with religion, especially Hindu religion and its interpretations, perhaps partly fuelled by the contestations that Bellenoit (2007) refers to. This was the period of social reforms in Bengal, often referred to as the Bengali Renaissance, saw emergence of movements that often included opening of schools based on particular philosophy. Social reformers such as Raja Rammohun Roy, who established the Brahmo Samaj, tried to question practices such as *Sati*[1] and also promoted reading of Hindu texts to non-Brahmins, also promoted girls' education and widow-remarriage, a cause that Christian missionaries had tried to champion. The Ramakrishna Mission established a chain of schools that celebrated Hindu religion but condemned practices that marginalized women and untouchables; similar to what the Christian missions were trying to use to enhance their outreach.

Parts of northern and western India saw the emergence of the Arya Samaj movement in the late nineteenth century, which focused on 'back to the Vedas' and established a chain of schools. These reform movements had close links with the national movement but that does not mean there was uniformity in terms of their position regarding many issues linked with education and religion. For instance, the analysis of archival materials on the issue of women's education in late nineteenth and early twentieth century revealed that 'there seems to be a deep schism in the national education movement on the issues of women's education....those who desired to create better opportunities for women were hampered by a number of constraints' (Bhattacharya et al., 2003, p. xix). While absence of agencyhood of women in public life itself was a major constraint, private contributions were also not as easily available for women's education as for men's education because of the firm belief in women's role within the family (Ibid.) and this also had its roots in religion.

Religion not only played a major role in private school initiatives, it also influenced the discourse of what is expected from public education among the nationalists. For instance, J.B.G. Tilak argued for religious education to be a necessary part of the national education because he considered secular education alone 'is not enough' to 'build up character' (Tilak, 1919). Lala Lajpat Rai, on the other hand, opposed the idea of mixing religion with education (Rai, 1919). While the references to Christian missions were common while taking either side of the debate, in later years, references to Hindu and Muslim religions became far more common (Bhattacharya et al., 2003). Irrespective of individual views and opinions, what is evident is that religion and its role had indeed been critical for private initiatives in education but they were by no means unimportant questions even for the nature of public education during the national movement.

What is also evident is that money or funding also entered as a major concern, though not as the main motivation, for religion-based educational institutions in this period. Christian missions received funds from their parent institutions and later also depended mainly on state funding and yet needed to charge fees that only the rich could afford. Even for the Indian initiatives, finding funding sources was a challenge and contributions as well as fees were important for survival. It was difficult to find teachers and others to work at low salaries. For instance, J.B.G. Tilak resigned from the management of the Deccan Education Society, which was formed on the lines of Christian Missions and proudly referred to themselves as Indian Jesuits, on grounds of deviation by many others from the principles of austerity and sacrifice (Tilak, 1919, pp. 4-6). The colonial government was also criticized for favouring Christian missionary schools by violating the principle of religious neutrality in providing grants-in-aid, as guided by the principles of Wood's Despatch. During the colonial rule, what is commonly known as Wood's Despatch of 1854, laid the foundation of state-sponsored mass education system in India by emphasizing the opening of schools across the entire country. For instance, the Bombay Provincial Committee criticized the provision of grants-in-aid to Christian Missionary schools in its submission to the Education Commission in 1882 (Apte, 1882, pp. 47-50). The colonial government supported the missionary schools by providing them grants leading to emergence of so-called private-aided schools, it also tried to influence these schools to underplay the faith issue to be able to continue its political grip.

The late nineteenth and early twentieth century also witnessed the opening of a few residential schools largely meant to serve the elite and rich. Princely states in central India had a role in this development as they wanted to have elitist Western education for their children on the lines of boarding schools in England. For instance, Mayo College in Ajmer and Sindhia School in Gwalior, both started in the latter half of the nineteenth century are two such examples. Similar initiatives also emerged though other sources later; a mix of philanthropy and commerce played a role and led to the starting of Doon School in Dehradun and Modern School in Delhi; these were meant for elites but also took the form of the nationalist idea of developing one's own institutions of high quality.

Four important points emerge for this period: (i) the notion of mass education and state responsibility to provide mass schooling entered India, and the private education, with or without state support was also to play a significant role in creating access to schooling, (ii) in the early phase, private education was largely confined to religious or religion-based civil society bodies where commerce was not the main motive but finding funding sources was a challenge; faith, beliefs and philosophy were still more important, (iii) plurality of thoughts existed within the national movement voices on the role of religion in education, as also on the issues of exclusion linked with gender and caste, and (iv) the emergence of elitist private schools in the later phase largely following the model of high fee-charging private schools in England.

Post-Colonial and Contemporary Phase

In the immediate post-independence period, Nehruvian ideology prevailed and the state became a major provider of school and higher education, where the dominant philosophy was guided by a liberal, democratic frame. Although not translated in reality, the thought that education is a state responsibility existed and guided the policies to an extent. Constitutional space was created for protection of religious minorities and education institutions being run by them but the state schools were conceptualized as secular spaces with no overt role of education. However, the plurality of thoughts and positions on education and its vision for independent India influenced the discourse as well as policies of independent India. Although discussed at length in the Constituent Assembly, primary education was not made a free and compulsory right under the fundamental rights section of the Constitution, and it remained under the section on directive principles. The Government of India continued with the system of three kinds of schools: publicly-funded government schools, aided private schools and unaided private schools. Education was first placed under the State List and later transferred under the Concurrent List with state governments largely deciding the regulatory frames for both public and private schools.

While many indigenous social reform movements that had started earlier were either merged or slowed down with the nationalist movement coming to the fore, educational institutions created by such movements survived and mostly worked within the constitutional norms and contemporary governance structures. For instance, Dayanand Anglo-Vedic (DAV) management runs a few hundred schools and colleges, and the schools are generally affiliated to the Central Board of School Examination (CBSE). Similarly, Ramakrishna Mission schools and other educational institutions are also active in some parts of India, and follow the respective states' affiliations and norms, as applicable. While tracing their roots to 'Indian' philosophy, culture and practices, they also adopted certain 'modern' practices, and operated within a secular and multi-cultural ethos that had guided the spirit of the Indian Constitution. But there also entered a number of new players who eventually became very important in terms of their influences and polity.

Rashtriya Swayamsevak Sangha (RSS), which was somewhat marginalized in the nationalist movement, and especially so after facing a ban in the aftermath of Gandhi's assassination at the hands of Nathuram Godse, who was believed to be an RSS follower, found a new and important tool in the form of opening a chain of schools named Shishu Shiksha Mandir (SSM). Starting its first school in 1952, it expanded to almost all parts of the country and now runs more than 11,000 schools, employing more than 150,000 teachers and enrolling almost three and a half million children. In addition, it also runs nearly ten thousand single teacher informal schools, known as *ekal vidyalayas*, in tribal areas and *sanskriti kendras* in slums, enrolling more than 300,000 students and employing as many teachers (source: http://vidyabharti.net/schools). The interesting part about this chain is that though they are affiliated with either state or central boards, and follow the respective curriculum, they have added subject areas that promote a very unitary and distorted view of the past as well as the present of India, and adopt pedagogies that reinforce and promote patriarchal and 'nationalist' notions, which are often at conflict with the fundamental philosophy of the Indian Constitution that is committed to equality, freedom and secularism (Sunder, 2005).

It is obvious that SSMs were conceptualized on the lines of Church-based schools in the colonial era, where propagation of religious doctrines was the main objective. However, many argue that these are worse, as SSMs are distorting Indian history to inculcate hatred towards Muslims and Christians, and portray them as outsiders to India (Ibid.), and which is defended in the name of *prabhu bhakti* or devotion to God and *desh bhakti*—devotion to nation (Nair, 2009). An important point to note is that unlike other social reform movements such as the Arya Samaj and Brahmo Samaj, who took to Indian culture and philosophy to counter the uncritical acceptance of Western or Christian values but also critiqued the Indian practices that they considered antithetical to their understanding of Hindu or Indian philosophy, the RSS does not have any history of engagement with social reform in the colonial period.

An important aspect of SSMs is their linkage with the RSS and the Bharatiya Janata Party (BJP)—widely known as the political wing of the RSS, and its emergence as a major force in electoral politics of contemporary India. Vidya Bharati, which is the main institution to develop curriculum, training and other such guiding principles and materials for SSMs and Vidya Mandirs (high schools known as VM) is said to have benefited wherever and wherever BJP or BJP-led governments have ruled; these appear in various forms such as allotment of prime land on a priority basis, allocation of grants under various schemes such as Local Area Development grants, a fund that is managed exclusively by the local Member of Parliament, fast approvals and sanctions, and in getting recognition from the government. However, donations and fees have remained their main source of revenue (Ibid., pp. 55-57).

More importantly, closeness to the RSS and BJP allowed them to gain credibility and enter the premier institutions responsible for designing the school curriculum, National Council for Educational Research and Training (NCERT). It is ironical that in 1996, NCERT in one of its reviews observed that 'many of the books being used by the Vidya Bharati schools were designed to promote "bigotry and religious fanaticism" in the guise of culture. Despite this, some of these textbooks were subsequently introduced in government schools in BJP-run states' (Ibid., p. 58). With the rise of the BJP as a major political force in the electoral politics with successive wins with a clear majority in the national elections in 2014 and 2019, Vidya Bharati and the affiliated schools are going to be much more entrenched in the national institutions and their influence as well as penetration in the public schooling system is also likely to be much deeper alongside perhaps their own expansion and flourishment. What we see here is that religion, in some form, continued to play a very important role not only in private but also started influencing the public education, something that was far less visible in early post-independent years. Money also entered this sphere but perhaps still remained a secondary motivation as compared to internalization of 'values'. However, the same period of the last three decades also witnessed exponential growth of schools that were predominantly guided by commercial interests. But before discussing that, it is important to discuss the rise in the number of schools based on Islamic ideology, and the change in the nature of such schools from earlier phases.

An important distinction between schools such as SSMs and Madrasas is that while SSMs are regular schools that promote one particular perspective of the majority Hindu religious ideology in India, Madrasas are openly religious schools of a major minority in India. Scholarly engagement with Madrasas in India has been somewhat to a lesser degree as compared to the huge amount of grey literature that is easily accessible. It is difficult to estimate the real number of Madrasas in absence of any authentic data, and also in absence of a clear definition. Each mosque runs a maqtab for religious teaching of young children. Some Madrasas operate at primary level while others are meant for higher level learning, that can be somehow equated with upper primary, secondary and tertiary levels. Although primarily confined to religious teaching, they also cover other areas depending on affiliation and location. Separate Madrasa Boards exist in certain Indian states such Assam, Bihar, West Bengal and UP. These states and a few others like Kerala also provide them state aid if they follow the state curriculum in addition to religious teaching (Jha and Jhingran, 2005).

The need for religious education is only one of the factors that drive the demand for Madrasa education; some are similar to what others from deprived backgrounds face while some are specific to being a Muslim. Lack of schooling-employment linkages and the lack of government or affordable schools within physical reach are common factors but in addition cultural isolation and suspicion of being 'the other' also drives Muslims away from regular schools (Jha and Jhingran, 2005; Asma and Shazli, 2015; Borker, 2015). Muslims are also not a monolithic group; caste, class location influence their schooling related behaviour significantly (Ahmad, 2001; Jha and Jhingran, 2005). State policies expressed through schemes such as Modernisation of Madrasas tends to view all Madrasas as a 'backward' place that carries the danger of radicalizing the Muslim youth and therefore needs to be modernized with minimal interventions such as provision of one science teacher and some equipment, and therefore fail in their objectives (Jha and Jhingran, 2005; Asma and Shazli, 2015; Borker, 2015).

In reality, Madrasas are not necessarily the same and those who choose private Madrasas that are well-funded and fully functional, do so as a conscious choice for livelihood as well as for asserting their identity (Jha and Jhingran, 2005; Borker, 2015; Taylor, 2015). Many private Madrasas have already adopted modern subjects and skills, and made efforts to establish linkages with universities, which simplistic schemes such as Modernization of Madrasas does not acknowledge (Borker, 2015). Most Madrasas offer free education largely through donations from within and outside the country, and those that are well-funded also provide relevant education that helps in social and economic mobility of Muslim young people, mostly boys but also sometimes girls. For instance, Nadwa Madrasa in Lucknow 'provides free education to significant numbers of Muslim students, resulting in perceived employment opportunities, as well as in other forms of social mobility that are highly salient such as gains in social status and overcoming caste barriers' (Taylor, 2015, p. 11). Employment prospects include religious jobs as well as ease in finding jobs in the Middle East, as the education in this and similar other Madrasas include Arabic teaching and teaching of many subjects beyond religious teaching (Taylor, 2015).

What emerges is that the number of Madrasas has indeed increased and so has the funding for private Madrasas. The funding is through donations and includes international funding. The motivation is to promote religious teaching and promote the well-being of Muslim youth by enabling them to develop skills that are more amenable to new economic opportunities, and perhaps also to combat the isolation they face and develop a more homogeneous Muslim identity as compared to what it has historically been. Available evidence based on ethnographic work with Madrasas and students is limited, but they do not provide pointers towards their radicalization but indicates the need for assertion of identity on the face of isolation and hostility faced in regular schools (Borker, 2015; Taylor, 2015). Commercial interests do not play a role as earning profit does not enter here as a motive but easy access to funding matters in smooth functioning. Dependence on any favour from the state is almost non-existent except in case of aided Madrasas.

In the post-independent period, Christian missionary schools became more secular in terms of their curriculum and teaching, and the demand for these schools has been driven by the popular belief, especially among the middle class in urban areas, that it was high quality English medium education. The number of schools has remained confined to a few hundred and other than cities, there is larger concentration in tribal areas and in cities and states where the proportion of Christian population is relatively higher. While they have faced allegations of forced conversions in some remote rural areas by right wing Hindu groups, in most cases, it is denied by respective missionary activists. In absence of any authentic source, it is difficult to ascertain the veracity of such allegations but perhaps the fact somewhere lies in between—there could be a few cases of involuntary conversion but there has also been a persistent fear of 'majoritarian' harassment among religious minorities for being falsely indicted of promoting involuntary conversion, especially Muslims and Christians, since the political rise of the BJP and its affiliated institutions.

Although the story of religion-based or religion-inspired private schools are critical to understand the landscape, the rise of non-denominational, trust-based private schools is a no less important phenomenon in contemporary India. What started as a part nationalist and part philanthropist venture with Doon School in Dehradun and Modern School in Delhi, evolved into opening of a series of such schools, now guided more by pure commercial interests than any philanthropical motivation. Delhi Public School is one such example that started soon after independence as Naveen Bharath School at Mathura Road in Delhi; it had no other branch till the early 1970s but the school now has more than 200 schools, most of them running through franchise, across India and a number of other countries. Many other similar chains have emerged in different parts of the country. One of the most sought-after schools by the Indian middle class, one particular such chain openly practises 'streaming' by putting together high-performing students together before public examinations, and weeding out 'low-performing' students to go for other options such as open schooling in order to keep the average performance rates high, as that is their selling point.[2] A number of similar private schools, focusing on academic performance in public examinations as the main achievement, started and succeeded commercially across the country till the 1990s. Although not necessarily started with commerce as the main motive, commerce entered as an important consideration in their expansion. These are largely, though not necessarily, secular in their ideology and serve urban and peri-urban upper and middle classes.

During the 1990s and later years, in the wake of liberalization, the private sector started expanding in many sectors, including school education. Two new kinds of private schools entered: low cost budget schools and high cost elite schools. These elite schools unlike those of the past offer international certifications and charge extremely high fees. They also followed the inquiry-based approach aimed at developing thinking, analytical and reflective skills amongst students using highly qualified, well-paid teachers. On the other hand, the lower end budget schools encourage the use of technology-based solutions with the help of low-paid, less-trained teachers (Jha, 2016). The entry of the so-called budget schools at one end of the spectrum and that of the high-fee, high-end 'international' schools offering IB (International Baccalaureate) curriculum and also the choices of Indian as well as external Board certifications, e.g. the British General Certificate of Education (GCE), giving O-Ordinary and A-Advance level certificates, added a new dimension to the nature of private schooling in India, and created new forms of divides, that can also be described as an apartheid in education: at the highest level are the elite schools and at the lowest level the government schools, with the traditional private sector being the second, and the new so-called budget private schools at the third rung of this hierarchy (Ibid.). The rich, who could afford, shifted from the traditional private schools and patronized the high-end alternatives as a deviation from the rigid, rote-learning-based schooling system, whereas the budget private schools run largely by 'education managers' were vociferously advocated as 'an affordable and effective' alternative to the 'dysfunctional, low-quality state schools' for the poor' (Ibid., pp. 42-43).

The primacy of commercial interests surfaces in many ways: charging various forms of fees from students that remain largely hidden and lack transparency, persistent and motivated advocacy in favour of policy support and public investment for affordable private schools in the name of offering 'school choice' to the poor, often backed by powerful networks to promote market-based interventions in education and therefore with obvious business interests. These institutions have also entered public schools through the mode of public-private partnership which has become the new name of contracting out work by public entities to private bodies using public money (Jha, 2016; Nambissan and Hall, 2010; Nambissan, 2012). Religion took a back seat in these cases with commerce being the primary motive. But with the BJP in power and RSS-backed organizations gaining credibility and access to national institutions and mechanisms, majoritarian religious ideology and political agendas are entering the education space including both public and private schools in many ways: overt and hidden curricula, surveillance, regulation and threat. While so far religion was one of the major motivations for private education but public education had remained, at least in its intention, secular. Now with public itself guided by a different ideology, the differences seem to be blurring on that count. Also, encouraged by the political signals, recent years have also witnessed the emergence of new high-fee-charging elite schools that are combining commerce with religion: any review of school advertisements in English language newspapers and magazines establishes this.

It is also important to add that the Indian state and the state governments have also been largely unengaged or have allowed a wilfully negligent attitude in developing any clear and transparent regulatory mechanism for either public or private schooling systems that enables understanding and growth of a secular space for learning. The quality discourse in the last one decade has remained almost uninformed by issues of caste, class, gender and religion, and learning outcomes have emerged as a single measure, with no connection to the context, of quality. The school monitoring mechanisms have also focused much more on the presence of defined inputs and learning outcomes; processes and relationships that could help us understand the pedagogy and hidden curriculum aspects are rarely studied by the state.

So, we see four major trends in post-independent India: (i) continued importance but changing faces of religion-based private education, (ii) emergence of major private players that are different from the initial phase of trust-based education; these are far more guided by commercial interest than anything else, (iii) absence of clear and transparent regulatory mechanisms, indicators and processes for 'school' to act as a secular space of learning (iv) religious and political ideologies joining hands to promote a particular kind of private schools and overt entry of majoritarian religious ideology and political agendas in the public educational spaces.

Conclusion

It is clear that religion has played a pivotal role in the emergence of private schools in India throughout history. Commerce is also an important motivation and we are not also witnessing these two motivations coming together though traditionally, these were not necessarily united. However, what distinguishes the contemporary from the colonial and even pre-colonial is that unlike those phases, there is no space for reason and dialogic education in the contemporary space of education ideology, institutions and practices. In ancient India, though formal education was exclusive, it was the focus on reason and dialogic tradition in education, that allowed discourses on caste, class and gender to take place (Sen, 2005). In colonial India, Indian scholars, especially social reformers and philosophers reflected on their own practices and questioned the supremacy of Western education by locating 'traditions of reasons and logic in Indian thoughts' (Bellenoit, 2007, p. 393) and therefore, 'rather than serving as a hegemonic colonial undertaking, mission schools were subject to Indian agency and contestation' (Ibid.). Unlike the past, the place for reason and dialogic tradition has shrunk in the education-related discourse in the contemporary phase and I argue that this is also a result of, among other things, a lack of focus on a comprehensive definition of quality. The focus on reason and argumentative tradition that Sen (2005) refers to as the defining character of being an 'Indian' seemed to have shrunk gradually and widely. Mere reproduction of mugged 'knowledge' became important for success and it coincided with internalization of values and thoughts without questioning becoming the norm in schools. While public schools have not necessarily been overtly religious, they also lack the power and wherewithal to become secular and resilient spaces for knowledge creation. And now, with the boundaries between public and private being blurred in more than one way: private commercial interests entering public though public-private partnerships, and majoritarian singular ideology entering major educational institutions that guide the curriculum, textbooks and teacher-training, and with opaque processes and practices, education in India is perhaps going to be even more influenced by religion and·commerce bereft of any focus on reason and dialogue, in days and years to come.

Notes

1. The practice of sati refers to the act of committing public suicide by jumping into the funeral pyre of dead husband; this was common and considered desirable for widows among Hindus in some parts of India.
2. ODL Hyderabad workshop reference.

References

Ahmad, Imtiaz (2001). *Muslim Empowerment,* mimeo.

Apte, V.S. (1882). Education Committee Bombay Provincial Committee submission, as Document No. 17 in Bhattacharya et al., 2003, *Educating the Nation,* Kanishka Publishers and Jawaharlal Nehru University, New Delhi, pp. 47-53.

Asma, Sana and Tasneem Shazli, Role of Madarsa Education in Empowerment of Muslims in India, *IOSR Journal of Humanities and Social Science (IOSR-JHSS),* Vol. 20, Issue 2, Ver. V (February 2015), pp. 10-15.

Bellenoit, Hayden J.A. (2007). Missionary Education, Religion and Knowledge in India, c.1880-1915, *Modern Asian Studies* 41, 2 (2007) pp. 369-394.

Bhattacharya, Sabyasachi (2003). Introduction in Sabyasachi Bhattacharya, Joseph Bara and Chinna Rao Yagati, 2003, *Educating the Nation*, Kanishka Publishers and Jawaharlal Nehru University, New Delhi.

Borker, Hem (2015). The State's Flawed Focus on Madrasas, *The Hindu*, July 20, 2015 https://www.thehindu.com/opinion/lead/maharashtras-flawed-focus-on-madrasas/article7440862.ece

Chancey, Karen (1998). The Star in the East: The Controversy over Christian Missions to India, 1805-1813, *The Historian*, Vol. 60, No. 3 (Spring 1998), pp. 507-522.

Jha, Jyotsna (2016). Education India Private Limited, *Education at the Crossroad, IIC Quarterly*, Winter 2015-Spring 2016, New Delhi.

Jha, Jyotsna and Dhir Jhingran (2005). *Elementary Education for the Poorest and Other Deprived Groups,* Manohar Publications, New Delhi.

Kumar, Krishna (2005). *Political Agenda of Education,* Second Edition, Sage Publications.

Nair, Padmaja (2009). Religious Political Parties and their Welfare Work: Relations Between the RSS, the Bharatiya Janata Party and the Vidya Bharati Schools in India, Religions and Development Working Paper No. 37, International Development Department, University of Birmingham.

Nambissan, Geetha B. (2012). Private Schools for the Poor: Business as Usual, *Economic and Political Weekly,* October 13, Vol. xlvii, No. 41 for a review of papers and articles supporting low-cost budget schools.

Nambissan, Geetha B. and Stephen J. Hall (2010). Advocacy Networks, Choice and Private.

Rai, Lala Lajpat (1919). *The Modern Review*, March-April, 1999, as Document No. 9 in Bhattacharya et al., 2003, *Educating the Nation*, Kanishka Publishers and Jawaharlal Nehru University, New Delhi, pp. 21-27.

Sen, Amartya (2005). *The Argumentative Indian*, Penguin Books.

Subramaniam, V. (1979). Consequences of Christian Missionary Education, *Third World Quarterly*, Vol. 1, No. 3 (July 1979), pp. 129-131.

Sunder, Nandini (2004). Teaching to Hate, *Economic and Political Weekly*, April 17, pp. 1605-1612.

Taylor, Christopher B. 'Madrasas and Social Mobility in the Religious Economy: The Case of Nadwat al-'Ulama in Lucknow', *South Asia Multidisciplinary Academic Journal* [Online], 11 | 2015, Online since July 15, 2015, connection on April 30, 2019. URL: http://journals.openedition.org/samaj/3932 ; DOI: 10.4000/samaj.3932

Thapar, Romila (1966). *A History of India*, Vol. 1, Penguin Books.

Tilak, Bal Gangadhar (1890). The History of the Deccan Education Society, Poona, 1935, Part III, as Document No. 2, in Bhattacharya et al., 2003, *Educating the Nation*, Kanishka Publishers and Jawaharlal Nehru University, New Delhi, pp. 12-14.

Tilak, Bal Gangadhar (1919). Bal Gangadhar Tilak: His Writing and Speeches, as Document No. 6 in Bhattacharya et al., 2003, *Educating the Nation*, Kanishka Publishers and Jawaharlal Nehru University, New Delhi, pp. 4-7

Vennila, G. (2018). Role of Missionaries in Indian Education, *International Journal of Advance Research and Development*, Vol. 3, Issue 4, Available online at: www.ijarnd.com.

Weiner, Myron (1991). *The Child and the State in India*, Oxford Paperbacks, Oxford University Press.

5

Public versus Private Provisioning of Elementary Education in India: A Trend in Privatization

Ashok Pankaj and Poornima M.

With the commencement of modern education in India in the colonial period, private players have been actively engaged in the field of providing school education. However, the nature of their involvement has been changing. In the initial years of the colonial period, Christian missionaries were encouraged to open schools in large numbers, especially in inaccessible areas where government machinery had a thin presence. The then government was least interested in the educational development of these areas. Missionaries were also invited to open schools for providing education to the children of British and Indian officials. This gave birth to the residential elite in English medium schools. With the establishments of municipalities and local-self-government by Lord Rippon in 1882, the colonial government entrusted them with the responsibilities of providing school education. Lord Rippon also constituted an Education Commission under the chairmanship of William Hunter in 1882 that recommended entrusting the responsibility of managing school education to local-self-government. It also recommended providing grants-in-aid to private organizations. In the 1920s and 1930s, fired by the zeal of Swadeshi and on the call of the non-cooperation movement, nationalist organizations and charitable societies opened schools in large numbers. By the time of independence, a sizeable proportion of elementary schools were either run by municipalities or local bodies or were aided by the government.

In the post-independence period, there was massive expansion of school education in the decades of the 1960s and 1970s, so much so that the total number of schools opened in the two decades was equal to the total number of schools opened up to independence. The government took this responsibility in a big way considering the significance of education, even though the constitution makers had decided to place right to education of 6-14-year children under the Directive Principles of State Policy (Article 45), a non-justiciable right. At the same time, the government continued with the policy of encouraging private players, mostly charitable and philanthropic organizations, to open up schools and promoted them through grants-in-aid and other assistances. In the 1960s, the Kothari Commission irrevocably asserted that the government should take the main responsibility of providing free and compulsory universal elementary education. In the 1970s and 1980s, although the government opened fewer schools compared to the decades of the 1950s and 1960s, the government remained committed to providing universal elementary education. The situation remained the same in the 1980s. Till the 1980s, the rate of growth of government schools was greater than that of private schools.

The situation changed in the 1990s. With the adoption of the new economic policy in 1990-91, there was a shift in policy approach. The government decided to minimalize its role in social sector development including education and encouraged private players to take greater responsibility. A reflection on the shift in approach can be seen in the various Five Year Plan documents. The Ninth Five Year Plan (1997-2002) emphasized the need for creating a conducive and supportive environment for private players (Government of India, 1999). The Tenth Plan (2002-07) made it more explicit by saying that the role of government should decline in public sectors, including the social sector (Government of India, 2002). The Eleventh Plan (2007-12) reiterated and emphasized that private players should be encouraged to achieve excellence in education (Government of India, 2008). The Twelfth Five Year Plan (2012-17) went one step further and constituted a Working Group on Private Sector Participation in School Education with an objective of tapping private sector capabilities and promoting their role in providing school education (Government of India, 2013).

The NITI Aayog that replaced the erstwhile Planning Commission, in its Three Year Action Agenda made a more radical proposal and suggested the education voucher system to tap the private sector (Government of India, 2017). The Draft National Education Policy, 2019, on the one hand, lays a great deal of emphasis on public provisioning of education, especially at early childhood care and education (ECCC), and on the other hand, also provides space for private players by suggesting multiple models of school and allowing healthy competition between public and private players, including giving options to parents to send their children to either (Government of India, 2019).

When the government withdrew from public provisioning of school education, an important development took place. The 86th Constitutional Amendment Act, 2002, made right to education a Fundamental Right by inserting Article 21-A in the Constitution of India. This was followed by the enactment of the Right of Children to Free and Compulsory Education Act, 2009, that made comprehensive provisions for providing free and compulsory education to 6-14-year-old children. The Right to Education (RTE) Act, 2009, came into force in April 2010, although different states notified it on different dates and years. With the insertion of Article 21A in the Constitution and the enactment of the RTE Act, 2009, it became obligatory on the part of the state to ensure right to free and compulsory education to 6-14-year-old children.

Paradoxically, the number of private schools in the elementary section and the total number of children enrolled in them that have been growing since the 1990s, increased dramatically in the 2010s. Private schools constituted 5.58 per cent of the total elementary schools in 1993-94 that increased to 8.43 per cent in 2001-02, 11.42 per cent in 2009-10, and further, to 19.04 per cent in 2016-17. They constituted 3.25 per cent of the total schools in 1949-50 and declined to 1.86 per cent in 1960-61. The share of private schools is greater in terms of total enrolled children. In 2016-17, private schools constituted 19.52 per cent of the total elementary schools, but 31.37 per cent of the total elementary school children.[1]

It is argued here that given India's socio-economic conditions, the increasing reach of private schools and greater level of reliance on them by the government are fraught with serious socio-economic consequences. Firstly, the withdrawal of the government from public provisioning of schools would lead to the denial of the right to free and compulsory education and defeat the objectives of the Right to Education Act, 2009. This is because, while government schools are accessible to all; private schools are not. The former provide free education; the latter charge fees, based on commercial considerations, which are unaffordable by most of the poor and low income population. Secondly, largely because of the first, there would be unequal access to school education. A vast number of children belonging to the low economic strata, who invariably belong to a low social class, would be deprived of education. The RTE Act though makes provision for the admission of children belonging to economically weaker sections (EWS) of population into private schools [Section 12(1)(c)], not all are able to secure the access. Further, this provision has been flagrantly violated, and there have been malpractices in its implementation. Most importantly, this provision is a supplementary provision to ensure that private players share the responsibility of providing elementary school education for the fulfilment of the RTE Act objective. Thirdly, education is a social good which provides socio-economic mobility to a large section of marginalized population. However, their avenues of mobility would be restricted with increasing privatization. Fourthly, the society would get divided between educated and non-educated. Much of the success in terms of achieving equality through education would be wiped out. Fifthly, with a sizeable section of population, deprived of elementary education, economic growth and development would be adversely affected. Sixthly, educated population are essential elements for success of democracy and nation building. However, privatization limits the access and increases the non-educated lot, thereby weakening democracy.

II

The significance of education for society has been underlined by many scholars. Schultz (1971) and Sen (1990) have argued for investment in education for human capital formation that, in turn, would lead to economic growth and development. Sen has emphasized the importance of education for opening up opportunities and increasing choices what he calls "freedom for development" (Sen, 1999). Sen and Dréze (2002) have identified five distinct ways through which education helps in socio-economic development of an individual and society. For them education plays five important roles. These are: intrinsic importance, instrumental personal role, instrumental social role, process role, and empowerment role. Tilak (2017) has emphasized equalizing role of education, and argued that it is a great equalizer in society. Beteille (2008) too emphasized equalizing role of education, as it bridges the gap between school educated and non-educated. Amin (1996) and Mukhopadhyay and Garimella (1998) have argued that education improves the status of marginalized communities by giving them decision-making power. It also increases opportunity for equal participation. It increases their ability to overcome or resist cultural biases.

The Kothari Commission (1964) stated that education has a social objective that is to equalize opportunity and enable the backward or underprivileged classes and individuals to improve their socio-economic conditions (Government of India, 1966). The National Policy on Education (NPE), 1968, emphasized the importance of equalization of educational opportunity to address issues like regional imbalance and problems of education of girls, backward classes, tribal and handicapped population (Government of India, 1968). The National Policy on Education (NPE), 1986, and the subsequent Plan of Action, 1992, reiterated the relevance of education in attaining equality and laid down a roadmap to address the educational deprivations of SCs, STs, OBCs, religious minorities, girls and children with special needs (Government of India, 1986). The 1986 policy went further to emphasize the role of education and its contribution for all-round development of individuals, society and economy and for strengthening the goals of socialism, secularism and democracy. The Draft National Education Policy (NEP), 2019, envisaged the role of education for creating "a just and equitable society (Government of India, 2019: 24)." The protagonists of privatization of school education plead that the private sector would supplement government efforts in providing school education. It would also provide more options to parents to choose between different types of schools (Shah and Miranda, 2013). It is further argued that private schools provide better education, good infrastructure, quality teachers, which results in better learning outcomes (Kingdon and Teal, 2007). They also argue for privatization on efficiency and outcome considerations. The draft NEP 2019 also argued that it would lead to healthy competition between public and private schools that will also force public schools to improve (Government of India, 2019).

Those who favour public provisioning of school education counter the arguments of protagonists of privatization. Winch (1996) argues that education is not a marketable good. It is a social good which has externalities. Muralidharan and Sundararaman (2015) show that there are no clear differences in learning outcomes of government and low-fee private schools, which constitute a sizeable proportion of the total private schools in India. Härmä (2011), Srivastava (2007) and Lahoti and Mukhopadhaya (2019) have shown that the parental choice of school is not necessarily based on a rational decision. Apart from the lack of information, parental choices are influenced by various other considerations. Lahoti and Mukhopadhaya (2019) have shown that parental choice of school is a complex process.

Apart from learning outcomes, discipline and safety, the language of instruction, expenses, and marketing strategy like advertisements by private schools determine parental choice of public and private schools. Pankaj and Poornima (2019) have shown through a large-scale household survey that English medium education, tailor-made school uniforms, and school vans have been a major attraction for private schools. Above all, there is a general negative perception about government schools as providers of poor quality education that has pushed children out of government schools.

This paper argues that public provisioning of school education in India is not only a constitutional goal, but a necessary condition for socio-economic development. Increasing privatization of school education is not only against the spirit of Article 21A of the Constitution and the broad objective of the RTE Act, 2009, but is bound to widen socio-economic inequality. The previous section discussed the significance of education for society. Section III of this paper shows differential access to public and private schools in India, using U-DISE data for 2016-17 and our own survey data collected from four districts of four states[2]. These are: Ghazipur from UP, Sikar from Rajasthan, Bellary from Karnataka and Kanyakumari from Tamil Nadu. Section IV examines the social and economic cost of private education. The concluding section sums up the main arguments of this paper.

III

Decline in Government and Increase in Private Schools

There has been a decline in the share of government schools and increase in the share of private schools. For example, between 2010-11 and 2014-15, in 20 major states, government schools increased by 16,376, whereas private schools increased by 71,360, which was almost five times more than the increase in the number of government schools. In some states, there has been a negative growth in the number of government schools. These are Andhra Pradesh (including Telangana), Haryana, Karnataka, Maharashtra and Rajasthan. In contrast to the above, in states like Bihar, UP, West Bengal, Madhya Pradesh and Chhattisgarh there has been an increase in the number of both government and private schools, but the increase has been more in case of the private than government schools (Kingdon, 2017: 15).

In 2016-17, 77.25 per cent of the total elementary schools were government and the rest were private. The proportion of government and private schools varied across rural and urban areas across states. Government schools constituted 82.76 per cent of the total elementary schools in rural areas, but only 46.49 per cent in urban areas. Government schools dominate in numbers in rural areas in most of the states. Private schools constitute more than 50 per cent in urban areas of Uttarakhand, Uttar Pradesh, Sikkim, Rajasthan, Punjab, Nagaland, Madhya Pradesh, Karnataka, Himachal Pradesh, Haryana, Gujarat and Andhra Pradesh. The state-wise proportion of government and private schools across rural and urban areas has been shown in Table 1.

Enrolment in Government and Private Schools

Government schools constitute 77.25 per cent of the total elementary schools in India, but enrol only 65.95 per cent of the total elementary school children. In rural areas, government schools constitute 82.76 per cent of the total elementary schools and enrol 73.09 per cent of the total children. In urban areas, government schools constitute 46.49 per cent of the total elementary schools and enrol 47.38 per cent of the total children. This shows that the private schools attract more number of students than government schools.

Table 2 shows state-wise proportion of children enrolled in government and private schools across rural and urban areas. It shows that in Assam, Bihar, Goa, Tripura and West Bengal, more than 80 per cent of the total elementary school children were in government schools. It is between 60 and 80 per cent in Arunachal Pradesh, Chhattisgarh, Gujarat, Himachal Pradesh, Jharkhand, Karnataka, Kerala, Madhya Pradesh, Maharashtra, Meghalaya, Sikkim and Tamil Nadu. The enrolment of students in private schools is the highest in Nagaland followed by Manipur, Haryana, Rajasthan, Uttar Pradesh, Uttarakhand, Andhra Pradesh and Jammu & Kashmir.

Differential Access to Government and Private Schools

There are differential accesses to government and private schools. They are pronounced in terms of caste, gender and economic class category.

Caste and Gender-Wise

Caste and gender-wise access to government and private schools varies. A relatively greater proportion of low castes and girls than their counterpart upper castes and boys are enrolled in government schools. It means they continue to depend on government schools for elementary education. In 2016-17, 76.39 per cent of the SC and 84.89 per cent of the ST against 66.28 per cent of the general students were enrolled in government schools. In

Table 1: Percentage Share of Government and Private Schools in Rural and Urban Areas

	Rural			Urban			Total		
State	Government*	Private	Others**	Government*	Private	Others**	Government*	Private	Others**
Andaman & Nicobar Islands	87.64	12.36		57.63	42.37		83.37	16.63	
Andhra Pradesh	84.42	15.05	0.53	41.66	55.46	2.88	76.26	22.76	0.98
Arunachal Pradesh	90.33	8.90	0.77	56.95	39.41	3.64	86.72	12.20	1.08
Assam	81.80	5.72	12.49	72.47	22.08	5.45	81.27	6.64	12.09
Bihar	91.14	3.77	5.09	61.88	18.89	19.23	88.46	5.16	6.39
Chandigarh$	100.00			57.84	39.46	2.70	61.19	36.32	2.49
Chhattisgarh	91.95	7.86	0.19	54.11	43.44	2.45	87.82	11.75	0.44
Dadar & Nagar Haveli	92.58	6.77	0.65	64.86	32.43	2.70	89.63	9.51	0.86
Daman & Diu	88.89	11.11		76.09	23.91		84.83	15.17	
Delhi	63.56	36.44		52.69	47.22	0.09	53.11	46.80	0.09
Goa	93.25	6.75		79.77	20.23		90.20	9.80	
Gujarat	86.24	13.58	0.18	41.32	58.59	0.09	76.38	23.46	0.16
Haryana	73.13	23.57	3.29	33.22	59.42	7.37	64.50	31.32	4.17
Himachal Pradesh	86.68	13.31	0.01	48.10	51.90		85.07	14.93	0.01
Jammu & Kashmir	85.02	14.97	0.01	52.90	47.10		81.61	18.38	0.01
Jharkhand	89.48	2.28	8.24	54.59	13.75	31.65	86.67	3.20	10.12
Karnataka	85.51	14.45	0.04	47.51	52.23	0.25	75.24	24.66	0.10

Kerala	73.23	17.40	9.37	65.48	25.62	8.90	71.70	19.02	9.28
Lakshadweep[$]	100.00			100.00			100.00		
Madhya Pradesh	88.68	11.03	0.30	38.09	56.01	5.90	81.06	17.80	1.14
Maharashtra	88.91	10.72	0.37	61.58	36.85	1.57	82.72	16.64	0.64
Manipur	81.68	15.84	2.48	60.60	35.56	3.84	78.71	18.62	2.67
Meghalaya	83.23	15.21	1.56	72.84	25.78	1.37	82.50	15.95	1.55
Mizoram	62.49	19.82	17.70	54.42	38.29	7.29	59.81	25.94	14.25
Nagaland	80.76	19.16	0.09	41.08	58.92		74.00	25.93	0.07
Odisha	92.52	4.54	2.94	65.44	21.70	12.86	90.41	5.87	3.72
Puducherry	64.01	35.99		59.77	40.23		62.01	37.99	
Punjab	78.69	17.63	3.68	36.07	47.11	16.82	69.05	24.30	6.65
Rajasthan	73.53	24.87	1.59	18.99	73.92	7.09	64.34	33.14	2.52
Sikkim	68.89	30.03	1.07	27.62	71.43	0.95	65.60	33.33	1.06
Tamil Nadu	86.23	12.79	0.98	61.12	36.84	2.04	80.04	18.72	1.24
Tripura	91.03	5.16	3.81	75.62	16.92	7.46	89.76	6.13	4.11
Uttar Pradesh	69.64	26.95	3.41	26.27	64.95	8.78	64.60	31.37	4.03
Uttarakhand	80.81	17.82	1.38	34.63	60.02	5.35	76.29	21.95	1.77
West Bengal	87.81	9.21	2.98	75.72	20.03	4.25	86.19	10.66	3.15
All India	82.76	14.45	2.79	46.49	47.85	5.66	77.25	19.52	3.22

Source: U-DISE, 2016-17; Note: * Government includes private aided by government; ** Unrecognized and others; $ Due to low number of schools in rural areas, the figure is 100 per cent

Table 2: Enrolment of School-Going Children by Type of School in Rural and Urban Areas (in %)

State	Rural			Urban			Total		
	Government*	Private	Others**	Government*	Private	Others**	Government*	Private	Others**
Andaman & Nicobar Islands	88.57	11.43		67.96	32.04		80.08	19.92	
Andhra Pradesh	71.84	27.79	0.37	31.04	67.79	1.18	58.43	40.94	0.63
Arunachal Pradesh	81.60	17.56	0.84	73.77	25.29	0.93	79.03	20.10	0.87
Assam	82.81	10.81	6.39	62.31	35.35	2.34	80.11	14.03	5.85
Bihar	93.60	3.50	2.90	76.89	15.87	7.24	91.90	4.76	3.34
Chandigarh$	100.00			64.67	35.06	0.28	67.99	31.76	0.25
Chhattisgarh	85.10	14.79	0.11	42.43	56.83	0.74	74.93	24.81	0.26
Dadar & Nagar Haveli	83.56	16.25	0.19	60.59	39.13	0.28	75.83	23.95	0.22
Daman & Diu	62.00	38.00		81.98	18.02		70.81	29.19	
Delhi	50.55	49.45		62.17	37.71	0.12	61.93	37.95	0.12
Goa	92.33	7.67		86.25	13.75		89.80	10.20	
Gujarat	81.23	18.68	0.09	39.81	60.15	0.04	65.47	34.46	0.07
Haryana	52.85	45.19	1.96	27.78	70.09	2.14	43.36	54.62	2.03
Himachal Pradesh	70.96	29.04	0.00	34.67	65.33		65.66	34.34	0.00
Jammu & Kashmir	68.75	31.24	0.01	32.74	67.26		59.97	40.03	0.00
Jharkhand	82.55	8.83	8.62	46.07	36.56	17.37	76.08	13.75	10.17

Karnataka	78.00	22.00	0.01	40.33	59.58	0.09	62.11	37.84	0.04
Kerala	73.07	23.37	3.55	61.84	35.83	2.33	70.13	26.64	3.23
Lakshadweep$	100.00			100.00			100.00		
Madhya Pradesh	77.63	22.12	0.25	30.28	67.87	1.85	61.72	37.50	0.78
Maharashtra	85.17	14.59	0.23	66.00	33.48	0.53	76.13	23.49	0.37
Manipur	43.32	54.32	2.36	25.82	71.82	2.36	38.85	58.79	2.36
Meghalaya	81.64	16.86	1.50	67.82	31.48	0.70	79.21	19.43	1.36
Mizoram	58.48	30.30	11.22	41.18	55.76	3.06	49.99	42.79	7.22
Nagaland	54.43	45.32	0.24	22.09	77.91		40.34	59.52	0.14
Odisha	89.17	7.91	2.92	52.63	36.99	10.38	83.43	12.48	4.09
Puducherry	47.12	52.88		42.94	57.06		44.70	55.30	
Punjab	59.98	32.74	7.28	34.52	48.39	17.10	49.45	39.21	11.34
Rajasthan	61.67	37.65	0.68	18.22	79.11	2.67	50.35	48.45	1.20
Sikkim	78.94	20.81	0.25	62.42	37.56	0.02	75.59	24.21	0.20
Tamil Nadu	73.66	25.57	0.77	59.43	39.49	1.09	67.36	31.73	0.91
Tripura	88.52	9.19	2.29	81.37	17.03	1.60	87.03	10.82	2.15
Uttar Pradesh	50.04	46.39	3.57	27.75	66.41	5.84	46.15	49.88	3.97
Uttarakhand	58.92	39.16	1.92	33.87	62.83	3.31	52.74	45.00	2.26
West Bengal	89.95	5.43	4.62	89.75	8.04	2.21	89.92	5.89	4.20
All India	73.09	24.34	2.57	47.38	49.66	2.96	65.95	31.37	2.68

Source: U-DISE 2016-17; Note: * Government includes private aided by government; ** Unrecognized and others; $ Due to low number of schools in rural areas, the figure is 100 per cent.

rural areas, the proportion of SC and ST children enrolled in government schools was even more. For example, 81.30 per cent of the SC and 88.56 per cent of the ST students were enrolled in government schools. In contrast to that, only 52.71 of general caste students were enrolled in government schools. In urban areas, 43.89 per cent of boys and 51.31 per cent of girls were enrolled in government schools. But more of SC, ST and girl students were enrolled in government schools.

Like SC and ST children, relatively greater numbers of girls compared to boys from all caste categories were enrolled in government schools. As against 63.06 per cent of boys, 69.07 per cent of girls were enrolled in government schools. The phenomenon of relatively greater proportion of boys attending private schools and girls attending government schools is found across rural and urban areas and in most of the states.

Caste, Class, Gender and Religion-Wise

The section below examines differential access to government and private schools using data collected through a survey conducted by the authors in 2016 and 2017. It shows that access to private schools was generally high in the survey regions: 57.92 per cent of the boys and 54.32 per cent of the girls attended private schools. However, the proportion of boys and girls attending private schools varied. Relatively greater proportion of boys than girls attended private schools in all other surveyed districts except Bellary. Further, except Bellary, the majority of boys and girls attended private schools in other surveyed districts. In Ghazipur, a much greater proportion of boys and girls (68.15 per cent of girls and 73.24 per cent of boys) attended private schools than in Kanyakumari and Sikar Districts.

Social category-wise access to government and private schools shows that a very large proportion of general and OBC boys and girls attended private schools and SC, ST boys and girls attended government schools. The differential access to government and private schools by caste groups was found across all the four surveyed districts.

Religion-wise, relatively greater proportions of Christian and Hindu both boys and girls attended private schools. While 66.73 per cent of Christian girls and 64.69 per cent of Christian boys attended private schools, only 43.05 per cent of Muslim girls and 46.69 per cent of Muslim boys attended private schools. The proportion of Hindu boys and girls attending private schools was 56.62 and 50.99 per cent respectively.

Table 3: Gender and Caste-wise Access to Government and Private Schools in Rural and Urban Areas (in %)

	Types of Schools	SC		ST		OBC		General		Total	
		Boys	Girls	Boys	Girls	Boys	Girls	Boys	Girls	Boys	Girls
Rural	Government*	78.59	82.34	86.83	89.67	69.64	75.31	50.63	57.07	70.62	75.72
	Private	20.45	16.83	11.80	9.12	27.74	22.14	43.87	36.84	26.80	21.71
	Other**	0.97	0.84	1.37	1.21	2.62	2.55	5.50	6.08	2.58	2.57
Urban	Government*	57.32	63.93	54.33	61.47	44.02	51.93	36.65	43.38	43.89	51.31
	Private	41.08	34.68	43.76	36.88	52.91	45.07	59.61	53.04	53.08	45.82
	Other**	1.60	1.39	1.91	1.65	3.06	3.01	3.74	3.57	3.03	2.87
Total	Government*	73.76	78.19	82.71	86.22	63.24	69.68	43.99	50.79	63.06	69.07
	Private	25.13	20.85	15.85	12.52	34.03	27.67	51.35	44.28	34.23	28.28
	Other**	1.11	0.96	1.44	1.26	2.73	2.66	4.67	4.93	2.70	2.66

Source: U-DISE, 2016-17.

Note: * Government includes private-aided by government; ** Unrecognized and others

Table 4: Differential Access to Government and Private Schools by Boys and Girls

Districts	Girls in:					Boys in:				
	Government Schools		Private Schools		Total	Government Schools		Private Schools		Total
	Nos.	%	Nos.	%		Nos.	%	Nos.	%	
Bellary	3390	69.06	1519	30.94	4909	3076	63.10	1799	36.90	4875
Ghazipur	603	31.85	1290	68.15	1893	571	26.76	1563	73.24	2134
Kanyakumari	3057	35.18	5633	64.82	8690	2841	35.59	5141	64.41	7982
Sikar	1832	46.38	2118	53.62	3950	1677	38.02	2734	61.98	4411
Total	8882	45.68	10560	54.32	19442	8165	42.08	11237	57.92	19402

Source: Survey, 2017.

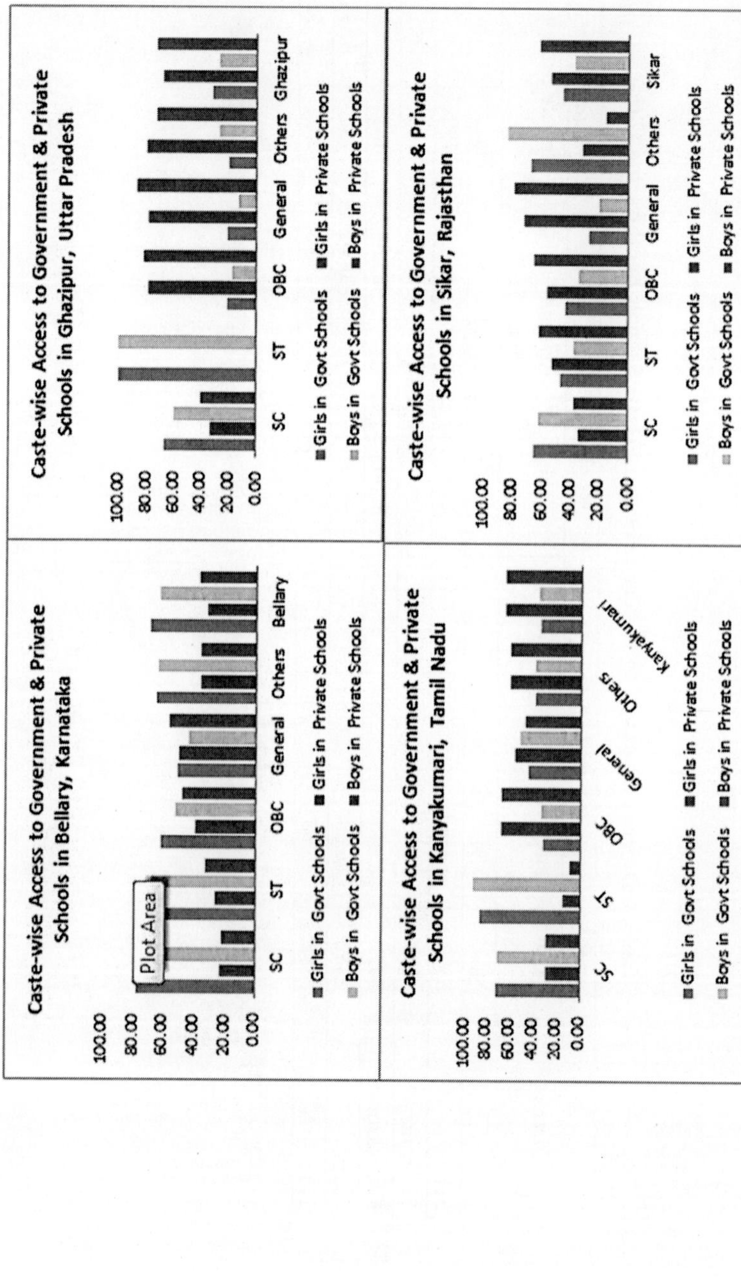

Fig. 1: Social Category-wise Access to Government and Private Schools in Sample Districts

Source: Survey, 2017.

Table 5: Caste, Religion and Income Category-Wise Access to Government and Private Schools (In No. and %)

Districts	Categories	Girls					Boys				
		Govt Schools		Private Schools		Total	Govt Schools		Private Schools		Total
		Nos.	%	Nos.	%		Nos.	%	Nos.	%	
Caste	SC	1948	71.75	767	28.25	2715	1902	69.70	827	30.30	2729
	ST	1518	72.70	570	27.30	2088	1252	66.99	617	33.01	1869
	OBC	4761	37.07	8081	62.93	12842	4408	34.12	8513	65.88	12921
	General	580	34.77	1088	65.23	1668	527	29.88	1237	70.12	1764
	Others	75	58.14	54	41.86	129	76	63.87	43	36.13	119
	Total	8882	45.68	10560	54.32	19442	8165	42.08	11237	57.92	19402
Religion	Hindu	6919	49.01	7199	50.99	14118	6278	43.38	8195	56.62	14473
	Muslim	471	56.95	356	43.05	827	443	53.31	388	46.69	831
	Christian	1480	33.27	2969	66.73	4449	1432	35.31	2624	64.69	4056
	Others	12	25.00	36	75.00	48	12	28.57	30	71.43	42
	Total	8882	45.68	10560	54.32	19442	8165	42.08	11237	57.92	19402

Income	Less than Rs. 50,000	4729	54.43	3959	45.57	8688	4321	50.49	4237	49.51	8558
	Rs. 50,000 to 1 Lakh	3359	42.12	4615	57.88	7974	3155	40.10	4712	59.90	7867
	1 to 2 Lakhs	505	28.02	1297	71.98	1802	451	23.53	1466	76.47	1917
	2 to 4 Lakhs	105	18.36	467	81.64	572	74	12.35	525	87.65	599
	Above 4 Lakhs	26	20.16	103	79.84	129	16	10.46	137	89.54	153
	Total	8724	45.52	10441	54.48	19165	8017	41.99	11077	58.01	19094

Source: Survey, 2017.

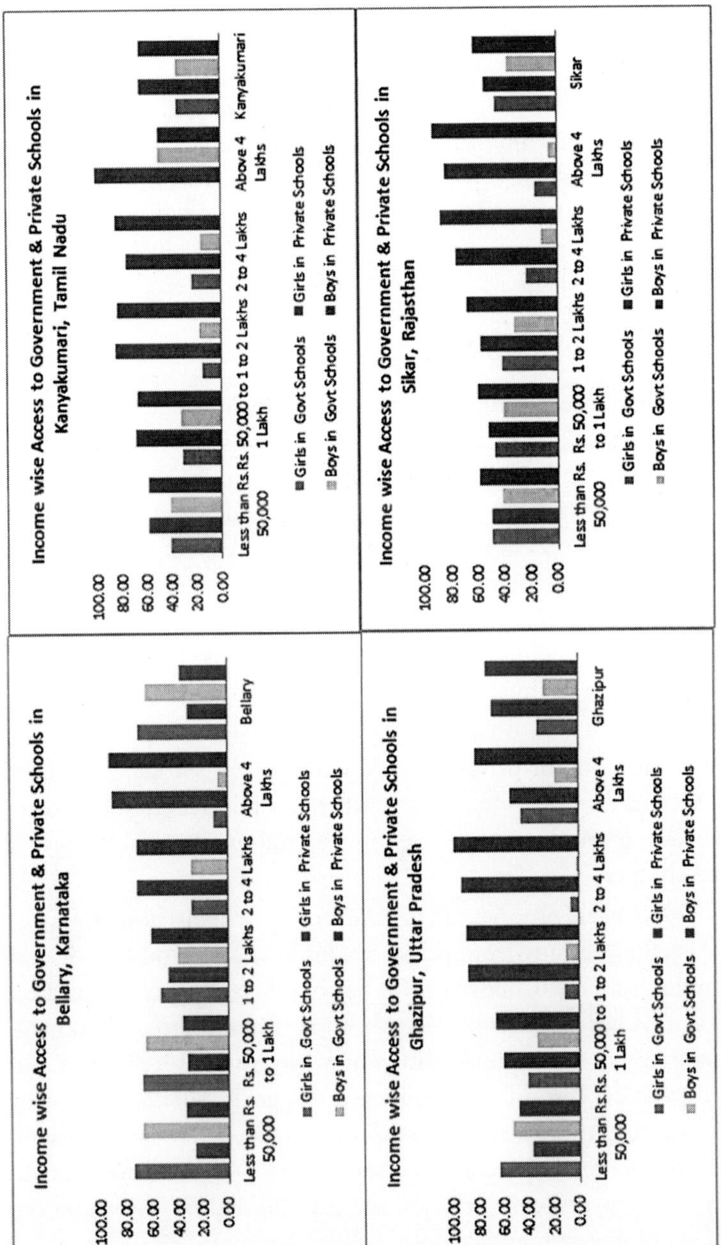

Fig. 2: Income-wise Access to Government and Private Schools in Sample Districts

Source: Survey, 2017.

Income category-wise, a clear correlation between income level and access to private schools was found across the surveyed districts. With the rise in income, the tendency to send both boys and girls to private schools was pronounced. For example, 79.84 per cent of the girls and 89.54 per cent of the boys who attended private schools were from households with income level above Rs. 4 lakhs per annum. In contrast to that, 45.57 per cent of the girls and 49.51 per cent of the boys who attended private schools belonged to the lowest income group.

IV

Social Cost of Privatization

The previous section shows differential access to government and private schools by different sections of society. Private schools have increased in number and so is the number of children enrolled in them. Nevertheless, a large proportion of SC, ST, and girl children are dependent on government schools for their elementary education. Also, a relatively greater proportion of rural than urban children attend government schools, even though private schools have made rapid inroads into rural areas. The majority of households with low income send their children to government schools. The dependence on government schools is much higher in remote and inaccessible areas like the Bastar region of Chhattisgarh, southern districts of Rajasthan, etc.

There are social costs of privatization. Firstly, there is a class division between those children who attend government schools and those who attend private schools. With greater level of privatization, this class division would become sharper.

Secondly, it has been observed that government schools head towards ghettoization, as children only from poor sections, low caste and low classes attend government schools. Children from better off classes have moved to private schools. This has also resulted in much less attention to government schools, as parents of the children attending government schools have less social and political resources to influence the government for greater allocation of resources to government schools and for better facilities and infrastructure. The better off sections of society, as they have withdrawn their children from government schools, are not affected by deterioration in the conditions of government schools.

Thirdly, schooling is not only a process of learning from textbooks of mathematics, languages and different subjects. It is a process of developing social consciences, empathy, mutual respect, sense of justice and moral values. In a classroom consisting of children from various socio-economic backgrounds, children learn about others through mutual interaction. They also learn to respect each other's culture, customs and traditions. However, all these experiences are missed out because of privatization. Protagonists of the common school system forcefully argue for common schools on social grounds as well.

Fourthly, privatization of school education has the danger of denying school education altogether to a large number of children belonging to poor sections and low social classes. While government schools provide free education, private schools charge fees which are beyond the means of many. One can argue that there are low-fee private schools which charge a minimal amount, but there are serious questions about the quality of teachers, and learning outcome of such low-fee private schools. Most of them lack even basic facilities like proper classrooms, playgrounds and, above all, trained teachers. Moreover, even the low-fee schools are unaffordable for a large number of the population.

Opportunity Cost of Private Schooling

There are opportunity costs of private schooling for poor families. The median fee per child of a private unaided school is Rs. 5,000 per annum that varies across states. For example, it is Rs. 8,000 per annum in Andhra Pradesh, 10,800 in Tamil Nadu, 8,400 in Kerala, 8,200 in Karnataka, 7,200 in Uttarakhand, 7,150 in West Bengal (Kingdon, 2017). Of course, in states like UP (1,800), Rajasthan (4,500), Odisha (4,000), MP (3,700), Bihar (4,200) and Chhattisgarh (4,300) it is relatively lower and lower than the national average. Given the fact that about one-fifth of India's population live below the poverty line, or have a miserably low income level, even this much of expenditure per child is beyond their means.

On the other hand, government schools charge hardly any fees and other expenses are also nominal. A comparison of educational expenditure incurred by parents per child in private and government schools shows a huge difference, which is demonstrated here from our data. For example, while the average educational expenditure[3] incurred in government schools per annum was Rs. 2,073, the corresponding expenditure for private schools was Rs. 12,335. This figure varies across states. In Kanyakumari district of Tamil Nadu, the average annual expenditure incurred for education in government schools was Rs. 2,807 per child, which was Rs. 19,607 per child in private schools. In Bellary district of Karnataka, the average annual expenditure incurred for government school education was Rs. 1,088, while it was Rs. 6,239 for private school education.

Many of the poor households meet the expenses of private schools by cutting expenditure on necessary items; many of them borrow money; and yet many others sell household assets to meet expenditure incurred for sending wards to private schools. Härmä (2009) shows that 64 per cent of the parents cut expenditure on clothes, healthcare, and livelihood items to send their wards to private schools. Akaguri (2013) shows high incidence of borrowing for sending wards to private schools in Ghana. In our own study of four states, it was found that a number of families in Karnataka and Tamil Nadu mortgaged their household jewellery; a number of families in all the four surveyed states, viz. Karnataka, Tamil Nadu, Rajasthan and Uttar Pradesh borrowed money, and a number of families in Karnataka and Rajasthan also sold assets to meet expenditure on private education. But for school expenditure, these households would have used this money for meeting basic needs, making savings in future productive investments, and for their economic mobility. They are deprived of this because of the cost of private education.

V

Although government and private schools have existed since the commencement of modern education in India, yet the nature of involvement of private players in providing school education has been changing. A major shift has taken place in the decade of the 1990s. The government has indicated through various policy documents its intention to withdraw from the social sector and greater dependence on market and private players for promoting the social sector. This shift in policy, especially in the field of school education continues notwithstanding the 86th Constitutional Amendment Act and subsequent Right to Education Act. Notwithstanding the above amendment and legislation for right to education, paradoxically, the share of government schools in total elementary schools has declined and that of the private schools has increased. The share of private schools in terms of total children enrolled in elementary schools is greater than their share in the total number of schools.

The examination of caste, and class profile of children attending government and private schools shows a clear class division. More SC,

ST, girl, poor and rural children attend government schools. Government schools are heading towards "ghettoization".

There are social costs of privatization of school education. Apart from class division, there are social costs. A large number of low caste, poor, girl and rural children are likely to be deprived of education amidst increasing privatization. The cost of private education has opportunity cost for many parents. They would have used the money forced to spend on education because of privatization on other necessities, savings and investments and for their economic uplift. Many of these poor households are forced to sell their household assets, mortgaged their properties and borrow money with long-term adverse consequences for them.

[Acknowledgements: This paper is part of our larger study on Reach and Role of Private Schools in India, sponsored by Cambridge Malaysian Education and Development Trust, Trinity College, Cambridge. A part of this paper has been reproduced from our previously published article on "Unequal Access to Elementary Education in India: Government Versus Private Schools", in T. Haque and N. Reddy. *India Social Development Report 2018: Rising Inequalities in India*, Oxford University Press.]

Notes

1. By adding the share of others, i.e. unrecognized, and Madrasa, the share of private schools and total enrolled children in them were 22.74 per cent and 34.05 per cent respectively.
2. The survey was conducted in Tamil Nadu and Karnataka from South India and Uttar Pradesh and Rajasthan from North India. These states were selected on the basis of the level of privatization of elementary schools and educational development of the states. Tamil Nadu and Karnataka were selected on the basis of high privatization and high level of education development, while Uttar Pradesh and Rajasthan were selected on the basis of high privatization and low level of education development. One district with high privatization was selected from each selected state. Thus, Bellary district of Karnataka, Ghazipur district of Uttar Pradesh, Kanyakumari district of Tamil Nadu and Sikar district of Rajasthan were selected for the survey. From each selected district, one Block with high level of privatization was chosen. From the selected Block, five villages were randomly chosen. All the households of the selected villages were surveyed. Thus a total of 20 villages and 35,462

households were surveyed. The sample consisted of OBCs (65.69 per cent), SCs (13.90 per cent), STs (13.90 per cent) and general (8.89 per cent).

3. The average annual expenditure includes fees collected which includes tuition fees, development fees, etc., other expenditure incurred, such as books, stationery, uniforms, transport, etc. and other out-of-school expenditure, which includes amounts such as payment made by parents for private tuitions, personal books and stationeries, etc.

References

Akaguri, L. (2013). Fee-free Public or Low-fee Private Basic Education in Rural Ghana: How Does the Cost Influence the Choice of the Poor? *Compare: A Journal of Comparative and International Education*, 1-22.

Amin, S. (1996). Female Education and Fertility in Bangladesh: The Influence of Marriage and the Family. In R. Jeffery, and A. Basu, *Girl's Schooling, Women's Autonomy and Fertility Change in South Asia* (pp. 184-204). New Delhi: Sage.

Béteille, A. (2008). Access to Education. *Economic and Political Weekly, 43*(20), 40-48.

Government of India (1966). *Report of the Education Commission 1964-66: Education and National Development.* New Delhi: Government of India: Ministry of Education.

Government of India (1968). *National Policy on Education, 1968.* New Delhi: Government of India.

Government of India (1986). *The National Policy on Education (NPE), 1986.* New Delhi: Government of India.

Government of India (1999). *Ninth Five Year Plan (1997-2002): Development Goals, Strategies and Policies.* New Delhi: Planning Commission, Government of India.

Government of India (2002). *Tenth Five Year Plan 2002-07 Volume II: Sectoral Policies and Programmes.* New Delhi: Planning Commission, Government of India.

Government of India (2008). *Eleventh Five Year Plan 2007-12 Volume II: Social Sector.* New Delhi: Planning Commission and Oxford University Press.

Government of India (2013). *Twelfth Five Year Plan (2012-17)—Social Sectors Volume III.* New Delhi: Planning Commission and Sage.

Government of India (2017). *India: Three Year Action Agenda 2017-18 to 2019-20.* New Delhi: NITI Aayog, Government of India.

Government of India (2019). *Draft National Education Policy 2019.* New Delhi: Ministry of Human Resources Development, Government of India.

Härmä, J. (2009). Can Choice Promote Education for All? Evidence from Growth in Private Primary Schooling in India. *Compare: A Journal of Comparative and International Education, 39*(2), 151-165.

Härmä, J. (2011). Low Cost Private Schooling in India: Is it Pro-Poor and Equitable? *International Journal of Educational Development, 31*(4), 350-56.

Kingdon, G.G. (2017). The Emptying of Public Schools and Growth of Private Schools in India. In CCS, *Report on Budget Private Schools in India 2017* (pp. 12-31). New Delhi: Centre for Civil Society.

Kingdon, G.G., and Teal, F. (2007). Does Performance related Pay for Teachers improve Student Performance? Some Evidence from India. *Economics of Education Review, 26*(4), 473-86.

Lahoti, R., and Mukhopadhyay, R. (2019). School Choice in Rural India: Perceptions and Realities in Four States. *Economic and Political Weekly, 54*(49), 51-57.

Mukhopadhyay, S., and Garimella, S. (1998). The Contours of Reproductive Choice for Poor Women: Findings from a Micro Survey. In S. Mukhopadhyay, *Women's Health, Public Policy and Community Action* (pp. 98-121). New Delhi: Manohar.

Muralidharan, K., and Sundararaman, V. (2015). The Aggregate Effect of Scool Choice: Evidence from a Two-Stage Experiment in India. *Quarterly Journal of Economics, 130*(3), 1011-66.

Pankaj, A., and Poornima, M. (2019). Unequal Access to Elementary Education in India: Government versus Private Schools. In T. Haque, and N. Reddy, *India Social Development Report 2018: Rising Inequalities in India* (pp. 203-215). New Delhi: Oxford University Press.

Schultz, T.W. (1971). *Investment in Human Capital: The Role of Education and of Research.* New York: Free Press.

Sen, A. (1990). Gender and Cooperative Conflicts. In I. Tinker, *Persistent Inequalities* (pp. 123-49). New York: Oxford University Press.

Sen, A. (1999). *Development as Freedom.* New Delhi: Oxford University Press.

Sen, A., and Dréze, J. (2002). *India: Development and Participation.* New Delhi: Oxford University Press.

Shah, P., and Miranda, L. (2013). Private Initiative in India's Education Miracle. In I. Foundation, *India Infrastructure Report 2012: Private Sector in Education* (pp. 74-83). New Delhi: Routledge.

Srivastava, P. (2007). Neither Voice Nor Loyalty: School Choice and the Low-Fee Private Sector in India. Occasional Paper 134, National Center for the Study of Privatisation in Education. New York: Teachers' College, Columbia University.

Tilak, J.B. (2017). Rejuvenation of Public Schools. *Summer, 44*(1), pp. 149-163.

Winch, C. (1996). *Quality and Education.* Oxford: Wiley-Blackwell.

6

Low-Fee Private Schools: A Global and Indian Perspective

Anjela Taneja[1]

Introduction

Ensuring a quality education for all its citizens—including girls, women and the most marginalized—is a core responsibly of the state as enshrined in international law. However, nearly 70 years after governments recognized education as a fundamental right and despite the fact that over 85 per cent countries recognize education as a fundamental right nationally, education systems in many low- and middle-income countries are far from delivering universal primary school education. Children from the poorest families are four times more likely to be out of school, compared to those from the richest 20 per cent of households in low- and middle-income countries.[2] When poverty intersects with other forms of inequality, the chances of being denied an education rise considerably. Quality of education available to those enrolled is also often poor. In the meantime, member states are now also committed to universalize secondary education by 2030 in line with the SDG commitments. Similar debates are underway in India where concerns are frequently voiced about the quality of education in government schools at the time when the demand has been raised for ensuring universal secondary education.

A number of think tanks, commentators, policy-makers and donor agencies argue that failings in public education systems can and should be remedied by increased involvement of private actors in education and/or the introduction of privatization policies in education. Where the government is not providing—or at least not sufficiently—then, the argument goes, the private sector can do so. The argument, furthermore, goes that these schools deliver better quality for the poor then the "failing" public education. India has seen a clamour[3] for deregulation of private schools from proponents of private schools who often proposed as alternatives to public education.

This paper examines some of the claims about private education- and especially low-fee private schools—to assess whether such schools do, as is often claimed, provide higher quality education and (more) accountable service delivery, expand access for the poorest, provide a more efficient delivery of education and response the best to parental demand. It also considers the evidence on private education—and again, specifically low-fee private schools—in light of rights-based concerns about whether expansion of and investment in such schools is an effective route to universal, equitable, non-discriminatory education of high quality. In so doing, emphasis is particularly given to evidence from India, although global evidence provides the background to this analysis.

Testing the Evidence

Given this expansion of and advocacy for certain forms of private education—notably low-fee private schools—and the actual and potential impact on education provision, it is vital that claims made in favour of such approaches are tested against available evidence and in light of overall policy objectives.

Do Low-Fee Private Schools Offer Better Quality Education?

Argument 1. Low-fee private schools enhance the quality of education through increased choice, competition and accountability.

Advocates of low-fee private schools argue that they deliver a better quality education than government schools. This is partly explained as an outcome of parents paying fees and a result of being more willing to please those who pay them (parents), or risk losing customers (students). It is also argued that doing so creates competition between schools for students and resources, leading to improved school quality and efficiency, thus driving up quality across the education system.[4] Many studies also point towards comparisons between government and private schools in terms of test scores as a proxy for quality.

Is there a private school advantage in learning outcomes?

There are fundamental questions as to whether performance of students on standardized tests of learning outcomes is the best measure of quality. However, even by this imperfect measure, there is no robust evidence to back the claim that all private schools offer consistently better quality education than all public schools.

While there are indeed studies showing a private school advantage, many of these fail to adequately control for the full range of factors related to children's backgrounds that influence outcomes. Children from higher socio-economic groups, with educated parents, have an advantage over their poorer peers.[5] Students from poor homes are more likely to be malnourished, less likely to support educational support at home or afford extra tutoring to compensate. Once these factors are accounted for, much of the quality advantage disappears. Thus, while one analysis of national reading data in India, comparing test scores for children from the same families where some children were attending public schools and others were in private schools, found (without examining the rationale for or impact of having related children in different types of school[6]) advantages in fee-paying schools.[7] Another study of (the same) reading data, showed that once students' socio-economic background and other factors had been controlled for, the difference in reading outcomes between government and private schools disappeared in some states, widened in others, and reversed in a few.[8] A more recent study in India using a methodology designed to isolate causal effects found that the difference in test scores of children in private and government schools invariably disappears when a broad set of factors are controlled for; while it found some difference in rural outcomes, it found "no evidence of a causal private school premium in urban areas."[9]

Fee-charging private school systems are selective through the fees that they charge. Some also undertake direct screening tests for admission, directly cream skimming the best students from the public education system (and other private schools). This skews their intake admitting the best performing students, widening the gap between them and the rest of the population. PISA studies looking at the factors behind learning found that there were no significant differences in student performance between public and private schools (both independent and government dependent) when socio-economic criteria are controlled for.[10] The 2012 round of PISA showed that even before socio-economic status was controlled for, students in public out performed those in private schools in Chinese Taipei, Hong Kong-China, Thailand and Luxembourg.[11]

Academic performance of students who earlier attended public schools also does not necessarily improve when they move into private schools. Evidence from India (Karopady, 2014) based on a five-year-long randomized control study on the impact of school vouchers suggests that private school enrolment provides no value addition to learning outcomes as compared to government schools.[12] Children shifting to private schools under a scholarship programme were found to perform no better than their government school counterparts even after five years of private schooling.

More recent research on private school enrolment on psychosocial skills shows no differential impact;[13] the same study found some positive effects of private rural enrolment on English, but not other subjects.

Do low-fee private schools really provide quality education?

Every child has the right to be educated in the best possible environment and there are reasons to question whether private schools uniformly deliver on this expectation. A study in the state of Andhra Pradesh found that at the age of eight, 72 per cent of private school pupils could not solve a basic two-digit by one-digit multiplication problem, while 79 per cent could not divide—results that were only slightly better than those for government school students.[14] They concluded: "it would be a fallacy to propose that low-fee private unregulated schools, which serve poor people are a panacea for ensuring equitable quality education for all children."[15]

At the same time, achievement of learning outcomes is not the only definition of quality education. The presence of a trained, qualified and well-supported educator is a critical determinant of learning. Evidence of classroom practice in low fees schools is limited and research is not always in agreement. Lall (2000)[16] found that the pedagogy practised in low-fee private schools was nothing more than reading from the text and copying of answers by children from the textbooks into their notebooks with unfinished lessons given as homework; space for children's participation was limited; with untrained teachers working under pressure from management, corporal punishment was frequent when children did not meet their teachers' expectations. Similarly, high levels of corporal punishment and rote memorization were found to be prevalent in India's top rated 89 elite private schools.[17]

An argument is made that the number of private schools is increasing because of teacher absence and poor time on tasks in public schools. However, teacher absence is the result of poor working conditions, low pay and erratic payment of salaries and additional (non-teaching) duties required by public schools and is, in turn, caused by poor governance, management and professional support systems. These factors should be addressed. Furthermore, teacher absence is not a unique feature of government schools. One study in India, for example, finds that government teachers have absence rates of 24 per cent, and those at private schools 17 per cent[18].

Research does suggest that private (especially low-fee) schools do have smaller class sizes. In Patna, there are 22 students for every private school teacher, compared with 42 for every teacher in government schools.[19] This argument is not, therefore, that private schools are inevitably better, but that smaller class sizes can yield higher learning outcomes.

In contrast, many of the teachers, especially in low-fee private schools are unqualified, poorly paid and on temporary contracts. Salaries in low-fee private schools[20] are low and sometimes even below the minimum wage or even the international poverty line of a dollar a day. Aslam and Kingdon (2011)[21] note that private schools often favour hiring female staff that can be paid less than males, are younger and often unmarried, and less experienced and less trained (though not necessarily less certified). Low wages and uncertain job tenure is a clear disincentive for qualified candidates to join the teaching profession. Furthermore, the practice is permitted to exist in the absence of regulation on the part of the state that permits exploitation of labour.

Do (low-fee) private schools contribute to improving the quality of education more generally?

Proponents of private education at times argue that the existence of the private sector in education helps improve quality across the system. There is no research to support this proposition and middle and higher-income countries having higher proportion of private sector provision do not outperform systems with greater public and less private involvement.[22] There is, at best, a lack of evidence for the claim that widespread private education drives up system-wide quality. In contrast, there is evidence that the growth of private schools is much more likely in areas with decent public educational infrastructure. Thus, evidence from Pakistan (Andrabi, Das and Khwaja, 2008[23]) suggests that private schools (especially low-fee private schools) are more likely to be located in villages with sufficient populations of younger, unmarried women who had a secondary school education that then become teachers in low-fee schools. Such an educated female labour force was said to be available in the villages where the government had invested in girls' secondary education in the last 20 years (Chudgar, 2012).[24]

Conclusion: There is no reliable evidence to show that low-fee private schools provide better quality education, let alone good quality education, than government schools. Some low-fee private schools may offer something better than the worst government schools, but the education they provide—offered at significant expense to families—is often far from what could be considered 'good quality education'.

Do Low-Free Private Schools Expand Access to the Poorest?

Argument 2. Low-fee private schools expand access to education for the poorest, by being affordable for all.

The operators and promoters of low-cost schools frequently refer to these schools as "affordable", emphasizing that the fees are within reach of poorest families, and claim that—in a context where hundreds of millions of children are still out of school—such schools can help expand access to all. These claims raise two factual questions: are low-cost schools 'affordable' for the poorest, and are they expanding access by enrolling out-of-school children from low-income families?

Are Low-Fee Private Schools Affordable?

Research into the quantum of fees charged by PFPSs across India is lacking. However, research from Delhi suggests that parents are discontented with the tuition fees and additional charges including overpriced textbooks and uniform and other expenses; children whose parents were unable to pay are penalized.[25]

Are low-fee schools reaching out to the remotest, under-served areas and the poorest families?

Children currently out-of-school are often the "hardest to reach", the poorest and most marginalized. Children with disabilities are much more likely to be out-of-school: in Nepal, for example, it is estimated that 85 per cent of all children out-of-school are disabled.[26] One-third of countries with data are still not enrolling girls in primary school at an equal rate to boys.[27] Similar trends prevail in India where girls, Dalits, tribals, minorities, child labourers and children with disabilities form the largest share of the out-of-school population. These are the children that any private schools will need to be able to enrol to reach the unreached.

Fee-charging private schools (except religious private schools) are unlikely to be located in the most geographically remote areas being disproportionately likely to be established in urban and peri-urban areas. Indeed, nationally representative evidence from rural India suggests that private schools are disproportionately likely to be established in areas with good public infrastructure and indeed, require such infrastructure to exist.[28]

Where private schools do exist, most low-cost private schools do not meet any reasonable definition of "affordability" for the poorest families. When poor families manage to pay, this creates potential for serious poverty spill-over effects, reducing available income for other essentials and making fees unsustainable over longer periods of time. In India, a study in Uttar Pradesh showed that the likelihood of a child in the second quintile accessing a low-cost private school was twice the chance of a poorest child, and for children in the third and fourth quintiles the likelihood increases to approximately 7.5 times. In the richest quintile the likelihood of a child attending LFP schools is 10.7 times that for a poorest child (Härmä, 2010).[29]

Affordable for whom? Do private schools exacerbate gender and other inequalities?

Inequalities in access to private education are evident not just between families, but also within families. The charging of fees creates a strong disincentive to educate children whose families are considered least likely to be seen as "productive", such as girls and children with disabilities. The gender gap in private school enrolment in India is rising, even as it is closing in government schools.[30] The World Bank's Living Standards Measurement Study in Uttar Pradesh clearly shows that the gender gap in enrolment even in private schools is increasing over the years. The gender gap in enrolment in private schools for the age group 6-19 years was 1 in 1997-98, which increased to 6 in 2007-08 and further rose to 10 in 2010-11.[31] Girls have been shown to be significantly less likely to be enrolled in low-fee schools because the poorest rural families often choose to invest in private education for their sons over their daughters.[32] The most comprehensive cross-country review of the literature on privatization in education finds that "girls are less likely than boys to be enrolled in private schools."[33] When education is provided not as a universal good to which everyone has free access by right, but a private good which parents must buy, poor parents are likely to make a difficult, but rational decision not to buy that service for the children—girls, children with disabilities—whom labour markets are less likely to reward for their education.

There is direct evidence of the deleterious effects of the fees such schools charge. Research from India points towards loans taken out for educational expenditure as being one of the greatest reasons for rural indebtedness. The state of Andhra Pradesh saw over 3,000 suicides by indebted farmers between 2002 and 2007; educational costs appear to be among the reasons behind the same.[34]

This analysis is further substantiated by the DFID-commissioned review of evidence on private schools, which found that, of the evidence on whether private schools are affordable for the poor, "most is neutral, some is negative, but there is no positive evidence..... Financial constraints are a key factor limiting or preventing poorer households enrolling their children in private schools. Where children of poorer households do attend private schools, research indicates that welfare sacrifices are made and continued attendance is difficult to sustain."[35] The last words on this go to Watkins (2004): "Should the world's poorest people really be expected to choose between health and the education of their children? And what is the market rationale to suggest that such choices make sense for the rest of society?" (p. 9).[36]

Furthermore, those who do manage to pay private fees face a triple burden. First, poorer families generally pay more than their fair share of taxes because of regressive tax systems that typically rely on consumption taxes such as VAT. Second, these tax contributions go in part to pay for a public education system from which they are not benefiting. Finally, they must pay a substantial additional proportion of family income to finance the cost of private schools. This phenomenon is the very opposite of the virtuous cycle that is created when governments invest tax dollars in quality public education, placing "virtual income" into the pockets of the poorest via the provision of a free education that will deliver economic and social benefits in the future.[37]

So, can low-fee private schools support expansion to out-of-school children?

Overall, there is evidence that children entering low-fee private schools are not those who were previously excluded from education. Another argument made by the proponents and operators of low-fee private schools is that the fees they charge make them no more expensive than public schools if hidden costs like charges for uniforms, books or examinations, or "unofficial" fees charged at community or school level are included. However, in India, for example, sending a child to a private school is approximately nine times as much as the cost of a government school, including all indirect costs associated with schooling, such as buying books, and transport.[38] The charging of fees—both official and unofficial, direct and indirect—in government schools should be treated as a problem to be addressed, not an excuse to justify and normalize the expectation that poor people can and should pay for education.

Conclusion: Low-fee private schools are not affordable to the poorest. These schools offer no meaningful options for expanding access to the most marginalized or those out-of-school.

Are Low-Fee Private Schools More Efficient and Innovative?

Argument 3. Low-fee private schools are more efficient and support greater innovation.

Private school supporters and operators claim that their schools tend to be more efficient and innovative than public schools—often with an implicit or explicit contrast to a supposedly inefficient public sector. The argument thus goes that these schools are not just low-fee, but low-cost, and that they produce comparatively better results for less investment, allowing investors and owners to make a profit without diverting funds from the provision of education services.

Are low-fee private schools more efficient?

Arguments about the efficiency of low-fee private schools often calculate "efficiency" in terms of per pupil spending, compared against learning outcomes in terms of test results. According to Milton Friedman (1962),[39] efficiency is created through competition between private providers of education which makes them more receptive to customers' demands. However, the DFID-commissioned review of evidence on private schools warned about the loose justification for these claims.[40]

In contrast, there is considerable evidence of wastage. The low-fee private school sector is extremely financially volatile, with frequent closures[41] impacting the continuity of the teaching and learning experience of students.

As noted in the *Affordable Private Schools (APS) Sector Analysis* produced by the hedge fund (and investor in low-fee private schools) Gray Matters Capital (GMC): "It appears that below a certain threshold of fees, APS [low-fee private schools] might find it difficult to perform well. From the sample of 200 APS, it is observed that none of the schools charging below Rs. 400 per month are able to perform well. They either lack basic facilities and resources required to create a conducive learning environment or are financially unsustainable."[42] Indeed, in their study in rural India, Härmä and Rose (2012) observed that LFPs in their dataset were operating for short periods of time, with as many as a quarter of the sample closing within 18 months of the end of the study period. Sixteen per cent of 7-8 year-olds had already changed schools at least once in one study looking at school choice in India. While 50 per cent of the movement was from government to private schools, there was also considerable movement within private schools and return to the government sector (frequently in the face of escalating annual fees).[43] In urban areas, 81 per cent of the students changing one private school for another by the age of 8 (Woodhead et al., 2012). An educational system that is based on the churn in the education sector where old schools constantly close and new schools emerge, is neither efficient nor effective in offering an uninterrupted and smooth learning environment to students.

The argument for poorly resourced schools for the poor appears to be morally wrong, denying poor children opportunities they deserve. Cheaper is not always better and is not synonymous with efficiency.

Finally, the push for greater efficiency creates perverse incentives to show results. Thus, the fact that many such schools rely on test scores to attract "customers" may make them more likely to discriminate against children whose backgrounds and circumstances create barriers to learning and academic success. This has indeed, frequently been the case with evidence emerging from different parts of the world, including among India.[44] Thus, children with disability or linguistic minority students are disproportionately unlikely to be admitted in private schools.

Does the private sector foster innovation through low-fee schools?

Another argument made is that these schools are innovative. There is no basis against which to test this assumption, but the comparable evidence that does exist—of private schools in higher-income countries—does not support this hypothesis. A cross-country analysis by the OECD of whether market-based reforms and increased private sector involvement in education had fostered innovation found only limited and marginal cases where reforms had promoted innovations, and only at certain levels of the school organisation, rather than within the classroom. In fact, they noted that the evidence suggested that economic forces tended to play a larger role in promoting uniformity, as schools tend to compete for a certain type of student, and standardize as such to attract that type."[45] This deviates from international human rights obligation of schools as enshrined in the General Comment 17 of the Committee on the rights of the child on the right of the child to rest, leisure, play, recreational activities, cultural life and the arts (Article 31 of the CRC), namely, the obligation to provide adequate space, including for play, school curriculum that allots adequate opportunity for children to learn, participate in and generate cultural and artistic activities, including music, drama, literature, poetry and art, as well as sports and games and provide learning environments which are active and participatory and offer, especially in the early years, playful activities and forms of engagement.[46]

Conclusion: There is no evidence that low-fee private schools are more efficient than public schools, or that they promote desirable innovation.

Should Low-Fee Private Schools be Supported as an Appropriate Response to Parental Demand?

Argument 4. Private schools are more accountable to parents and parents want to send their children to low-fee private schools. It is undemocratic to oppose this demand.

The argument is that private schools perform better than public schools because private schools—including low-fee private schools—are more accountable to fee-paying parents. If schools are not responsive or fail to deliver, their "consumers"—parents and students—will withdraw their "custom". Given that private schools respond to their demands, parents choose and want to send their children to such schools. This choice should be respected and supported by the state. The work hinges on the work of Hirschman (1970) that suggests that consumers in the face of deteriorating quality of goods: either "exit" (in this case, leaving the school) or "voice" (challenging and negotiating the system).[47]

Are low-fee private schools more accountable?

The World Bank's 2004 *World Development Report, Making Services Work for Poor People,* identified a "long route" of accountability in public education—from schools and teachers to elected officials to taxpayers and parents—as the crux of the quality problem, an argument repeated many times since.[48] In contrast, private schools are directly and more strongly accountable to parents. The theory is that dissatisfied 'consumers'—i.e. parents—have the choice of complaining and demanding change if they are unhappy with the service they are receiving. If that fails, and they remain sufficiently unhappy, they can leave the school (exercise the option to exit).[49]

There appears to be little evidence that parents exercise either voice or exit. In India the strategies adopted were staying (due to perceived obligation to the school's owners, not a commitment to the school), fee-bargaining (to reduce the individual fees charged, not improve the quality of the school), exiting, and fee-jumping (Srivastava, 2007). The DFID-commissioned study reviewing the latest evidence on private schools (not just low-fee private schools) concluded there was weak evidence of parental engagement in decision-making and of school responsiveness to such engagement, and "no evidence" that parents change schools, or are more likely to do so in the case of private schools than government schools. The authors concluded there was a need for more research to understand the politics of local community choice, and whether and how parental school choice actually operates, in order to "help clarify the prevalent but largely untested assumptions of accountability [in market systems]."[50]

Increased demand for private schools by parents: is it genuine or limited choice?

Low-fee private schools often tend to emerge in locations where either government schools are lacking or where they are perceived to be of very low quality, suggesting that they are filling a gap left by inadequate government supply. Low-fee private schools seem to flourish in illegal slum settlements, where governments fail to provide public schools, especially when they do not recognize the settlements. Thus evidence from India suggest that private schools are used as "interim schools during primary or elementary grades" because of the perceived danger of sending younger children to distant government schools; Muslim parents prefer sending their children to government schools, prefer faith-based teaching in an Islamic environment, which they expect from government schools but not from private schools.[51]

Structural factors in how educational systems are designed may also play a role; where private schools form the major providers of secondary or post-secondary education, parents may prefer to admit their wards in such schools from the beginning to maximize the chances of getting admission (e.g. in Mumbai, India[52]). Such situations certainly suggest that the government needs to respond urgently to expanding enrolment: but by providing decent public education in the poorest areas, not by supporting private schools.

A study in India, for example, found that, despite apparently widespread preference expressed by parents for private schooling, when parents are asked to specify what they are seeking, it is '…well-functioning, well-staffed government schools, inspected regularly and sincerely to ensure accountability'.[53] So, in actuality, the choice they are making here is *against* poor quality.

What are the other drivers of parental choice?

Another argument that is frequently made by proponents of private schools is that the growth of private, including low-fee private schools is a tacit endorsement of them as being of good quality. However, research into the drivers of choice does not substantiate this claim.

One fundamental assumption is that everyone has equal access to information about the quality of the school. This is clearly not the case. Indeed, a case can be made that the eventual outcomes of a particular school (in terms of learning achieved or employment prospects) at the end of the entire school cycle are inherently unknowable since the educational experience of cohort currently leaving school at the end of 5-12 years of schooling is bound to be fundamentally different from that of entering school now. Furthermore, research on impact of educational interventions suggest that not programmes that have short-term benefits yield long-term gains.[54]

There is no consistent definition of the term quality and parents and students make use of their own mental models of what constitutes quality, models that frequently do not match the factors that drive learning. Thus, high classes as an indicator of high popularity and strict discipline (Srivastava, 2007) were among the criteria voiced as being influential in parental choice of low-fee schools; extent of student learning did not appear to be high on the list of criteria utilized. PISA shows that for disadvantaged parents, cost-related factors often weigh as much as, if not more than, the factors related to the quality of instruction.[55] There is also some evidence of perverse incentives to show improved academic performance. Thus, in India, high promotion rates (without considering whether these were based on student mastery of concepts or lenient grading) lead to lenient marking (Srivastava, 2007).

Parents prefer private to public schools where the former provide education in English (or another language seen to be more "useful") and the public schools in a local or national language.[56] This speaks to the need for informed dialogue and consultation with parents about the implications of mother-tongue instruction and strengthening the process of transition to the majority language prevailing in the country in government schools. It is not an argument for government investment in private schools.

Conclusion: What parents want is a good education for their children and evidence fails to show that private schools is what poor parents really seek or that low-fee private schools offer a responsive and sustainable option.

Do Low-Fee Private Schools Provide a Route to Equitable and Universal Access to Education?

Argument 5: In a context where education goals are not being met, the private sector can provide a route to good quality education, equitably and for all.

Low-fee private education is often presented as the best option in a bad situation; in contexts where public systems are over-stretched and of poor quality, the argument is made that private operators can "step in, to fulfil a demand that the public sector is unable to meet",[57] offering an adequate education within reach of the poor. The evidence presented so far—on quality, equity, efficiency and demand—calls this assumption into question, suggesting that the education on offer in private schools is still of poor quality, and often also unaffordable.

Growth of the private schools for some: what impact does it have on schooling for all?

According to international law, states have the obligation to respect the freedom of parents to choose for their children schools other than public schools but they do not have the obligation to support it neither to finance it.[58] This provision exists to allow minorities to receive education that is in line with their beliefs, but which continues to be delivered in educational institutions that adhere to national standards. The existence of this protection, however, does not in any shape minimize the role of the state towards ensuring public education for all. Indeed, no OECD or rapidly developing country has depended on non-government provision to achieve universal attendance in basic education.

Impact on equity and social cohesion

As the evidence presented previously suggests, levying of school fees in private schools excludes learners from marginalized backgrounds and creates rifts within families. In contrast, when schools provide spaces for rich and poor students to mix, as has been envisaged under Section 12(1)(c) of the RTE Act, 3 research suggests that this makes rich students more pro-social, generous, and egalitarian, less likely to discriminate against poor students, and more willing to socialize with them.[59]

However, at a more structural level, school systems with low levels of competition among schools often have high levels of social inclusion, meaning that students from diverse social backgrounds attend the same schools. In contrast, in systems where parents can choose schools, and schools compete for enrolment, schools are often more socially segregated (PISA, 2014).[60] Public education systems are better suited to ensure intergenerational mobility which is higher in public education systems than in private schools; greater private provisioning, in contrast, reduces mobility in both the short and the long run (Davies, Zhang and Zeng, 2003). Education systems that have significant private participation have been found to both reflect and intensify existing inequalities in society. Data from India,[61] shows an extremely high correlation between high family income and likelihood of attending a private school. The schools favoured by the wealthy are those with better facilities, smaller class sizes and highly paid teachers, all of which are likely to contribute towards better educational outcomes and thus, ultimately, extend the economic and social advantages of the already-privileged children who have access to them. There is no evidence that the expansion of low-end budget private schools for the poor will address this social segregation.

Countries that stream their populations in childhood into private schools (for the rich or relatively richer) and government schools (for the poor or most poor) run the risk of dividing the society across class lines. Doing so is not only bad for the national social fabric as a whole, but also deprives the rich of critical learning opportunities. In the words of India's 1964-66 National Education Commission popularly called the Kothari Commission,[62] "The National System of Education (must) bring the different social classes and groups together and thus promote the emergence of an egalitarian and integrated society…(However,) instead of doing so, education itself is tending to increase social segregation and to perpetuate and widen class distinctions… this is bad not only for the children of the poor but also for the children of the rich and the privileged groups (since) by segregating their children, such privileged parents prevent them from sharing the life and experiences of the children of the poor and coming into contact with the realities of life... also render the education of their own children anaemic and incomplete."

A system that encourages abandonment of the public school system by all but the very poorest can further exacerbate educational stratification and inequalities. The economist Albert Hirschman highlighted this concern over 30 years ago,[63] pointing out that middle-class exit from public education systems results in poorer school quality and equity, as those with economic and political influence end up without a stake in defending public education, contributing to its deterioration. The lack of political capital in improving public education contributes to state retreat from mainstream education provision, leaving the poorest marginalized children behind in substandard public schools, effectively building a glass ceiling against moving out of poverty.[64]

This abandonment of public schools by the middle class is in fact already underway in India. Worldwide, this tends to lead to ever more poorly funded public schools offering even more substandard education. On the one hand, private schools that operate in a highly stratified system (socially and economically), themselves become stratified offering varying degrees of quality from "low-cost" to elite. This stacks the odds against children from families on very low incomes, rural and marginalized communities who are left behind as a result of the "pauperization of public schools."[65]

Not only does this have the potential to have a corrosive impact on equity in education systems, but can also erode society's cohesion, exacerbate broader patterns of inequality and generate conflict and have a negative impact on social democracy. Investment in public education is one of the most powerful tools to level the playing field. It also thwarts social mobility, further entrenches disadvantage and solidifies pre-existing social inequalities.

Less equitable education also widens income inequalities. For example, in the United States over the past three decades, increasing wage gaps between secondary school graduates and secondary school dropouts has been a major source of rising inequality.[66] In Morocco, the UN Committee on the Rights of the Child has recognized it to be a human rights violation where the growing privatization of education—actively encouraged by public policy—has widened the gap in access to quality education and inequalities between the most advantaged and the most disadvantaged families.

Is Privatization of Education and Private Sector Participation in Education Should be Encouraged, Not Opposed?

Argument 5: Growing privatization of education is universal, impossible to resist and the state should step aside to allow private schools to deliver.

Is privatization truly increasing worldwide?

In 40 per cent of countries for which there are data, official statistics indicate that fewer than 5 per cent of the children enrolled in primary schools are in private schools, and the median is just over 8 per cent. Malawi, Vietnam and Papua New Guinea have fewer than 1 per cent primary school students in private schools, while in 10 countries (none of which are low-income) private enrolment is more than 50 per cent of the total.[67] These statistics in all probability underestimate private school enrolment since many private schools are not recognized or not counted, however, public schools remain overwhelmingly the main providers of education in most countries of the world.

Going by official statistics, most countries have more children enrolled in private schools in real terms now than a decade ago (with exceptions being some high- and upper middle-income countries, along with Bolivia, El Salvador, Eritrea and Syria). However, this must be seen against the backdrop of growing overall enrolment and does not necessarily translate into greater share of the population attending private schools.[68] In most countries for which there are data, there is little notable shift in the proportion of primary school children being privately educated. In a few countries, however, there have been increases of more than 5 percentage points—these include eight low-income and lower-middle-income countries, almost all in Africa (Benin, Congo, Gambia, Guinea, Guinea Bissau, Mali, Mauritania and Nepal). In the same period, Bolivia, Cameroon and Togo have all seen decreases of more than 5 percentage points in the proportion of primary school students enrolled in private schools.[69] Growth of private provisioning is, therefore, not universal and while some countries have seen a considerable rise in private education, others are reversing this trend. India is one of the countries experiencing a growth in private school enrolment.

Then there is the lesson of history. Universalization of education has rarely, if ever, been ensured through for profit provision. In the countries being offered as examples of private involvement in education (e.g. US and UK), strong state education programmes and public education systems have been responsible for improvement in public systems.

State intervention to regulate schools or freeing schools to do the right thing?

Under international human rights law governments are responsible for guaranteeing the right to education[70] and are expected to be principally responsible for delivering education.[71] However, private actors have the liberty to establish and direct educational institutions provided they are subject to the requirement that they must conform to minimum standards laid down by the state.[72] This is a right provided to protect minorities and provide them an option to receive culturally or linguistically appropriate education.

The problem is not the fact that private schools exist, but that privatization and commercialization of education is increasing, creating a negative impact. The opposition is not ideological, but based on the evidence listed above. It is fundamentally based on the fact that the growth of private involvement in education risks a decline in quality and equity. The 2015 Global Education Monitoring Report highlighting the instances of Chile, New Zealand, Sweden, and the United States shows that "substantial freedom to choose schools often leads to increased inequality... The wealthier and higher ability students... end up with the most benefits, and public schools increasingly serve disadvantaged populations."[73] In Sweden, a country with strong institutions and systems, the voucher-based system there contributes to segregation, which required further reforms and intervention by the government.[74] In Chile, the country with the most substantial experience of voucher schemes and OECF's most educationally unequal system,[75] there has been a pushback against vouchers[76] due to severe stratification of the education system that it created. There is no reason to suppose the experience will be different in an already highly socially stratified country like India.

Private schools' poor track record on regulation

Evidence suggests that private schools in India have not adhered to existing regulatory frameworks. Thus, they have been found to misuse government concessions granted to them.[77] The average amount foregone in providing fee concessions by these private schools per student annually was Rs. 71.63 in 2001-02—in schools were the annual fee of these schools for a single child ranged between Rs. 12,000 to Rs. 30,000—meaning a huge amount of government funds are not reaching their intended beneficiaries or delivering intended objectives. Thirty per cent did not admit children with disabilities in their schools as a matter of policy; 41 per cent of schools do not have any disabled children in practice. For every Rs. 100 subsidy or incentive given by government to private schools, only Rs. 27 were spent towards socially useful activities. Government financial audits point towards financial malpractices: payment to fictitious employees, unauthorized fees, unauthorized transfers between different budget heads and a host of other problems.[78] An independent system for monitoring the financial and performance of schools is therefore essential. Attempts at regulation are often resisted. Indeed, many low-fee private schools simply ignore, or in some cases contest, government regulation.[79]

Things have not improved since the introduction of the Right of Children to Free and Compulsory Education Act, 2009 that requires 25 per cent of places in all private schools go to children from poor and marginalized families. This met with fierce opposition from private school providers, who challenged the provision in the Indian Supreme Court. Fortunately, in this case, it was constitutionality upheld.[80] Subsequent evidence points to continued evasion of private schools of their obligation to fill seats[81, 82] and a spate of instances of acute discrimination against children thus admitted.[83]

Similarly, several states have regulatory frameworks for regulation of school fees. These provisions too are often not adhered to, forcing the courts[84] and the state to intervene.

So what is the alternative?

In the end state political decisions—rather than parents' demand—drive privatization. Fundamentally, only 12.7 per cent government schools currently comply with even the minimum quality provisions of the RTE Act and India's investment on public education has never crossed 4 per cent[85] despite repeated policy commitments to investing 6 per cent GDP to education. This is a policy choice that consecutive governments have made in India.

Conclusion

India and China started their journey as independent nations at approximately the same time. China nearly tripled its primary school net between 1950 and 1965 and made robust investments in public financing for education and the expansion of the public education net. In the early 1950s, Chinese public education expenditure (2.0 per cent of GDP) was three times higher than in India (0.6 per cent of GDP). The Government of China consequently continued to invest more heavily on elementary education than in India and invested more in basic than tertiary education. The result is that whereas China is close to completing universal basic education, primary school attendance in India was only 76.2 per cent in 2012-2013. Research suggests that while the presence of a large private school sector at the primary level risks creating several decades of delay in implementing universal basic education.[86]

It is undeniable that there are failings—in some cases huge failings—in India's public education system. These are rooted in old and well known problems—weak institutions, poor governance and chronic under-funding of education. Despite these constraints, public schools remain the major providers of education worldwide and the best and only hope for universal, quality education for all. If we care about equality, socially mobility, stable and democratic nations and the right of everyone to a good quality education, we must build strong and good quality public education systems that work for everyone.

Notes

1. The author currently works for Oxfam India on education and inequality. Views expressed are personal. This paper draws extensively on GCE's 2016 Thematic report addressing functioning of Low-Fee Private Schools globally on which the author worked. Walker, Taneja, Abuel-Ealeh, and Pearce (2016) "Private Profit, Public Loss: Why the push for low-fee private schools is throwing quality education off track." The full text of the report can be accessed athttp://bit.ly/PPPLE
2. UNESCO Institute of Statistics (UIS), (2012). *Reaching Out-of-School Children is Crucial for Development.* www.uis.unesco.org/FactSheets/Documents/fs-18-OOSC-2.pd
3. Including a Save Education Campaign by the National Independent Schools Alliance: http://nisaindia.org/sites/default/files/appeal-from-nisa.pdf

4. See Tooley, J. and P. Dixon (2006). '"De facto" privatisation of education and the poor: Implications of a study from sub-Saharan Africa and India', *Compare*, 36 (4), 443-462. Tooley, J. and P. Dixon (2007), 'Private education for low-income families: Results from a global research project', in P. Srivastava and G. Walford (eds.), *Private Schooling in Less Economically Developed Countries*, Oxford: Symposium Books.
5. For instance, see this useful summary of evidence: http://www.jrf.org.uk/publications/does-money-affect-childrens-outcomes
6. Although this may well be skewed as some parents may have been selecting on perceived 'investment' in a more intelligent child, as will later be shown is a common pattern.
7. French, R., Kingdon, G. (2010). *The Relative Effectiveness of Private and Government Schools in Rural India: Evidence from ASER Data*. London: Institute of Education.
8. Wadhwa W. (2009). *Are Private Schools Really Performing Better Than Government Schools?* New Delhi: ASER.
9. http://www.isid.ac.in/~pu/conference/dec_12_conf/Papers/AbhijeetSingh.pdf
10. http://www.oecd.org/pisa/pisaproducts/pisainfocus/48482894.pdf
11. http://gpseducation.oecd.org/revieweducationpolicies/#!node=44129&filter=all
12. http://www.periglobal.org/sites/periglobal.org/files/Does_School_Choice_Help_Rural_Children_from_Disadvantaged_Sections.pdf
13. Singh, A. (2014). Private school effects in urban and rural India: Panel estimates at primary and secondary school ages. https://ora.ox.ac.uk/objects/uuid:5eda87d1-03d5-47a5-9a41-44c639f2c696/download_file?safe_filename=2014_Singh_JDE_OA.pdf&file_format=application%2Fpdf&type_of_work=Journal+article
14. Singh, R., Sarkar S. (2012). *Teaching Quality Counts: How Student Outcomes Relate to Quality of Teaching in Private and Public Schools in India*. Oxford: University of Oxford. Young Lives Working Paper 91.
15. http://www.younglives.org.uk/files/working-papers/wp91-singh-sarkar
16. Lall, Jyotsna (2000). *Schools for Thought: A Study of Small Private Schools in Jaipur*. Jaipur: Bodh Shiksha Samiti.
17. http://www.ei-india.com/wp-content/uploads/Main_Report.pdf
18. Kingdon, G., Aslam, M., Rawal, S. and Das, S. (2013). *Are Contract Teachers and Para-teachers a Cost effective Intervention to Address Teacher Shortage and Improve Learning Outcomes?* London, Evidence for Policy and Practice

Information and Co-ordinating Centre, Institute of Education, University of London.

19. UNESCO 2013/14 Global Monitoring Report: Teaching and Learning: Achieving Quality for.
20. Stern, J.M.B. and Heyneman, S.P. (2013). Low-fee private schooling: the case of Kenya in Srivastava, P. (ed.), *Low-fee Private Schooling: Aggravating Equity or Mitigating Disadvantage?* Oxford, UK, Symposium Books, pp. 105-28.
21. Aslam, Monazza and Kingdon, Geeta, (2011). "What can teachers do to raise pupil achievement?," *Economics of Education Review*, Elsevier, Vol. 30(3), pp. 559-574, June.
22. OECD, 2011, PISA in focus: http://www.oecd.org/pisa/pisaproducts/pisainfocus/48482894.pdf
23. Das, Jishnu, Tahir Andrabi, and Asim I. Khwaja. (2008). "A Dime a Day: The Possibilities and Limits of Private Schooling in Pakistan." *Comparative Education Review* 52(3): 329-345.
24. Chudgar, Amita, (2012). "Variation in private school performance: The importance of village context" *Economic and Political Weekly*, 47 (11), 52-59.
25. Manjuma Akhtar Mousumi and Tatsuya Kusakabe (2017). The dilemmas of school choice: do parents really 'choose' low-fee private schools in Delhi, India?, *Compare: A Journal of Comparative and International Education*, DOI: 10.1080/03057925.2017.1401451
26. Jo Walker, Global Campaign for Education, (2014). Equal Education, Equal Rights: Education for Children with Disabilities.
27. GMR 2013/2014.
28. Chudgar, Amita, B. Creed, "How does demand for private schooling vary across locations with different private school supply? Analysis of data from Rural India" National Centre for the Study of Privatization in Education, Working Paper, 222.
29. http://files.eric.ed.gov/fulltext/ED508748.pdf
30. Sahoo, S. (2015). Intra-household gender disparity in school choice: evidence from private schooling in India. www.isid. ac.in/~soham9r/ doc/pvt_paper.pdf
31. Ibid.
32. Martin Woodhead, Melanie Frost, and Zoe James, 'Does growth in private schooling contribute to Education for All? Evidence from a longitudinal, two cohort study in Andhra Pradesh, India,' *International Journal of Educational Development*, Vol. 33, No. 1, 2013, pp. 65-73.

33. Day, Ashley L., Mcloughlin, C., Aslam, M., Engel, J., Wales, J., Rawal, S., Batley, R., Kingdon, G., Nicolai, S., Rose, P. (2014). The role and impact of private schools in developing countries: A rigorous review of the evidence. Final Report. *Education Rigorous Literature Review*. Department for International Development.
34. http://www.younglives.org.uk/files/journal-articles/Singh%20Bangay%20%20IJED%20Low%20Fee%20Private%20Schooling%20in%20India.pdf
35. Härmä, J., Rose, P. (2012). Is low-fee private primary schooling affordable for the poor? Evidence from rural India in: Robertson, S., Mundy, K. (eds.) *Public-Private Partnerships in Education: New Actors and Modes of Governance in a Globalizing World.*
36. Watkins, K., (2004). Private education and "Education For All"—or how not to construct an evidence-based argument: A reply to Tooley. *Economic Affairs* 24 (4), 8-11.
37. Emma Seery, *Working for the Many: Public Services Fight Inequality*, OXFAM Briefing Paper No. 182, (Oxford, Oxfam, 2014). Available from www.oxfam.org).
38. Härmä, J. (2009). Can choice promote Education for All? Evidence from growth in private primary schooling in India. *Compare: A Journal of Comparative and International Education* 39(2): 151-165.
39. Friedman, M. (1962). *Capitalism and Freedom*. Chicago: University of Chicago Press.
40. Day, Ashley L., Mcloughlin, C., Aslam, M., Engel, J., Wales, J., Rawal, S., Batley, R., Kingdon, G., Nicolai, S., Rose, P. (2014). The role and impact of private schools in developing countries: A rigorous review of the evidence. Final Report. *Education Rigorous Literature Review*. Department for International Development.
41. Harma and Rose, Taken from the book, Susan L. Robertson, Karen Mundy, Antoni Verger and Francine Menashy (2012). *Public-Private Partnerships in Education: New Actors and Modes of Governance in a Globalizing World.*
42. Gray Matters Capital (GMC) Report Affordable Private Schools (APS) Sector Analysis (2012): taken from: http://r4d.dfid.

    gov.uk/pdf/outputs/ORIE/Guidance_Note_Low_Fee_Private_Schools_June_2013.pdf
43. http://oro.open.ac.uk/39150/3/ORE%20school%20changes%20ZJ%20MW%20250913.pdf
44. http://www.vivekbharadwaj.in/public%20utility%20final%20report.pdf

45. Lubienski, C. (2009). "Do Quasi-markets Foster Innovation in Education?: A Comparative Perspective", OECD Education Working Papers, No. 25, OECD Publishing. http://dx.doi.org/10.1787/221583463325. Quote from NZ study in paper.
46. General Comment 17 of the Committee on the rights of the child on the right of the child to rest, leisure, play, recreational activities, cultural life and the arts (Article 31 of the CRC).
47. Hirschman, A.O. (1970). *Exit, Voice, and Loyalty: Responses to Decline in Firms, Organizations, and States.* Cambridge, MA: Harvard University Press.
48. 2004 *World Development Report.*
49. Based on Albert O. Hirschman (1970). *Exit, Voice, and Loyalty: Responses to Decline in Firms, Organizations, and States.* Cambridge, MA: Harvard University Press.
50. Day, Ashley L., Mcloughlin, C., Aslam, M., Engel, J., Wales, J., Rawal, S., Batley, R., Kingdon, G., Nicolai, S., Rose, P. (2014). The role and impact of private schools in developing countries: Rigorous review of the evidence. Final Report. *Education Rigorous Literature Review.* Department for International Development.
51. Manjuma Akhtar Mousumi and Tatsuya Kusakabe (2017). The dilemmas of school choice: do parents really 'choose' low-fee private schools in Delhi, India?, *Compare: A Journal of Comparative and International Education,* DOI: 10.1080/03057925.2017.1401451
52. Juneja, N. (2007). Private Management and Public Responsibility of Education of the Poor: Concerns raised by the "Blocked Chimney" Theory. *Education Dialogue,* 5(1), 5.
53. Härmä, J. (2009). Can choice promote education for all? Evidence from growth in private primary schooling in India. *Compare: A Journal of Comparative and International Education* 39(2): 151-165.
54. http://aspe.hhs.gov/hsp/14/longtermimpact/rb_longtermimpact.cfm
55. http://www.oecd.org/pisa/pisaproducts/pisainfocus/PISA%20in%20Focus%20N42%20%28eng%29--Final.pdf
56. Sucharita V. (2013). Negotiating between family, peers and school: understanding the world of government school and private school students. *Compare: A Journal of Comparative and International Education.* Härmä, J. (2009) Can choice promote education for all? Evidence from growth in private primary schooling in India. *Compare: A Journal of Comparative and International Education* 39(2):151-165.

57. Harry Patrinos, http://blogs.worldbank.org/education/innovative-approaches-to-low-cost-education-examples-from-around-the-globe, accessed September 2014.
58. http://www.right-to-education.org/issue-page/educational-academic-freedoms
59. Rao, G. (2018). Familiarity does not breed contempt: Generosity, Discrimination and Diversity in Delhi schools. bit.ly/2QDKg8n 5 https://timesofindia.indiatimes.com/city/delhi/with-just-3-monthsleft-in-session-doe-yet-to-fill-over-1200-seats-for-children-withspecial-needs/articleshow/67222271.cms
60. http://www.oecd.org/pisa/pisaproducts/pisainfocus/PISA%20in%20Focus%20N42%20%28eng%29--Final.pdf
61. Singh, R. and Sarkar, S. (2012). *Teaching Quality Counts: How Student Outcomes Relate to Quality of Teaching in Private and Public Schools in India.* Oxford, UK, Young Lives, Department of International Development, University of Oxford.
62. Cited in http://mhrd.gov.in/sites/upload_files/mhrd/files/document-reports/Girls%20Education.pdf
63. Hirschman, A.O. (1970). *Exit, Voice and Loyalty: Responses to Decline in Firms, Organizations and States.* Cambridge, Mass./London, Harvard University Press.
64. UNESCO, (2009). Inequality: Why Governance Matters EFA Global Monitoring Report.
65. Term used in Bhatta and Budathoki's study in Nepal looking at family perceptions of education.
66. UNESCO, (2009). Inequality: Why Governance Matters EFA Global Monitoring Report.
67. UIS database, accessed September 2014 cited in Walker, Taneja, Abuel-Ealeh, and Pearce (2016) "Private Profit, Public Loss: Why the push for low-fee private schools is throwing quality education off track" The full text of the report can be accessed athttp://bit.ly/PPPLE
68. Ibid.
69. Ibid.
70. Right to Education Project http://www.right-to-education. org/issue-page/privatisation-education
71. CESR General Comment 13: The Right to Education (Article 13). Accessed at https://www.right-to-education.org/node/155
72. ICESCR, 1966, Article 13; CESCR General Comment 13, 1999: Para. 30

73. UNESCO GEMR (2015a). EFA Global Monitoring Report 2015: Education For All 2000-2015: Achievements and Challenges. Paris: UNESCO
74. http:// www.regeringen.se/content/1/c6/22/15/13/4bd84e37.pdf
75. González, P.; Mizala, A., and Romaguera, P. (2004), *Vouchers, Inequalities, and the Chilean Experience.* Santiago, Chile: Centre for Applied Economics, University of Chile.
76. For more information read: http://www.emol.com/especiales/pagina_ protesta_ estudiantes/index.htm, http://www.theguardian.com/commentis free/2011/jun/22/ students-march-chile-education-protests and http:// www.washingtonpost.com/world/chile-tax-reform-plan-to-tackle-inequalitythrough-education-boost/2014/05/04/b5d52c71-9f0c-4a46-9867-6e86dcdf5b4c_story.html, http://www.brookings. edu/blogs/ education-plus-development/posts/2014/05/09-education-reform-inequality-middle-class-frustration-chileatinc-graham
77. Bhatnagar, D. and Omer, D. (N.D.). Public Utility of Private Schools: A Study of Eighty Elite Private Schools of India http:// www.vivekbharadwaj. in/public%20utility%20final%20report.pdf [Accessed September 2016]
78. 5 http://timesofindia.indiatimes.com/city/delhi/CAG-slams25-top-Delhis-private-schools/articleshow/7050173.cms
79. Srivastava, P. (2008). School choice in India: Disadvantaged Groups and Low-Fee Private schools, in Forsey, M., Davies, S., and Walford, G. (eds.) *The Globalisation of School Choice?* Oxford: Symposium Books.
80. http://www.bbc.co.uk/news/world-asia-india-17687204
81. https://www.thenewsminute.com/article/are-cbse-schools-tn-gaming-their-admission-schedule-evade-rte-quota-102804
82. https://www.thehindu.com/news/national/other-states/Private-schools-violating-RTE-norms-over-EWS-admissions/article14400433.ece
83. There are also problems with how states are rolling out these provisions. Sarin, A., Dongre, A., Khanghta, P., Varshney, N., Gaur, A. and Sengai, A. (2018). Implementation of Section 12 (1)© of the Right to Education Act. *EPW.* 53 (8) Accessed on https://www.epw.in/journal/2018/8/special-articles/implementation-section-121c-right-education-act.html
84. https://www.firstpost.com/india/sc-ruling-on-private-school-fees-govt-regulation-is-important-but-cant-be-long-term-strategy-3273652.html
85. https://www.oxfamindia.org/sites/default/files/Davos-India-Supplement. pdf
86. Smith, W.C. and Joshi, D.K. (2015). Public vs Private Schooling as a Route of Universal Basic Education: A Comparison of China and India. *International Journal of Educational Development*, 46, 153-165.

7

Learning Crisis in School Education in India and Telangana: A Brief Analysis

D. Narasimha Reddy

I

For decades now it has been increasingly realized that the ultimate goal of development in any country is the well-being of its citizens. The basis for such a development achievement lies in the improved capabilities of the people. The path towards improved capabilities is built on the foundation of access to universal equitable quality education. However, apathy towards universal equitable education turned out to be one of the grave failures of the Indian development process, in spite of dreams about education for all from the pre-independence times. The demand for free and compulsory education was originally raised more than a hundred years ago in the "Gokhale Bill" presented in the Legislative Council of Colonial India in 1911 and finally passed in 1913 (Mundle, 2017). Though not much came out, hopes were rekindled in independent India when the Constitution provided, though not as a fundamental right, for universalization of education up to the age of 14 years within a period of ten years of the commencement of the Constitution. The process of pushing universal education not as fundamental right but as part of Directive Principles of State Policy could be seen as a reflection of the nature of social forces behind it and their political power to resist any drastic social transformation.

After more than a decade of the constitutional deadline what was achieved was not much in the direction of universal elementary education but a National Commission for Education in 1966, which has become famous as the Kothari Commission because of its progressive recommendations including free and compulsory education for all until the age of 14, special attention to education of girls and children of deprived communities and increase in the allocation of resources to education to the tune of 6 per cent of the GDP. Though the report was accepted by the Parliament and included in the National Policy on Education 1968, there was hardly any effort to provide adequate funding to match the lofty mandate of the policy. On the contrary, the allocation to education was much less in the Fifth and Sixth Plans compared to previous Plans (Tilak, 2019). There was also a resolution as a part of the International Convention on Economic, Social and Cultural Rights (1966) making it obligatory to governments to submit within two years a detailed Plan of Action for the progressive implementation of the principle of free and compulsory education within a reasonable number of years (Mehendale, 2019). It is not surprising such resolutions are left to benign neglect by countries like India. After almost two decades, a new National Policy on Education was announced in 1986. There was some awakening when in 1992, the Supreme Court, in the case of Mohini Jain Vs State of Karnataka pronounced education as a Fundamental Right, without indicating any age cohort, which left room for restricted adoption for policy.

After a prolonged debate and dithering on the judgment of the Court for over a decade, finally the Constitution was amended in 2002 to include education as a fundamental right under Article 21C. But it was not followed by any legislative guarantee but came out only in the form of introduction of the programme of Sarva Shiksha Abhiyan (SSA) in a mission mode with time-bound action. But it turned out to be neither. SSA ended up erecting parallel structures, sidelined the whole government machinery. It turned more into promotion of a non-formal scheme with para-teachers and diluted the 'noble mission of universal elementary education', killing the very spirit behind it. It took seven years after amending the Constitution, to pass the Right of Children to Free and Compulsory Education (RTE) Act in 2009 that raised expectations of equitable quality education. But it came with several limitations. First, it provided for free and compulsory education for the age group of 6 to 14, and ignored the recommendations of the Central Advisory Board on Education to include the early child group of 3-6 years and to extend it up to at least 16 years but desirably 18 years. Second, it did not provide for the Common School System (CSS) as recommended by earlier Education Commissions and as in practice in most of the countries with universal free and compulsory education. Third, it had no concern for equitable and quality education. It left stimulus for private education at all levels. Fourth, provided for 25 per cent reservation in private schools for disadvantaged sections which promotes neglect and poor quality of government schools. The Act does not clearly recognize that education is a public good with a very special social role as a human right (Tilak, 2019).

This history of prolonged dithering and dysfunctional policies relating to such a vital aspect of quality education for all, raises two questions: one is what explains such a disastrous neglect of school education in India? Second, what are the consequences of such a neglect for the learning capabilities of the children? For the first question Myron Weiner gave an insightful explanation of the indifference towards free and compulsory legislation: "India's low per capita income and economic situation is less relevant as an explanation than the belief systems of the state bureaucracy, a set of beliefs that are widely shared by educators, social activists, trade unionists, academic researchers, and, more broadly, by members of the Indian middle class. At the core of these beliefs is the Indian view of the social order, notions concerning the respective roles of upper and lower social strata, the role of education as a means of maintaining differentiations among social classes, and concerns that 'excessive' and 'inappropriate' education for the poor would disrupt existing social arrangements". (Weiner, 1991, quoted in Mehendale, 2019, (276)).

I would like to leave Weiner's observation for your reflection whether this mind-set is waning or entrenching in the context of the unfolding regimes of growing intolerance against the voices of more freedom. Now, let me turn to my central question: What has been the impact of decades of dysfunctional policies towards universal equitable quality school education? This is presented in two parts one as it could be seen at the national level and the other in its manifestation at the state level.

II

Manifestation of Learning Crisis: All India

For assessing the learning performance of children at the school level there have been internationally comparable surveys like PISA (Programme of International Student Assessment) PIRLS (Progress in International Reading Literacy Survey), and TIMSS (Trends in International Mathematics and Science Study). Though India has been obviously afraid of being exposed but by accusing these surveys of being based on indicators that are inappropriate for India, it never became a part of any globally comparable survey of the status of school education in India. Recently, India seems to have decided to slowly raise its head from this ostrichism by deciding to join PISA last year but the survey is yet to happen.

However, for assessing the performance of school education in Indian schools there emerged two fairly credible national surveys, viz. the National Achievement Survey (NAS) conducted by the National Council for Educational Research and Training (NCERT) periodically since 2001 for Classes III, V, VIII and X; and the other is an independent initiative of nation-wide assessment surveys that brought out Annual Status of Education Reports (ASER) annually during 2004-14, and biannually since 2016. The NAS covers both rural and urban areas but is confined to government schools including aided ones. The ASER covers both government and private schools but confined to rural areas. For the present analysis the latest reports of both ASER and NAS are the main sources. The ASER 2018 also brings together the earlier survey results of every two years from 2008 to 2018 which enables us to gauge the learning trends over a period. The focus of the ASER surveys have been on two dimensions, viz. reading and arithmetic. Table 1 refers to "reading achievement" of Class V and VIII students in terms of their ability to read II standard text; and Table 2 presents the arithmetic ability in terms of recognition of numbers, ability to do 2-digit subtraction or simple division. It shows that almost half the Class V students in government schools are not able to read a Class II text, about two-thirds of Class V students in private schools are able to do it. It seems that one has to reach Class VIII to be able to read Class II text. Even after reaching Class VIII, about one-fifth of students are not able to read Class II text. Though the performance in arithmetic is poor for Class V in both government and private schools with more than half of the class failing the test, it is dismal for those in the government schools.

What is somewhat puzzling is that these two Tables show that there was a trend decline in reading and arithmetic achievement scores from 2008 to 2012 in both government and private schools. It could be seen as a consequence of the operationalization of the RTE Act from 2010 which pushed enrolment in schools. The government schools suffered resource deficiencies with inadequate public funding, while private schools proliferated with limited resources and growing enrolments that pushed them towards a trend from high-fee-high-quality elite exclusivity to low-free-low-quality mass commercialization. There was a marginal recovery from the 2008-14 fall but even in 2018 the scores were much lower than in 2008, forcing one of the experts involved in the survey to observe: "we are far from an educated country."

Table 1: Reading Achievement in Indian Schools: 2008-18 Percentage of Children Who Can Read a Standard II Text at Standards V and VIII

Level	2008	2010	2012	2014	2016	2018
Standard V						
i. Government Schools	53.1	50.7	41.7	42.2	41.7	44.2
ii. Private Schools	67.9	64.2	61.2	62.6	63.0	65.1
Standard VIII						
i. Government Schools	83.6	82.0	73.4	71.5	70.0	69.0

Notes: 1. Reading Text assesses whether a child can read a 'story' of Standard II language text.

2. There is no data for private schools for Standard VIII.

Source: *Annual Status of Education Report (Rural) 2018 (Provisional)*, January 15, 2019.

Table 2: Arithmetic Achievement in Indian Schools: 2008-18 Percentage of Children Who Can Do Division* at Standards V and VIII

Level	2008	2010	2012	2014	2016	2018
Standard V						
i. Government Schools	34.4	33.9	20.3	20.7	21.1	22.7
ii. Private Schools	47.1	44.2	37.8	39.3	38.0	39.8
Standard VIII						
i. Government Schools	65.2	67.0	44.5	40.0	40.2	40.0
ii. Private Schools	71.8	72.0	57.1	54.2	51.2	54.2

Notes: 1. The ASER arithmetic test assesses whether a child can recognize numbers 1 to 9, recognize numbers 10 to 19, do a 2-digit subtraction or solve division of 3-digit by 1-digit.

Source: *Annual Status of Education Report (Rural) 2018 (Provisional)*, Pratham, January 2019.

The ASER (2018) also extended a part of the survey to children of 14 to 16 with the objective of finding out as to what are the academic capabilities acquired by those who completed Class VIII. The responses sought related a few tasks carried out in an every day context. The tasks included (with the percentage of correct responses in parentheses) are: calculating time difference (less 50 per cent), application of unitary method of arithmetic (52 per cent), financial decision like purchase of books (37 per cent) and calculation of discount (30 per cent). The weak foundational learning seems to lead to deteriorating arithmetic abilities with increase in age. The ASER (2017) also undertook a survey with a focus on 14-18 age group to find out "beyond basics" of foundational readership and arithmetic. It was aimed at four domains: Activity, Ability, Awareness and Aspirations with a large sample of 30,800. Findings on the "activity" showed that about 86 per cent were still in either school, plus-two or a small section in college. Since the sample is of rural students, 42 per cent of all, in school or not, are working, mostly (80 per cent) in agriculture. But it is "ability" after eight years of schooling expected to acquire certain foundation capabilities that exposed the shallowness of the school education: 76 per cent could not count money correctly; 44 per cent could not convert weight in grams to kilos; 60 per cent could not calculate time between two periods; 25 per cent still cannot read basic text fluently in their own language; more than 50 per cent struggle with division; and only 43 per cent complete division of 3 digit by one digit! On "awareness" and aspirations there was some gadget obsession but still the majority of them cannot use a computer.

Reference to one more assessment, and I am done with the scenario of the learning crisis of the country as a whole. The NAS 2017-18 focussed on subject-wise achievement in five subjects at the Class X. Table 3 shows under each subject the proportion of students who had correct answers (A), and (B) those with less than 35 per cent correct answers grouped as "at risk". What is surprising is that in all the states listed, and in all the subjects except in Modern Indian Language (MIL), that too only in 2 states, the proportion of students with correct answers is less than 50 per cent. And in mathematics one-half to two-thirds of the students were in the red. Overall it is a clear signal that if we go by the results of the critical threshold of school education, at the X Class the performance of the students is distressingly low across the country. This is a clear signal that it is not merely the country's "foundational education" that is at risk but the future of the workforce.

Table 3: Performance of Students of Class X: 2017-18

India/Status	Mathematics		Science		Social Science		English		Modern Indian Language	
	A	B	A	B	A	B	A	B	A	B
INDIA	34	*66*	34	*62*	39	*44*	36	*61*	49	*27*
Andhra Pradesh	41	*51*	41	*42*	43	*35*	43	*42*	43	*33*
Karnataka	38	*53*	38	*47*	45	*29*	42	*41*	55	*14*
Kerala	33	*66*	35	*57*	41	*35*	40	*48*	55	*13*
Tamil Nadu	31	*56*	34	*63*	39	*41*	36	*63*	47	*24*
Telangana	34	*66*	37	*52*	39	*44*	38	*56*	47	*27*

A: Percentage with correct answers.

B: Percent of "students at risk" with a score of 35 per cent or less correct answers.

Source: National Achievement Survey (NAS) Class X, 2017-18, Educational Survey Division, NCERT, New Delhi.

Privatization

The crisis in school education intensified with the shift to the neoliberal regime and explicit policy of private provision public goods like education. It manifested in two processes: one is the unbridled and unregulated expansion of privatization of education and the other is increasing resistance to increase budgetary resources for education. Despite the fact that SSA vision documents did not articulate the role of the private sector, especially in enabling access to the disadvantaged, the interventions by private interests including certain civil society organizations, resulted in the spread of private schooling, including low-fee private schooling in the decade of universalizing elementary education under SSA (Srivastava and Fennell, 2013). Beginning with the Eleventh, and especially from the Twelfth Five Year Plan, there was increasing space provided to private participation in education, and decreased role for the state in education financing, management, and regulation (Srivastava, 2016; Tilak, 2019). This has happened in spite of the fact that private school students did not universally achieve better results in every subject, taking into account the background variables; that the most disadvantaged, described as orphans, migrants, and financially unstable families, could not afford the 'low' fees charged, and that the work of some of the private schools revealed education corruption at the highest levels, showing such schools in India gained recognition through bribery (a critical summary account from Srivastava, 2016).

Privatization took certain strange *avatars* in states like Uttar Pradesh. In fulfilling the task of universalizing elementary education, i.e. from Standard I to VIII, the rapid expansion of private unaided (PUA) schools which mostly offered up to Class 8. The secondary education from Class 9 was largely left to private schools. A case study, contrasting the situation in a district in UP with that of one in Odisha where both elementary and secondary schools are in the government sector, shows that the wide prevalence of fee-charging private schools lead to lower enrolments at the elementary level and higher dropout after Class 8 in UP. In contrast, in the Odisha districts, enrolments at elementary level are near universal, and dropouts after Class 9 negligible, because of the government schools at both the levels (Banerjee, 2018). The equity dimension of the distorted school institutional structure in UP is highlighted in an earlier study by Kindron (1996): "The abundance of PUA elementary schools and the relative lack of PUA secondary schools in UP (rural and urban) and urban India is inequitable. It gives the well-off better chances of acquiring primary education and it obliges a number of students to carry a financial hurdle in order to access junior and secondary education subsidies. Moreover, government subsidies to a large proportion of secondary schools but only a smaller proportion of elementary schools represents an inequitable expenditure of scarce educational resources since children of the poor are better represented in elementary than in secondary education".

Yet another larger study on the limits of marketization of primary education in rural India, in the context of the spread of the so-called 'low-fee private' (LFP) schools shows "that the equity effects of the market in education are negative in that with the exit of all wealthier families more capable of exercising voice to the private sector, the government sector has become a ghettoized option of last resort for the poorest and most marginalized in society. Those accessing government schools, the choice of the last resort, are not achieving meaningful access leading to real learning. All traditionally privileged groups in society are favoured by the market in education, leaving behind those of low caste or minority religion, the landless, girls, and children born later in families and children of large families. ... to raise the prospects of the poorest, the standards at government schools must be raised through increased accountability of teachers for the work that they do. Marketized options are neither sustainable in the context of rural villages, nor are they, most importantly, socially equitable" (Srivastava and Fennell, (2013)).

Geetha Gandhi Kindron (2017) in her path-breaking analysis of "emptying of public schools" brings out how the government schools are thrown into strangely high resource, high cost but low achievement situation because of the onslaught of privatization. In an exceptional effort she pools together on schools, enrolments and resources for all the 20 major states from the District Information Systems on Education (DISE). She shows that during the period between 2010-11 and 2014-15 the total government schools increased by 16,376 but enrolments in government schools decreased by 11.1 million, while private unaided schools increased by 71,360 and enrolments in private schools also increased by 16.0 million. The increase in enrolments in private schools was largely due to 'emptying' of the government schools. The result was that government schools across the country started experiencing shrinking in size. The proportion of "small schools" (with a strength of 50 or less) and "tiny schools" (with a strength of 20 or less). Table 4 shows the number, average size and per pupil teacher cost in the 'small' and 'tiny' government schools between 2010-11 and 2015-16. The tragedy or the irony is the government schools end up spending huge overhead costs per pupil without benefiting many students who are on migration mode. It is not that all those who migrate to private schools are better-off sections. The range is from the children of the rich elite to the children of casual labour. The supply is expensive private schools with per pupil fees running into lakhs of rupees per annum to budget private schools with fees at the extreme in Uttar Pradesh as low as 3.2 per cent of the annual earnings of wage labourers (Kindron, 2017). The result is that most of these schools can hardly afford any infrastructure and better paid teachers to impart quality education. On the one hand, the poor in budget schools end up learning hardly anything, while the government schools face closures. This state of affairs would further ruin the learners, especially from the disadvantaged sections. Strengthening government schools through better human and infrastructural resources is the answer to reverse the trend. Augmenting public investment is a desideratum. But the budgetary resource flow to education seems to be still an aspiration than realization.

Table 4: Growing Share of "Small" and 'Tiny' Government Schools in India (20 Large States)

Year	Small Schools (50 or less students)				
	Number	Average Size	% Total Government Schools	Pupil-Teacher Ratio	Per Pupil Teacher Salary per month (Rs.)
2010-11	313169	30	30	15	1887
2014-15	372163	28	35	12.7	3191
2015-16	418825	-	40	-	3430

1. "Tiny Schools" (with 20 or less students): Increased from 71,189 in 2010-11 to 95,637 in 2014-15 to 1,08,183 in 2015-16.

   The per pupil teacher salary cost per month in these schools increased from Rs. 4,250 to Rs. 6,522 in this period.
2. During this period MP, Maharashtra, West Bengal and UP experienced greatest 'emptying' and highest increase in 'small' schools.

Source: Kindron, 2017.

For years now there have been recommendations by several commissions, and repeated demands by the stakeholders in public education and people at large that the education sector needs public investment of at least 6 per cent of the GDP, and to facilitate the same the budgetary allocations at the state level should be at least 20 per cent of the state budget, and 10 per cent of the Union budget. These demands are in tune with the recent pattern of education expenditure suggested by the International Commission on Financing Global Education Opportunity (2016), in the context of reaching educational achievement under SDGs in lower-middle income countries like India. Table 5 shows that over the years, even after the RTE, there has hardly been any increase in the total government expenditure on education, as a ratio of GDP. It continues to hover around 3 per cent. Worse still, in recent years there has been a marginal decline in the union government education expenditure as a share of GDP. The budgetary share of the union government showed a marginal increase after the RTE but there seems to be resistance thereafter (Table 6).

Table 5: Public Expenditure on Education* as a Percentage of GDP

Year	States on Education as % of GDP	Centre on Education as % of GDP	States and Centre as % of GDP
2009-10	2.46	0.65	3.11
2010-11	2.51	0.72	3.22
2011-12	2.40	0.69	3.09
2012-13	2.34	0.66	3.01
2013-14	2.33	0.64	2.97
2014-15	2.35	0.55	2.90
2015-16 (RE)	2.44	0.49	2.93
2016-17 BE)	2.56	0.47	3.03

* Expenditure by Education Departments.

Source: GoI (2018). *Analysis of Budgeted Expenditure on Education, 2014-15 to 2016-17*, MHRD, Department of Higher Education, New Delhi.

Table 6: Trends in Total Budegtary Spending on Education by Union and State Governments

Year	Education Share in Union Budget Expenditure (%)	Education Share in Combined Union and State Budget Expenditure (%)
2004-05	2.6	9.7
2005-06	3.5	10.0
2006-07	4.1	10.3
2007-08	3.8	9.8
2008-09	3.9	10.1
2009-10	3.8	10.6
2010-11	4.3	11.4
2011-12	4.6	11.4
2012-13	4.7	11.8
2013-14 (RE)	4.7	11.7
2014-15 (BE)	4.6	-

Source: 2004-05 to 2014-15 (BE): "Budget for Education Sector in India", Lok Sabha Secretariat, 2014.

There are some who argue that school education is denied of resources because of excessive higher allocations per student in higher education (Mundle, 2017). They also propound a hypothesis of "distorted allocation" of resources for education. But Table 7 shows that the resource allocation to higher education has been low and stagnant over the years in spite of the fact that the gross enrolment rate in higher education has more than doubled during the past decade. Here again, there have been deliberate efforts to promote private provision on a massive scale, by posting a thesis that higher education is not a merit good, and that higher education has an elite bias. Again just at a time most of the disadvantaged started entering the portals of higher education, public institutions of higher learning fail to expand.

Table 7: Combined Expenditure on Education by Union and State Governments (as % of GDP)

Sector	2012-13	2013-14	2014-15	2015-16 (RE)	2016-17 (BE)
Elementary Education	1.60	1.62	1.81	1.79	1.82
Secondary Education	0.90	0.95	0.98	1.01	1.05
Adult Education	0.01	0.01	0.01	0.01	0.01
University and Higher Education	0.63	0.67	0.57	0.65	0.64
Technical Education	0.56	0.58	0.70	0.80	0.87
Total	3.70	3.84	4.07	4.27	4.39

Note: These estimates include expenditure on education by the Education Department as well as other departments.

Source: Lok Sabha Unstarred Question No. 19 on February 4, 2019.

III

Unfolding School Education Crisis in Telangana

When Telangana was achieved as a separate state after prolonged struggles and many sacrifices, there were great expectations by the people which was matched by great promises by the new government. One that raised hopes and widespread appreciation was free education for all from KG to PG and the promise to move to the common school system. But for the reasons known to the powers that be, not much has been heard about this great promise much to the disappointment of many. In this context and in the context of what is transpiring in the domain of school education at the national level as analysed above, it would be instructive to have a few glimpses at the state of school education in Telangana. The two main sources for the study of learning performance in school education in India are, as shown earlier, ASER and the National Achievement Surveys (NAS) of the NCERT. In addition, the State Council of Education Research and Training (SCERT) also conducted an assessment of school education in Telangana. There is a fairly detailed study of Telangana school learning achievement using all these three sources (Reddy and Reddy, 2017). The present analysis focuses on certain aspects and is confined to NASs of NCERT. But the limitation of the NAS is that it is confined to government schools only. Thus we do not have other independent sources for assessing the status of learning in fast expanding private schools in Telangana.

Recently, NITI Aayog using the extensive data based on district level achievement surveys of the NAS prepared School Education Quality Index (SEQI) for each state. The purported aim of the SEQI is "to drive the policy reforms that will improve the quality of school education". SEQI consists of 30 critical indicators, 16 of them relating to "outcome domains" of learning, access, infrastructure and equity, and 14 relating to "Governance Process". The "outcomes" and "Governance" are combined to derive "overall performance". The SEQI of NITI Aayog are confined to the NAS data relating to only Classes 3, 5 and 8. SEQI does not include Class X data nor does it present subject-wise performance separately. We will first look at NITI Aayog data relating to Telangana, and the neighbouring southern states wherever relevant. And then turn to NAS for Class X and subject performance.

Table 8: School Education Quality Index
Performance of Telangana Compared to Southern States (2016-17)

State	Overall Performance		Performance in "Outcomes Domains"		"Governance Process Aiding Outcomes"	
	Score	Rank	Score	Rank	Score	Rank
1. Andhra Pradesh	56.1	11	65.4	8	49.3	12
2. Karnataka	52.9	13	71.5	6	39.3	16
3. Kerala	82.2	1	87.1	2	79.0	1
4. Tamil Nadu	73.4	2	87.3	1	63.2	3
5. Telangana	39.0	18	55.9	20	35.4	18

Note: Ranks refer to the 20 large states.
Source: NITI Aayog (2019).

Table 8 presents three indices, viz. 'Overall Performance' performance in terms of 'Outcomes' and 'Governance Process' for Telangana and the other four southern states with the respective scores and ranks that refer to 20 large states. The 'overall performance', as mentioned earlier, is a combination of 'outcomes' and 'governance'. In terms of 'overall' performance Telangana has the lowest score and a rank of 18 which is just above the bottom performers Jharkhand and Bihar. Of the 20 states only two states had their ranks decline between 2015-16 and 2016-17, and Telangana is one of the two falling from the rank of 17 to 18. In the case of "outcomes," Telangana is placed at the bottom with a rank of 20. In the "Governance" too Telangana has a very low score and a rank of 18. "Governance" includes a number of critical domains covering student and teacher attendance, teacher availability, administrative adequacy, training, accountability and transparency. It has the second highest weightage in the index next to 'learning outcomes' which reflect student performance.

Table 9: School Education Quality Index Outcomes Domain Scores and Ranks: Telangana in Comparison with Other Southern States 2016-17

State	Access Domain		Infrastructure and Facilities		Equity Domain	
	Score	Rank	Score	Rank	Score	Rank
1. Andhra Pradesh	58.2	14	18.7	17	88.9	5
2. Karnataka	79.9	5	26.0	13	75.3	8
3. Kerala	88.7	2	54.6	5	95.4	1
4. Tamil Nadu	93.1	1	50.8	6	91.1	4
5. Telangana	61.0	11	20.5	16	30.0	20

Note: Ranks refer to the 20 large states.
Source: NITI Aayog (2019).

Table 9 shows the performance in terms of domains which constitute the 'Outcomes'. Telangana does better than Andhra Pradesh in 'Access', but does poorly in both 'Infrastructure' and 'equity'. The SEQI does not give a feel of the situation in terms of the critical school education level of Class X nor does it reveal the subject-wise performance for which we shall turn to NAS data. Table 10 shows the subject-wise achievement of students in Classes 3, 5 and 8. There is an interesting aspect that comes of these class-wise scores. Achievement of Class 3 students in all the three subjects is at a high level. But as one moves up the class ladder from 3 to 8 the performance gradually declines in all the subjects. This has a strong message that unless the students get quality instruction and facilities their abilities may not improve with the progression from one class to the next. Table 11 apparently confirms this insight as we see the proportion of students with 50 per cent or more gradually decreasing and the proportion with 30 per cent or less increasing in both mathematics and language as they move from Class 3 to Class 8. At Class 8, there are more in 30 per cent or less category both in Science and Social Sciences.

Table 10: Class-wise Average Percentage of Students with Correct Responses to the Subjects: Class: 3, 5 and 8

Class	Mathematics (%)	EVS (%)	Language (%)	Science (%)	Social Science (%)
Class 3	69	67	68	-	-
Class 5	56	54	57	-	-
Class 8	37	-	53	38	40

Source: NCERT (2017) NAS 2017, Classes 3, 5 and 8: Telangana State Learning Report.

Table 11: Distribution of Students' Achievements by Classes and Subjects: Certain Disturbing Trends (2017) Telangana—(NAS: 2017)

Subject / Score	Class 3	Class 5	Class 8
Mathematics			
% of students with 50% and above	78.2	58.6	22.8
% of students with 30% or below	6.5	15.2	43.4
Language			
% of students with 50% and above	76.1	59.9	54.4
% of students with 30% or below	7.2	13.8	17.0
Science			
% of students with 50% and above	-	-	23.4
% of students with 30% or below	-	-	*40.3*
Social Science			
% of students with 50% and above	-	-	27.8
% of students with 30% or below	-	-	*36.9*

Source: NCERT (2017) NAS 2017: Telangana State Learning Report.

Table 12 seems to further prove the observation as the students progress to higher classes their performance may get affected if what we saw as "infrastructure and facilities" domain is weak. The X Class students both in Telangana and at the national level have very low scores in all the subjects except MIL. Table 13 shows subject-wise achievement of Class X students in Telangana. Except in the case of MIL and to an extent in Social Sciences, the majority of students at Class X are in the category of "students at risk" with scores less than 35 per cent. This is a very disconcerting situation, because many of them are likely to leave school with very poor abilities and may even relapse into 'illiteracy' with such a poor learning achievement.

Table 12: Performance of Students in Telangana Class X (2017-18) (Average Per cent Correct)

Subject	State Average	National Average
Mathematics	34	34 ↔
Science	37	34 ↑
Social Science	39	39 ↔
English	38	36 ↑
Modern Indian Language	47	49 ↓

State average ↑ (above) ↓ (below) ↔ (No difference) National average
Source: MHRD-NCERT (2017-18) NAS Cycle 2: Class X.

Table 13: Performance Distribution of Students by Range Telangana (Per cent Correct) Class X

Subject	0-35 (%)	36-50 (%)	>50 (%)
Mathematics	68	20	12
Science	52	34	14
Social Science	44	39	17
English	56	22	22
Modern Indian Language	27	33	40

0—35: "Students at Risk"—Maximum Intervention Required
36—50: "Students Need Improvement"
Source: MHRD-NCERT (2018).

We may now turn to examine as to what difference place, gender and social group make to learning achievement. Table 14 shows place and gender-wise performance of Class X students. Though the overall performance of all students in all the subjects, with some exception of MIL, is poor, there is one positive aspect that there is no gender difference. As could be expected, the urban-rural difference does exist, especially in English. But it is the social group differences in performance that can clearly be seen. Table 15 shows the graded differences. The low scores of "others" gradually moves down to further lower in the OBC category and further down in Scheduled Castes followed by Scheduled Tribes. Schools still appear to be far from enabling institutions to overcome the social disabilities even after spending 10 ten years post-RTE in the hope of learning better.

Table 14: Performance by Location and Gender Class X (2017-18), Telangana

Subject	Rural (% correct)	Urban (% correct)	Girls (% correct)	Boys (% correct)
Mathematics	33	37	34	34
Science	36	39	37	37
Social Science	38	40	39	39
English	35	45	38	38
Modern Indian Language	46	49	48	46

Source: MHRD-NCERT (2018).

Table 15: Performance by Social Group Class X (2017-18), Telangana

Subject	SC (% correct)	ST (% correct)	OBC (% correct)	Others (% correct)
Mathematics	31	31	34	41
Science	35	35	37	41
Social Science	37	36	39	42
English	35	32	38	50
Modern Indian Language	46	43	48	51

Source: MHRD-NCERT (2018).

The facts reveal that the learning situation in Telangana schools is grave. Of the several factors, the growing privatization and poor resource availability, as we have seen in the national context, could be some of the causes for the crisis. Though we do not have comprehensive studies on the privatization and its impact on school education in general and the state of government school education, the available data, not as detailed that of Geeta Gandhi, show that there has been rampant expansion of private schools in Telangana, possibly with all the adverse effects encompassing government schools, huge wastage that goes with tiny schools with the threat of being closed, mushrooming of budget schools together denying quality education to a vast majority of children whose proportion from poor and disadvantaged sections in Telangana is very high. There has been a steep increase in the privatization of school education in Telangana. The share of enrolments in private schools of levels increased from 49.9 per cent in 2011-12 to 53.94 per cent in 2015-16. In 2015-16, about two-thirds of all primary schools have less than 60 students each, and 61 per cent of upper primary schools have a strength of less than 100. There were as many as 400 schools (all government) without any students (Reddy and Reddy, 2017). Table 16 provides a static picture of management-wise schools and enrolments in Telangana in 2018-19. About 72 per cent of government and aided schools accounting for only 45 per cent of enrolments, and with about 27 per cent of schools in the private sector with 55 per cent of enrolments are indications enough to the possible distortions in the learning achievements including equity considerations.

Table 16: Proliferation of Privatization: Management-wise Distribution of Schools and Enrolments in Telangana 2018-19

Management Type	Rural	Urban	All
I. Schools			
Government	26,252 (84.47)	3,570 (31.39)	29,822 (70.41)
Aided	110 (-)	597 (5.20)	707 (-)
Private-Unaided	4,554 (14.70)	7,067 (62.14)	11,621 (27.44)
Others	205 (0.66)	66 (-)	205 (-)
All	30,982 (100.00)	11,373 (100.00)	42,355 (100.00)

II. Enrolments			
Government	21,81,875 (65.86)	6,40,560 (19.75)	28,22,435 (43.05)
Aided	10,659 (-)	96,872 (2.99)	1,07,531 (1.64)
Private-Unaided	11,16,637 (33.71)	24,96,715 (76.97)	36,13,352 (55.11)
Others	3,742 (-)	9,641 (-)	13,383 (-)
All	33,12,913 (100.00)	32,43,783 (100.00)	65,56,707 (100.00)

Note: Figures in parantheses are percentages.
Source: Dash Board, Department of School Education, MHRD, GoI, New Delhi.

Let us have a quick look at the other critical aspect of education, viz. public resource provision. Table 17 provides details about the budgetary share of education in the past six years, comparative budget provision in terms of an average of all states and also Telangana's education expenditure as a proportion of gross state domestic project (GSDP). The figures are revealing and also disturbing. The steep decline in the budgetary share of education expenditure is nothing short of gross negligence. That Telangana budget allocation has deteriorated within a short period to less than half of the average of budgetary allocations of all the states cannot be justified in any way. Worse is the fact shown by Table 18 that per capita public expenditure on education in Telangana is one of the lowest in the country with a bottom rank of 18 among 20 large states. The engulfing learning crisis in school education in the state may not be entirely due to less allocation of resources. But these are challenging times as to why allocation to school education, including early childhood education, as a part of building investment in human capital, we shall examine in the next section.

Table 17: Telangana Budgetary Expenditure on Education in Comparative Perspective

Year	Share of Education Expenditure in Total Budget Expenditure: Telangana (%)	Average Share of Budgetary Expenditure for All States (%)	Education Expenditure as Ratio of State GSDP: Telangana (%)
2014-15	10.88	15.05	1.38
2015-16	9.69	13.82	1.83
2016-17	8.23	14.51	1.85
2017-18	8.49	16.10*	1.66
2018-19 (RE)	7.61	15.90*	1.46
2019-20 (BE)	6.57	NA	1.21

* Average for 19 States.

Source: 1. Centre for Budget and Policy Studies, New Delhi.
2. GoI (2018).

Table 18: Per Capita Expenditure on Education in Telangana and Other States 2014-15

State	Per Capita Public Expenditure on Education (Rs.)	Rank*
Sikkim	12,364	1
Mizoram	10,979	2
Himachal Pradesh	6,200	3
Nagaland	6,163	4
Uttarakhand	5,651	5
Jammu & Kashmir	4,728	6
Meghalaya	4,498	7
Kerala	4,246	8
Tamil Nadu	3,470	12
Andhra Pradesh	3,364	13
Karnataka	3,028	15
Telangana	2,799	18

* Ranking is for select 24 States.

Source: Bhattacharya, P. and T. Kundu (2017).

IV

The Challenge of Learning Crisis in Perspective

The whole world is gearing up to the emerging technological revolution and its impact on work and workforce. There is a growing concern about the unfolding, what is called, 'Fourth Industrial Revolution'. "The First Industrial Revolution used water and steam power to mechanize production. The Second used electric power to create mass production. The Third used electronics and information technology to automate production. Now a Fourth Industrial Revolution that has occurred since the middle of the last century. It is characterized by a fusion of technologies that is blurring the lines between the physical, digital and biological spheres" (Schwab 2016). The challenge is that it is likely to fundamentally alter the way we live, work and relate to one another. We do not yet know just how it will unfold. There are two extreme views on the impact of the new technology on the future of employment. There are those who suggest that the impact of new technologies like robotics, automation, artificial intelligence (AI) and internet of things would drastically displace jobs, suggesting a kind of apocalypse. There are others who criticize this 'automation anxiety' and suggest that there would be possibilities for creation of new jobs. (Islam, 2019). There is somewhere a balanced type of view that either way what is needed is to build resilient and adoptable human capabilities. There are already clear indications even in the Indian economy which is supposed to be a slow adopter of technology, that lack of proper education would lead to loss of employment. This process has already started as can be seen from the changes in employment between 2011-12 and 2017-18. During this period, 38.84 million who lost jobs are with poor education below secondary level. At the same time there were 32.70 million jobs into which those with education levels of secondary and above were absorbed (Kannan and Ravindran, 2019). But the future is more uncertain and the need is for strengthening foundational level education (Reddy, 2019).

In India, there appears to be yet another dysfunctional policy strategy to face the challenge of the emerging technological revolution in the form of "skill development", with continued neglect of the deteriorating learning process at the foundational school education. It is pointed out that while "education is not the same as skill, education is what enables workers to acquire new skills with ease, whether on jobs or through participation in training programmes" (Ghose, 2016). Thus lack of foundational education actually restricts movement of workers from traditional to modern jobs. Instead mere emphasis on skill development could end up as some kind of "band-aid response" to the present learning crisis in school education in India (Sandhu, 2020). Reviewing the experience of skill development programmes in India, Mundle (2017) concludes: "No skill development programme, however well designed, can succeed without an underlying foundation of basic education. But India's long standing neglect of primary and secondary education has greatly limited access to quality basic education".

The answer to the emerging challenge of technological transformation and its impact on future employment, it is suggested by many studies lies in improved foundational domain of education that would impact basic abilities as how to interpreter written passages, basic arithmetic that enables one to understand how numbers work, and reasoning and creativity built on these basic foundational skills (World Bank, 2018). The foundational education should be capable of equipping the young with an ability to reinvent themselves as they grow and face changes in their work requirements. There has been a sea change in thinking on development and well-being and multilateral institutions like the World Bank emphasize the need for strengthening early childhood and school education. The last two *World Development Reports* (2018, 2019) are basically focused on changing the nature of work and the preparedness of countries to face it through more in investment in strengthening school education. The *World Development Report 2019* begins with this observation : "When we prepare for the future of work, it is important to understand that many children currently in primary school will work in jobs as adults that do not even exist today". Referring to rapid and often disruptive changes in the nature of work, the then President of the World Bank, Jim Yong Kim goes on to observe: "Three types of skills are increasingly important in labour markets: advanced cognitive skills such as complex problem solving, socio-behavioural skills such as team work, and skill combinations that are capable of adoptability such as reasoning and self-efficiency. Building these skills requires strong human capital foundations and lifelong learning". "The foundations of human capital, created in early childhood, have thus become more important. Yet governments in developing countries do not give priority to early childhood development, and the human capital outcomes of basic schooling are suboptimal" (World Bank, 2019). There cannot be a more damning indictment than this on countries like India for the neglect of school education.

Table 19: Learning Proficiency in India Compared to Select Asian Countries

Country	Below Minimum Proficiency in Schools (%)	Learning Poverty (%)
India	53.7	54.8
China	18.2	18.2
Malaysia	11.7	12.9
Sri Lanka	14.0	14.8
Thailand	21.9	23.5
Vietnam	1.1	1.7

Source: World Bank (2019)

Building on the emphasis on investing more on human capital in the form of strengthening early childhood and school education, the World Bank launched a campaign on ending "learning poverty". The relevant report points out: "Age 10, when children are expected to be in the fourth grade, is when many children finish mastering "the mechanics" of basic reading in high-performing systems. By then, they can decode most words and start to grow as independent readers ...". But "without a systematic and intensive approach to early intervention, the majority of *at-risk* readers rarely catch up. Failure to read by nine years of age portends a lifetime of illiteracy for at least 70 per cent of struggling readers."

The World Bank launched a human capital project based on the estimates of investments made on education and health, on certain outcomes, the project arrived at Human Capital Index for 157 countries in which India had a rank of 115. The Government of India rejected this as being based on indicators not relevant for India. One would have expected a saner approach to go with the rank and approach the World Bank for concessional finance which the Bank was eager to provide if it is meant for investment in overcoming the crisis in school education.

References

ASER (2019). *Annual Status of Education Report 2018*, Pratham.

ASER (2019). *Annual Status of Education Survey (Rural) 2018*, Pratham.

ASER (2018). *12th Annual Status of Education Survey (2017): Beyond Basics*, Pratham.

ASER (2017). *Annual Status of Education Survey (2016)*, Pratham.

Bhattacharya, P. and T. Kundu (2017). "How State Governments are Spending on Education, Health and Irrigation" *Live Mint*, April 26.

Banerjee, Rukmini (2018). "Betrayal or Benefit", *Seminar*, No. 706.

Dubey, Muchkund and Susmita Mitra (2019). "Introduction" in Muchkund Dubey and Susmita Mitra (eds.) *Visions of Education in India*, Aakar Books, Delhi.

Ghose, A.K. (2016). *India Employment Report 2016*, OUP and Institute for Human Development, New Delhi.

GoI (2018). *Analysis of Budgeted Expenditure on Education: 2014-15 to 2016-17*, MHRD, Department of Higher Education, New Delhi.

Harma, Joanna (2010). *School Choice for the Poor? The Limits of Marketisation of Primary Education in Rural India*, Creative Pathways to Access, Research Monograph No. 23.

International Commission (2016). *The Learning Generation: Investing in Education for a Changing World: A Report*, The International Commission on Financing Global Education Opportunity.

Islam, Iyenatul (2019). "Growth, New Technology and the Future of Work: International Evidence and Implications for India", *The Indian Journal of Labour Economics*, Vol. 62, Issue 1, January-March, 31-53.

Kannan, K.P. and G. Ravindran (2019). "From Jobless to Job-loss Growth: Gainers and Losers During 2012-18", *Economic and Political Weekly*, Vol. LIV, No. 44, November 9.

Kindron, Geeta G. (1996). "Private Schooling in India: Size, Nature and Equity-Effects", *Economic and Political Weekly*, Vol. 51, No. 31, December 21.

Kindron, Geeta Gandhi (2017). "The Emptying of Public Schools and Growth of Private Schools in India", in *Report on Budget Schools in India*, Centre for Civil Society, New Delhi.

Lok Sabha Secretariat (2015). "Budget for Education Sector in India".

Mehta, A.C. (2019). *Elementary Education in India: Analytical Tables 2016-17: Progress Towards UEE*, NIEPA, New Delhi.

Mehendale, Archana (2019). "RTE Act from View Point of the Right to Education and Law" in Dubey and Mitra (eds.) op. cit.

Mundle, Sudipto (2017). "Employment Education and the State", *The Indian Journal of Labour Economics*, Vol. 62, No. 1, January-March, 17-31.

NCERT (2019). National Achievement Survey—Class X, Cycle 2 (2017-18).

NITI Aayog (2019). *The Success of Our Schools: School Education Quality Index* (SEQI), NITI-Aayog, New Delhi.

PRS (2019). *Telangana Budget Analysis: For Years 2016-17 to 2019-20*, PRS Legislative Research, New Delhi.

Rao, Srinivas et al. (2017). *School Closures and Mergers: A Multi-State Study of Policy and Mergers: A Multi-State Study of Policy and Its Impact on Public Education System—Telangana. Odisha and Rajasthan*, MA Centre for Education Studies, JNU, New Delhi.

Reddy, D. Narasimha (2019). "Future of Work and Challenges to the Capabilities of Emerging Indian Labour Force", Radhakamal Mukherjee Memorial Lecture, 62nd Annual Conference of the Indian Society of Labour Economics, Department of Economics, Patiala University, Patiala, December 7-9, 2019.

Reddy, B. Shiva, and K. Anji Reddy (2017). "Social Sector in Telangana", Telangana Economic Association, Conference Papers (February 2017).

Sandhu, Rohan (2020). "India Needs a New Education Paradigm", *The Hindu Business Line*, February 5, 2020.

Schwab, Klaus (2016). "The Fourth Industrial Revolution: What it Means, How to Respond", *World Economic Forum*.

Srivastava, Prachi (2016). "Questioning the Global Scaling Up of Lowe-Fee Private Schooling: The Nexus Between Business, Philanthrophy and PPPs", *Education Publications*, 132, https://in.lib.uwo.ca/edupub/132.

Srivastava, Prachi and Shailaja Fennell (2013). "Private Sector Sudy: Sarva Shiksha Abhiyan: A Report submitted to DFID India on the Government of India's Universal Elementary Edcuation Programme".

Tilak, Jandhyala B.G. (2019). "The Policy Crisis in Education" in Muchkund Dubey and Susmita Mitra (eds.), op. cit.

World Bank (2019). *Ending Learning Poverty: What Will it Take?* The World Bank, Washington.

World Bank (2018). *The Human Capital Index and Components*, The World Bank Group, Washington.

World Bank (2018). *World's Development Report 2018: Learning to Realise Education's Promise*, World Bank, Washington, DC.

8

Public versus Private Provision of Elementary Education: Challenges Facing the Right to Education in India

Kiran Bhatty

Introduction

The growing disenchantment with low quality education in the public sector has resulted in increasing numbers of children leaving state schools in recent years, fuelling an increase in demand for private education, and a ceding of space for it by the state. The most recent estimates show that 30 per cent of elementary schools are private unaided schools (UDISE, 2016-17).[1] While we still do not have accurate estimates of the proportion of children studying in private schools, the number is increasing every year. This shift has engendered heated debates around public versus private provision of basic education, with sharp lines being drawn between supporters of each. For instance, private schools are perceived to be cost-effective and accountable, especially in relation to teacher performance, which state schools are not. However, state schools have to cater to a wider range of concerns, including equity, which the private schools do not.

These discussions have been further complicated by the 86th amendment to the Constitution, which led to the addition of Article 21A, and the subsequent passage of the Right of Children to Free and Compulsory Education Act, 2009 (RTE). Article 21A makes elementary education a fundamental right of every child,[2] placing the primary legal obligation for its provision on the state, and the RTE Act provides the legal framework for operationalizing the right.[3] In so doing, the RTE Act, sets standards and norms for the quality of elementary education, and delineates the roles and responsibilities for different levels of government in implementing or enforcing these norms. Thus, the state governments have been given the primary responsibility for ensuring that every child is in school and able to avail his or her fundamental right to education, while the panchayats have the added responsibility of being the first point of call for grievance redress.[4] Similarly, the National Commission of Protection of Child Rights [NCPCR], has been designated the monitoring agency in the Act. But the RTE Act also includes the private sector within its ambit through a series of regulatory clauses that in effect extend the right horizontally to private provision as well.[5] In other words, private schools also have to abide by the standards and norms set out in the RTE legislation. While, this might seem like a straightforward inclusion, it has given rise to a plethora of questions, both legal and social, some of which continue to remain unanswered.

The passage of the RTE Act was intended to give a boost to public provision of education, since it caters to a majority of the country's child population. By mandating improvements in the system of provision through the setting of standards for infrastructure as well as norms for teacher education and training, teaching hours, non-teaching duties, curriculum and system of evaluation, it was hoped that the quality of public schools would improve attracting more children to them.[6] As the right has been enunciated as a fundamental right and thus extends to all children such standards could not be limited to public schools alone. Hence, private schools have also been obliged to adopt the same standards, and in addition have to admit 25 per cent of their incoming class from the socially and economically backward communities. The latter to improve the diversity in the classrooms of private schools. However, private schools are also granted exemption from certain other provisions that allows them independence in management, such as charging of fees from the 75 per cent students that do not come from under-privileged families, and from setting up School Management Committees in the manner mandated for public schools.

Unfortunately, the Act has not had the desired impact, in terms of the intended improvements in quality of public schools, or the judicial push that was expected towards ensuring it. In fact, on none of the norms mandated in the RTE Act, has there been universal compliance, and millions of children still remain out of school.[7] As a result, children continue to exit public schools. Unfortunately, private schools have failed equally to comply with the mandatory provisions imposed on them. The 25 per cent reservation clause 12 1(c) has in particular generated a lot of controversy and even been challenged by private school associations in the Supreme Court.

This paper is thus an attempt to look at some of the challenges faced in making RTE effective. It does not purport to address all the challenges imposed by the Act, but merely to highlight some that are manifest in the text of the legislation and in the capacity of the state to implement and enforce its basic mandate. It shows that while some loopholes in the text of the Act affect public and private schools symmetrically, there are others that have a differential impact on them. For instance, while justiciability is a common issue for both, the hierarchies of access within the state system presents a challenge for state schools alone. It further questions the capacity of the state to ensure that the right is ensured to all children, whether in private or public schools.

The paper is organized around the following questions:

i) What are the implications of transferring a constitutional obligation under a fundamental right to the private sector? Are there sufficient safeguards in the Act (or Rules) to ensure that the right is not compromised, especially for children from marginalized backgrounds?
ii) Can the state, in exercising its right to choose how it fulfils its obligations, distinguish between state institutions of provision? In other words, is the right, as currently drafted, neutral in its application to all children?
iii) Does judicial enforcement constitute the only or main form of grievance redress for violations under RTE? What form of systemic redress does the Act or Rules provide for? Are these available symmetrically to children from public and private schools?

I. Challenges for Private Provision of Education as a Fundamental Right: The Case of RTE

The provision of education as a fundamental right raises a set of tricky questions as far as private provision of education is concerned, as the Constitution of India (as well as international conventions) place the primary obligation on the state to deliver fundamental rights, but there is no reason per se that private provision cannot be included under the purview of a fundamental right. In fact, the manner in which Article 21A has been phrased, in principle allows for the possibility of private provision. It states: "***The state shall provide free and compulsory education to all children of***

the age of six to fourteen years in such a manner as the state may, by law, determine." What this implies is that not only can the legislative arm of the state enact laws and policies to give effect to the right, but also, if it so determines, elicit non-state participation in the realization of the right. This is reflected, in the 2009, Right to Free and Compulsory Education Act (RTE), which specifically recognizes non-state participation in education through the inclusion of different categories of private schools.

While the intent of the amendment as stated in Article 21A seems straightforward, it raises a series of questions. For instance, there is implicit potential conflict among the following i) the right to free and compulsory quality education without discrimination for every child; ii) the liberty of parents to choose non-government schools and ii) the liberty of citizens to set up private schools as part of their right to practise any profession or trade of their choosing.

In addition to the mandatory application of norms and standards to private provision, the now 'infamous' clause 12(1)(c) of the RTE, that requires private schools to admit, as 25 per cent of their incoming class, children from socially and economically deprived backgrounds, has been met with a great deal of opposition.[8] These children are to be given the same education, free of cost, but with the government subsidizing the private school to the extent of per child expenditure in the local public school. This reservation and the overall applicability of the RTE was challenged in the Indian Supreme Court by a private school association on the grounds that it violated the provider's freedom, as a private agent, under Article 19(1)(g) of the Constitution (the freedom to follow any profession), to organize his or her profession as he or she deems fit. The reservation clause in particular was seen as interfering with such a right. Arguments were also made, by the private school association, that parents had a right to choose a private or a public school for their child, which choice was implicitly being affected by the restrictions imposed on private schools by the norms and standards of RTE.[9]

i) The Supreme Court's Response to the general applicability of RTE to private schools

The Court in this matter dismissed the private school association's arguments and upheld the constitutionality of RTE including the reservation clause, 12(1)(c).[10] This landmark judgment made significant contributions to the understanding of the right to education in India. For instance, the Court held that the RTE is "child-centric, not institution-centric" and therefore every barrier to the child's access, including financial barriers, must be removed to allow the child to access his or her right.[11] However, because the state has been given discretion under Article 21 A on how to fulfil the right to education, the Court recognized that it can choose to do so through statutory obligations on the private sector, as has been done through the standards and norms mandated in the RTE.[12] While Article 19(1)(g) provides citizens the freedom to pursue a profession or trade, this "freedom is not absolute" but could be subjected to "social control in the interest of the general public", through the imposition of "reasonable restrictions."[13] The Court also held that education falls under the category of "charity" and therefore, according to a previous judgement (the *T.M.A. Pai* case),[14] if an educational institution goes beyond charity into commercialization, it would not be entitled to protection of Article 19(1)(g).

ii) Questions that remain

While the interpretation of Article 19 and Article 21A of the Constitution and of the RTE by the Supreme Court in *Society for Unaided Schools* settled the issue of the state legally including the private sector in the fulfilment of a fundamental right, another set of questions remain regarding the manner in which that legality has been conferred on the private sector. For instance, have safeguards been built into the text of the Act, or otherwise through Rules and Guidelines that ensure that the obligations are understood and followed in letter and spirit? This is particularly important for the issue of equality.

1. One of the loopholes in the text of the Act regarding private provision of education is the many different forms that privatization can take that neither the RTE nor the Court have adequately addressed. For instance, different forms of 'horizontality' potentially arise in relation to the different types of private schools. These are:

   a) *Private unaided* schools, which the government regulates by imposing norms and standards. This has been done through the conditions laid out in the schedule and upheld by the Supreme Court in *Rajasthan.* This category of schools has been listed in the RTE. Private unaided minority schools have however been exempt from the RTE following the Supreme Court's order in the same case.

   b) *Private-aided* schools, where the government provides aid in the form of salaries for teachers and other schools staff in a privately owned and managed school. The norms and standards of the RTE apply in such schools. This category of schools has been listed in the RTE.

c) *Public-private Partnerships [PPP1]*, Here the government enters into an agreement with the private sector by way of a "partnership," for jointly running or managing public schools, where all the norms of the RTE, including free education, would apply by virtue of a contractual relationship between the private provider and the state. The RTE itself does not oblige the private provider to uphold the legislated norms and standards.
d) *Public-private Partnerships [PPP2]*, where there is *complete handover* of public schools to the private sector, and the latter is free to charge fees. The RTE does not refer to these types of private schools and there is concern that they may be exempt from the provisions of the Act as the contract in this situation does not import the terms of the RTE.

The rights implications are very different for these four types of private education facilities. While private aided and unaided schools have been explicitly included in the Act, the different forms of PPPs lie in a grey area, as they are not explicitly recognized. The omission of the PPPs from the RTE has created an ambiguity about the extent to which they need comply with the norms and standards in the Act, particularly around PPP2. This has serious implications for the manner in which privatization is likely to proceed in the future. For instance, while private unaided schools must comply with norms and standards set out in RTE, as well as the clause that relates to reservation of seats for disadvantaged children (clause 12(1)(c)), it is not clear that schools functioning under PPPs need do the same. Hence, it is very likely that more and more private agencies wanting to set up schools might choose the PPP model in order to avoid having to meet the RTE's norms and standards and to avoid having to reserve seats for disadvantaged children. There is a very real risk then that the privatization wave may well proceed along this route, to the detriment of children who will be devoid of the cover of the rights guaranteed under RTE. The contracts entered into by the private agencies in PPP2 type scenarios are not available in the public domain, so it is not known if any safeguards have been put into place to ensure that the rights of children are not tampered with or that these schools are RTE compliant.

II. Judicial vs Bureaucratic Recourse or Justiciability vs State Capacity

The second question raised in this paper relates to enforcement of the provisions in the RTE as they apply to private and public schools. It is interesting to note that punitive clauses in the RTE are restricted to non-compliance in respect of "capitation fees"[15] and screening procedures (Section 13), but no other provisions. Furthermore, private schools are faced with de-recognition for non-compliance with standards and norms, but public schools are not. In effect, there are no punitive clauses for non-compliance by public schools. In fact, there is a "good faith" clause (clause 31) that states, "No suit or other legal proceedings shall lie against the central government, the state governments, the National Commission for Protection of Child Rights, the State Commissions for Protection of Child Rights, the local authority, the School Management Committee or any other person, in respect of anything, which is in good faith done or intended to be done or intended to be done in pursuance of this Act, or any rules or order made thereunder". This provides a blanket protection to the entire public administration.

Further, as no grievance redress rules or mechanisms have been established within the public education system to deal with violations or non-compliance, the citizen or child is virtually at a loss for where and how to complain if his/her right is not being upheld. For instance, in some states, like Odisha, a helpline has been established. However, while complaints get registered through it, this system has not yielded positive results. This is in large part due to the inadequacies in the governance architecture, mentioned earlier, including huge shortfalls in state capacity to ensure entitlements are provided to all children. It would appear then that the courts are the only recourse available. But, as a violation of RTE entitlement would now be seen as a violation of a fundamental right to education the complaint can only be admitted at the level of the higher judiciary—that is, the High Courts or Supreme Court. But as the majority of the population attending public schools belongs to the lower end of the economic strata, accessing the higher judiciary—both physically and financially—is not easy. This is evident from the limited use of this judicial route by ordinary citizens.[16] It highlights instead the need for a robust grievance redress mechanism within the bureaucratic system that is accessible to all people. The absence of it is another example of the neglect by the state in upholding a fundamental right to education. Implicit in this situation is a marginalization of the poor from the justiciability of their right to education. It has implications not just for equity but for the quality of government schools as well, as it is the poor that overwhelmingly populate the public schools and the quality of which cannot easily be appealed for in the current design of the RTE or its justiciability.

As far as the justiciability of private schools is concerned, it suffers equally from the inadequacies in the grievance redress and judicial arrangements governing the RTE. This is starkly evident in the manner of implementation of the reservation clause 12(1)(c), perhaps the most radical measure thus far to promote inclusion and diversity in the classroom. It provides for inclusion of children from socially and economically under privileged backgrounds into private schools that would otherwise not be affordable for them. Specifically, it requires private unaided schools to admit 25 per cent children in their starting class (Class 1 or pre-primary as the case may be) from economically weaker and socially disadvantaged backgrounds, free of all costs, while extending all benefits and privileges that fee-paying children obtain in the school. But, as mentioned earlier, this provision has met with unprecedented (though not unsurprising) resistance from private schools. In addition to trying to have it legally removed, as discussed above, other measures to circumvent the requirement, or avoid it altogether, have also been employed by private school managements. These measures range from withholding information about admission procedures from parents, to turning them away from the gate of the school or demanding documents they are unable to provide. The social resistance is such that private schools are even willing to have a separate "shift" (evening classes) for children from disadvantaged backgrounds, rather than have them attend the same classes with privileged children. Another ploy being attempted by private schools is to apply for "minority" status, often on very specious grounds—to avoid having to follow the clause 12(1)(c) and admit children from disadvantaged sections, since minority institutions have been exempt from the RTE. Great care needs to be taken to ensure this exemption is not exploited, while also considering a judicial review of the exclusion of minority institutions from RTE.

Even in cases where the provision has been followed in letter, it falters in spirit. Thus, children admitted under this provision are reported to face discrimination in various forms.[17] In fact, discrimination of children from disadvantaged backgrounds in private schools has been documented in other studies as well. For instance, a well-known study on the use of vouchers that allowed children from economically disadvantaged families to access private school education, found that after 5 years of the programme nearly 30 per cent chose to go back to public schools, despite the acknowledgement of better quality in the private schools.[18] Preliminary analysis in the same study shows an inability to keep up with homework and the feeling of being discriminated against as reasons for the shift back to public school.

While monitoring mechanisms could conceivably capture non-compliance of the reservation clause, discrimination is much harder to catch. It is an area that requires more creative methods to document and handle in private schools, but also in public schools. In the absence of better vigilance on discriminatory practices, especially by parents of disadvantaged children, the only option available to children and their parents is exit, as seen in the study mentioned above. In many ways this strengthens the hands of the private providers, who see this as both a vindication of their position that such social engineering 'does not work' and also as an underhand means of edging out the disadvantaged children. The lack of a robust grievance redress mechanism makes it even harder to fight exclusionary practices. In other words, despite legal provisions or monetary incentives, in the form of vouchers, a greater effort is needed to sensitize teachers and students to the advantage of diversity in the classroom, before it can have its desired impact

The growth of PPPs and their nebulous status with respect to the RTE are also an indication of the attempts being made by the private sector to exit from the standards and norms within the RTE and state regulation generally. In the context of education as a fundamental right, this has significant implications, not least for the role of the state itself in ensuring the right to all children. Unfortunately, case law from India or elsewhere has not been able to definitively settle these issues. It is possible that accountability clauses could be built into the contractual arrangements between the state and the private entity to ensure that the private provider is equally liable with the state for the provision of education. However, even as PPPs abound, little is known about the legal arrangements governing them. A simple search will show that the memorandum of understanding (MOUs) signed by the state and the private entity are not publicly available and hence beyond public scrutiny. This opacity highlights the larger issue of regulation of private schools and the growing resistance to it. Currently, regulation is seen as a form of interference leading to market failure and thus sub-optimal outcomes. However, given the growing presence of private schools, it will be necessary to look more closely at the issues that need regulation and the most appropriate agencies for the job.

Ambiguities are related to the implementation structures for RTE and the lack of resources mandated for its realization. While, the RTE legislation was meant to provide the details for operationalizing the right, in effect it has left many gaps in enunciating the implementation architecture for RTE.

The first of these relates to the financial allocations under the RTE. In fact, the text of the RTE makes no mention of finances that need to be committed to education to ensure that the standards and norms mandated can be adhered to. Nor does it specify an administrative structure that would be accountable for ensuring the right is delivered. In effect, the governance architecture did not expand to include the special services covered under the Act, such as special training for out-of-school children or a designated RTE officer to oversee implementation. Budget allocations too have remained below the levels required to meet the norms set out in the RTE.

The lacuna in the financial commitment to RTE in fact goes back to its passage in Parliament and a lesser known or discussed procedural anomaly. Parliamentary procedures in India require that all Bills, which have financial implications—like the RTE—be moved along with a finance note, so that both are simultaneously passed and the legislation can be put into effect accordingly. Accordingly, only non-money Bills may be moved through the Upper House (Rajya Sabha), and do not require the finance note. For reasons, not yet clarified, the RTE was moved as a non-money Bill, with a proviso that the financial implications would be subsequently presented and passed by the legislature. Thus, the Bill became an Act of Parliament without the costs being either worked out or included in the text. Subsequently the exercise of determining the cost was undertaken, but a highly diluted version was presented to Parliament, in order to ensure it was passed and did not present any obstacles with the rolling out of the RTE itself. As a result, to date the real cost of RTE implementation is neither known nor has been actualized. In fact, the budgetary allocations, as a percentage of GDP, have even fallen since 2010, when the RTE came into effect.

As is well established, it is the economically and socially marginalized children that access the public education system by a large majority in India[19]. The extremely low budgetary allocations, and the subsequent impact on quality, imply that the education of the poor is being given short shrift by excluding them from quality education, belying the principle of inclusion. Further, the RTE has not made any special provisions for marginalized groups, including minority communities. In fact, by not including a budgetary provision to meet the requirements of the RTE in the legislation, it has de facto allowed the system to continue to provide subpar financial provisions to public schools, as before, without legal consequences. Even though as far back as 1966, the Education Commission under Mr. Kothari recommended 6 per cent of GDP as an appropriate budgetary allocation for education, India is yet to exceed even 4 per cent (currently less than 3 per cent).

With demand for education, especially from the marginalized groups, increasing like never before, such low budgets are simply not enough. The impact of the low resource base for RTE has affected minority children the most. In fact, while the government has followed a policy of providing incentives in the form of scholarships, bicycles, and other inducements to get children of socially and economically deprived backgrounds to come to school, these tend to be restricted to children of SC and ST backgrounds and girls. Minorities, especially Muslims are provided incentives by the Minority Affairs Ministry, which has far fewer financial resources and is unable to provide the same level of support. Often, they restrict their support to children in *madrasas*, even though a majority of Muslim children study in secular government schools.[20] The latest NSS (National Sample Survey) round data (2014) unsurprisingly shows that the education attainment of Muslim children has fallen to the bottom of the social hierarchy—below all other social groups in India.

Unfortunately, the financial shortfalls, as extreme and debilitating as they are, tend not to reach the courts for redress. Even if they did, courts in India have a tendency to defer to the executive for such matters, citing the separation of powers principle. Thus, even though this lacuna is critical to RTE implementation, no solution has yet been found.

The second issue related to the gap in the implementation structure refers to the data and information regime within education. Although this does not have a constitutional basis, it has strong implications for the manner in which the right is implemented, especially in terms of bringing out-of-school children into the mainstream. One way of gauging the government's efforts to fulfil its obligation towards education for all, including disadvantaged learners, is to see how carefully and adequately data is collected on excluded groups and children. In the context of a fundamental right, one would imagine that determining the number of children that are out-of-school—both the total magnitude as well as distribution by social category—would count as the starting point for such a purpose. However, at present, there are three official sources of information on out-of-school children [OOSC] and all provide vastly different estimates, ranging from 6 million (Ministry of Human Resource Development) to 40 million (Census, 2011). The situation becomes worse when we look for disaggregated estimates across social categories. While caste-based estimates are now available, data on minorities is conspicuous by its inadequacy, if not absence. The SRI-IMRB survey (2014) does provide an estimate of OOSC by social category that shows the following percentages:

Table 1: Out-of-School Children by Social Category

Scheduled Castes[1]	3.24%
Scheduled Tribes[2]	4.2%
Muslims	4.43%
Christians	1.52%

Source: MHRD website

Even the District Information System for Education [DISE], which is the official database for education, does not collect any data on minorities. What it does collect is data on what is rather oddly labelled as "Madrasas and Unrecognized Schools, "and within that too, only the number of such schools is included (without distinguishing between madrasas and unrecognized schools), and without giving the distribution of children within these categories of schools. What this implies is that the state has no estimate of how many children from minority families are studying in the different categories of schools and therefore enjoying access to education. This puts into serious question the state's commitment to combatting the exclusion of minority children from the public education system and indeed the fundamental right of these children.

III. Reinforcing Hierarchies of Access within the Public-School System

The second question raised by this paper refers to the fact that within the government school system itself, there is a hierarchy of schools that puts into question the neutrality of the RTE as far as children are concerned. The constitutional guarantee applies *equally* to *all children* between 6-14 years, but the RTE differentiates between types of school and thereby implicitly differentiates between the children studying in them. There are two forms of differentiations made in the Act that in effect discriminate against children on the basis of the school type they study in.

The *first* differentiation concerns the division of schools into distinct categories, with the provisions of the Act not applying uniformly to all categories of schools.[21] As outlined above, the Act differentiates schools into the following categories: i) Government schools and aided schools (i.e. privately run but government aided); ii) Private unaided schools; iii) Specified category schools (Kendriya Vidyalayas, Sainik schools, and Navodaya Vidyalayas[22]); and iv) Unaided Minority schools which, while not mentioned in the Act, have subsequently been identified for removal altogether from the ambit of the Act on the basis of a Constitutional provision that allows them to run educational institutions [Article 30].[23] This decision was made by the Supreme Court as part of the ruling in *Rajasthan*.

While all provisions of the Act are applicable to the first category, i.e. government and government-aided schools, they are not all applicable to the second and third categories, which have been given "exemptions" from certain provisions. For instance, private unaided schools are exempt from forming school management committees and are also allowed to charge fees [other than from those children who come through the 12(1)(c)]. The so-called "specified category" government schools, on the other hand, are also exempt from providing free education[24] and further have been given the freedom to choose children based on merit—a provision denied to *all* other categories of schools. While the exemptions given to private schools can perhaps be justified even though they do put to question the full import of the horizontal applicability of the right to education, the exemptions to special category schools—all of which are entirely under government management—is inexplicable. It essentially implies that schools set up by the government for children of government employees are entitled to differential treatment by being better resourced and exempt from the need to treat all children equally at the time of admission. This does not sit squarely with the equality or inclusion principle implicit in the RTE. The fourth category of unaided private minority run institutions, which has been removed completely from the ambit of the Act, seriously questions the RTE as a fundamental right for all children. Should children studying in minority institutions not be entitled to the same standards and norms of elementary education as other children?

The issue of differential and unequal access to state resources extends to a further categorization within government schools, which I shall not go into here for lack of time, but mention in passing only. This differentiation relates to schools run by different state departments with the express purpose of catering to different social groups. For example, there are schools run by the Tribal Welfare department for Scheduled Tribe children and by the Social Welfare department for Scheduled Caste children. It is a well-documented fact that the resources available to these departments fall far short of what would be required to maintain basic standards in line with RTE requirements.[25] But lacking convergence mechanisms with the primary department, i.e. the Ministry of Human Resource Development [MHRD], these schools have in effect fallen off the radar of RTE as well, to the obvious detriment of children studying in them—mostly the socially and economically marginalized.

Through the separation of schools, the RTE in effect segregates children and calls into question the equality and universality of the right to education. Worse, it signals a hierarchy within the government system and, when looking at the budget allocation and quality of education in the schools, these differences are pernicious and amount to discrimination. The following subsections examine how different categories vary in terms of costs, quality and the inclusion of minority and disadvantaged groups.

A. Costs

The cost per pupil ratio in the different schools makes clear the discrimination that is built into the government school system itself. The specified categories of schools—the first three in the table below—get from twice to almost six times the resources per student that the average government school gets. In some states, like Bihar, with the highest population of children, the government's expenditure per child is a fraction of the national average.

Table 2: Per Student Expenditure by Type of School

	Type of Government School	Expenditure/Student [Annual][3]
1.	Kendriya Vidyalayas	25,898 [2014-15]
2.	Jawahar Navodaya Vidyalayas	70,033 [2011-12]
3.	Sainik Schools	79,962[4] [2006-7]
4.	Regular Government Schools	12,768 [2013-14] [Bihar: 4515]

Source: MHRD website. The first three are specified category schools.

B. *Quality*

The limited information available shows that specified category schools have no incidence of single teacher schools or multi-grade teaching—in fact the pupil to classroom ratio is as low as 1:18—while regular government have a national average of 10 per cent single teacher schools, with some states, like Rajasthan having almost 20 per cent of its schools managed by a single teacher and a much higher incidence of multi-grade teaching.[26] A full complement of one teacher for every grade is rarely to be found in rural government schools. Multi-grade classes are never to be found in specified category schools. In fact, they possess the full complement of subject teachers as well as teachers for sports, art, music, etc.—a luxury in most government schools.

This raises a very fundamental question: Can the state legitimately provide differential quality of education to different classes of children under its statutory obligation? It also calls into question the Court's observation that the RTE is "child-centric" and not "institution-centric". This remark was made in the context of a distinction between public and private schools. But it should also apply to the different types of state schools. In fact, an improvement in the quality of government schools would not only set a benchmark for all schools, including the private, it would put a brake on the transfer of children from public to private in search of better quality. However, an improvement in public provision, which is the *raison d'etre* of the RTE, cannot be selectively applied to specified category or "model" schools only.

C. *Segregation*

Based on the differences discussed above, it is not surprising that the children going to the specified category schools are from different communities to children attending regular government schools. Further, the merit-based selection process adopted by the specified category schools (i.e. the Navodayas, Kendriya Vidyalayas and Sainik schools) is another violation of a fundamental principal of the RTE that all children be treated as equally meritorious at the beginning of their educational life. The idea of merit-based selection that has been repeatedly upheld for these [and other so-called "model" schools] is in effect a way of discriminating against children from disadvantaged backgrounds who do not have the exposure or home-support that equips them to compete in entrance procedures designed to test knowledge acquired through resources they do not have access to.

Unfortunately, figures are available only for the Navodaya Vidyalayas, as given below:

Table 3: Distribution of Students by Social Category in Navodaya Vidyalayas

General Category:	57%
Schedule Castes:[5]	24.8%
Schedule Tribes:[6]	18.2%
Minorities:[7]	? [not available or not collected]

Source: MHRD website

From the table above, it is clear that the disadvantaged communities (i.e. the Scheduled Castes and Scheduled Tribes), are under-represented in the Navodaya schools. While Muslim children do attend the Navodayas, it appears that statistics related to them are not collected. I shall refer to this issue in the next section but suffice to say that there is a clear bias in the social distribution of children attending these elite government schools.

Conclusion

In conclusion, it would be fair to say that the RTE has been remiss in addressing the issues of privatization adequately, especially in the transfer of obligations from the public to the private sector and the implications of this transfer for accountability. This is particularly problematic in situations arising from PPPs, which is the new form that private initiatives in education are taking in India. Without clarifying the principles of horizontality or the conditions under which a fundamental right can be delivered by private institutions, the Act and the Supreme Court have left wide-open the possibilities of interpreting the law and allowing private institutions to escape from under its radar. The unfortunate exclusion of privately run minority institutions from the ambit of RTE has added another layer to the segregated education system in India, while also sending a highly pernicious message to minorities in keeping them from enjoying their fundamental right to education.

Further, despite adopting the rights framework, the state continues to play a less than benign role in reproducing inequalities through a hierarchical education system that it legitimizes even within the public education system, thus ignoring the special needs of minority and disadvantaged children within it.

This paper shows further that the state has failed to put into place adequate implementation or enforcement structures that would enable the state to fulfil its obligation under the right. In fact, loopholes in the enforcement mechanisms for RTE in both private and public schools have led to gross violations of the rights of children, with the impact on disadvantaged children being magnified. This problem is compounded by the lack of punitive measures on public school violations defeating the purpose of improving quality in public schools to the benefit of the disadvantaged who populate the public schools in larger proportions.

Finally, this paper argues that to realize the right to education for every child, especially the poorest and the most marginalized, the focus of action should be on the public sector, and not on the private sector, which has neither the motivation nor the scale of operations to deliver what is required. However, since private provision is on the rise, better regulatory mechanisms will have to be considered to ensure that the rights of the child within private schools are also protected.

Notes

1. According to UDISE there are 293 recognized private unaided schools in India (2016-17) and 6,612 unrecognized private school (2015-16).
2. In fact, the right to education is the only "social" right that has been formally moved to Part III of the Constitution, that contains the fundamental rights, such as Article 21A. The judicial enforcement of this right thus assumes a different status, from other social rights that have sought cover under Article 21, such as the right to food, the right to housing, or employment guarantee.
3. Article 12 of the Constitution: In this part, unless the context otherwise requires, the state includes the Government and Parliament of India and the Government and the Legislature of each of the states and all local or other authorities within the territory of India or under the control of the Government of India
4. It is an 'added' responsibility, as the role assigned to panchayats are identical to those of the state government. This raises several questions about state capacity, which are discussed later in this paper.
5. In fact, one of the reasons for the delay in enacting the law was the issue of private schools with sharp lines drawn between the drafters on whether to include them within the legislation and if so, what role to assign them. While, one side preferred a "common school" system the

other was reluctant to diminish the role of private schools. In the end, a "consensus" was achieved by abandoning the common school idea and opting for regulation of private schools instead.

6. Except those constitutionally mandated, i.e. census enumeration, elections and disaster management.
7. There are only about 16 per cent schools across the country that are RTE compliant [DISE 2013-14].
8. Clause 12 1(c) of the RTE states: For purposes of this Act, a school-specified under sub-clauses (iii) and (iv) of clause in Section 2 shall admit in Class 1 to the extent of at least 25 per cent of the strength of that class, children belonging to weaker sections and disadvantaged groups in the neighbourhood, and provide free and compulsory elementary education till its completion. Provided further that where a school specified in clause in Section 2 imparts pre-primary education the provisions of clauses (a) to (c) shall apply for admission to such pre-primary school.
9. The International Convention of Economic Cultural and Social Rights (ICECSR), to which India is a signatory, recognizes the rights of parents to send their children to schools, other than those run by the state [Article 13, para 3]. But, this provision is subject to principles set out by the state's right to education, as well as the minimum standards laid down by the state.
10. *Society for Unaided Private Schools of Rajasthan v Union of India & Another* (2012) 6 SCC; Writ Petition (C) No. 95 of 2010. Decision in April 2012.
11. Ibid., Para 9.
12. The Constitution at the time of drafting recognized the need to extend horizontality to private sectors, with respect to fundamental rights, but limited it to a small class of cases, namely discrimination [Article 15(9)(2) and 19(2)]; forced labour [Article 23]; child labour [Article 24]; untouchability [Article 17]; and freedom of expression and religion [Article 28(3)]. Article 21A has added elementary education to that list as well. See Wahi (2007) for more on horizontality.
13. Article 19(6): Nothing in sub clause (g) of the said clause shall affect the operation of any existing law in so far as it imposes, or prevents the state from making any law imposing, in the interests of the general public, reasonable restrictions on the exercise of the right conferred by the said sub clause, and, in particular, nothing in the said sub clause shall affect the operation of any existing law in so far as it relates to, or prevent the State from making any law relating to, (i) the professional or technical qualifications necessary for practising any profession or carrying on any

occupation, trade or business, or (ii) the carrying on by the state, or by a corporation owned or controlled by the state, of any trade, business, industry or service, whether to the exclusion, complete or partial, of citizens or otherwise.

14. TMA Pai vs State of Karnataka (2002). Besides Article 21A and the passage of the RTE Act, which follows *TMA Pai*, nullifies the import of the latter as far as elementary schools are concerned.
15. Capitation Fees is defined in the RTE Act as follows: "any kind of donation or contribution or payment other than the fee notified by the school". This applies to private unaided schools, especially as they are allowed to charge fees under the RTE.
16. A cursory look at the number of cases filed in the High Court and the Supreme Court—45-shows that litigation is the not the route being taken by parents for the rights violations of their children. Based on author's ongoing research at the Centre for Policy Research.
17. Namala Annie, Archana Mehendale, Rahul Mukhopadhyay (2015). "Right to Education and Inclusion in Private Unaided Schools", *Economic and Political Weekly*, February 2015.
18. Muralidharan, K. and Venkatesh Sundaraman. "The Aggregate Effect of School Choice: Evidence from a Two-Stage Experiment in India", *Quarterly Journal of Economics*, Vol. 130, No. 3, pp. 1011-66.
19. According to NSSO data [64th round] 56 per cent of the students in government schools are from the two lowest expenditure quintiles in rural areas and 77 per cent in urban areas.

20 Bhatty, Kiran and Ambrish Dongre (2016). "India' Education Policy and its Development Over Time: How Has Social Inequality Been Addressed?" Background Paper for the International Commission for Financing Education Opportunities. http://report.educationcommission.org/resources/

21. The RTE Act, in clause 2 (n) defines a school as: any recognized school imparting elementary education and includes (i) a school established or controlled by the appropriate government or local authority; (ii) an aided school receiving aids or grants to meet whole or parts of its expenses from the appropriate government or local authority; (iii) a school belonging to a specified category; (iv) an un-aided school not receiving any kind of aid or grants to meet its expenses from the appropriate government or local authority.

    Clause 2 (p) defines the specified category schools mentioned in (iii) above as: a school known as Kendriya Vidyalaya, Navodaya Vidyalaya or Sainik

School or any other having a distinct character which may be specified, by notification, by the appropriate government.

22. These three types of schools—classified as "specified category schools", by the RTE Act are schools set up by the government for children of central government employees (Kendriya Vidyalayas) and Armed Forces (Sainik Schools). The Navodaya schools are special schools set up for so-called meritorious children from economically deprived families.
23. Article 30 (1): All minorities, whether based on religion or language, shall have the right to establish and administer educational institutions of their choice.
24. Clause 3 (1) of the RTE states, "every child of the age of six to fourteen years shall have a right to free and compulsory education.in a neighbourhood school till completion of elementary education".
25. Sujatha, K. (2002). India Education Report: Education Among Scheduled Tribes.
26. DISE 2014-15.

Endnotes

1. Scheduled Caste is the official term used for the lowest castes groups in India. Technically the term is derived from the list of such groups living in the "scheduled areas" as demarcated in the Constitution of India. However, over time, they have come to denote the "untouchable" caste now referred to also as the Dalits.
2. Scheduled Tribes similarly refers to tribal groups living in the scheduled areas, but now commonly to all tribal groups, irrespective of location.
3. As seen in the Table, the data are not available on an annual basis for all the schools, as they are not collected either regularly or by a common agency. Thus, there is a discrepancy in the years for which data has been presented.
4. These fall into a somewhat different category as most of these fees are to be paid by the parents.
5. Scheduled Caste is the official term used for the lowest castes groups in India. Technically the term is derived from the list of such groups living in the "scheduled areas" as demarcated in the Constitution of India. However, over time, they have come to denote the "untouchable" caste now referred to also as the Dalits.
6. Scheduled Tribes similarly refers to tribal groups living in the scheduled areas, but now commonly to all tribal groups, irrespective of location.

7. Minorities: This term refers to religious minorities, including Muslims, Sikhs, Buddhists, etc., However, since Muslims constitute the largest minority group it usually refers to them. In this paper too, it is used to refer to them. Also, as other Minority groups have fared much better in social and economic terms, including educational achievements.

9

Enhancing Quality of Education Through Partnership: A Case Study of Vodafone Idea CSR Initiative in Education

Nilay Ranjan

Primary Education in India

Primary education is the most important phase of compulsory education for developing the cognitive, emotional and social skills of children for their future school career. India has one of the largest primary education systems in the world with around 1.5 million schools and over 180 million students enrolled. Scores of measures have been taken by the government for the education sector right from building schools, providing midday meals to Right to Education.

The Right of Children to Free and Compulsory Education Act or Right to Education Act (RTE), aims to make education a fundamental right of every child between the ages of 6 and 14 irrespective of gender and social category. This historic act was passed by the Indian parliament on August 4, 2009. The act provided a legal framework that entitles a child to an education of reasonable quality, based on principles of equity and non-discrimination. The act came into effect in the whole of India except the state of Jammu and Kashmir from April 1, 2010.

Over the years, the government has worked on various initiatives to strengthen the country's elementary education system which in turn has resulted in six times growth in the number of schools offering primary education and sustained rise in the Gross Enrolment Ratio from 1950 to 2018. In the process we have been able to build a sizeable number of schools because of an emphasis on enrolment, resulting in a proliferation of schools with tiny populations and inadequate resources. India has almost 3-4 times the number of schools (15 lakh) than China nearly (5 lakh) despite a similar population. Nearly 4 lakh schools have less than 50 students each and a maximum of 2 teachers (*ToI*, March 30, 2019). The government spending on education by both central and state governments, currently, is close to 3 per cent of GDP which is less than the world average (according to the World Bank) of 4.7 per cent of GDP. Still quality, equity and access are the key challenges in the primary education.

Key Challenges to Achieve Quality Education to All

While the enrolment rate in primary schools has risen substantially, the learning outcomes have not seen a commensurate increase in alignment with higher enrolment rates and have rather declined over the past decade giving rise to a learning crisis. However, this momentum has not been maintained once we move to upper classes. Dropout rates increase as children move up. Around 30 per cent enrolled in Class I graduate from Class 12 of these who are the majority do not possess the requisite skills to be readily employable. According to Annual Status of Education Reports (ASER) 2018 only 64.3 per cent in Class 3 could answer a Maths question correctly; and the proportion continued to drift downwards to 54.14 per cent in Class 5 and a mere 42.07 per cent in Class 8. The subsequent numbers in English are not particularly good either, 67.7 per cent could answer in Class 3; 58.43 per cent in Class 5 and 56.7 per cent in Class 8. The possible reasons for the low learning outcome are:

- There is a shortage of nearly 10 lakh teachers while the existing teachers are inadequately distributed.
- Over 100,000 schools in the country are single-teacher schools as per the District Information System for Education (DISE).
- The absenteeism of teachers either for administrative or non-academic duties is another major issue as teachers spend a lot of time outside the classroom.
- There are over 11 lakh teachers yet to be properly trained. The deadline to train teachers under the RTE Act, 2009 has already been extended from 2015 to 2019.
- Outdated curriculum, inadequate infrastructure facilities, lack of accounting and monitoring mechanisms, and skewed pupil-teacher ratio.

- The focus remains on completing the curriculum and there are hardly systems and structures in place to provide extra help to those children who fall behind. Without the learning support that is critical, a large fraction of students lag in learning outcomes.
- 74 per cent teachers still use homework as a top tool to assess students in every lesson. The rote method is followed by the students and teachers. Teachers struggle with subject knowledge and ability to teach it. Also the curriculum lacks relevance, particularly at the secondary level.
- Only 24.3 per cent of teachers depend on project-based or experiential learning to assess students.
- India has just 14 teachers per 1,000 children under age 15, whereas Denmark has 253 teachers per 1,000 children under age 15.

All the above mentioned challenges have had a huge impact on the early education and in the absence of addressing these critical issues we are not able to participate in knowledge economy. Poor learning outcome among elementary school students has also a direct bearing on the efficiency of the country's workforce. Parents are forced to pay for extra tuition and are overburdened. According to the 2017 report by the Praja Foundation, 61 per cent of parents with children studying in Delhi government schools and 63 per cent in private schools had to send their children for extra tuition because of absence of quality teachers in school.

Taking the above issues into consideration the time has come to explore and experiment with methods to improve the learning outcomes of the children. One of the approaches is engagement of corporates through corporate social responsibility (CSR) activities.

Role of CSR and Right to Education

Education has been one of the favourite domains of corporates under corporate social responsibility. It is estimated that between FY 15-18 corporates have spent over Rs. 50,000 crore (CRISL Foundation). In the process corporates have gained a lot of experience to bring transformation in the education sector. This is also true for effective implementation of the RTE Act. Much before the RTE Act was announced, many corporates and NGOs were already working towards the improvement of the education standard of the children of our country in a different way like opening and running schools. These noble initiatives are already contributing towards meeting some of the RTE objectives. Hence it is important to recognize these initiatives and learn from the best practices that corporates/NGOs follow. The paper aims to highlight some of the Vodafone Idea Limited CSR initiative in the area of education and identify some key learnings from these initiatives. The paper will also highlight how these initiatives have followed different approaches to meet certain objectives of the RTE Act.

CSR Initiative in Education: Corporate Engagement Models

After the introduction of the CSR provision in the Companies Act 2013, there has been an increasing push by the government towards engaging the private sector as partners for achieving the goal of universalization of elementary education. As per Section 135 (1) of the Companies Act 2013, every company having net worth of rupees five hundred crore or more, or turnover of rupees one thousand crore or more or a net profit of five crore or more during any financial year, at least two per cent of the average net profits of the company made during the three immediate preceding financial year.

Vodafone Idea believing in bringing transformation in the learning environment and improving learning among students through use of technology has taken a number of initiatives related to education. Its education initiatives have led to a positive impact in learning among students and bringing overall transformation in the project schools. Its intervention has inculcated culture of joyful learning among the schools.

Like the Vodafone Idea many other corporates have taken significant steps through their CSR initiatives in improving the education standard of the children in our country. Although the objective might be the same for most of the corporates, the engagement model varies. In terms of the existing model, generally there are three models in which the corporates carry out their CSR activities in the field of education.

Model 1

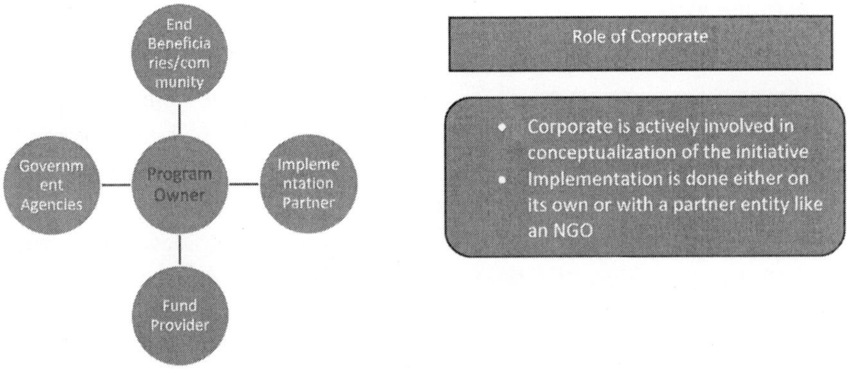

Model 2

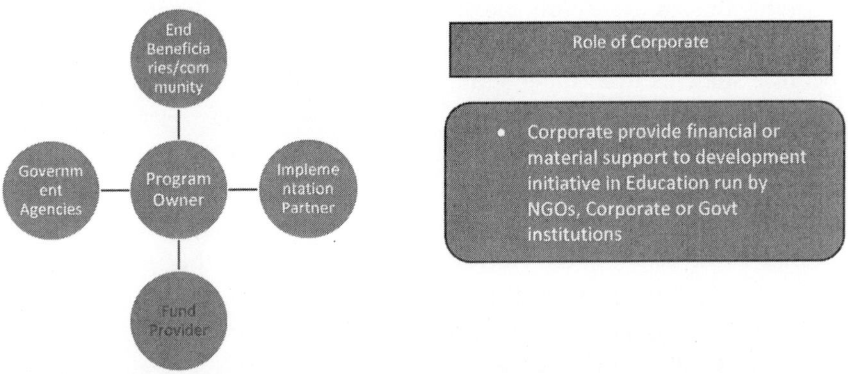

Model 3

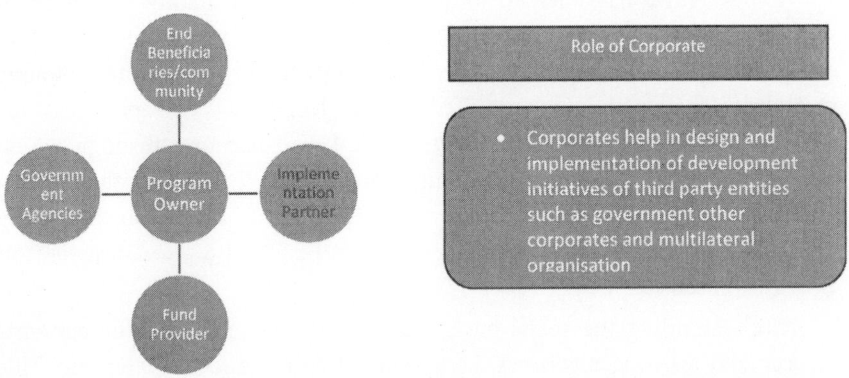

Improving Education Through Digital Content and Game-Based Learning—A Case Study of VIL CSR Project

Education is one of the priority themes under the CSR activities of the company. The activities under the education domain range from development and usage of digital content for Classes 1 to 8 to infrastructure works that support a good learning environment. One of the significant projects under the education domain has been development of digital content for Classes 1 to 8 for Science and Maths subjects. This project aims at developing frugal and appropriate interactive physical tools that address curricular objectives and can be interfaced with mobile phones or can be adopted on desktops, Virtual and Augmented Reality devices, as well as hands-on- tasks to enable and enhance sustained learning capabilities. We believe in bringing the highest standard of education to the citizens at the bottom of the pyramid. Keeping this into account the focus of the initiative is on low income group schools and government schools. This has been done consciously because students from other strata (slightly better off) of the society get an opportunity to access internet and come across various learning methods available on the internet. Other important aspects of the initiative is that students from low income groups and government schools (generally from the lower middle class) take an interest in these things because they generally do not come across such content either at home or other places because of ill affordability. As a result they take a keen interest in learning through digital media at school. In a way this has helped in bringing these students at par with others though for a limited time, i.e. during school hours. It has tried to bridge or narrow the gap between the haves and haves not.

The activities have helped to address the issue of quality education in schools which is a major concern for India especially, when the majority of our population is young. The project has adopted three level methodology to address challenges of primary education. In phase 1, the pedagogy for Classes 1 to 3 were designed on the game-based learning through which basic concepts were developed among the children. In Phase 2, the content for Classes 4 to 6 were developed on video and games-based problem solving approach and in Phase 3 content for Classes 6, 7 and 8 were designed on activities-based learning.

Understanding the social background of the beneficiaries the contents have mixed learning resources, i.e. animated video, inforgraphics, etc. This not only helps to develop an interest among the students but also makes them to use more and more and in the process their learning is improved. In a similar way acknowledging the importance of teachers in improving the learning outcomes of the children under the initiative a special focus has been put on building the capacity of the teachers on the use of content in the classroom. During the training teachers are also oriented on how to engage students in the classroom through different learning activities. In addition to learning content, teachers especially of Classes 6 and 8 are encouraged to develop a teaching plan as per the interest and likes/dislikes of the students. In addition to their plan, teacher have also been provided different teaching pedagogy through the online and offline mode. This not only helps teachers to tackle day-to-day issues in the classroom but also helps to inculcate interest among the teachers. In addition supportive infrastructure like television, tablets, etc. have been provided in the school.

The sections and paragraphs below provide details of the initiative undertaken in a phased manner.

Phase 1: Khel-Reaching Education Direct to Learners

Khel aims at improving the quality of learning through creative use of digital technologies. Two fold strategies have been followed, i.e. it provides the infrastructure for using technology. It supports the development of educational software as learning content that can be disseminated and used by learners, irrespective of their educational background and their resources.

Under the initiative 800 laptops have been provided to the Government of Madhya Pradesh through its implementing partners -IIT Bombay and IIT Kanpur. The laptops have been distributed to government primary schools in Madhya Pradesh (MP) in the districts of Sehore, and Khandwa. The laptops enable dissemination and use of educational content. In addition development of teaching-learning modules have also been supported. The Khel modules aim at reinforcing the teaching-learning of English and Hindi language and Mathematics in Classes 1 to 3.

In the second and successive phases, Khel modules aim at strengthening the knowledge and understanding of Science and Maths or (STEM) subjects from Classes 4 upwards, covering a competency cluster of 3 classes in a year. This is designed and developed in partnership with IIT Kanpur.

Design Innovations in Khel

To ensure that the modules are being used by the children and help in improving learning outcomes, story-based games have been designed in a modular manner so as to enable flexible, non-linear, and learner-paced pedagogy. They embed concurrent evaluation with in-built user feedback mechanisms to give regular feedback reports to the user- both students and teachers on a dashboard. They are adaptive to personalized learning, group learning, self and teacher-led learning. Using vernacular medium to support learning, the games are easily assimilated in schools, where there is a dearth of good quality supplementary learning resources. The game-based pedagogy mapped to the school curriculum enables easy integration into the actual school time-table and assists the teachers in providing easy solutions for remedial, diagnostic learning as well. Khel, thus, seeks to overcome several typical school handicaps such as erratic student attendance, inability to absorb knowledge through traditional teaching methods and unequal learning levels.

In terms of content, the learning objectives are aligned with the school curriculum. The academic content is identified on the basis of the diagnostic analysis of the learning process with the identification of 'hard spots' in the learning process such as:

- abstract concepts,
- content which is hard to visualize,
- content which has a broader context and presupposes inter-connected ideas at different levels,
- linguistic and cultural disconnect
- concepts not easily associated with familiar contexts

The content of the games in Khel is mapped on baseline tests conducted in a hundred government schools in MP, along with the teachers generating 'hard spots' that students experience in learning. For the Khel games, text books are intensively analysed, teaching-learning processes are closely observed, and learning difficulties are mapped.

In English, children had problems recalling alphabets out of sequence, spellings, full sentences, capital and small letters. The remedial plan in Khel focuses on listening, spelling, comprehending and writing full sentences, using a bilingual interplay with choices, visually reinforcing the alphabet, word and sentences throughout the game will expose the child to correct formation of letters and also teach them where the capital letter or the small letter is to be used.

Games designed for STEM subjects address a range of concepts mapped on the curriculum and design creative interactions through mobile phones or computers, virtual and augmented experiences through observation, experimentation, inference, drawing, model-building strengthening the capacity for scientific and mathematical reasoning.

Khel content is available on-line and off-line. The content is dynamically improved and customized based on field feedback.

Vodafone-IDEA CSR Khel has been quite successful and is making it possible for most of the teachers and the children to get their first opportunity of a direct interface with computers. Students in the schools are able to overcome their initial hesitation in handling the laptops and are able to intuitively navigate the keyboard and the lessons.

Phase 2: Enhancing Problem Solving Abilities to Learners

In the second phase the project focused on children for Classes 4 to 6. These educational Internet of Things[1] (IoTs) act as learning objects to inculcate problem-solving abilities of students by facilitating comprehension, recall as well as application of concepts in a playful and engaging manner. IoT-based learning are designed on a narrative that is scalable to multiple levels for the same competencies optimizing the challenge level for players in STEM (Science Technology Engineering and Maths) education for Classes 4-6. The primary objective is to inculcate problem-solving abilities in STEM subjects for Standards 4 to 6 by creating, using, and managing appropriate technological processes and resources for learning. Under the initiative below are the focus areas:

- Building a multi-sensory learning environment which supports multiple learning styles to strengthen government tutelage of the current curriculum.
- Design and development of low cost digital/internet interfaces connected with physical objects for accessing STEM knowledge through hands on pedagogy.
- Encouraging context-specific learning, well adapted to the unique situations of the rural school environment. (Erratic attendance, insufficient educational material and parental guidance, part-time learning etc.)

STEM Education

Science, Technology, Engineering and Mathematics (STEM) education forms the bedrock for technological progress and sustained development. However, the current trends of viewing STEM education as part of the competitive race for economic productivity alone, while increasingly disengaging it from skills of knowledge acquisition, reasoning, and processing is a cause of concern.

STEM consists of a body of knowledge, concepts and principles as well as a set of processes and skills (Clayden and Peacock, 1994), and are thus considered difficult learning concepts to grasp. Unfortunately, the present education scenario lays major emphasis on memorization of facts and methods, giving students the impression that memorizing and recollection of facts are the essence of STEM subjects. The PISA (Programme for International Student Assessment) test data from 13 million fifteen-year-olds across the world argues that children who focus on memorization score the lowest. (PISA, 2014) There is also an exaggerated emphasis on rapid or quick Maths calculations which raises anxiety amongst children. 'Rapidity' does not have a precise relation to intelligence, and such 'speed' driven classrooms demoralize the slow and deep thinkers spreading the belief that Maths or more generally STEM subjects are difficult to grasp.

The need of the hour is to promote scientific temperament and create enquiry-based hands-on-learning environment for children, instead of encouraging them to memorize facts. It is extremely important to obliterate the fear and anxiety in children associated with STEM subjects, and encourage them to tinker and play with concepts and methods, to let them explore multiple ways of arriving at the same solution and model, and to substitute rote learning with reason.

Acknowledging the fact that learning is stimulated when curiosity and creativity are sparked. Factors identified as making for effective teaching-learning include stimulating enquiry and exploration, interactive learning, problem-solving factors that enable learners not only to comprehend what is taught but more importantly, to learn how to learn. But, in the absence or lack of qualified teachers, what kind of frugal tools—digital and physical could be designed to enable children to become motivated and engaged in STEM subjects through observation, experimentation, inference, drawing, model, building, rational reasoning, testability, etc.?

To circumvent these problems, we have designed e-learning as well as physical tools to create a culture of thinking, inventing, tinkering and doing to promote enquiry-based learning in schools. After multiple product designs in the context of school education, game-based learning has been designed in the form of

I. ICT enabled learning through development of Multimedia Rich Lessons (MMRLs) designed as interactive and creative problem-solving games on desktops, mobiles, etc.

II. Frugal, cost-effective games as experiential learning enabling exploration of significant concepts through hands-on activities.

The rationale for this is to tap the potential of interactive games as a medium for learning STEM subjects and to use it for designing problem-solving pedagogies. Unlike lectures, games can be adapted to the pace of the user. Games also simultaneously present information in multiple visual and auditory modes, which capitalizes on different learning styles. Games are also particularly adept at doing information delivery. Complex tasks are presented first as a small core experience that is practised multiple times before being progressively extended into a longer, more complex sequence. Games are also useful for reinforcing information acquisition. (Mayo, 2009)

Phase 3: Activity Based Learning

Taking the initiative forward on the basis of our learnings, the next phase of the initiative is focused on activity-based learning and target group for this initiative is students of Classes 4 and 8. Under the initiative digital content for Science and Maths subjects have been developed to promote activity-based learning. This is interactive content framework which enables learning by seeing, thinking and doing and to provide more contextual understanding of the concepts by demonstrating them using graphics-thereby helping students to visualize complex concepts and to also facilitate transition from rote learning to learning by doing.

The programme was introduced in 1020 low income schools across 8 states in India in the year 2016 and provided content for Maths and Science for Classes 6, 7 and 8 by typically engaging two teachers from each school. Hardware in the form of tablets and LED screen were provided in all schools for display of content and classroom sessions. The intervention in these 1020 schools focus is on strengthening teacher capacities and pedagogical knowledge, benefiting around 1.5 lakh students and over 5000 teachers.

The main objective of the initiative is to positively impact the learning levels of students in low income schools through the introduction of technology in classrooms. Enabling teachers to use technology and group learning methodologies for teaching. Providing access to teachers to online teaching modules, digital content and a platform to network through an integrated web portal. Providing an individual experience to the students for interacting with technology.

The initiative has two aspects—first establishing technology in the classroom as an amiable aid in the teaching learning process. Aspects like technology handling, technology integration and group learning pedagogies have been the key components of the implementation strategy.

Being a new aspect for the teachers and students, capacity of the teachers was built through training and hand-holding support. Similarly, for the students who are primarily from low income schools were encouraged to do as many activity-based learning as possible. The whole method adopted under this initiative is based on three pillars—Relate, Explore and Assess. To keep the intervention relevant in fast changing teaching pedagogy and methodology offline digital content aligned to NCERT has been provided to teachers for Maths and Science for Classes 6-8 as a content bank to be used in the classroom. Regular call support provided to teachers for giving them hand-holding support on usage of self-learning modules, classroom strategies and use of digital content in the classroom.

Under the same phase another important initiative undertaken has been the development of teacher-learning platform—Gurushala https://gurushala.co. It focuses on providing teacher a holistic platform taking into account the increased exposure to technology of the teachers.

Teachers are central to the education ecosystem. Impacting their quality and capacity will directly impact the learning outcomes of children. While regular trainings are conducted in government schools to keep teachers apprised of developments in education and teaching methods, these are mostly limited to vacation periods and there are no mechanisms to keep them constantly engaged. The lack of follow up and practice renders the trainings less effective. Low income schools do not have budgets for teacher trainings. The limited budgets, infrastructure and resources, available with these schools do not permit many training programmes.

The teacher portal—Gurushala.co aims to overcome these gaps by empowering teachers through access to technology and methodologies for ensuring more participative and productive classroom sessions. The application directly delivers NCERT Mathematics and Science curriculum-aligned interactive digital content for Classes 6, 7 and 8 that can be accessed through desktop, laptop, tablet, smart mobile phone and used by the teacher both in the classroom and during lesson planning. The application has videos, images, quizzes, slideshows and classroom activity ideas stored in it to make learning creative and fun. Students get to explore learning via the See-Think-Do model and engage in experiments and activities. This improves their grasping power and encourages continuous engagement between teachers and students, inside and outside the classroom.

Self-learning modules on various linked aspects like learning difficulties, teaching strategies, classroom management, student engagement, etc. The attempt is to address a multitude of challenges being faced by the teacher in the classroom. Digital resource library providing teachers access to downloadable digital content on chapters of Maths and Science from Classes 6-8. Peer networking platform provides an opportunity to teachers to interact and engage with other teachers to share resources, cross-learn and network with the community of fellow teachers.

The portal provides an opportunity to teachers to keep the learning momentum going and also provides an opportunity to teachers to become students and encourages them to learn new happenings and development in the education sector, especially pertaining to teaching methodology. This is very important because teaching being a dynamic profession throws up various challenges in front of the teachers in classrooms. Often, they have little or no help in dealing with these issues as support and trainings are conducted at specific intervals and with pre-decided agendas. To address this number of courses are available on the portal which have 2-4 modules. The courses are free of cost only one has to enrol for the course and compete for it as per his/her time. These courses are designed keeping the challenge faced by the teachers in classes.

The teacher portal platform not only provides resources to the teachers but also a space to showcase their innovations, provide solutions to everyday common problems other teachers face all around the country. In addition it also works as an interactive platform virtual staffroom where teacher can learn from each others' experiences. Enrolled teachers can share his / her experience and also queries which can be answered by fellow teachers. This has one of its kind in present days.

The above mentioned shows that a great effort has been made to improve the learning outcomes of the students and improving teaching methodology of the teachers. Understanding the relevance of the initiative all the products and materials/contents developed have been placed on Gurushala portal for its maximum utilization and further enrichment. Enrichment of the portal is being carried out through the research corner where all relevant published articles, papers, innovation in educations, etc. are placed. This helps teachers and the general public to access these relevant research papers. Another important aspect of the intervention is teachers are consulted while developing new course content or teaching methodology. Under the project one of the important activities is SAMVAD which is conducted with groups of teachers at different locations to understand the issues in teaching and also to get inputs on the developed content or teaching methodology. This not only helps in understanding the new issues of teachers but also provides an opportunity to make necessary corrections in the content or teaching methodology which is being developed. As a whole, all issues related to student learning and teaching methodology have been tried to be answered under the CSR initiative of Vodafone Idea.

Monitoring

The initiative has led to improvement in children's learning and also in building the capacity of teachers in teaching pedagogy and methodology. A robust monitoring mechanism has been placed to ensure that initiative is sustained and carried for the years to come. The initiative is being monitored using different tools:

a. On call support to teachers—teachers are being regularly followed up through phone on call and are being provided regular support on teaching methodology, etc.
b. Whatsapp group: Around 10+ groups have been created comprising 200+ teachers. Teachers regularly share their innovative teaching practices, queries, etc. Apart from content provided during the initial phase of the project teachers are being provided videos and content on teaching pedagogy and are also provided handhold support.
c. Field visit and training: Regular field visits are being undertaken by the project team. School administration, teachers and students are being interacted.
d. Gurushala portal: Teachers' activities are monitored through portal, i.e. visits to portal and accessing content, enrolling for course, etc.
e. Courses available on the portal helps in monitoring of the teachers and their learning ability.

Conclusion

The initiative is not an end .... this journey is going to continue and will keep improvising as we move along with students and teachers. As per the need and requirement of students and teachers content and teaching pedagogy will be upgraded and shared with larger audience through the Gurushala portal. In days to come it will not be a close group initiative, rather it will be open for everyone to access the portal and assess her/himself by enrolling for the course. The efforts will continue to further improve the learning of students from government and low income groups. In the coming days focus will be more on building the capacity of teachers through courses and training on different aspects of teaching pedagogy and to keep the content relevant and remap it as per syllabus as and when required. In a nutshell a beginning with solid foundation has been laid for the better future of students.

Notes

1. Physical ordinary devices such a blackboards, refrigerators, televisions, and even pens can be connected to the Internet. Today, this trend is popularly known as the Internet of Things (IoT). Generally, the 'things' can be addressed uniquely, using a uniform resource identifier or an IP address. The objects can transmit data to each other and even perform physical acts using sensors. For instance, interactive boards can accelerate and simplify the learning experience by receiving, acknowledging and reciprocating information. Using similar devices, students sitting in classrooms can interact with educators, mentors and peers across the world. However, the immense potential of IoT to transform the educational panorama has been limited to passive devices, and not for direct learning amongst students or for increasing peer-to-peer collaboration.

10

Privatization of Teacher Education in India: Virtual Capture of the 'Public'

Poonam Batra

Mapping the Landscape of School Teachers

The non-availability of professionally qualified teachers in several states was a challenge amidst which the right to Free and Compulsory Education (RTE) was enacted in 2009. The cumulative shortfall of qualified teachers was due to the adoption of short-term policy measures and the gross neglect over several decades of developing institutional state capacity to prepare teachers. The huge demand for teachers to implement RTE compelled several states to seek exemption from adhering to norms of qualifications while recruiting teachers. Unqualified candidates were pumped into the teaching profession, adding to the large number of 'para teachers' that had overrun the state school system since international donor-supported educational reforms of the 1990s in some of the most educationally challenged states of India.

The Eighth All India Survey (NCERT, 2009) recorded a growth of 22 per cent in the total number of 67,47,466 teachers, including para teachers since the previous Survey. It noted a growth of 20 per cent in full-time primary school teachers; 23 per cent in the upper primary and 24 per cent in the secondary and higher secondary school teachers. The period between 2002 and 2009 saw a phenomenal growth of over 302 per cent in the number of para teachers and of about 210 per cent in the number of part-time teachers.

The total number of para teachers in the primary and upper primary sections at that time was estimated to be 8,09,256. Several of these did not have the requisite essential qualifications apart from not having a teacher education certification. Four per cent of the 5,60,492 para teachers at the primary stage did not have a secondary school certificate, when the essential requirement was higher secondary. Six per cent of the 2,48,764 para teachers at the upper primary stage had only secondary school qualification, when the essential requirement is graduation. Twenty per cent of the 12,67,000 teachers at the secondary stage did not have the requisite qualification of graduation; and 25 per cent of the 4,00,695 teachers at the higher secondary stage did not have the requisite qualification of postgraduation.

By the time the RTE Act was implemented in 2010, the country had accumulated not only a huge shortfall of professionally qualified teachers but also a large cadre of untrained teachers, many even lacking essential qualifications. The Bordia RTE-SSA Committee estimated 10.6 lakh teachers who worked without professional training; and would be required to acquire it within a maximum period of 5 years as per stipulations in the RTE Act (GoI, 2009).

The unpreparedness of the teacher and the teacher education system to meet the goals of NCF, 2005 (Batra, 2005), deepened with the studied silence in the RTE Act, on defining who an elementary school teacher ought to be. Some were of the view that the implementation of RTE would exacerbate inequities in access to quality teachers and teaching across India (Chugdar, 2013). Even today, several states face acute teacher shortage largely due to poor institutional capacity to prepare teachers. Many of these states continue to recruit teachers on contract, compromising on mandated essential qualifications. Currently, thirty-four per cent of the teachers in Delhi government schools alone, work as guest teachers and have sought cabinet approval to continue working as such until the retirement age of 60 years[1]. Several states have virtually abandoned the responsibility of creating professionally qualified teachers. Some have dispensed with the cadre of primary school teachers, as in the case of Madhya Pradesh, followed by Bihar.

While 11 per cent primary schools during the Eighth All India Survey were without full-time teachers, 33 per cent primary schools had less than two full-time teachers. Thus, four out of every ten primary schools had only two full-time teachers in position (NCERT, 2009).

The period from 2006 to 2012 (pre and post-RTE) saw marginal improvement in the overall percentage of professionally qualified regular teachers in the system from 78 per cent to 80 per cent. The overall percentage of contractual teachers (read para teachers), to the total number of teachers declined marginally at the primary level, from 17.01 in 2009-10 to 16.72 in 2011-12. The upper primary, secondary and higher secondary schools however, showed an increase in the percentage of contractual teachers, from 6.60 in 2009-10 to 7.48 in 2011-12.

The number of contractual teachers who acquired professional qualifications enhanced from 45 per cent in 2006-2007 to 62 per cent in 2011-12. Nevertheless, 38 per cent of the serving contractual teachers continued to teach in schools without any professional qualifications.

The average number of teachers in government primary schools remained more or less stagnant at 2.6 and 2.8 between 2005 and 2012 (DISE, 2011-12). In private primary schools the average number of teachers was much higher, and increased from 4.7 in 2005-2006 to 5.0 in 2011-12. The average number of teachers at the upper primary, secondary and higher secondary level in government schools however, indicated a steady growth from 9.0 in 2009-10 to 13.7 in 2011-12; but stagnated in private upper primary, secondary and high secondary schools at 9.0 in 2009-10 and 9.1 in 2011-12.

Two years past the RTE deadline of 2015, by when all untrained teachers in the system were expected to acquire the requisite professional qualifications, India had accumulated 11 lakh unqualified teachers in the school system as per the HRD minister's statement in Parliament[2]—higher than what it started with in 2009. Waking up to this reality, the central government passed an amendment to the RTE Act, providing elementary school teachers another small window to acquire the requisite professional qualifications under the legislation.[3] These 11 lakh teachers were to attain the required certification through massive open online courses on the Swayam Portal, launched for the purpose by the Government of India. However, there was enough ground for scepticism, given that distance learning measures via the involvement of IGNOU and the National Institute of Open Schooling, suggested in 2010, were found to be poorly operationalized, creating no real impact on the ground. Moreover, a distance learning architecture needed to be operationalized and monitored for transaction and evaluation of registered teachers, for the period September 2017 to March 2019 (Batra, 2019), we do not have data to indicate what has been achieved in this regard, so far.

The most recent estimates noted in the draft education policy (GoI, 2019), show that "the country faces over 10 lakh teacher vacancies—a large proportion of them in rural areas—leading to PTRs (pupil-teacher ratios)[4] that are even larger than 60:1 in certain areas." As per AISHE (2019) estimates,[5] a total of 5,16,463 candidates graduated in secondary teacher training and a total of 98,343 graduated in elementary teacher training. These are woefully inadequate figures given the challenge of the large number of teacher vacancies. Besides, it must be borne in mind that only 15 per cent graduates qualified (for elementary level) to become teachers as per the TET requirements[6]. What the system needs, as per UDISE data[7] and in alignment with RTE norms, is approximately 83 lakh teachers to cater to a school population of 2,500 lakh elementary and secondary children in the existing 15 lakh schools.

Glossing Over Intervention by the Supreme Court

Major Education Commissions and Committees on education[8] since independence have flagged the need to reform teacher education as a key concern. The sector remained stagnant despite several attempts to release it from colonial frames and ground it in prevailing school realities and frontiers of decolonized knowledge. As a result, the bulk of schoolteachers across the country are under-trained, under-compensated; and reduced to demotivated instruments of a mechanical system of education that was initially conceived to support a colonial regime.[9] Even today this system tends to strengthen rather than question the status quo on questions of caste, community and gender asymmetry.

The Supreme Court of India made a far-reaching intervention in teacher education in June, 2011, to address complaints of widespread malpractice, policy distortions and regulatory conflicts. After uncovering a viper's nest of vested interests from widespread corruption, dummy colleges, a moribund teacher educator community to malpractice and widespread political patronage—it constituted a High Powered Commission headed by J.S. Verma, a former Chief Justice of India. The Justice Verma Commission (JVC), after a year-long nationwide consultations, presented a comprehensive report and Action Plan to reform the sector, to the Supreme Court in August 2012.

One of the most critical observations made by the JVC was that "...close to 90 per cent of pre-service teacher training institutions are in the private sector...(while) around 80 per cent of children enrolled in state schools are the direct responsibility of the state as per the RTE Act." The Commission noted that the National Council for Teacher Education (NCTE) had failed to control the proliferation of substandard TEIs, leading to rampant privatization and commercialization. This in their view had adversely affected the quality of teacher education (p. 21) as the bulk of those who qualify to be teachers through a substandard private system of 'teaching shops', fail to address the pedagogic needs of diverse classrooms.

Analysis of the data on recognized teacher education institutes (TEIs) updated by NCTE in 2019 reveals that the number of private TEIs has increased further since the JVC submitted its report. Data[10] indicates that 46 per cent (7,725 out of a total 16,917) of recognized TEIs across the country are located in the northern region (see figure below). The southern region has 26 per cent TEIs; the western region, 18 per cent and the eastern region about 10 per cent of total TEIs in India. Figures indicate a total private share of over 91 of all TEIs across the country. Of these, northern and the western regions have the maximum number of private TEIs—96 and 93 per cent respectively. The southern region has 89 per cent of TEIs in the private sector. The relatively lower percentage of private TEIs in the eastern region (77 per cent) is largely because two states—Odisha and Mizoram—do not have any TEI in the private sector.

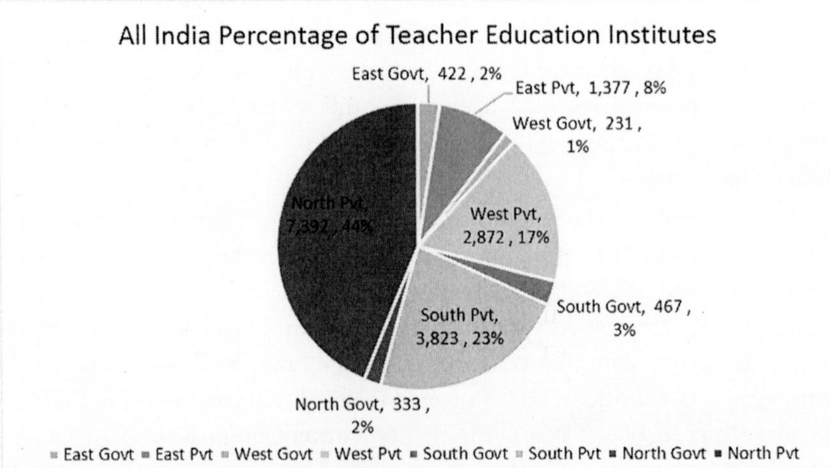

The largest share of private TEIs are located in the larger states of each region. In ERC, the largest share of TEIs is within West Bengal (48 per cent), of which, 96 per cent are in the private sector. In the northern region Uttar Pradesh (UP) has the largest number of TEIs (61 per cent). TEIs in UP offer a total of 6,123 courses, including the MEd. Ninety-four per cent of these courses (5,736) are offered through private TEIs.

In SRC, the states of Tamil Nadu, Andhra Pradesh and Karnataka together have 79 per cent of all TEIs in this region. Tamil Nadu alone offers

87 per cent of all teacher education courses through private institutions. In the western region, two states—Madhya Pradesh and Maharashtra—hold the bulk of TEIs (90 per cent); and 90 per cent of the courses offered in Maharashtra alone are through private institutions. This suggests that for large and small states, barring Odisha and Mizoram, private TEIs continue to be the norm as was highlighted by JVC.

This is a virtual business takeover of teacher education via contracts between state and national governments with support from the apex regulatory body and private providers. Private TEIs are sustained on a network of rent-seeking activities, beginning with the requirement of formal institutional recognition and the provision of certification to aspiring students. The award of degrees and diplomas without the need to attend classes is accepted practice.[11] Several private TEIs have commercial motives but poor facilities and a lean teaching staff. Visiting one of the private colleges in Jharkhand, the Joint Review Mission Report (JRM) team found that while the college apparently fulfilled all NCTE norms, it had an attendance of 19 students out of the 100 enrolled and very few teachers. The teaching faculty in private and even University-based self-financed MEd programmes in Jharkhand was found to be on contract with a consolidated salary (GoI, 2013b). The JRM visiting Bihar noted that while 90 per cent TEIs had buildings, office rooms and lecture halls were not usable, and the majority of institutions were without electricity connections. Only a few toilets were usable and 50 per cent institutes lacked drinking water facilities (GoI, 2013a).

The period between 2007 and 2011 saw an exponential rise in the number of private TEIs; the number more than doubled from 7,300 in 2007 to 14,704 in 2011,[12] with a total intake of ~10 lakh students. Currently, there are a total of 16,917 TEIs offering 24,199 courses[13] with an intake of over 12 lakh potential seats.

Estimates indicate that 51 per cent of TEIs trained secondary school teachers and 43 per cent trained elementary level school teachers. Of the total of 5 lakh potential seats (intake) in pre-service teacher education, 3 lakh (64 per cent) were for training secondary teachers to cater to 27 per cent of secondary level students and 1 lakh (34 per cent) to train elementary level teachers to cater to 73 per cent of primary level students.[14] As per current estimates of the NCTE, percentage intake for DElEd ranges from 29.81 in NRC to 40.79 in ERC; and percentage intake for BEd ranges from 45.25 in SRC to 56.27 in NRC. Clearly, the system of teacher education is geared to produce a far larger number of secondary teachers than what the school system can absorb. In contrast, the number of primary level teacher graduates are far less than the existing need. This systemic imbalance[15] continues to remain in the blind spot of policy makers.

Of the total current intake, a mere 40,000 seats[16] are in District Institutes of Education and Training (DIETs)—state institutions that prepare elementary school teachers. This implies that mushrooming substandard teacher training institutes are expected to fill the unfilled demand of ~1,60,000 (81 per cent) elementary school teachers.

Corresponding figures for 2019 indicate an enhanced share of teachers trained in the private sector with a further increase of 13 per cent TEIs since 2011. While the relative arrest of private expansion of TEIs post-2011 can be attributed to JVC's expressed disapproval of sub-standard private 'teaching shops'; its recommendation to increase state investment in teacher education goes unheeded and finds no mention in the draft education policy of 2019.

The Problem of Intellectual Isolation

The second critical observation made by JVC was the intellectual isolation of institutional environments in which teachers are prepared. The bulk of TEIs (91 per cent of which are private) exist as standalone institutions offering a single course, such as the Bachelor of Education (BEd) or Diploma in Education[17] (DEd). NCTE estimated that, in 2011 only 20,000 of the 3 lakh secondary level seats approved, were university-based. According to AISHE data for 2015-16, nearly 90 per cent of 17,000 colleges in India that teach a single programme, are teacher training institutes (GoI, 2019).

JVC noted that the standalone nature of TEIs is a "direct consequence of stipulated norms that require separate independent campuses for teacher education institutes even within universities" (2012: 14). Also, most colleges of teacher education (CTEs that offer BEd) have marginal scope for engagement across disciplines due to lack of physical and academic proximity to the affiliated university. About half of the total number of TEIs that train elementary school teachers via a Diploma in Elementary Education (DElEd) in any case fall outside universities and the higher education system of the country.[18] The bulk of teacher preparation therefore happens in isolation of centres of higher learning. As a result of their 'standalone' nature, noted JVC, TEIs "remain severed from activities of knowledge generation and a culture of research and interdisciplinary studies". This helps us understand why TEIs remain impoverished in terms of professional capacity and curricular change. "It is therefore desirable", observed JVC, "that new teacher education institutions are located in a multi and inter-disciplinary academic environment." The Commission therefore emphasised that "apart from augmenting the required capacity to prepare teachers, pre-service programmes require a radical shift in curriculum[19] and institutional design."

A critical way forward suggested by JVC to address three of its crucial recommendations, namely, (a) increase government investment; (b) prepare high quality teachers through integrated programmes of general and professional education; and (c) remove the intellectual isolation that characterizes school teachers and their preparation, was to locate teacher education programmes of secondary and elementary education in university-based colleges of liberal arts and sciences.

With the revision of NCTE norms in 2014, based on JVC recommendations, all teacher education courses were supposed to have become part of 'composite institutions' defined (by the JVC) as multi-disciplinary institutions that offer diverse courses in the liberal arts and sciences. One of the several sub-committees[20] set up to provide road maps for the implementation of JVC recommendations, outlined concrete strategies to address this specific recommendation, drawing upon UGC database that listed over 35,000 affiliated and constituent colleges of liberal arts and sciences across the country.[21] The sub-committee[22] observed that the large number of undergraduate colleges could potentially offer pre-service teacher education programmes beginning with states in urgent need of teachers, but having poor institutional capacity. It recommended that locating teacher education programmes in liberal arts and science colleges would enable the gradual transition of the preparation of teachers from standalone institutions to multi-disciplinary institutions as recommended by JVC.

However, in the revised norms of 2014, the term 'composite institutions' was reinterpreted by the NCTE to also mean institutions with more than one teacher education course/programme. Consequentially, the insular nature of TEIs as pointed out by the JVC remained unaddressed and unresolved, despite revision in regulatory norms.

With a change in the political regime at the centre in 2014, the JVC recommendations were set aside despite their approval by the CABE committee and a ruling by the Supreme Court to ensure their implementation via an Implementation Committee[23] (IC) constituted at the behest of the apex court in 2012. The JVC, its recommendations and the road maps proposed by various sub-committees find no mention in any of the policy provisions and modifications made by NCTE under the new dispensation, since 2014.

The draft education policy, 2019 too, merely mentions the Commission's observation that a majority of "the standalone teaching institutes—over 10,000 in number[24]—are not even attempting serious teacher education, but are essentially selling degrees for a price" (GoI, 2019: 283). The only academic strategy it proposes to enhance professionalism amongst teachers and build their capacity is to set up national level Teacher Education Universities, a concept that many argued against during the national level JVC deliberations. Such a move, the Commission noted, would further augment the existing problem of preparing teachers in an intellectual vacuum through stand-alone institutions.

The Problem of Poor State Investment in Teacher Education

The gross financial neglect of teacher education, though characteristic of education policy, rarely finds critical mention in educational debates. The district-based infrastructure for pre and in-service of elementary school teachers (DIETs), established under the centrally sponsored scheme of teacher education in the Seventh Five-Year Plan (1985-90) is a glaring example of such neglect. Established post-1986 policy, DIETs have remained under plan funds for over three decades until the Twelfth Plan (2012-17). During this long period most DIETs were allowed to languish[25] because of inadequate funds; and the meagre and untimely release of allocated funds. DIETs also faced academic marginalization during the nation-wide reforms under DPEP.[26] With the discontinuation of Five-Year Plans[27] post-2017, the centrally—sponsored scheme of teacher education has since been merged with the SSA and RMSA under Samagra Shiksha (GoI, 2018), implying a further decline in fund allocations. It is important to reiterate that DIETs form a minuscule part (a mere 600+) of the total number of 17,000 existing TEIs.

Taking note of this and the enrolment rate of over 80 per cent children in elementary state schools, the Justice Verma Commission recommended a substantive increase in government spending on teacher education. As indicated earlier, to increase state presence in the teacher education sector, the IC via its subcommittees suggested economically viable models such as locating programmes of teacher education in undergraduate colleges of liberal arts and sciences. The Commission also saw in this the possibility of shutting down large numbers of substandard standalone institutions without exacerbating the problem of inadequate institutional capacity.

However, budget allocations for school education, including teacher education, continue to be inadequate. According to one estimate, even though India stepped up its spending on school education by 9.35 per cent from 2014-15 to 2018-19; the education share in the total union budget reduced from 2.55 per cent to 2.05 per cent in this period. Spending on education has fallen from 1 per cent of the national income in 2014-15 to 0.62 per cent in 2017-18. The overall share of educational financing in the budget has been slashed from 6.1 per cent to 3.7 per cent (Vivek, 2018). Also, the union government's budgetary spending on education accounts for a much smaller share than state governments' total budgetary spending on education. This puts higher fiscal responsibility on state governments without offering any specific solutions to the existing challenges facing the education sector (Kundu, 2017, p. 33).

Kundu (2019) notes that the share of teachers' education budget in the overall school budget declined from 1.3 per cent in 2009-10 to 1.1 per cent in 2018-19. Uttar Pradesh, Chhattisgarh, Bihar and West Bengal—states with large numbers of professionally unqualified teachers do not spend even 1 per cent of their school education budgets on teacher training.[28] While on the recommendations of the 14th Finance Commission, Bihar and Chhattisgarh did increase allocations for the training of teachers, these were as low as 0.001 per cent in Uttar Pradesh and 1.3 per cent in Bihar.

Despite JVC recommendations, the central as well as state governments have both failed to invest enough to create institutional capacity for training teachers. Government of India estimates[29] indicate that DIETs, the nodal agencies for elementary teacher education have over 45 per cent faculty (teacher educators) vacancies.[30] Also, DIETs are often staffed with people who are not appropriate for these roles, leading to ineffective use of budget allocations (GoI, 2019). Paucity of teacher educators is yet another critical manifestation of the poor fiscal health of the teacher education sector.

Preparation of Teacher Educators: A Weak Link and the Absence of Critical Discourse

A large number of teacher educator vacancies is characteristic of not only state-run TEIs but of the bulk of private run TEIs[31] as well. Clearly, the extraordinarily large presence of TEIs in the private space has neither solved the chronic problem of teacher shortage nor the problem of acute shortfall of teacher educators across several states. The paucity and unpreparedness of teacher educators is usually glossed over in policy debates and is rarely seen to be critical to the preparation of quality teachers.

The all India figures of NCTE 2013 (cited in Batra, 2017) revealed that of all the institutes recognized by the NCTE, less than 6 per cent offer MEd programmes amounting to a total intake of about 2 per cent. Current NCTE estimates indicate that the total capacity of institutions that offer a master's degree in education (MEd)—the essential qualification for becoming a teacher educator[32]—is a mere 1,204 with a total student intake of 51,180. The ERC intake for MEd is 4,600 of which 58 per cent is offered in private institutes. For SRC the intake for MEd is 9,970 of which 74 per cent is offered in private institutes. The intake for MEd is highest for NRC at 26,910, of which 90 per cent is located in private institutions; and for WRC it is 9,700, 86 per cent of which are in the private sector.

If all 51,180 graduates of MEd were to be accommodated as teacher educators, an ideal system would need 3,198 TEIs to conduct pre-service programmes, taking 16 faculty members per institution as per NCTE norms, 2014. In order to meet the requirement of 10 lakh school teachers (teacher vacancies as per draft education policy, 2019) a projected institutional capacity to develop teacher educators would need to be six times higher than what exists.

Currently, only 3.32 per cent of TEIs offer MEd courses in the Eastern region; 4.75 per cent in the western region; 5.07 per cent in the northern region and 5.61 per cent in the southern region. Of these, the lowest intake for the MEd course is 1.91 per cent in ERC; and 3.05, 3.28 and 3.96 per cent each in NRC, WRC and NRC. While most MEd courses are offered in university-based government institutions, states with high MEd intake in private institutions are: Haryana, Uttarakhand, Himachal Pradesh, Kerala, Chhattisgarh and the union territories of Chandigarh and Goa.

JVC suggested several concrete ways to fill the massive deficit in teacher educators. This was reiterated by the 12th Plan Working Group (GoI, 2011). Recommendations include (a) enhancing the capacity of existing institutions by increasing the annual intake of students in MEd programmes; (b) creating capacity in new universities to offer MEd programmes[33]; and (c) diversifying the eligibility criteria for recruiting teacher educators. JVC observed that the key problem of 'intellectual isolation', plaguing the sector of teacher education, impacts the preparation of teacher educators as well. Data indicates that even though much less than the required number, teacher educators are nevertheless, being prepared largely in 'standalone' institutions.

Commercial substandard institutions disseminate practices rested in an unchanged frame of duration, and curriculum and pedagogic approaches, that remain largely uncontested. In the absence of a robust teacher educator community within and across institutions, a culture of uncritical engagement with questions of educational theory and practice is normalised.

The Commission unequivocally noted that the "preparation of teacher educators has remained a weak link in ensuring the quality of pre-service teacher education, and therefore, the issue of the profile of a teacher educator should receive due attention, transcending the existing thinking on the subject" (p. 17). It observed that the current institutional norm of requiring an MEd degree for the recruitment of teacher educators is limiting and needs to change; and recommended a strong grounding in the social sciences for the teaching of foundation courses.

Enabling a multi and inter-disciplinary faculty to become teacher educators, with strong theoretical and epistemological grounding in major foundational disciplines will provide the opportunity for wider and deeper engagement with issues of educational theory and practice. Hence, linkages with higher education need to become deeper and lateral, observed the Commission. It suggested that the essential qualification framework for teacher educators be broadened to ensure the entry of specialized faculty to become teacher educators.

The Twelfth Plan also observed that the 'restrictive norm' of MEd as an essential qualification 'needs to be reviewed in the light of the following two aspects: (a) the repertoire of skills and capacities required of teacher educators to respond to the demands of a curriculum outlined in the National Curriculum Framework for Teacher Education (NCTE, 2009); and (b) international practice in respect of teacher education institutions...the central idea (of which) is to offer alternate paths for persons from various disciplines to become teacher educators.' This comes from the understanding that the requirement of teacher educators who can engage with questions around aims of education, epistemological basis of knowledge, learners, learning and curriculum design can be fulfilled via rigorous theoretical engagement with foundational disciplines and not within frameworks of educational practice alone.

The Commission recognised the need to combine the study of education as a liberal discipline and as professional practice. To do this would require bridging the popularly held conceptual distinction between education as professional practice and liberal study. A close scrutiny of the Master of Arts programmes in Education and the MEd programmes reveal that this distinction remains blurred[34] and is difficult to articulate. Not only do professional concerns and liberal ideas inform each other to enrich educational discourse as well as practice; their confluence is also necessary to develop a language of praxis. To enable this, structural provisions will need to be made at two broad levels: (1) open direct entry of students of social sciences, sciences, mathematics and humanities into postgraduate educational studies and research, without the existing prerequisite of a degree in teacher education;[35] (2) offer education as an elective subject in undergraduate programmes of liberal arts and sciences to pool talent and steer them towards higher degrees in education. Equally critical to this is the inclusion of faculty trained in diverse disciplines, in programmes of teacher education and educational research.

Post-JVC, the revised norms did little by way of opening up the space in outlining faculty qualifications for teacher educators. On the contrary, space for those with post-graduate degrees in social science disciplines along with research experience/research degrees in education, that existed in norms of 2009 for the BElEd, was effectively closed with the revisions notified in 2014. In the current norms, a teacher education degree has been made mandatory for being recruited as teacher educators, even in the few positions where MEd is not listed as an essential qualification. This was not only a regressive step, but was violative of the recommendations made by JVC.

The JVC report made far-reaching recommendations with the aim to revitalise the teacher education sector, improve pre-service and continuing professional development programmes for teachers; bring radical modifications to the statutory regulatory functions of the NCTE and make substantive revisions in the NCTE Act that would be commensurate with the recommendations. Specific recommendations focus on structural changes in institutional arrangements; attracting fresh talent to the field of teacher education; the redesign of teacher education curriculum to respond to and enhance diversity; develop knowledge and learning contextualised to Indian society and institute appropriate regulatory mechanisms to enable significant shifts on the ground. The draft education policy of 2019 has chosen to ignore the bulk of these recommendations that require structural rearrangements and major changes in the regulatory functions of teacher education, including the NCTE Act[36]. As this paper is being written, a

High Power Committee has been constituted by the Government of India[37] to 'suggest Sectoral Reforms in teacher education' starting from a clean slate.

The Changing Axis of the Quality Debate and Privatisation

While the state school system expanded to achieve the goal of universal enrolment, the simultaneous acute need for more teachers was left unaddressed. School enrolments gained ground, but the quality of teaching-learning posed several challenges in the absence of qualified teachers. The neglect of building institutional capacity to prepare teachers, especially in states with low literacy rates and the acute shortfall of teachers made the task of achieving quality education that much more difficult. The continued gross neglect of teachers and their education was a strong indication that the state was no longer interested in rejuvenating a fast declining state school system.

Large numbers of parents moved their children to private schools in search of quality education. Many low-fee paying schools (LFPS) mushroomed to meet parental aspirations of an English medium education—one of the perceived hallmarks of quality schooling. Continuing international pressures to achieve universal quality education paved the way for policy borrowing and seeking answers from the growing global policy community. Advocacy by global education networks and ideas of educational entrepreneurship caught the imagination of many national and international private players. Encouraged by the policy discourse on inviting the private[38] into the education space, non-state actors of various hues pitched in to meet the crying need for quality education. Srivastava (2010: 524) notes that privatization, which may once have been a default strategy, is becoming the strategy of design. The proliferation of the private in education was aided by several corporations that initiated education projects in the framework of corporate social responsibility (CSR). Towards the end of the second decade of reforms school enrolments in state schools started to decline sharply. This was despite the enactment of a central legislation to provide free and compulsory elementary education.

DISE data of 2012 indicates that the share of private school enrolment in rural primary schools is 31 per cent, 37 per cent in upper primary levels, 54 per cent at the secondary level and 60 per cent at the secondary and senior secondary school level (EY and FICCI, 2014). Currently, India is one of the four South Asian countries where about one-third of children from 6 to 18 years of age attend private schools (World Bank, 2017). The largest number of private schools is at the elementary and secondary level in the states of UP, Maharashtra, followed by Gujarat and West Bengal.

The impact of the proliferation of private schools, including low-fee paying schools led to further segregation of schools. State schools became largely homogenous spaces with the children of the economically and socially disadvantaged—a direct outcome of the policy neglect of the state schools. The proliferation of low-fee paying schools in particular, intensified inequality between regions and schools in terms of learning (Majumdar and Mooij, 2012; Srivastava and Oh, 2010). The absence of an adequate policy response in matters of institutional neglect in preparing qualified teachers added to the problem of impoverished school learning environments. A multi-tiered education system spawned by privatisation exacerbated inequality and legitimised the presence of unequal learning environments for children from different sections of society.

The increasing presence of unequal learning environments across different types of schools did not inform debates on quality education. Unable to address the complexity of diverse classrooms and teacher unpreparedness, the axis of the quality debate was effectively shifted to the operations of educational practice—especially those that were easy to measure and scale up, namely learning outcomes. Parameters to define quality were narrowed to close the contradictory gap between quality as a fundamental right and the neo-liberal thrust on teacher performativity and learning outcomes. As narrow concepts of quality were imposed, purposes of education started disengaging from long-term goals of commitment towards equity and social justice; also undercutting the core role of critical teacher knowledge in enabling socially just education.

Outcome-based notions of quality created a rationale for teachers to pay greater attention to learning assessments rather than on creating meaningful learning experiences for children. With policy emphasis on student learning outcomes, state schools too were rearranged into unequal learning environments. For instance, several state schools have English medium sections as well; and the entire school population in Delhi government schools has been streamed into ability-based[39] sections. The focus on learning outcomes is now part of the RTE via an amendment in 2019, justifying the NITI Ayog's position that the right to education should really be the 'right to learning' (GoI, 2017). This resulted in divorcing notions of 'learning' and 'teacher professional judgement' from 'pedagogic processes' (Batra, 2017); and dissociating notions of 'quality teacher' from 'quality teaching' (Sayed and Ahmed, 2015).

It can be argued that the trajectory of privatization hastened the process of institutionalizing outcome-based conceptions of quality—a discourse largely borrowed from a 'global education policy community' (Ball, 2017) and disseminated by non-state advocacy groups. This enabled the normalisation of a policy discourse that hinged on ensuring tangible but minimalist educational outcomes for the masses—learning achievement scores and teacher accountability. The policy focus on teacher performativity in ensuring learning outcomes reduced the teacher to a mere instrument of neoliberal reform.

Privatization of Teacher Education and Policy Propositions

Privatization of teacher education appears to have followed a slightly different trajectory—one, led by policy 'inaction' rather than 'action' as in the case of school education, wherein neoliberal reforms had institutionalised unequal learning environments. As teacher education was allowed to expand in the private space, the university-based teacher educator community shrunk and was pushed to the margins of school education policy. This was easy to effect as the NCTE Act itself undermines the role of universities in sustaining the quality of teacher preparation[40]. Years of gross neglect, regulatory inaction, followed by withdrawal from the responsibility of preparing teachers, despite judicial intervention, led to a de facto public policy that emasculates the potential role of teachers and teacher education in achieving equitable, quality education. While intervention of the Supreme Court of India led to an increase in the duration of pre-service teacher education, precious little was done to translate the curriculum[41] vision into reality.

The reform process had succeeded in constructing utilitarian notions of teachers and their education, corresponding to anti-intellectualism (Hofstadter cited in Sindelar and Rosenberg, 2000). Teachers were reduced to implement minimalist agendas and 'practical knowledge' was positioned as key to ensure student learning. The system continues to certify teachers largely ill-equipped to handle diverse classrooms due to poor theoretical grounding. The de-emphasis of theoretical knowledge in favour of 'practical knowledge' could be seen as an outcome of policy borrowing from contexts where neoliberal reforms had delinked theoretical markers from processes of teacher preparation.

In the absence of robust epistemological underpinnings of teacher knowledge, and the orchestrated absence of teachers in problematising conceptions of school knowledge, it was easy to essentialise teacher knowledge within the frame of neoliberal agendas. Reforms that undermined teacher's epistemic identity derived strength from the distanced policy position on teachers taken by the NCF, 2005 and RTE, 2009. The turn of policy discourse towards the centrality of teachers in fulfilling the neoliberal agenda continued unabated; making teachers complicit in taking forward narrow school-based reforms (Biesta, 2015); leaving very little latitude for them to exercise agency in real classrooms (Long, et al., 2017).

While the bulk of pre-service teacher education continues to happen in private 'teaching shops', well into 7 years post-JVC, most of in-service training of teachers in many states is also being outsourced to private edupreneurs. The Central Square Foundation (CSF) for instance, is actively involved in creating ecosystems to enable and accelerate the digitization of existing non-digital teacher development solutions, working closely with central and state governments. In 2017, MHRD and NCTE with support from IT led organizations launched a teacher education platform called Digital Infrastructure for Knowledge Sharing (DIKSHA). This platform is being projected as a unique initiative which leverages existing highly scalable and flexible digital infrastructures, with teachers at the centre. Several non-state actors, through PPP arrangements continue to validate standardised pedagogical approaches and influence policy debates on reforming teacher education.

The most recent example is the Boston Consulting Group (BCG) that works with the Government of India across several states. Their intervention in Haryana started with the observation that the state suffers an "anaemic teacher-student ratio where 2,500 primary schools are with either one or two teachers... large number of teacher vacancies and lack of focus on the quality of academics". Without addressing any of the systemic challenges it highlights, BCG claims[42] that of the 1.8 million students assessed on every subject, every month, grade I through VIII students show an improvement of 3-6 per cent in learning outcomes. BCG and Piramal Foundation are also 'knowledge partners' with NITI Aayog in implementing its SATH-Education programme[43] in Jharkhand, Madhya Pradesh and Odisha. Critical interventions in this programme include 'school mergers, remediation programme, training, monitoring teacher recruitment/rationalization, institutional reorganization at district and state level via the proper utilization of MIS'. None of these measures address either the structural problems of teacher shortage or that of poor teacher capacity.

Clearly then, the preparation and in-service support of school teachers in India is almost entirely in the hands of private players. Privatisation of teacher education has paved the way for instituting several measures within the neoliberal frame of 'governing' education. Foremost among these is reconfiguring the role of the state in line with the logic of the market—as a form of governance and 'regulator' rather than 'service provider'. This is evident in the draft education policy of 2019. In its bid to enhance the quality of teacher education, the draft policy proposes the need to tighten control via a set of 'professional standards' for teachers and periodic performance appraisal of teachers. It views 'teacher absenteeism and indiscipline' as a major problem of governance that needs to be managed via instituting measures of accountability, assisted by technology such as recording attendance with mobile phones and biometric devices; the periodic assessment of teachers linked to their future promotions and release of increments.

Though the policy draft takes cognisance of some of the critical gaps in the preparedness of school teachers, including 'the lack of professionalism in teacher training institutes, mismatch between training and practice', it chooses to maintain a studied silence on the critical recommendations made around several of these gaps by the Justice Verma Commission. It merely acknowledges the need to move teacher education "into multi-disciplinary colleges and universities", as proposed by JVC. But recommends the provisioning of "special short-term local teacher education programmes... at BITEs, DIETs and school complexes" as a measure to prepare teachers for children of 'underrepresented groups', strategies that will exacerbate inequities in access to quality teachers and teaching.

Conclusion

Unprepared teachers and a stagnant teacher education sector characterized the landscape of school education when elementary education was declared a fundamental right. A large number of teacher vacancies and the sizeable presence of professionally unqualified teachers posed critical challenges to the task of universalizing quality education. Private teacher education institutions increased manifold in the years preceding the RTE. JVC noted that over 90 per cent teachers were being prepared in private TEIs, while 80 per cent elementary school children were enrolled in state schools. There has been a 13 per cent rise in private TEIs since then.

This paper argues that privatization of teacher education is largely an outcome of policy inaction characterized by gross neglect of the need for institutional capacity development and the professional development of serving school teachers. Teacher education suffered from years of intellectual isolation as a result of rigid and unimaginative regulatory norms and the proliferation of sub-standard private TEIs that were severed from universities. The gross state neglect of institutional capacity building left major gaps in the preparation of teacher educators as well. In the absence of a robust teacher educator community, a culture of uncritical engagement with questions of educational theory and practice normalised.

As a result of state inability to address the complexity of diverse classrooms and teacher unpreparedness, policy debates on quality education shifted to measures that were easy to scale up, namely, learning outcomes. This enabled the normalization of a policy discourse that hinged on ensuring tangible but minimalist educational outcomes for the masses—learning achievement scores and teacher accountability. The focus on learning outcomes essentialized teacher knowledge and undermined teachers' epistemic identity.

The Justice Verma Commission made far-reaching recommendations with the aim to revitalise the teacher education sector: prioritise state investment in the education of teachers, bring pre-service and continuing professional development programmes in line with NCFTE; bring radical modifications to the statutory regulatory functions of the NCTE and make substantive revisions in the NCTE Act to commensurate with the recommendations. However, poor state investment and lack of policy attention to the several problems that plague this sector continue despite Supreme Court intervention in 2011-12.

The virtual business takeover of teacher education has happened via contracts between national and state governments with support from the apex regulatory body and private providers. The presence of the 'private' in school education cannot be seen in isolation of the proliferation of private TEIs. Neither can it be seen as impacting adversely the quality of teaching and learning alone. The expansion of the 'private' needs to be recognized as a network of the larger 'global education industry' that has made comfortable entry into spaces of government policy. National as well as state governments are now relying exclusively on this new 'policy community' that focuses on providing digital solutions to enhance learning outcomes.

The capture of the school teacher by private interests has led to a subversion of the commitment to the Constitution-led policy frame of equity and social justice. Even as the Supreme Court stepped in to disrupt the subversion of the Constitutional agenda, an institutionalized nexus between an entrenched private sector in teacher education and a compromised state system shapes teacher education policy.

Drawing on Arendt's (1958) sense of the 'public', the crucial questions that need to be asked in this context are: How do we see the teacher education space that is dominated by the 'private', as a space of debate and contestation required for critical teacher education? Can we see prospective teachers being prepared in private institutes, as social and political subjects or as mere 'consumers'?

Notes

1. Source: *Hindustan Times*, Delhi Cabinet Allows Guest Teachers to Work Till 60 Years, March 7, 2019. URL: https://www.hindustantimes.com/education/delhi-cabinet-allows-guest-teachers-to-work-till-60-years/story-M47J4biurBceX8gZaiZdbM.html Accessed on February 4, 2020.
2. Source: HRD Minister's statement on Prakash Javadekar "Over the Last Chance to Unqualified Teachers In Schools" URL: https://www.youtube.com/watch?v=MByBftdM6po
3. The Rajya Sabha unanimously passed the RTR (Amendment) Bill, 2017, which aims to provide a two-year window to around 11 lakh private and government teachers to get prescribed minimum qualifications for appointment, August 2, 2017. https://www.thehindu.com/news/national/rajya-sabha-passes-rte-amendments/article19403014.ece
4. The mandated pupil-student ratio is 30:1 as per RTE norms.
5. This includes BEd, BSc/BA-BEd for secondary teacher education and DEd or DElEd for elementary teacher education. AISHE data does not make mention of the BElEd degree of elementary education that could account for a few thousands of graduates every year.
6. Out of a total of 23.77 lakhs who appeared for the CTET exam in July 2019, 14.80 per cent qualified. This an improvement over the past years when percentage of those qualifying STET and CTET have been as low as 5-7 percent. https://www.businesstoday.in/latest/trends/cbse-ctet-2019-results-out-in-record-23-days-35-lakh-candidates-qualify-here-is-how-to-check-scores/story/369103.html Accessed on March 2, 2020.

7. Source: http://udiseplus.gov.in/mainhome# Accessed on January 8, 2020.
8. The Education Commission (1964-66) recommended professionalization of teacher education; The National Commission on Teachers (1983-85) recommended five-year integrated courses and internship; and The National Policy on Education (NPE) (1986) recommended the overhaul of teacher education. The NPE Review Committee (1990) and the National Advisory Committee on Learning without Burden (1993) have also drawn attention to the need for qualitative reform of teacher education and suggested various measures.
9. Scholars have argued how the concept and content of teacher training; the model lesson and supervision norms have remained unchanged for over a century. See Krishna Kumar Kumar, *Political Agenda of Education*, Sage Publications, New Delhi, 2005 and Poonam Batra, Voice and Agency of Teachers, *Economic and Political Weekly*, October 2005.
10. Source: https://www.ncte.gov.in/Website/RecognizedInstitutions.aspx Accessed on January 6, 2020.
11. Behar (2015) notes that several private TEIs award degrees without the need to attend classes and that this is a generally accepted practice. Several private TEIs have commercial motives, practically no facilities and no teaching staff, only a licence from NCTE to operate.
12. This analysis is based on NCTE data accessed in 2007 (See Batra, 2017).
13. Source: https://www.ncte.gov.in/Website/statewiseTEI.aspx Accessed on January 6, 2020.
14. Data generated using the Census 2001 and 2006 figures and adjusted with the initial results of the NCERT 7th Educational Survey of 2002, indicates a strong skew in the supply of teachers at both the elementary and secondary stage of education. (See Batra, 2017).
15. Estimates of intake in TEIs for 2019 juxtaposed with the number of secondary and elementary level school populations will strengthen this argument.
16. Computed on the basis of AISHE (2019) data, which mentions a total of 3,759 institutions of elementary teacher training, including DIETs. NCTE (2019) data reveals a much higher percentage intake for DElEd. The bulk of this is nevertheless in private TEIs.
17. The nomenclature of DEd has now changed to DElEd (Diploma in Elementary Education).
18. AISHE (2019) lists DIETs (private and government) as 'standalone' institutions, p. 8.

19. JVC recommends that teacher education curriculum be redesigned in consonance with NCFTE, 2009.
20. Subcommittees set up at the behest of the Implementation Committee.
21. Date of UGC data access. This number has gone up since then. According to 2018 estimates of AISHE, there are a total of 39,931 undergraduate colleges. Although majority colleges are private, over 22 percent are state-run and about 10 per cent are government aided.
22. Poonam Batra Committee Report on Implementation of Justice Verma Commission Recommendations, July 2014. National Council for Teacher Education: New Delhi. F.No. 79-4/2013/NCTE/Acad/PUBLIC NOTICE.
23. Supreme Court of India Record of Proceedings: Petition(s) for Special Leave to Appeal (Civil) No(s). 4247-4248/2009 (From the judgement and order dated 07/01/2009 in WP No.2701/2008 dated 16/01/2009 in WP No. 2701/2008, CAW No. 52/2009 of The High Court of Bombay at Nagpur). RASHTRASANT T.M.S. & S.B.V.M.C.A.VID. & ORS. Petitioner(s) VERSUS GANGADAR NILKANT SHENDE and ORS. Respondent(s).
24. The number of standalone institutions appear to be grossly underestimated in the draft policy.
25. GoI (2013). Report of the Joint Review Mission on Teacher Education, Jharkhand, February 17-23, 2013; GoI (2013). Report of the Joint Review Mission on Teacher Education, Bihar, February 17-23, 2013.
26. See Batra, P. (2019).
27. The NDA government disbanded the Planning Commission and with it the practice of developing Five-year Plans, post-2014. The Planning Commission of India was replaced by NITI Ayog.
28. Protiva Kundu (2018) Budgeting for School Education: What Has Changed and What Has Not? Analysis of Six States in the 14th Finance Commission Recommendation Period. New Delhi: Centre for Budget and Governance Accountability (CBGA) and Child Rights and You (CRY). http://www.cbgaindia.org/study-report/budgeting-school-education-changed-not/ Accessed on February 4, 2020.
29. GoI (2018). Draft Framework for the Implementation of Samagra Shiksha Abhiyan—An Integrated Scheme for School Education, MHRD. http://samagra.mhrd.gov.in/docs/Framework_IISE%20_F.pdf Accessed on February 4, 2020.
30. These vacancies are of faculty of DIETs that are teacher educators who are meant to train teachers. Concept Paper on Strengthening District Institutes of Education and Training, MHRD, 2017, cited in Draft Education Policy, 2019.

31. For instance, Amity Institute of Education affiliated to Guru Gobind Singh University in Delhi lists only 9 faculty members for teaching the BEd programme. The NCTE norms suggest a minimum of 16 faculty for an intake of 50 students for a two-year programme. URL: https://www.amity.edu/aie/Faculty.aspx
32. The 2014 NCTE norms recognize MA Education as equivalent to MEd. The small number of MA Education courses existing across the country do not add substantially to the existing need of teacher educators.
33. During the Twelfth Plan, there were only 108 University-based Departments of Education. The Twelfth Plan suggested opening schools of education in new universities, including the newly developed central universities.
34. Based on this rationale articulated by the JVC, the NCTE revised norms of 2014 regard MA Education as equivalent to MEd.
35. Currently, as per NCTE norms, only students with a diploma or degree in teacher education are eligible for pursuing an MEd programme. Likewise a degree in education is essential to pursue doctoral research in education.
36. A separate Task Force on Restructuring of the NCTE, recommended by the JVC submitted its report on how the NCTE needs to reorganize itself administratively and academically to become a more robust regulatory body with academically driven purposes.
37. Government of India, MHRD F. No. 11-1/2020-IS.14, dated February 21, 2020.
38. Starting during the DPEP, the initial discourse was an advocacy to involve NGOs and civil society initiatives in country-wide reforms. This eventually led to opening the school sector to other initiatives, prominent among this was the CSR sector.
39. Government of National Capital Territory of Delhi issued a circular dated 29/6/2016 about re-grouping of children according to achievement levels. http://edudel.nic.in/upload_2015_16/230_dt_29062016.pdf Accessed on March 2, 2020.
40. The National Council for Teacher Education Act, 1993. Act No. 73 of 1993. https://ncte.gov.in/ITEP/Recognition/NCTEAct1993.pdf Accessed on March 2, 2020.
41. The JVC recommended that teacher education curriculum be revised in line with the NCFTE. However, NCFTE finds no mention in the Draft Education Policy, 2009.
42. Source: https://www.bcg.com/industries/education/transforming-education-on-massive-scale.aspx Accessed on March 2, 2020.

43. SATH is Sustainable Action for Transforming Human Capital. See https://niti.gov.in/sustainable-action-transforming-human-capital-sath Accessed on March 2, 2020.

References

Arendt, H. (1958), *The Human Condition*, Chicago: University of Chicago Press.

Ball, S.J. (2017). Labouring to Relate: Neoliberalism, Embodied Policy and Network Dynamics. *Peabody Journal of Education, 92*(1), 29-41.

Batra, P. (2019). Comparative Education in South Asia: Contribution, Contestation, and Possibilities. *Comparative and International Education: Survey of an Infinite Field (International Perspectives on Education and Society, Vol. 36)*, Emerald Publishing Limited, 183-211.

Batra, P. (2017). Reclaiming the Space for Teachers to Address the UEE Teaching-Learning Quality Deficit. In R. Govinda, and M. Sedwal, *India Education Report: Progress of Basic Education.* New Delhi: Oxford University Press.

Batra, P. (2005). Voice and Agency of Teachers: Missing Link in National Curriculum Framework, *Economic and Political Weekly*, 4347-4356.

Biesta, G. (2015). What is Education For? On Good Education, Teacher Judgement, and Educational Professionalism, *European Journal of Education, 50*(1), 75-87.

Chudgar, A. (2013). Teacher Labour Force and Teacher Education in India: An Analysis of a Recent Policy Change and its Potential Implications. *Teacher Reforms Around the World: Implementations and Outcomes, 19*, 55-76.

EY, and FICCI. (2014). *Private Sector's Contribution to K12 Education in India: Current Impact Challenges and Way Forward.* Retrieved from (http://www.ey.com/Publication/vwLUAssets/roleof-private-sector-on-K-12-education-in-India/$FILE/EY-role-of-private-sector-on-K-12-education-in-India.pdf).

GoI. (Government of India, 2019). Draft National Education Policy, New Delhi: Department of School Education and Literacy, MHRD.

GoI. (2019). All India Survey on Higher Education (AISHE) 2018-19, Department of Higher Education, New Delhi: MHRD.

GoI. (2018). Samagra Shiksha Abhiyan: An Integrated Scheme for School Education Framework for Implementation. New Delhi: Department of School Education and Literacy, MHRD.

GoI. (2017). *Three Year Action Agenda: 2017-18 TO 2019-20.* New Delhi: NITI Aayog.

GoI (2013a). Report of the Joint Review Mission on Teacher Education, Bihar, March 17-23, 2013. New Delhi, MHRD.

GoI (2013b). Report of the Joint Review Mission on Teacher Education, Jharkhand, March 17-23, 2013. New Delhi, MHRD.

GoI. (2012). Vision of Teacher Education in India: Quality and Regulatory Perspective, Report of the High-Powered Commission on Teacher Education Constituted by the Hon'ble Supreme Court of India. New Delhi: MHRD.

GoI. (2011). Report of the Working Group on Teacher Education for the 12th Five Year Plan, Department of School Education and Literacy, October 2011. New Delhi: MHRD. https://niti.gov.in/planningcommission.gov.in/docs/aboutus/committee/wrkgrp12/hrd/wg_teacher1708.pdf Accessed on March 2, 2020.

GoI. (2009). *The Right of Children to Free and Compulsory Education Act.* New Delhi: Gazette of India, Government Press.

GoI. (2009). SSA-RTE Report. Anil Bordia Committee, New Delhi: Ministry of Human Resource Development.

Kundu, Protiva (2019). To Improve Quality of School Education India Must Spend More on its Teachers. January 30, 2019: IndiaSpend.

https://www.indiaspend.com/to-fix-poor-quality-of-school-education-teacher-training-holds-the-key/ Accessed on February 4, 2020.

Kundu, P. (2017). Education Budget Lacks Imagination. *Economic and Political Weekly, 52*(27), 31-33.

Long, C., et al. (2017). Enabling and Constraining Conditions of Professional Teacher Agency: The South African Context. *Contemporary Education Dialogue, 14*(1), 5-21.

Majumdar, M., and Mooij, J. (2012). *Education and Inequality in India: A Classroom View.* London: Routledge.

NCERT (National Council of Education Research and Training, 2009). *Eighth All India School Education Survey*, New Delhi: NCERT.

NCTE (National Council For Teacher Education, 2014). Report on Implementation of Justice Verma Commission Recommendations. Poonam Batra Committee. July, 2014. New Delhi: NCTE.

NCTE (2009). *National Curriculum for Teacher Education (NCFTE): Towards a Humane and Professional Teacher.* New Delhi: NCTE.

NUEPA (National University for Educational Planning and Administration, 2012). DISE Graphic Presentation 2011-12 Teachers, New Delhi: NUEPA.

Sayed, Y., and Ahmed, R. (2015). Education Quality, and Teaching and Learning in the Post-2015 Education Agenda. *International Journal of Educational Development, 40*(1), 330-338.

Sindelar, P.T., and Rosenberg, M.S. (2000). Serving Too Many Masters: The Proliferation of Ill-Conceived and Contradictory Policies and Practices in Teacher Education. *Journal of Teacher Education, 51*(3), 188-193.

Srivastava, P. (2010). Privatization and Education for All: Unravelling the Mobilizing Frames. *Development, 53*(4), 522-528.

Srivastava, P., and Oh, S.A. (2010). Private Foundations, Philanthropy, and Partnership in Education and Development: Mapping the Terrain. *International Journal of Educational Development, 30*(5), 460-471.

Vivek, V. (2018). *Budget 2018: Falling Education Spending Aggravates India's Learning Crisis, Wastes Its Demographic Dividend.* IndiaSpend. Retrieved April 10, 2019, from https://www.indiaspend.com/budget-2018-falling-education-spending-aggravates-indias-learning-crisis-wastes-its-demographic-dividend-96241/

World Bank. (2017). World Bank Open Data. Accessed on January 1, 2018. https://data.worldbank.org/indicator/SE.PRM.PRIV.ZS

Education—Secondary

11

Education in Public and Private Schools in Telangana

L. Reddeppa

Introduction

The Indian Constitution (Right to Education under Articles 21A and 41) mandates that the state provides free and compulsory education to all children in the country between the ages of 6 and 14 years. In view of the national and international commitments, at the beginning, the state envisaged the achievement of universal elementary education for all within the first 10 years (i.e. by 1960). But the Gross Enrolment Rate (GER) in elementary education (Classes 1-8) and the Drop-Out Rate (DOR) in upper primary education in the country in 1960-61 were only 48.7 per cent and 78.3 per cent respectively. The target of GER in elementary education has not been achieved even today—it was 97 per cent in 2016 (GOI, 2018: 28). The achievement of constitutional provisions in terms of targets and objectives requires a holistic approach in planning, allocation of adequate budget for school education, and development of an appropriate institutional mechanism for effective monitoring and implementation.

The Second Education Commission (Kothari Commission, 1966) advocated public education, with a common school system, in order to achieve access for all, with assurance of quality and quantity. The Commission also estimated the financial requirements of the education sector and recommended that budgetary provisions be raised to 6 per cent of GNP by 1985-86, if the sector is to develop adequately (Kundu, 2013: 25). Subsequently, several committees on education took this figure as a benchmark, but the total expenditure by all departments on education as a percentage of GDP at current prices (at factor cost) has been very low in the country. It was less than 2 per cent even up to the end of the 1960s, varied from 2 to 3 per cent during 1971-84, and hovered between 3.0 and 4.0 per cent for the next three decades (1985-2015). This shows that education has not been considered a priority by the state throughout the various plan periods. The Review Committee on National Education Policy, 1986 (Ramamurthy Committee) observed that the common people kept away from education owing to deep-rooted poverty and limitations in access to facilities, and the principal beneficiaries of owing education system in the early plan period were the upper and upper-middle classes only (GOI, 1990: V).

During the wave of Liberalization, Privatization and Globalization (LPG), the state allowed the private sector to expand the country's educational infrastructure after the 1990s. The state assumed that it could regulate and channelize private investments to complement its efforts. However, the state neither effectively monitored the private sector for complementing public sector efforts nor did it achieve the stated objectives of quality and equity in education. The abandonment of public schools and the shift of students towards private (PUA) schools have been clearly visible over time in the country (Kingdon, 2017; Bandhopadhyay, 2016). The private sector's' role in education and health has produced mixed results, more often negative results, in quality and equity, and other dimensions of education, jeopardizing the well-established goals of human development' (Tilak, 2018). 'Growing private education is a sure sign of commercialization of education, while weaker sections of society and rural students continue to patronize government institutions. Students from the urban and socially advanced sections attend private institutions' (Kannabiran et al., 2017). In view of the poor turnout of students, the Governments of Telangana and Andhra Pradesh have planned to close down public schools where student admission is very poor. The attempts of the states to close down public schools in the name of rationalization would negatively affect poor households.

Generally, the private sector operates on a for-profit basis and charges for the service provided by way of higher fees on account of the absence of and/or limitations of the public service delivery mechanism. Sometimes, this may lead to disruption/discontinuation of a student's education due to the lack of accessibility of the public facility and the lack of affordability of the private facility. Strengthening of the public sector is critical for achievement of National Development Goals. This needs to be investigated thoroughly from the point of view of the deficiencies in the public sector. It leads us to several questions: Why have the enrolments in public schools been declining over the years? Is the educational infrastructure in public schools adequate? Are the public schools providing quality education? Are the curriculum and pedagogy appropriate for improvement of learning skills? All these questions need to be answered, reflecting on the comparative picture in the private sector so as to strengthen education in the public sector. This paper is an attempt to analyse the trends of student enrolments, factors influencing enrolment in public and PUA schools, and the achievement of National Development Goals of equity and quality in education in the context of the presence of the private sector in school education.

Methodology of the Study

The study is based on existing literature, secondary and primary data. The collection of primary data for the study was from the major stakeholders in the system, i.e. the students and teachers in public and private secondary/high schools (Classes 6-10) and their parents in the study area of 10 sample districts in the state of Telangana. For the purpose of sampling, one district from each of the former 10 districts was chosen. Due diligence was done to ensure a fair level of geographical representation. From each district, two mandals were selected—one was a district headquarters mandal while the other was located away from the district headquarters. From each mandal, four to five schools were selected, giving due representation to Telugu and English medium high schools, residential schools, Kasturba Gandhi Balika Vidyalayas (KGBVs) and model schools. In all, primary data was collected from 92 schools—30 Zilla Parishad High Schools (ZPHS) of Telugu medium and 34 ZPHS Telugu-cum-English medium high schools, 10 KGBVs, 9 model schools and 9 residential/ashram high schools (AHS) from the 10 districts of the state. The primary data has been collected from February 20 to April 10, 2018. The results form a part of the study undertaken on 'Use of Digital Infrastructure in High School Education in Telangana'. As a part of the study, interactions were also held with the principals/teachers and students/parents of the Private Un-Aided (PUA) schools in all the study districts regarding their preference for PUA schools, and to gauge the strengthening merits offered by the schools.

The study is divided into four sections: (1) Trends in enrolment of students at various schools in public and private-aided and PUA schools, and the pattern of shift of students towards PUA schools; (2) Quality of educational infrastructure in public schools, reflecting the merits and demerits compared to the PUA schools; (3) Medium of instruction and quality of education in terms of teaching staff, pedagogy, student learning skills, reflecting the merits and demerits of the public schools compared to the PUA schools; (4) Conclusions.

Section I

Trends in Enrolment of Students in Public and PUA Schools in Telangana

The educational statistics for Telangana are available from 2006 to 2018. In all, there are about 60.36 lakh students enrolled in about 41,841 schools from primary to high level in all the three broad categories—public, private-aided and PUA, up to the year 2018. The third category of PUA schools includes unrecognized schools and madrasas as well, which is about 1 per cent. The year-wise data indicates that the growth of enrolments in PUA schools has increased constantly while that in public sector schools has declined during the period. The decline is 10.1 per cent in public schools in a 12-year period while the same has increased by 12.3 per cent in PUA schools (Table 1). This trend is not conducive for the cause of inclusive education as it indicates that the state was unable to control the growth of the private sector which is also widely criticized for high amounts of fees collection and low quality maintenance in schools, while the public sector continues to be insignificant in terms of enrolments and quality education.

The positive aspect of public schools is that their number is quite substantial (more than 70 per cent of the total number of schools) and they serve rural and tribal areas and slums in urban areas for primary and upper primary schools even for a small number of children. On the other hand, the proportion of PUA schools in the total is very limited (less than 30 per cent), but the student enrolments in them were more than half of the total enrolments in 2017-18. The average enrolments in public schools has declined from 122 students to 92 students between 2006-07 and 2017-18; the decline in private-aided schools was even higher (from 287 to 157 students) during the same period (Table 2).

Table 1: Management-Wise Proportion of Schools and Enrolments in Telangana

S.No.	Year	Total Number of Schools	Management-Wise Proportion of Schools (%)			Total Enrolment of Students	Management-Wise Proportion of Student Enrolments (%)		
			P	PA	PUA		P	PA	PUA
1	2006-07	40735	72.9	2.2	24.9	6614374	54.8	4.0	41.2
2	2010-11	42911	70.2	2.0	27.8	6255856	49.6	3.2	47.2
3	2014-15	43861	65.6	1.8	32.7	6153410	46.6	2.4	50.9
4	2017-18	40841	71.8	1.7	26.5	6036536	44.7	1.7	53.6

Note: P = Public; PA= Private-Aided; PUA= Private Un-Aided

Source: Secondary Data from the Commissioner of School Education, Government of Telangana

Table 2: Management-Wise Average Students Enrolments, and Student-Teacher Ratio

S.No.	Year	Management-Wise Average Students Enrolled in Schools				Management-Wise Student Teacher Ratio			
		P	PA	PUA	T	P	PA	PUA	T
1	2006-07	122.1	287.4	269.1	162.4	34.4	36.8	28.4	31.7
2	2010-11	103.0	231.6	247.5	145.8	28.0	33.1	28.9	28.6
3	2014-15	99.8	190.7	223.7	140.3	23.4	40.7	27.5	25.6
4	2017-18	92.1	157.2	297.8	147.8	22.9	38.1	31.0	26.8

Note: P = Public; PA= Private-Aided; PUA= Private Un-Aided; and T=Total
Source: Secondary Data from the Commissioner of School Education, Government of Telangana

The situation is quite different in PUA schools where the average enrolment was 269 students in 2006-07, which increased to 298 students in 2017-18, though there was a slight decline for a few years from 2009-2015. The student-teacher ratio is one of the indicators of quality education. The lower the ratio, the better would be the monitoring and attention towards the learning of each individual student. The student-teacher ratio is relatively higher in public-aided (PA) schools, moderate in PUA schools and lowest in public schools.

Within the public sector, there are three categories of schools operating under different managements—central, state and local bodies. Within local bodies, there are Zilla Parishad high (ZPH) schools and Mandal Praja Parishad (MPP) schools. The enrolment in these local bodies' schools is more than half of the total enrolment in public schools. The declining trend in enrolment of students is predominant in ZPH and MPP schools. The optimum size of any high school is 200 students (@ 40 students per class for five standards from Classes 6 to 10) without any sections. The data shows that about 30 per cent of the high schools operate with less than 100 students. However, there are a few public high schools which operate with more than 500 students mostly in urban areas, and they have been operating in both Telugu and English medium. The student strength in public schools has declined in most of the Telugu medium public schools after the establishment of private English medium schools.

There are about 15 lakh children studying in all public high schools, both in the day scholar and the residential school system in the state.

Among them, 26 per cent of the students studying in the residential school system—which includes KGBVs and minority residential schools—are SCs, STs, BCs and Minorities (Table 3). The minority residential schools were established only after the formation of the new Telangana state. Residential hostel facility is also available for 100 to 200 students for each model school, but the first preference is for girls and then for higher secondary students in that order of priority. Apart from these, there are about 1400 stay hostels in the state which provide lodging and boarding facilities for boys and girls of SC, ST, BC, minority and orphan/destitute children studying in public schools. In these stay hostels, there are about 1.4 lakh boarders and these hostels are located in close proximity to the public schools in all major towns. Thus, public schools play a critical role in promotion of secondary education among marginalized social groups, particularly the SCs, STs, BCs and Minorities.

Table 3: Management-wise Students Enrolled at High Schools in Telangana

S.No.	Management	High Schools		Students Enrolments		Average Students Per School
		Number	Per Cent	Number	Per Cent	
1	Central/State/ZPP/ MPP Schools	4697	74.4	970423	65.0	206.6
2	KGBV	475	7.5	87106	5.8	183.4
3	Model Schools	194	3.1	124034	8.3	639.4
4	Residential Schools of SC, ST, BCs*	746	11.8	264563	17.7	354.6
5	Minority Schools*	201	3.2	46286	3.1	230.3
	Total	6313	100.0	1492412	100.0	236.4

*Residential schools includes Telangana Residential Educational Institutions Society (TREIS), Social Welfare, Tribal Welfare, BC and Minority Welfare

Source: Secondary Data from the Commissioner of School Education, Government of Telangana

Residential hostel facility is also available for 100 to 200 students for each model school, but the first preference is for girls and then for higher secondary students in that order of priority. Apart from these, there are about 1,400 stay hostels in the state which provide lodging and boarding facilities for boys and girls of SC, ST, BC, minority and orphan/destitute children studying in public schools. In these stay hostels, there are about

1.4 lakh boarders and these hostels are located in close proximity to the public schools in all major towns. Thus, public schools play a critical role in promotion of secondary education among marginalized social groups, particularly the SCs, STs, BCs and Minorities.

Section II

Quality of Educational Infrastructure in Public and Private Schools

2.1 Building Space, Playground, Compound Wall and Ramp

Adequate building space and required classrooms, playground and regular physical education teacher (PET/PD) are essential for creating interest and ability in games/sports among the students which is an essential extra-curricular activity for the students from the point of view of health, recreation and sports-filled approach to life. It was observed that the buildings were very old and in a dilapidated condition in half of the public high schools. In a majority of the schools, a serious issue is the inadequacy of rooms for facilities such as library, science lab, computers and sports equipment. This is due to both the lack of additional rooms and the lack of repair/renovation of old buildings. During the rains, the leakage of water from the roofs of some of the rooms is a common problem, as revealed by the school headmasters in most of the schools. The buildings in model schools, KGBVs and residential schools are mostly recent constructions. However, here too, there are roof leakages and space problems, particularly in the KGBVs. In the case of PUA schools, the buildings are in good condition, complete with recent whitewash or painting, but there is overcrowding in these schools as compared to public schools.

While, as per records, the majority of the students (about 80 per cent) in public schools and PUA schools (Table 4) do have access to a playground, it was observed that for many of the PUA schools, the space for the playground is very limited, particularly for outdoor games. A few schools have a playground away from the school, but this is not helpful for regular use of the students. However, a few PUA schools operating in the periphery of the towns have a good playground, but even these were not being used properly for the benefit of students as reported during the interactions with the students and parents in the study. The availability of sports and games, however, was not found to be a significant factor that influenced the parents' decision to enrol their child in a particular school.

Table 4: Availability of School Infrastructure in Different Managements of High Schools

S.No.	Management of the School	Playground	Electricity	Compound Wall	Ramp	Total
1	Central & State Govt./Govt. Local Bodies	3722(79.2)	4644(98.9)	2286(48.7)	2943(62.7)	4697(100)
2	KGBV	332(69.9)	475(100)	401(84.4)	198(41.7)	475(100)
3	Model Schools	155(79.9)	191(98.5)	146(75.3)	97(50.3)	194(100)
5	Residential Schools*	668(70.5)	941(99.4)	677(71.5)	258(27.2)	947(27.2)
6	Private-Aided	242(91.7)	252(95.5)	231(87.5)	48(18.2)	264(100)
7	Private Un-aided (PUA)	4852(82.1)	5847(98.9)	5259(89.0)	1487(25.1)	5911(100)
	Total	9972(79.9)	12348(98.9)	9000(72.1)	5031(40.3)	12488(100)

* Residential schools includes Telangana Residential Educational Institutions Society (TREIS), Social Welfare, Tribal Welfare, BC and Minority Welfare

Source: Secondary Data from the Commissioner of School Education, Government of Telangana

The situation of the playground, PET/PD and participation in sports/ games is relatively better in residential, ashram and KGBV schools as compared to the PUA schools. The residential schools especially promote all kinds of sports and adventurous activities through their regular grand annual sports event. Since they are established in spacious campuses, all the residential schools have huge playgrounds with adequate facilities. However, many high schools face problems of a shortage of regular or permanent teacher for sports, particularly in girls' schools, while in some schools they are run on a contract basis or by temporary teachers who may not devote their full time and interest to training the students.

The Ministry of Human Resource Development (MHRD) had issued various instructions to all centrally-funded educational institutions to ensure a barrier-free environment in buildings, which would include provision of ramps, rails, lifts, adaptation of toilets for wheelchair users, braille signages and auditory signals, tactile flooring, etc. as envisaged in the PWD Act, 2016. As per the Unified District Information Systems for Education (UDISE), ramps are available in a majority of the public high schools (62.7 per cent) as these schools are mostly located on the ground floor where it is easy to build a ramp. But the ramp facility is very limited in both PA (18.2 per cent) and PUA (25.1 per cent) schools and also in residential schools (27.2 per cent).

A permanent compound wall is available in 72.1 per cent of the schools, and it is relatively better in PUA schools as compared to public schools. In many public schools, the compound wall is either partly available or broken and in some cases, it is only a wire fencing. This may result in increased scope for the entry of miscreants who could indulge in illegal activities at night and the menace of the entry of pigs and other animals, leading to the dirtying of the area, particularly during school holidays. Though electricity is officially available in 99 per cent of the schools, many rooms have no power supply. This could be due to burnt electrical wiring, or theft of electrical wires, lack of proper wiring and pending repairs. In many classrooms, there was no power supply for fans, lights and for other purposes such as computer operation or overhead projector. However, all these facilities are relatively better in PUA schools due to their regular and timely maintenance.

2.2 Computer Facilities in Public and PUA Schools in Telangana

Use of computers and electronic devices has become a part of life, and access to information and knowledge has become relatively easier. Throughout the world, Information and Communication Technology (ICT) enabled teaching is considered one of the most effective teaching tools to raise the quality of education. In view of this, the government has provided computers (a 10-seater computer lab with two desktop PCs and eight computing systems) for most of the high schools. These computers were found to be defunct and outdated, and thus not operational any longer. The average number of working computers available is very poor in high schools (4.0) and KGBVs (2.11) when compared to residential schools (11.0) and model schools (9.13). However, in a majority of the high schools, the computers were not being used by the students for learning the basics of computers due to the lack of trained teachers or instructors.

Computer teacher-cum-instructors are available in KGBVs and model schools, but the systems are insufficient in both the cases. Hence, all KGBVs and model schools are compelled to ration the computer lab hours for students. This method is hardly sufficient to promote quality of teaching, digital skills and education. A minimum of 10 working computers are required for each high school. Such a facility is available in only 23.3 per cent of the sample Telugu medium high schools, 47.1 per cent of Telugu-cum-English medium high schools, zero in KGBVs, and one-third each in model and residential schools (Table 5).

Table 5: Status of Computers in Use in Schools

Type of Schools	Sample Schools	No. of Computers in Use in Schools				
		Nil	1	2-5	5-10	10+
ZPHS (Telugu)	30(100)	7(23.3)	5(16.7)	5(16.7)	6(20.0)	7(23.3)
ZPHS (T&E)	34(100)	3(8.8)	5(14.7)	6(17.6)	4(11.8)	16(47.1)
KGBV	10(100)	0	0	9(90.0)	1(10.0)	0
Residential/AHS	9(100)	3(33.3)	0	2(22.2)	1(11.1)	3(33.3)
Model	9(100)	0	0	0	6(66.7)	3(33.3)
Total	92(100)	13(14.1)	10(10.9)	22(23.9)	18(19.6)	29(31.5)

Source: Primary Data Collected from the Schools.

The computers have been lying idle for months and years together as observed in many schools. The main issue is that there is a long procedure to assess the problem and offer a rectification due to delay in identification of technicians, cost estimation, approval for budget sanction and release. Even the technicians are not inclined to do repairs or service as they do not get paid in a timely manner as revealed in the interactions with teachers and headmasters. Thus, resolving the technical problems in public schools is a delayed process and, often, the issues do not even get resolved.

On the other hand, in PUA schools, it was observed that the computer centre is furnished with 10 to 20 computers, depending on the student strength in the school and they provide the opportunity to every student to learn the basics of computers. They have a regular time table for computer theory and practice in the school and have allocated a minimum of three periods (45 minutes each) per week to the subject. There are two different systems for maintenance of computers and operation of classes in PUA schools—one system is that the total investment on computers, teacher-cum-instructor salaries and maintenance of computers is borne by the school management and the other one is that the job is outsourced to an agency by paying service charges, with a lump sum amount of Rs. 60,000 to Rs. 1,00,000 per month, depending on the strength of the students and the number of computers installed in the school. In the second option, there is no risk for the school management in terms of investment on computers, their maintenance and payment of salaries to the staff. In both the systems, the fees would be collected from the students (either included in the school fees or collected separately from the parents). In both the systems, there was no disruption of classes on technical grounds as the management resolved the issues very quickly and promptly as noted in the discussion with students, teachers and principals.

2.3 Toilets and Clean Environment in Public and PUA Schools

Provision of clean toilets in the school is essential for hygiene, good health and human dignity. The Right to Education (RTE) Act, 2009 emphasized the provision of separate toilets for boys and girls in all recognized schools. The Sarva Shiksha Abhiyan framework also clearly mandates that all new school buildings be equipped with an adequate number of separate toilets and drinking water facilities for boys and girls. Accordingly, the Government of India recently launched the 'Swachh Vidyalaya' initiative across the country for construction of separate girls' and boys' toilets in all government schools. It was observed from the data that toilets are available for girls in most of the schools (99.6 per cent). However, the availability is only up to two toilets in 75 per cent of the public schools, whereas there are over three such toilets in 62 per cent of the PUA schools. Again, the availability of six and above toilets is only in 5.3 per cent of the public high schools while their proportion is 29.2 per cent in PUA schools, residential schools (75.4 per cent) and KGBVs (79.8 per cent). For details, see Table 6.

The mere availability of toilets in schools is not enough; their cleanliness is equally important for the health and well-being of the students. It was observed during fieldwork that toilet maintenance is very poor in public schools due to the lack of running water and cleaning materials. The public schools mostly depend on municipal/gram panchayat water supply and bore wells. In some schools, they have both the sources, but lack storage facility. Thus, toilet maintenance is very poor due to the inadequacy of water supply or source, the absence of electric motor and power supply problems, and the lack of regular staff/workers to make use of the available water with proper planning.

Table 6: Toilet Facilities in Girls' Schools in 2017-18

S.No.	Management of the School	Toilet for Girls				Total
		Nil	Up to 2	3 to 5	6 +	
1	Central and State Govt./ Govt. Local Bodies	32 (0.7)	3440 (75.0)	873 (19.0)	243 (5.3)	4588 (100)
2	KGBV	0	38 (8.0)	58 (12.2)	379 (79.8)	475 (100)
3	Model Schools	0	24 (12.4)	69 (35.6)	101 (52.1)	194 (100
4	Residential Schools of SC, ST, and BCs, and Minority	2 (0.4)	64 (12.5)	60 (11.7)	386 (75.4)	512 (100)
6	Private-Aided	4 (1.6)	108 (42.4)	76 (29.8)	67 (26.2)	255 (100)
7	Private Un-aided	14 (0.2)	2233 (37.9)	1932 (32.8)	1717 (29.2)	5896 (100)
8	Unrecognized Private Schools and Madrasas	0	2 (100)	0	0	2 (100)
	Total	52 (0.4)	5909 (49.6)	3068 (25.7)	2893 (24.2)	11922 (100)

Source: Secondary Data from the Commissioner of School Education, Government of Telangana

The main issue in public schools is that the budget for cleaning and scavenging work is Rs. 2,500 per school and they get an additional Rs. 2,500 if the strength is above 300 students in the high school. The budget provision for model schools, i.e. Rs. 4,000 per month (Rs. 2,500 from the state and Rs. 1,500 from the residential hostel) is insufficient as the average strength is more than 600 students. The budget provision is very meagre given that the task involves sweeping the school premises/rooms as well as getting the scavenging work done. One full-time worker is required for each school to monitor the students to keep the school premises clean and hygienic. The budget provision is made available only for part-time work which is insufficient for a majority of the high schools. If any worker is engaged full-time for the available budget provision (Rs. 2,500), it is in violation of the Minimum Wages Act. However, the situation is different in residential schools, where the cleaning work is outsourced (with or without materials) for sweeping and scavenging/toilet cleaning. The budget provision for both the tasks would be Rs. 25,000 to Rs. 35,000, depending on the school strength, the school area and the number of toilets in the school. Though the budget provision is less than the quantum of cleaning work, the cleaners still opt to work in residential schools as they get a regular salary and also food—which is free of cost—in the hostel.

The situation is quite different in PUA schools where they engage an adequate number of sweepers, maids, scavengers, watchmen, drivers and supporting staff. All the staff are paid a regular salary and the cleaning is monitored by the management. Usually, the floor in PUA schools is made of either ceramic tiles or marble and the management gets the premises, rooms and toilets cleaned on a daily basis or multiple times within a day if needed. Such staff provision or budget and water use efficiency is not available in public schools.

Section III

Medium of Teaching and Pedagogy and Quality of Education in Public and PUA Schools

3.1: Medium of Instruction in Schools

It is widely accepted that the English medium of instruction is the main motivating factor to opt for a school. It was clearly observed from the interaction with parents that they prefer that their ward studies in English medium at the primary level with a view to join an English medium school at the high school level in the sixth standard, either in a residential or a model school. It was clearly noticed in the study that 30 to 60 per cent of the students in model and residential schools have studied in English medium, mostly in PUA schools at the primary level. It shows that there is a tendency among parents to send their children to English medium schools. It is even proved in a study that there is no statistical relationship to region and wealth as the children in the slums of Hyderabad city and of Mumbai prefer to join private English medium schools (Baird, 2009: 2).

It was observed in the study that an amount of Rs. 15,000 to Rs.20,000 per annum (inclusive of fees, transport and books) is required to educate a child in an average English medium PUA school. Many parents of average income and middle income group have lamented that the fees paid to the PUA schools is beyond their capacity. However, irrespective of whether they can afford the fees, parents are lured by the promise of English medium and quality of education. But the choice of the parents is not always a sound one when it comes to educating their children (Roy Chowdhury, 2019). There are many cases of parents who are in a debt trap due to the hefty fees payable to PUA schools.

Keeping in view the demand for English medium, public high schools (ZPP/MPP) in the state introduced English medium education in mostly urban areas such as district headquarters and big towns in the second half of the 2000s. But the proportion of primary level students studying in PUA English medium schools turning to public English medium high schools is very limited (10 to 15 per cent). The low turnout of students is attributed to the poor command over language of the teachers in public English medium schools, their lack of fluency of thought while trying to express themselves in English, and the apprehension that the students would lose even the limited knowledge in English that they had gained earlier in a PUA school. In spite of these limitations, they had nevertheless opted for a public school due to the unaffordability of PUA schools. Still, the teachers display a keenness to teach in English as a means to stay on in the school and to avoid transfers, according to the headmasters in some schools.

3.2 Teaching with the Support of Digital Aids

Teaching with the support of digital aids in all high schools of the state has been in operation since the academic year 2016-17. An external disk loaded with digital lessons was also supplied to all high schools for offline use. The quality of content of the digital lessons relayed on Mana TV is very good and useful, according to most of the students and the majority of the teachers in the schools. More specifically, the teachers pointed out that the digital lessons for mathematics pertaining to the chapters on 3D shapes, constructions—triangles and quadruples, Geo-Zebra (tools software) and graphs; all the science themes with pictures and diagrammatic explanations, lab experiments; pictorial explanations of geography, etc. are rather useful. They said that it is easier to understand the subject, gain knowledge, remember, think innovatively and perform in examinations because of digital teaching. Though the digital mode of teaching is limited in PUA schools, the teachers are involved in educating the children and imparting basic knowledge in the subjects even if they do not adopt the digital mode of teaching.

3.3 Pedagogy and Learning Levels of Students in Public and PUA Schools

Promotion of quality education is very critical for nation building and it directly contributes to 'the goals of addressing poverty reduction and reduced inequalities, health and nutrition, economic growth and labour market opportunities, as well as peace building and the promotion of democratic institutions' (EAC and FHI, 2016). The indicators for assessment of the quality dimensions of education include 'academic progress and social development of students; the quality of teaching; the assessment of learning; the physical resources available; students' health and safety; and, the quality of leadership' (NCERT, 2015.).

According to the Annual Status of Education Report (ASER) 2014, only a fourth of all children in Standard III could read a Standard II text fluently. This number rises to just under half in Standard V. Even in Standard VIII, around 25 per cent of the children could not read a Standard II level text (Bhamra et al., 2015). Based on the latest ASER report (2017), several studies even pointed out that the learning levels of children in reading and arithmetic skills had deteriorated in government schools in recent years at the national level (Kundu, 2017; Bhat, 2017; Joshi, 2019). Based on the ASER data, the children's learning levels in both private and public schools are low, but relatively better in private than public schools (Kingdon, 2017). Kingdon observes that the better academic performance is mainly due to the students typically come from better-off and more educated homes. Thus it is argued that comparing raw learning levels in private and public schools could lead to a potentially false inference that private schools are higher quality.

In Telangana, the high school teachers have conducted tests for all the students from Classes 6-9 at the beginning of each year to assess the performance of students on the 3 Rs Test—Reading and Writing(in English and Telugu), and Arithmetic, starting from the academic year 2016-17. The students who do not qualify in the 3 Rs Test have to be given special classes in the afternoon session for improvement of their basic knowledge in English, Telugu and Mathematics. In spite of all the efforts for the past two to three years, there are students who have failed to qualify in the 3 Rs Test as on February 2019. The proportion of children not qualified to read and write in the first language (mother tongue) is 36.3 per cent out of the students appearing for the test in public schools in Telangana. In the case of the English language, half the students are not able to read and write simple words of the level of their textbooks. The same is the case as far as doing simple arithmetic (51.1 per cent) is concerned. More than half (52.3 per cent) of the students were not qualified in all the three tasks (Table 7).

Table 7: Students Qualified in Reading, Writing and Arithmetic in Year 2018-19

S.No.	Indicator	Boys	Girls	Total
1	Total no. of children attending the test(III to IX) based on the data uploaded by the school as on 05-02-2019 for the year 2018-19 (in Lakh)	3.43	3.76	7.19
2	% of children not qualified in first language (Telugu)	39.3	33.6	36.3
3	% of children not qualified in the English language	52.9	48.4	50.6
3	% of children not qualified in four arithmetic operations	53.3	49.1	51.1
4	% of children not qualified in all the three—reading, writing and doing four arithmetic operations	54.6	50.3	52.3

Source: Data Compiled by Commissioner, School Education, Government of Telangana

The high school teachers have complained that the primary teachers have not paid adequate attention to children to enable their learning of the basics of reading, writing and arithmetic. The intensity of this problem is highly prevalent in ST students and in schools where there is a language divide between the mother tongue and the academic language (Telugu). There are attempts by the state to teach children in their own language by teachers recruited from the same community, but this has had a positive impact on the improvement in the learning of English and Telugu subjects only in a limited number of schools where the teachers are academically strong in the subject and have shown special and community interest for promotion of education (CSD, 2016).

Within the public schools, the student performance is also better in residential and model schools and moderate in KGBVs. The better performance of the students in residential, model schools and KGBVs is mainly due to regular monitoring and periodic personal visits by the top management to assess the conditions of infrastructure, delivery of food provisions, student learning and teachers' activity in promotion of education. Even the teachers are made accountable for the poor results in exams and there is a penalty in the form of increment cut in the salary of the principal and teachers if the annual result in Standard 10 is found to be less than 60 per cent. Such a system is not available in public high schools, particularly in ZPP/MPP schools.

All teachers in public high schools are technically qualified with a BEd, which is the basic degree for eligibility for teaching in public schools. However, the PUA school teachers have been mostly recruited with a graduation degree qualification and subsequently only a few are technically qualified with a BEd degree. The gross salary of a high school teacher starts from Rs 30,000 per month after completing the initial probationary period and it could cross Rs. 1 lakh per month; the average salary of a high school teacher in Telangana is about Rs. 50,000 per month. The teachers in PUA high schools mostly get a salary in the range of Rs. 5,000 to Rs 30,000 per month as noted in the interactions with teachers and headmasters. A salary above Rs. 20,000 is paid mostly for supposedly 'important' subjects such as science and mathematics depending on the need or if the teacher is good in teaching and has worked for a longer period in the school. Though the teachers' salaries in PUA schools are lower than those in public high schools, the PUA management ensures quality in teaching as well as regular attendance and timings of the school.

In the interaction with headmasters during the informal discussions, it emerged that about 20 per cent of the teachers are not regular in attending school and are not committed to monitoring the studies of their students, their main concern being conducting their own private work and being constantly engaged in private phone conversations. It was argued in a study that there is a major statistical link between teacher absence in government schools and PUA enrolment (Baird, 2009).The situation is totally different in PUA schools where the teachers are diligent in timings and attendance, and in the monitoring of reading, writing and homework verification of the students. Also, the parents show keen interest in monitoring their children and question the teacher about the poor performance of their child and demand the facilities and quality education that they are paying for.

Section IV

Conclusions

After the LPG policies of the 1990s, the PUA sector expanded by filling the gap in demand created due to the limitations of public school education—partly due to factors such as English as a medium of instruction, administrative efficiency in school attendance and cleanliness of school premises including toilets, and partly due to teachers' commitment to teaching and marketing strategies in terms of conducting periodic meetings with parents to discuss the progress of their wards. On the other hand, public schools' performance has been characterized by poor school infrastructure due to the lack of adequate maintenance budget and cleaning staff, inadequacy of rooms for science lab, computers and digital classes. Though the teachers are professionally qualified in public high schools, they could not bring in quality education, partly due to a lack of accountability and institutional mechanism for good governance, and partly due to the poor socio-economic background of the parents. However, the residential school system has been strengthened significantly in recent years with introduction of English as a mode of teaching, better infrastructure and maintenance, use of technology and digital equipment in pedagogy, efficient monitoring mechanism to bring quality in education even among the poor and marginalized social groups. But, the majority of the economically poor children have no option but to be admitted in day scholar schools due to limited availability seats in the residential school system.

The children from poor economic backgrounds and the children of marginalized groups, particularly the SCs and STs in rural areas, cannot access and afford the PUA school education. However, many parents who are attracted by the marketing strategies of PUA school managements get caught in a debt trap and have to return to public schools as a midcourse correction. Such transformation is clearly visible in isolated pockets, depending on the schools teachers' sincerity and commitment to teaching and student monitoring to improve the learning levels of the students. In many public schools, there are sincere and committed efforts from the headmaster, teachers and parents, with close cooperation of the community to improve school education. In certain cases, the parents even restricted the entry of PUA school buses in their villages. There is a realization among the public for the need to protect public schools, but the attempts are sporadic and need leadership from the community and teachers to rebuild faith in public school education. Thus, all the day scholar schools being operated by the local self-government need to be equipped with adequate infrastructure, and incorporate choice to English as a mode of teaching. Otherwise, it would be difficult to achieve the objectives of inclusive and equitable quality education as enshrined in the Constitution and the SDGs.

References

Baird, Ross (2009). 'Private Schools for the Poor Development, Provision, and Choice in India.' A Report for Gray Matters Capital, May; http://dise.in/downloads/use%20of%20dise%20data/ross%20baird.pdf (accessed on 9 October 2019).

Bandhopadhyay, M. (2016). 'Present Status of Infrastructure Facilities in Schools in India: From National and State Level Perspective,' National University of Educational Planning and Administration, NewDelhi; http://www.dise.in/Downloads/Paper_on_Physcial_Facilities_(Draft_prepared_for_CABE)_-_Report.pdf- (accessed on 9 October 2019).

Bhamra, Anshul, Harshini Shanker and Zeenat Niazi (eds.) (2015). 'Ensure Inclusive and Equitable Quality Education and Promote Life-Long Learning Opportunities for All,' *Achieving the Sustainable Development Goals in India: A Study of Financial Requirements and Gaps*, Technology and Action for Rural Advancement, New Delhi.

Bhat, Dhruva (2017). 'Harbinger of a New Era? Evaluating the Effect of India's Right to Education Act on Learning Outcomes'. M-RCBG Associate Working Paper Series | No. 76.

Council for Social Development (CSD) (2016). 'Third Party Evaluation of Welfare Hostels and Residential Schools in Telangana State'. A Study Sponsored by the Department of Planning, Government of Telangana, Hyderabad.

Educate A Child (EAC) and FHI 360 (2016) 'Education and SDGs,' *Occasional Paper #2*, October; https://educationaboveall.org/uploads/library/file/2a8e15847d.pdf- (accessed July 5, 2019).

Government of India (GOI) (1990). 'Towards an Enlightened and Humane Society,' Committee for Review of New Policy on Education 1986 (Ramamurthy Report). New Delhi: Ministry of Human Resource Development.

Government of India (GOI) (2018). 'Educational Statistics at a Glance,' Ministry of Human Resource Development, Department of School Education and Literacy, New Delhi.

Joshi, Natasha (2019). 'No-Detention: Why Did a Popular Policy Get Scrapped?' *India Development Review*, 10 April; https://idronline.org/no-detention-why-did-a-popular-policy-get-scrapped/ (accessed on July 5, 2019).

Kannabiran, Kalpana, J. Jeyaranjan and Padmini Swaminathan (2017). *Telangana Social Development Report-2017*, Council for Social Development, Hyderabad.

Kingdon, Geeta Gandhi, (2017). 'The Private Schooling Phenomenon in India: A Review.' IZA Discussion Paper No. 10612; https://ssrn.com/abstract=2940602(accessed on July 5, 2019).

Kundu, Protiva (2013). 'Budget for Education: A Factsheet,' *Yojana*, September, p. 25.

Kundu, Protiva (2017). 'Education Budget Lacks Imagination,' *Economic and Political Weekly*, July 8, Vol. II, No. 27.

NCERT (National Council of Educational Research and Training) (2015). "Quality Assessment Tools", August; https://studylib.net/doc/11668275/quality-assessment-tools--qat-(accessed on October 9, 2019).

Roy Chowdhury, Shreya (2019). 'Are Private Schools Really Better Than Government Schools?' January 18; (https://idronline.org/are-private-schools-really-better-than-government-schools/- Accessed on July 5, 2019).

Tilak, JBG (2018). 'What Matters for Outcomes in Elementary Education in India?' In: *Education and Development in India*, Palgrave Macmillan, Singapore.

World Bank (2018). *World Development Report: Learning to Realise Education's Promise.* Washington, DC.

Education—Higher

12

Private Higher Education in India*

Jandhyala B.G. Tilak

Introduction

The theme of private higher education is not only an unavoidable issue while debating on the current state of higher education in India, but also—and more importantly—is an extremely important theme when conferring on knowledge, equity and democratic rights, as private education impinges on all three aspects significantly. Drawing on my earlier research, a few important aspects relating to private higher education in India are highlighted here.

If one looks at public policies in higher education in India during the past quarter century, one necessarily feels that there has been confusion all over, in some sense. At the beginning of the 1990s, widespread laissez-faireism could be noted with respect to higher education policies. In fact, there was no policy on private higher education, because we were perhaps confused about whether it would be good or bad to opt for private education on a large scale. This laissezfaireism, that is, non-intervention by the state and the absence of any policy, which had been the characteristic feature of the few decades beginning with the 1990s (Tilak, 2004), helped in the rapid growth of private higher education and the emergence of large-scale markets in higher education. This period was followed by clear pro-private approaches.

Simultaneous 'Yes' and 'No'

However, confusion remained as to whether privatization was good or bad. From even a quick look at several documents of the government—plan

* Earlier published in *Economic and Political Weekly*, Vol. 49, Issue No. 40, October 4, 2014.

documents, policy documents and other statements—one can note several confusing statements being simultaneously made. The government was found saying "yes" and "no" very often, almost simultaneously. For example, the government stated that privatization was good, but not commercialization; therefore, privatization would be allowed but not commercialization, although they are two sides of the same coin and are based on the same principle—of making and maximizing profits. By definition, the private sector is for profit, and it is not possible, either theoretically or empirically, to make a distinction between the two.

Further observations then found that privatization was not necessarily desirable, even from a market perspective; however, private participation had to be encouraged, without making any clear distinction between private participation and privatization in education. At another point the government stated that private participation was also not desirable, but that we should encourage something along the lines of a public-private partnership. The confusing statements continued: privatization of higher education was good and needed to be encouraged; commercialization was not bad, but profit-making in higher education should not be allowed. Therefore, it was emphatically stated that profit-making private educational institutes were not to be permitted, that educational activities motivated by profit have no place at all in society.

Some courts announced in the same context that making "surplus" in private higher educational institutions is acceptable, but not profits, without clarifying the difference between the two. They did not note that, following Karl Marx, surplus means profits. It was later felt that profit might, after all, be tolerated, but not exorbitant profits. There was, however, no definition provided for "exorbitant profits". All of this shows just how confusing the state approach has been, with no proper understanding of the nature or the consequences of private higher education (Tilak, 2005a, 2005b). In more recent years, the government seems to have gained greater clarity, and has come out with strong pro-private policies in higher education.

During the past three decades, some policies have been formulated and adopted out of compulsion (possibly the reason for the prevailing confusion), while others have been adopted out of conviction. There is a big difference between the two approaches. In the first phase of policy with regard to privatization during the early 1990s, I believed that governments in various states and at the centre in India were not in favour of private education; however, neoliberal forces have actually compelled them to adopt policies of privatization. After all, it is well known that privatization is an important component of the neoliberal policies associated with the World Bank and the International Monetary Fund (IMF), which we adopted in the early 1990s. Compelled by these policies of the World Bank and the IMF on the one hand, and by the emergence of strong markets and the corporate sector in the country on the other, the state in India had no choice but to reluctantly accept privatization as an important policy instrument in the development of higher education.

That phase is now over; so perhaps one can state that policies at present are being formulated out of a conviction that privatization is good in itself. The state is convinced that privatization is necessarily desirable: it would promote access, quality and equity in higher education, and is an effective solution to most of the ills plaguing our higher education system. It is because of this change in perception that the state began adopting clear policies that strongly favoured private education. As a result, today we note very dominant tendencies towards a high degree of privatization of the higher education system in the country. A big non-violent shift has taken place—from policies of welfare-statism in higher education to a market-based approach to higher education.

There are several myths around private education. I (Tilak, 1991, 2009) have exploded some of them; and Dhanwanti Nayak (2014) did the same by focusing on the arguments concerning access, inclusion and quality in favour of private education. Yet, private education has become a dominant phenomenon in higher education in India. Occasionally, the government states that privatization of higher education is irreversible, and all that it requires is a good regulatory framework (Basu, 2012; Goswami, 2012; Varghese, 2012); although it is also simultaneously argued that private higher education in India is over-regulated and needs to be relaxed (Sudarshan and Subramanian, 2012). Such statements imply that discussing the pros and cons of private education is an exercise in futility.

Others view the public-private divide as pointless and argue that it does not matter whether it is public or private, as long as education is delivered to the people. They overlook the point that the division of public and private sectors is an abiding concern of the political economy (Kamerman and Kahn, 1989). I believe these statements attempt to preempt any debate on private education; discussions on the regulatory framework brings about an abrupt end to any discussion on the consequences of private education.

In this context, I wish to describe a few major features of the growth of private education in India.

Unprecedented Growth

First, if we look at the trends in numbers with respect to higher education, we note that there has been a tremendous growth in private higher education from the beginning of the 1990s. This growth has been unprecedented; in fact, before 1990 there were very few private institutions. By private institutions, I do not mean the private-aided colleges and schools that have been in existence since before independence, but private, self-financing colleges, which started emerging during the last quarter century. The growth of self-financing colleges has been phenomenal: the number of private colleges in several states grew from a few in the late 1980s to several hundreds, particularly in the case of engineering colleges, and management and medical institutions. In all, private, self-financing colleges grew to such a level that in relative size, the public sector became infinitesimally small.

In some specific areas like engineering and management, more than 90 per cent of institutions are in the private sector. The private sector has also spread to arts and science colleges, and even to intermediate colleges and polytechnics. They are spread all over the country, from Andhra Pradesh, Karnataka, Tamil Nadu, Maharashtra and Kerala, to Odisha, Rajasthan, Punjab, Haryana, and Assam. In 2011-12, there were 191 degree-awarding (almost equivalent to a university) private, self-financing institutions in the country; 19,930 colleges (compared to 13,000 government and government-aided private colleges); and 9,500 diploma-level institutions (compared to 3,240 government institutions) (Planning Commission, 2013). The corresponding numbers of private unaided institutions at the end of the 1980s were close to zero. Of late, attempts have been made to transfer public institutions to the private sector under different modes of public-private partnership. This is already happening at a noticeable rate at the school, and even at the college level, in different states. For example, the Uttar Pradesh government was planning to transfer five government medical colleges to the private sector (http://zeenews.india. com/news/uttar-pradesh/up-to-transferfi ve-medical-colleges-to-private-sector_ 652189.html).

If such instances continue to occur on a large scale, we will soon end up with no public institutions of higher education at all. The unbelievably rapid growth of the private sector has resulted in crowding out or displacing the public sector in no time. Now, there is practically no space for the government to set up an institution—there is a dearth of physical space and no felt need for yet another institution, given the many private institutions in existence. Instead, the argument is to ensure that the existing (private) institutions work within a good regulatory and enabling framework.

Quite a few people argue that the simultaneous existence of public and private-sector institutions of higher education in our mixed economy poses no problem; rather, this would create competition, and competition in turn would produce efficiency. How correct is such an argument? There are a few aspects: first, there is no simultaneous existence of public and private institutions; what is found is a rapidly growing private sector and a fast declining public sector.

Different Forms of Privatization

Second, there cannot be competition between public and private institutions, which differ in most respects, starting from the objectives and goals of setting up the institutions to the method of functioning and delivery of services. It is well known that the objectives and motives of the public and the private sectors are completely different with respect to higher education.

There are a few other forms of privatization of higher education taking place in India. An important form of the privatization of our public system of higher education is financial in nature—public institutions are being subject to financial privatization, through the mobilization of finances from students and other non-governmental sources. Student fees of different types have been on the rise in most public institutions, with several items that used to be provided free of cost—or for a nominal fee—being charged heavily. Items in this category include application fees, examination fees, and fees for mark statements. These days, we have clear policy statements saying that we should increase the rates of cost recovery in higher education through student fees, much beyond 20 per cent of the university expenditure. It may be recalled that a committee of the University Grants Commission (UGC) chaired by Justice Punnayya, and a committee (UGC, 1993) constituted by the All-India Council for Technical Education (AICTE, 1994) in the early 1990s recommended that about 20 per cent of the university expenditure be generated from student and other sources. Going by the spirit of these two committees, the 20 per cent was to be considered an upper limit; however, the argument put forth by the National Knowledge Commission (2009) is to consider 20 per cent the minimum level.

The other instrument of financial privatization being adopted vigorously is the educational loan programme. Education loans have replaced scholarships in policy discourses on higher education. It is argued that even needy students need not be given scholarships; instead, they can be asked to opt for education loans. When the students' loan programme was restructured in the 1990s, the government argued that it should be developed in such a manner that a revolving fund could be formed out of loan repayments, which would be sufficient to finance higher education as a whole. This way, the government would not have to finance higher education from the public exchequer in the future.

A closely related form of financial privatization of public institutions is the large-scale introduction of self-financing courses in public institutions. The resources so generated are being used for other university activities, for which state funding has been inadequate or even missing. Self-financing courses have been introduced in almost all departments in universities and colleges, both central and state-level ones, including some of the best universities. These courses are run more efficiently than others, with teachers taking a greater interest; administrators, too, are far more interested in these courses because they generate revenues that can be used without formal permission from the state, or bodies like the UGC. Thus, public institutions are being fiancially privatized on a large scale, because of which the "public"-ness of public higher education has seemed to disappear. The UGC once constituted an Expert Committee for the Review of Unaided and Self-Financed Courses in Central/Deemed Universities (2002-04); however, it barely acted on the committee's report, which is not even available.

It is important to note that the higher education system in India is more privatized compared to other capitalist or market economies, for instance, the US, the UK, Canada, and Australia. Currently, we have more than 100 private deemed universities, a large number of private-aided colleges, and an even larger number of self-financing colleges, in addition to very many unrecognized private institutions, which do not necessarily offer recognized degree programmes and are basically coaching centres of different kinds. Even if one ignores the unrecognized institutions, and takes into account only the private, unaided, self-financing colleges, the private sector in India is one of the largest in the world.

In the US, as described by Altbach et al. (2009), one-fifth to one-fourth of the total number of students in higher education, and about 30 per cent of the global enrolment in higher education, are in private institutions; the remaining students go to public universities. On average, only 15 per cent of the enrolments in the tertiary education system in Organization for Economic Cooperation and Development countries, and a meagre 8 per cent in the countries of the EU21 group, are enrolled in independent private institutions, with a vast majority everywhere studying in the public sector. In contrast, in India, 66 per cent of students in general education and 75-80 per cent in technical education are enrolled in private, self-financing institutions (Planning Commission, 2013).

Based on the number of students and the institutions of higher education, private higher education is measured in different degrees—predominantly private, moderately private, and insignificantly private higher education systems (Gieger, 1987; Tilak, 1991). Our system can be described as predominantly private. If one includes the vast number of private, unrecognized institutions, one can conclude that the size of the private higher education sector has reached alarming levels in India, with our higher education system being privatized at a level that is much higher than in many other parts of the world (including the most privatized systems). Contrary to the general impression that Western countries have large private higher education systems, they actually strongly advocate privatization of higher education not for themselves, but for the developing countries. They have strong public higher education systems, while we are being encouraged to resort to private institutions.

Profits Replace Philanthropy

The third important feature of the higher education system refers to a very significant decline in philanthropy in India (Tilak, 2006). At the time of independence, philanthropic and voluntary contributions constituted a reasonably substantial proportion of the total education funding; but they have dried up over the years, and have come down to negligible levels in recent years. People with some money in the 1950s and the 1960s used to donate to public institutions or set up philanthropy-based private schools and colleges; today, though, those with even a small fraction of that money prefer to set up a private, self-financing college or university. This is because investment in colleges and universities is found to be the most rewarding, yielding quick and very high pay-offs, with minimal risk. Philanthropy and charity have been replaced with greed for profit and narrow, selfish financial interests. So the growth of profit-oriented commercial institutions has been an important feature of the 1990s and beyond, compared to the philanthropy-based private institutions of the past.

Fourth, there is a strong misconception that the quality of private higher education is very high, compared to public education. Such an impression is based mostly on impressive buildings. If one goes beyond the outer walls, one will conclude that the superiority of private institutions is a sham. Most private higher education institutions have no libraries, laboratories, or research programmes; they concentrate on saleable courses of study, prefer short-term to long-term programmes, and have underqualified and underpaid teachers. The teaching staff required to impart meaningful teaching is also inadequate.

Private educational enterprises are guided essentially by private demand, and prefer to concentrate on courses of study for which students are ready to pay heavily; in other words, those that are revenue-generating and surplus-generating, rather than those traditionally considered necessary for a good higher education system. As a result, some disciplines of study are sacrificed while some others are pampered. Subjects that currently flourish in India include engineering, management, and commerce, and disciplines like the social sciences, humanities, or basic sciences are ignored. This produces a distorted, unbalanced and unsustainable higher education system.

This is in addition to the values they inculcate, which revolve around selfishness and a lack of concern for social issues. It is precisely for this reason that globally, the need has been felt to strengthen liberal higher education (Nussbaum, 1997). Further, considering global rankings as indicative of the quality and standard of higher education, one would notice that very few private institutions feature in the global rankings. With the exception of a few in the US, no other private university in the world features in the top 300.

The Question of Equity

On the other hand, well-funded public institutions are indeed found to be performing well. The best examples we have are the central universities, the Indian Institutes of Technology, Indian Institute of Science, central medical institutions, and other specialized research institutions, including national science laboratories. Some of these institutions attract highly talented students and faculty, sometimes even from abroad, and feature in the global rankings of universities. So funding is a critical issue. The problem is that under neoliberal policies, public funding for higher education has come under attack (Tilak, 1996). Grants to the institutions have been slashed, and public institutions are not allowed to perform even basic functions satisfactorily. It is then misleadingly argued that as they do not perform well, there is no justification for continuing to provide public funds.

Even the champions of the private higher education system admit—while arguing strongly that private education would improve access and quality—that equity would be at stake. Equity in higher education is one aspect that will be seriously compromised. Private education widens inequalities not only in education, but also in economic and social spheres. After all, no private institution in India will be prepared to promote equity on a satisfactory level, grant access to the weaker sections, or provide liberal scholarships. The government's interventions in this regard, such as fee reimbursement schemes (which are similar to vouchers), access to loans, interest subsidy on loans, or even quotas in admissions to private institutions for weaker sections, would not help much; in fact, these misaligned initiatives would contribute more to strengthening the private sector than to reducing inequalities in higher education and in society.

Another important aspect is the argument relating to the regulation of private education. Those who recognize the problems with private education argue that the government should develop an enabling and regulatory framework, so that private educational institutions meet public standards and adhere to public goals. Given all our experience, we can say that the government's ability to regulate these politically and economically powerful institutions is extremely limited. The market forces are so strong that the government cannot do much. In fact, as many argue, market forces dictate government action. That is particularly true in developing societies, where markets are indeed strong but very imperfect. So while the government can formulate effective regulations, ensuring their proper implementation and a fair performance from private institutions, is a tall task. Some of the bills introduced in Parliament, such as those aimed at checking corrupt practices in higher education, and the setting up of tribunals and proper accreditation authorities, have remained unapproved for a long time (although many of these bills have their own weaknesses) (Tilak, 2010).

Return on Equity

The one important feature of private higher education institutions in India (as well as of those in other developing countries) is: they rely exclusively on students' fees. Student fees account for 100 per cent of the total costs of higher education in these institutions. They invest little to nothing of their own resources; and whatever they do invest is recovered soon, in a few years' time, from the students. Also, private institutions make no attempt to generate any additional sources of money, in contrast to some major private universities in Western countries like the US, where, according to available statistics, students' fees account for only a small fraction of the total costs of higher education.

In the US, for example, in private universities that do not get support from the federal government or the state, the fees contributed by students constitute less than 40 per cent, with the remaining 60 per cent met by non-state and non-student sources. In Japan, the fees in private universities form 59 per cent of their total expenditure; the remaining 41 per cent comes from non-state and state sources.

In India, though, higher education is either financed by the state and students (in the case of public higher education institutions), or solely by the students (in the case of private universities). There are no other (either non-student or non-state) sources of funds available for higher education. Private management, or the rest of society, do not contribute any financial resources to education, except for the initial investment that is returned with profits.

In the same context, it may be underlined that the fees in private universities in India are about 50 to 80 times higher than those in public institutions. In contrast, private universities in countries with a sizeable private sector, like Japan, Korea, or the US, charge a fee that is eight to 10 times higher than fees in public institutions. Therefore, there is a very significant difference between private education in India and private education in other parts of the world. In the US, Harvard University and Stanford University were founded essentially on philanthropic and educational considerations, and on considerations of providing good quality education. They are not motivated by profit; in fact, it is widely known that about one-third of the Harvard University budget goes towards scholarships, compared to almost zero in many private universities in India. More than 60 per cent of Harvard college students annually receive need-based scholarships towards the cost of tuition, room and board. As a result, approximately 20 per cent of the families pay nothing, and many college students graduate debt-free (http:// news. harvard.edu/ gazette/story/2013/03/ financial-aid-budget-increases-by-10m/). Private universities in the US use their autonomy to attract the best students and the best faculty from around the world, while private institutions in India use their autonomy mostly to breach state rules and regulations.

The private sector in Western countries grew historically, with a consideration to providing education to the people and complement public efforts. In India, however, the private sector is growing essentially because the public sector is not doing its job adequately; there is a public-sector disinvestment programme going on, and state withdrawal from higher education is becoming increasingly strong. The private sector takes advantage of this situation; unlike in the West, private institutions in India are not set up to complement public institutions, but to capitalize on the public sector's inadequacy.

Public-Private Partnership

One of the government's arguments in support of private education is: the government does not have enough money to meet the increasing demand for higher education. Yet, it seems to be aware of the problems that arise in the wake of private education—massive corrupt and unfair practices, unregulated expansion, and the production of low quality graduates. Hence, the government has proposed a few bills and regulations to check unfair practices in private institutions, which include the setting up of a proper accreditation authority, mandatory accreditation, new rules and regulations for private deemed universities, etc. It is not clear, though, just how effective these would be.

At the same time, realizing the need to generate more resources, the government proposes to rely on innovative methods of public-private partnership. However, as the experience of other countries has shown, public-private partnership models rarely succeed, particularly if their concerns are essentially financial. But in India, the government aims to mobilize 50 per cent of the required funds in states from the private sector, through various methods. Public-private partnerships are associated with several inherent contradictions. The motives of the two partners are bound to clash; there will be an increase in commercial and other revenue-generating activities on university campuses; an increased miserliness with regard to expensive academic programmes; markets will invade every sphere of the universities, and every activity would be seen as a cost-centre and as a source for generating profits.

This culture, which is alien to public higher education systems, will become a part of the systems modelled on public-private partnerships.

The casualty will be the academic culture of institutions engrossed in the production and dissemination of knowledge, and imbued with principles of equity and excellence. If the considerations are related to improving the relevance of the curriculum, imparting practical knowledge, and enhancing the employability of graduates, certain models of public-private partnership, like the university-industry cells already in existence in most universities, might work to some extent (although their experience has also been unsatisfactory). The models that the government has been proposing essentially involve a massive transfer of public resources to the private sector. This might lead to public pauperization and the enrichment of the private sector.

The bottom line is: active participation of the private sector in higher education institutions is likely to create different kinds of problems. Even countries like the US found that this might involve several compromises on core academic values, including distortions in the research agenda—and even the results of research—of universities, and might end in universities becoming endlessly preoccupied with money and competition (Bok, 2003, 2013).

Contradictions and Clashes of Interest

The Eleventh and Twelfth Five-Year Plans strongly argue in favour of privatization of higher education. So far, higher education institutions are, de jure, "not for profit". The Twelfth Five-Year Plan clearly proposes to remove the "not for profit" tag in the rules and regulations, stating that unless the private sector is allowed to grow, it will not become profitable. At the same time, the Ministry of Human Resource Development (2013), in the Rashtriya Ucchatar Shiksha Abhiyan, argues against allowing profits in higher education. This is an actual conflict of interest among two government bodies—the Planning Commission and the Ministry of Human Resource Development.

Such clashes are not uncommon; we have seen a similar clash of interest between different ministries with regard to the commitment of higher education to the General Agreement on Trade in Services, with the Department of Commerce and Trade making such a commitment, and the Ministry of Human Resource Development asking for its withdrawal. Further, to stimulate the growth of private higher education, it is proposed that public funds be provided to private institutions, and liberal fiscal incentives be offered to the corporate sector to entice them to invest in higher education. Given that public institutions are severely starved of resources, there is no rationale for providing public resources to private higher education institutions. The objective is merely to encourage the private sector to grow. Unfortunately, privatization of higher education has become a goal in itself, and is no longer a mere strategy for the development of higher education.

Lastly, a careful examination of the longitudinal data on enrolments and economic development in higher education in various countries, provided by the UNESCO Institute of Statistics (UIS), shows that no country—with the exception of Japan and Korea, which predominantly depend on the private sector in higher education—has progressed educationally in any significant way, or economically prospered; neither has it socially advanced nor politically flourished. Educationally, the total gross enrolment ratios in higher education show that higher education systems with a high proportion of private enrolments are still underdeveloped compared to other countries. In the familiar classification of the World Bank, many such countries, including countries in South America, which have a strong history of private higher education, are developing—low or middle income—countries; they have not yet economically progressed to the level of advanced countries.

On the political front, too, many such countries are beset with severe problems, with political instability being an important feature of these countries. Only those countries with strong public higher education systems have prospered in all dimensions, economically, politically, socially, and culturally. The best examples are North America and Western Europe; in Scandinavian countries, private higher education is virtually non-existent. Countries like Sweden and the UK still do not have any sizeable number of private universities.

Conclusion

We need to expand our higher education system, as countries with small higher education systems—public and private—cannot progress at all. The best examples are countries where enrolment ratios are between 10 per cent and 15 per cent; most of these countries are economically underdeveloped, with high levels of poverty and inequality. A look at advanced countries shows that the minimum desirable enrolment ratio appears to be around 30-40 per cent. India has set a target of reaching 30 per cent gross enrolment ratio in higher education by 2020. At the same time, however, it should be noted that the increase is to be achieved mainly through the expansion of the public higher education system, and not through the private education system.

The most disturbing development pertains to the fact that the state is gradually abdicating its responsibility towards higher education, including planning for higher education, policy-making for higher education, and of course, the funding and delivery of higher education in favour of the private sector, under the guise of private participation, public-private participation and private initiatives.

For a long time, the government advocated private education by stating that it did not have sufficient resources to meet the increasing demand for higher education. Today, though, it is arguing strongly that private education is good in itself; it will improve efficiency, quality and access.

In the present context of neoliberal policies, privatization is not seen as an instrument but as a goal in itself; it is not a strategy to develop higher education, but is itself seen as reflecting the development of higher education. This is another major shift in the approach of the state to the private sector, and I consider this the most unfortunate shift taking place in policy discourses on higher education in India.

The massive private higher education system in India has been detrimental to the character of education as a public good. Private education essentially views education as a private good, yielding benefits to the individual student, and is not concerned with social values or national concerns. The greater the extent of private higher education in the country, the faster the disappearance of the public nature of education. The social responsibility of higher education needs to be valued, protected and nurtured, and this is not possible in a system dominated by a profit-motivated private higher education system.

An education bazaar, no matter how big, is no substitute for a public higher education system. A strong, vibrant, high-quality public higher education system, accessible to all, is the solution to many of the ills plaguing the country. Along with this, a philanthropy-based private education ought to be encouraged. There is no place for a profit-seeking private higher education in a democratic society that aims to transform itself into a knowledge society and an advanced economy, with faster inclusive growth as its main maxim.

References

All-India Council for Technical Education (1994). "Report of the High-Power Committee for Mobilisation of Additional Resources for Technical Education", Swaminathan Committee Report (New Delhi: All-India Council for Technical Education).

Altbach, Philip G., Liz Reisberg and Laura E. Rumbley (2009). "Trends in Global Higher Education: Tracking an Academic Revolution", Report Prepared for the UNESCO 2009 World Conference on Higher Education, Paris, available at http://www.uis.unesco.org/Library/Documents/trendsglobal-higher-education-2009-world-conference-en.pdf

Basu, Sambit (2012). "Private Sector in Education: An Overview" in IDFC Foundation (ed.), *India Infrastructure Report 2012: Private Sector in Education* (New Delhi: Routlege for IDFC Foundation), xxiii-xxxviii.

Bok, Derek (2003). *Universities in the Marketplace: The Commercialization of Higher Education* (Princeton: Princeton University Press).

____ (2013). *Higher Education in America* (Princeton: Princeton University Press).

Bortolotti, Bernardo and Enrico Perotti (2007). "From Government to Regulatory Governance: Privatization and the Residual Role of the State", *World Bank Research Observer*, 22(1): 53-66.

Gieger, Robert L. (1987). *Private Sectors in Higher Education* (Ann Arbor: University of Michigan Press).

Goswami, Amlanjyoti (2012). "Higher Education Law and Privately-Funded University Education in India" in IDFC Foundation (ed.), *India Infrastructure Report 2012: Private Sector in Education* (New Delhi: Routlege for IDFC Foundation), 185-98.

Kamerman, S. and A. Kahn (eds.) (1989). *Privatization and the Welfare State* (Princeton, NJ: Princeton University Press).

Ministry of Human Resource Development (2013). *Rashtriya Uchchatar Shiksha Abhiyan* (New Delhi: Government of India), available at http://mhrd.gov.in/rusa

National Knowledge Commission (2009). *Report to the Nation 2006-2009* (New Delhi: Government of India).

Nayak, Dhanwanti (2014). "Understanding the Logic of Neo-liberalism in Education", *Economic and Political Weekly*, 49(13): 10-13.

Nussbaum, Martha C. (1997). *Cultivating Humanity* (Boston: Harvard University Press).

OECD (2013). *Education at a Glance 2013: OECD Indicators* (Paris: Organisation for Economic Cooperation and Development).

Planning Commission (2013). *Twelfth Five Year Plan: 2012-2015: Faster, More Inclusive and Sustainable Growth* (New Delhi: Planning Commission).

Sudarshan, Anand and Sandhya Subramanian (2012). "Private Sector's Role in Indian Higher Education" in IDFC Foundation (ed.), *India Infrastructure*

Report 2012: Private Sector in Education (New Delhi: Routlege for IDFC Foundation), 178-84.

Tilak, J.B.G. (1991). "Privatization of Higher Education", *Prospects: Quarterly Review of Education* (UNESCO), 21(2): 227-39.

____ (1996). "Higher Education Under Structural Adjustment", *Journal of Indian School of Political Economy*, 8(2): 266-93.

____ (1999). "Emerging Trends and Evolving Public Policies on Privatisation of Higher Education in India" in P.G. Altbach (ed.), *Private Prometheus: Private Higher Education and Development in the 21st Century* (Westport: Greenwood Publishing), 113-35.

____ (2004). "Absence of Policy and Perspective in Higher Education", *Economic and Political Weekly*, 39(21): 2159-64.

____ (2005a). "Are We Marching Towards Laissezfaireism in Higher Education Development?" *Journal of International Cooperation in Education*, 8(1): 153-65.

____ (2005b). "Higher Education in 'Trishanku': Hanging Between State and Market", *Economic and Political Weekly*, 40(37): 4029-37.

____ (2006). "Private Higher Education: Philanthropy to Profits" in *Higher Education in the World: The Financing of Universities* (Barcelona: Global University Network for Innovation and Palgrave Macmillan), 113-25.

____ (2009). "Current Trends in Private Sector in Higher Education in Asia" in Proceedings of the International Conference on Privatization in Higher Education (Haifa, Israel: Samuel Neaman Institute, Technion University, January, 5-8) 113-43, available at http://www.neaman.org.il/Neaman2011/userdata/SendFile.asp?DBID=1&LNGID=1&GID=2213

____ (2010). "Policy Crisis in Higher Education: Reform or Deform?", *Social Scientist*, 38(9-12): 61-90.

UGC (1993). "UGC Funding of Institutions of Higher Education", Report of Justice K. Punnayya Committee (1992-92) (New Delhi: University Grants Commission).

Varghese, N.V. (2012).: "Private Higher Education: The Global Surge and Indian Concerns" in IDFC Foundation (ed.), *India Infrastructure Report 2012: Private Sector in Education* (New Delhi: Routledge for IDFC Foundation), 145-56.

13

Public-Private Partnerships in Higher Education: An Interrogation of the Role of Private Sector Participation in the Context of India

Saumen Chattopadhyay

The policy makers in India have been advocating public-private partnership (PPP) in education as a major policy initiative as a part of ongoing education reform for both school education and higher education. However, there could be several types of such a partnership between the public and the private sector. This paper seeks to examine a select set of public-private partnership models to illustrate how different types of partnerships have varying implications for funding by the government and the objectives the government seeks to realize in the higher education sector. It is, therefore, an imperative to examine the implications of various types of such partnerships for the three objectives envisaged during the Eleventh Five Year Plan for the higher education sector, expansion, inclusion and excellence to throw light on some aspects of private sector financing in the context of education, and in particular, higher education.

In addition to this, the paper makes an attempt to consider two important dimensions of the implementation of PPP in higher education. The private sector is not a homogeneous entity and hence it matters whether the private party with whom a partnership is being forged has reputation and expertise or not to deliver in a sector like higher education. In other words, the true objective function of the private sector, which may be different from the stated one, is crucial for knowing how well the private sector would be able to address the two objectives of delivering quality education and earn 'reasonable surplus'. The issue is whether the pursuit of these two conflicting objectives is considered at all to be a challenge or not by the private investor depends on the character and the true objective of the private sector.

The second interesting dimension of the problem is the mode of funding. One major way the government would often wish to participate and contribute to the PPP is to extend financial support to keep the cost of education for the students affordable. But the question is how does the government extend financial support? The financial contribution could come in the form of direct funding of the students in terms of vouchers/scholarships, or, the funding support can be transferred directly to the private institute. In fact, this paper seeks to explore how the reputation factor and the mode of funding will jointly determine the quality of education.

We begin with a brief description of the rationale behind the PPP and various types of partnerships the policy makers think of and follow it up with our analysis of the possible implications along the lines we have argued above.

The Emerging Context

Though the number of institutions has grown rapidly in the recent years mainly being driven by the private sector participation, the gap in resources remains between what is required to achieve GER of 30 per cent by 2020 and what is being contributed by the government at present. The Draft of the National Education Policy (DNEP) (2019) has suggested that the present level of expenditure on education which constitutes 10 per cent of total public expenditure should be gradually raised to 20 per cent within a span of ten years. The DNEP has urged that a more philanthropic contribution is desirable and commercial motives are inimical to value-based quality education. Committees set up by the University Grants Commission and the RUSA, advocacy for PPP has been the recurrent theme of the policy discourse. PPP is being considered as the panacea for the misgovernance of the state-run enterprises and departments.[1]

Public-Private Partnership

Ball and Youdell (2008) distinguish between two main types of privatization, (i) privatization of public education which is called exogenous privatization and when public education is opened up to private sector participation generally on a for-profit basis, (ii) privatization in public education institutions or 'endogenous' privatization where public-funded institutions are governed more like a business entity. In this type, therefore, the public institutions, reform in governance is carried out in line with the new public management (NPM) which entails the adoption of managerialism, outcome-based incentives, inculcation of audit culture, a greater orientation towards family demands. As argued by (Verger, et al., 2016), these two modes can be seen as strongly interconnected. In exogenous privatization, as the public-funded institutions feel compelled to compete with the private institutions, the public institutions will undergo NPM type governance reform, private sector culture norms and ethos which have serious implications for what education is and what an educational institute is meant for the students and the teachers. In the process, a market for education emerges. The debate is that education is a complex social and political activity (Robertson and Verger, 2012). Education, strictly speaking, is not a typical commodity and an educational institution is not to be treated as a business entity either in the absence of a well-defined technology which renders the concept of economic efficiency rather untenable (Chattopadhyay, 2012).

Public-private partnership implies an arrangement between the government/statutory entity and the private party for a specified period of time for the provision of assets/services and management and delivery of goods and services with well-defined risk allocation. The private party will receive payments in conformity with the pre-specified performance standards decided by the public enterprise. The definition given by the UK Commission goes beyond a mere arrangement because of its emphasis on shared aspiration to achieve a desired public policy outcome. For rendering service in the social sector, the shared vision and commitment from both parties are essential under an ideal PPP set up.

PPPs represent a range of policy options and diverse rationales which renders this policy option as an ambiguous category (Verger and Moschetti, 2017). According to the World Bank, PPPs in education or ePPPs, the different policy arrangements can be viewed as a part of a continuum which ranges from low to high levels of engagement between the public and the private sector in an evolutionary way. The last category which implies 100 per cent private engagement is the voucher schemes where students are given vouchers to make informed choices and the public and the private compete with each other to provide good quality education in a cost-efficient manner (Patrinos, et al., 2009). However, as Verger and Moschetti (2017) point out that the last stage where the private sector engagement culminates in the implementation of the voucher scheme is rather problematic because this arrangement is not really in sync with the focus on partnership in the very idea of PPP where private sector knowledge is used by the public sector, risk is shared and learning is mutual in a cooperative ambience. Further, strict categorization is difficult as each model may mean different things. It all depends on the particular features of the arrangement, like the mode of government funding support, how much and to whom, the specific contract that defines the partnerships, the objective of the private sector, for-profit or not-for-profit.

The Rationale Behind Public-Private Partnerships

The rationale for PPP can be put forward from different theoretical standpoints. We discuss the various arguments. These arguments contrast the rationale behind public funding as compared to private funding of education.

Public Good, Mixed Good and Private Good

The role of the government in the provision of goods and services is mooted in case of merit goods and public goods. However, the line dividing the two categories of goods, private and public is blurred. Technically speaking, public goods are non-rival in consumption and non-excludable. However, the excludability principle for public goods is not readily applicable to all public goods. While some public goods are called pure public goods as the excludable principle remains readily applicable, for others, excludability is determined by policy decisions and the existing legal provisions and it is, after all, a social construct (Marginson, 2007). Higher education is best described as a mixed good/service as it is both a rival in consumption and excludable. The role of the private sector cannot, therefore, be ruled out even theoretically in case of higher education. Further, what the consumer or beneficiary of higher education stands to gain is the human capital formation which is embedded and individual as certified by the award of certificates but the students by virtue of being educated individuals generate positive externalities for the society. And these externalities along with the objective of equalization of access and nurture of merit, higher education calls for subsidization.

But in a developing country context like India with a low level of gross enrolment ratio (GER)[2], how can we conceive of the role of the private sector is a topical issue and poses a challenge for the policy makers. There have been many instances of private sector initiatives in setting up of universities and institutions of higher learning of repute in the past. However, at the present juncture, the issue of private sector participation is somewhat different and challenging. The government has tried to encourage the private sector to invest in higher education through many changes in policy making. It is not a case of charitable organization and the trusts who would have invested on their own with marginal support or otherwise from the government to participate in higher education.

Private Sector Efficiency

It is argued that the private sector can ensure efficiency in the use of resources which has the potential to guarantee quality education in a competitive and less regulated, enabling framework.

The private sector in pursuit of profit maximization is assumed to be engaged in the exercise of gaining efficiency through reallocation of inputs. But, education is not for business and profit maximization is discouraged. However reasonable surplus is allowed and it is for reinvestment in that sector. If not profit maximization, what is the driving force of the private sector to achieve efficiency in the use of resources for the delivery of education? As shown by Chattopadhyay (2012), the private sector inflates cost by loading illegitimate costs to show profit as zero but these inflated costs constitute the profit of the owners. In case of PPP, it depends on the kind of agreements the public and the private would enter into and therefore on the mode of partnerships. This will determine the recruitment of the teachers and their service conditions, their levels of motivation and the costs related to the financing of infrastructure.

Here, we need to go somewhat deeper to understand the concept of efficiency, particularly in the context of the specific nature of higher education. The human resources and physical resources constitute the inputs to a higher education institute. The quality of teaching, learning and research crucially depend on the quality of human resources, their motivation levels given the quality of human resources and physical infrastructure. Therefore, there are wide variations in the quality of human resources and they command differential prices. So an attempt to cut costs may lead to a compromise with the quality. Since teachers assume centre-stage in an educational institute, the service conditions, the freedom in what a teacher does would matter.

Education is also different from other public services where the students are not really the consumers. Since students are the co-producers of quality education and research, they need to earn their degrees by dint of hard work.

Since the students' fees recover the costs of education, in absence of public support, the private providers tend to appease the students.

In the literature, it is argued in general that the private party in the partnership would therefore deliver and the quality of delivery of public services can be improved. Some of the theoretical arguments are given below.

Transaction Costs Perspective

As per the transactions cost approach, for the public goods with modest contractual and probity hazards, the government can be at the centre with private forming the nodes engaged in the actual delivery of goods and services (Ojha, 2010). In case of education, market incentives are virtually absent and the government has to provide employment security. In case of education, the public sector can ensure probity but in practice, it fails the most. Though the private sector can provide a high level of executive autonomy but minimal security that the public sector organizations offer. In higher education, executive autonomy is most desirable and it is also related to the high level of security. Very often it is argued that high level of security can bring down the level of motivation among the teachers. Getting a tenure position in the higher education sector will become difficult in the government-funded universities. But autonomy has to come with accountability and security can be ensured as long as there is regulation. For education, the process is important and it remains a moot question whether a private organization can prevent subversion of the processes without falling into the trap of ritualizing the regulatory practices.

Knowledge Processing Perspective

A distinction is made between tacit knowledge or local knowledge and explicit knowledge or general knowledge. Public policies are made based on general knowledge. For effective with predominant public good characteristics, the government should be the authority to decide and make policy decisions. In case of education, as mentioned, the quality depends on the content and the delivery which depends on quality of human capital embedded in the individual and motivation level. Ojha (2010) argues that in such cases implementation can be left to the private who can deliver based on specific data.

Agency Cost Perspective

In this framework, there is a principal who delegates the work to the agencies to deliver. It can arise between a principal and a teacher and a public organization *vis a vis* a private organization. There are two sources of uncertainty: one is adverse selection and the second is moral hazard. Both are important in the case of education. The first one arises when the agency misleads the principal about her ability and the second one arises when the effort is lacking. Ojha (ibid.) argues that there is an obsession with the agency costs being over-emphasized while it is true that agency costs do exist which make the bureaucrats respond late to local needs even when they have knowledge. There is an intrinsic mechanism in place to deal with agency costs. Decentralization is a way out but it is not the case for education. In case of PPP, the government can be the principal and the private is the agent and the agency costs can be reduced only through proper monitoring of the delivery and the proper compliance with the regulatory requirements.

Fiscal Constraint

In addition, if the need of the hour is to expand the sector through massive investment, the government is argued to be substantially circumscribed by the fiscal constraint. Here comes the role of the private sector to invest in education to meet the resource gap and contribute to the expansion of the sector. PPP is an attempt to gain from the positives, arguably though, associated with the participation of both the private and the public sector. The rationale advanced for PPP with government support is, therefore, to allow only for moderate increase in cost and realize the benefits of efficiency gains and possible improvement in the quality of education due to the involvement of the private sector. The government retains the scope for moderating and regulating the role of the private sector in various ways. However, the assumption that the private sector can ensure efficiency in its use of resources needs deeper probe. The public participation in PPP highlights the importance of legitimacy, public ownership, minimized risk and pursuit for social goals (Ramesh et al., 2010).

Different Models of PPP

There could be various ways in which the public-private participation in education can be envisaged. As shown in Table 1 below, there are at least four different ways of blending the public and private sector the government can think of in connection with the delivery of education, as (i) the investor in land and building to begin the operation, (ii) as an employer of the teachers, the main input in this service sector, (iii) producer and the deliverer of services and having control over its delivery in terms of curriculum and pedagogy and finally, (iv) the buyer of services, i.e. education. It could be the students or the consumers who pay for education or it could be the government on behalf of the students to ensure affordability. The government can channelize subsidies either directly to the institution engaged in delivering education or directly to the students who can then decide and exercise their choices. In all the models, we envisage the role of the public sector in the form of financial support at the last stage, as a buyer other than as an investor or regulator. The models are as follows.

Table 1: Various Options of Public and Private Delivery

Type	Asset (Building) Owner	Labour (Teacher) Employer	Producer	Purchaser (Who Pays Producer)
Pure Public (no governance reform)	Public	Public	Public	Public
Pure Public (with governance reform)	Public	Public	Public	Public
Pure Private	Private	Private	Private	Private
Basic Models of Public-Private Partnership				
A. Basic infrastructure model	Private	Public	Public	Government to make annualized payment to the private sector. If an investment is made by the trust, it need not be so.
B. Outsourcing model, case of full scholarship	Private	Private	Private	Public
C. Reverse outsourcing model	Public	Private	Private	Private, or, Public to fund scholarship/or reimbursement to the private
D. Equity and hybrid model	Public-Private	Public-Private	Public-Private	Public-Private

Source: Adapted from Grout and Stevens, 2003: "The Assessment: Financing and Managing Public Services", *Oxford Review of Economic Policy*, 19(2), 215-34.

We can begin with the purest cases of public and private provisioning. In the purest form, the government invests and manages the functioning of the institutes. In the second form of public provisioning, the government can think of adopting corporate managerial practices to counter the accusation of being inefficient and delivery of poor quality education. Since, the institutions are owned and run by the government, the functioning becomes akin to the type of private sector functioning.

Basic infrastructure model: In Case A, government runs the school in a private set up as the government is the funder, employer and the producer while the land and the building are owned by the private party. The government-aided colleges in India belong to the category. But a majority of these colleges or the universities were set up by the Trust and the government need not make any payment to the Trust. But, if the private sector is invited to invest, the private party would hope to earn a profit. If the government comes forward to fund or run the institution entirely, the private sector would need to be compensated. Otherwise, there is no sound justification why the private sector would be willing to invest. Though the government allows for third party profit, it may not be adequate to lure the private sector to invest in education.

In case of B, Outsourcing model, the government appears in the chain of operation only at the end through funding for the delivery of services. The government can pay directly to the private institution on a per-student basis or may seek to provide education vouchers to the student aspirants.

In case of C, Reverse Outsourcing model, the government invests in land and building. But the institution is managed and run by the private sector. There can be two ways of looking at this. The government retains control over the recruitment process and delivery through regulation and the private sector runs the institution and recovers the cost from the users. The government can also provide scholarships to select students to negate the adverse impact of cost rise on access.

In case of D, the Equity and Hybrid model, during all the four stages, the public and private sector are jointly involved and they invest and run the institutions together. However, the extent of cooperation may vary with the different stages. Depending on the extent and nature of participation, the implications would therefore vary. The private sector would look forward to earning a profit and have a larger say in the delivery stage. Which means that they would wish to have some control over the fee structure and admission policies.

We would like to discuss three models of PPP in this paper, the basic infrastructure model, the outsourcing model and the reverse outsourcing model for working out the possible implications as referred to above. The analysis of all these options has to recognize the two important dimensions as pointed out above. One, the financial implications for the government, and, two, the realization of the three objectives, expansion, implications for access to education and the quality of education.

Financial Balance as a Framework for Analysis

In order to study the financial implications and realizations of the objectives, we can invoke the financial balances of the institution as suggested by Winston (1999). Though the financial balance is an identity, we can infuse causality in the balance depending on the types of partnerships to trace the possible implications.

If we use the financial balance identity used by Winston (ibid.),

Cost of education (c) + dividend/surplus (v) = prices charged (p) + donative revenues (dr) + grants (g)

$$c + v = p + dr + g$$

Prices charged should be interpreted as the extent of cost recovery including fees levied on the students. Cost of education is interpreted as the cost of education for maintenance including salaries of the teaching and non-teaching staffs. Since the identity has to remain in balance, a change in one of the components will effect changes in the other variables but there is no definite way of causal interpretation. It depends on the context and the policy initiative.

Government Financial Support and Realization of Objectives Under Different Models

We would now like to work out the implications for the extent of government support required under the PPP, impact on access and quality under different types of arrangement (Chattopadhyay, 2012). In order to contrast how the implications under various forms of partnerships would evolve, we begin with a university which is fully government-funded. As we proceed, we relax the assumption and work out the implications under different PPP arrangements.

Case 1: Pure Public Sector Provision

For capital formation in the social sector, the government does not look forward to earning a rate of return in cash but would definitely be keen that social benefits or positive externalities accrue to the society. For pure public provision, $dr = v = 0$, hence,

$$p + g = c, \text{ and, therefore } g = c - p$$

Fees p can be explained as the extent of cost recovery inclusive of tuition fees. We are not discussing the different components of g which can be non-recurrent or developmental and non-recurrent, meant for expansion and maintenance respectively. An increase in cost is to be matched by a commensurate increase in g given p. If the increase in g is not adequate, p has to be raised by raising fees and exploring from other sources of revenue. Depending on the sources of financing like offering of self-financing courses, online courses or projects, there would be some compromises with academic freedom that these universities would otherwise enjoy.

For pure private provision,

$$p + dr = c + v$$

To analyse the different implications, we may begin by considering that the objectives behind private sector investment may vary. Those with interest income from endowments (dr) or every year support from the owners or trusts, p can be less than the cost of education plus surplus. If the endowment is large, and the private institute is keen to be inclusive, p can be kept low which can enable them to attract meritorious and deserving students from the underprivileged economic background and good faculty which are essential prerequisites for good quality education and research. For pure private sector, dr can be thought of as CSR or transfer of surplus or investment out of black incomes to book profit in white. Otherwise, p has to be equal to $(c + v)$. The governance will be purely of corporate type which can affect quality of education as cost minimization is resorted to. The private providers driven by prestige maximization and provision of quality output, would not resort to blatant ways of cost minimization. That is why some private universities with good endowments are doing well. Corporate type management has potential for adverse implications for academic freedom and output.

Case 2. Basic Infrastructure Model

The private sector would take the plunge by undertaking investments in setting up the facilities required for the establishment of the institutions. The investment has to be in the form of land and buildings. In this case, the governmental support has to be as follows,

$$g = c - p + v$$

'Reasonable surplus', v is the extent of minimum compensation the private sector would require for their investment. In this case, the government runs the university and retains control but grants have to be raised. For all practical purposes, the private sector participation is restricted to initial investment and therefore without a reduction in c and a rise in p as the government assumes charge for running the show, g has to go up. However, the development component of g may remain low at the expense of a rise in g which is in the nature of subsidies for maintenance expenditure.

The question is why would the private sector be interested in investing without having any claim over revenue and therefore profit. One time saving of the cost of investment by the government as the private sector takes over would lead to a payment to the private sector forever, ceteris paribus to ensure sustained private sector engagement.

Case 3. Outsourcing Model

The private sector invests and runs the university and the government pays for the services as effectively the only consumer on behalf of the students. Therefore,

$$g = c - p + v$$

How does the government gain if the extent of financial support remains the same as compared to case 2, i.e. the basic infrastructure model is the question? The difference is in terms of who governs. In this case, it is the private sector who governs and therefore, the gain is in terms of efficiency gains. It is to be expected that c will come down as wastage is reduced. But any unfair reduction in c may lead to a compromise with the quality. Corporate type management may improve the output of the institution but it may come at the expense of academic freedom, corporate type ambience can be inimical to the concept of liberal education and a liberal university. The question remains whether v has to remain unchanged. If v remains unchanged as per the negotiation between the public and the private sector, either the private institute takes recourse to unfair cost compression or does not try hard enough for gaining efficiency. If v cannot be maximized, how would the private sector, ensure efficiency in resource usage remains, therefore, a moot point? The improvement in quality will come from corporate style management. The private sector may be interested in promoting the brand and earn credibility. Even, the private provider may look forward to expand their operations by setting up new institutions.

Case 4. Reverse Outsourcing Model

The government invests in land and buildings but hands over charge to the private sector to run the university. But in order to address the concern for equity, the government continues to provide for the services. There are two possibilities regarding the mode of funding by the government. One, the government pays a scholarship fee to the students or provides them with education vouchers to let the students decide on the courses and the institutions they intend to study. This develops a market-like situation and fosters competition. And two, the government pays directly to the institute irrespective of the number of students enrolled.

In the first case, education vouchers promote competition through encouragement for exercising choices. The private sector faces uncertainty and will seek to deliver quality to capture the market share. Though the government safeguards access issue, this is a move clearly towards marketization as both allocational efficiency and technical efficiency are addressed.

Now suppose the government is keen to reduce its fiscal burden by reducing g. This possibility is discussed below.

The private sector is now allowed to face the market and recover costs but the government will continue subsidization of the students albeit at a lower level. There are now two sources of revenue. One is the fees recovered from the students admitted under the management quota and otherwise, p_m, and the other is funded by the government. So, $p_r = g$.

$g + p_m = c + v$;

Since p_m is larger than p, g comes down. Given g, the private institute can now raise p_m to raise v given cost. Or, given $(g + p_m)$ the private sector now can suppress c in order to raise v.

Now the question is whether p_m is regulated or not. If p_m is regulated, the focus would be on unfair reduction of c. If p_m is not regulated, v can be raised by both a reduction in c as well as by raising p_m. This is pure commercialization. Since g is lower, access suffers, and quality suffers on two counts, pursuit for cost minimization and corporate style of governance. Of course, there could be a positive impact on output. If p_m is unregulated, admission is determined more by money power than merit. This is an undesirable scenario. The divide between g and p_m matters for access and quality as well.

Education is a process. There could be various ways of subverting quality as the cost of delivery is reduced. The objective function of the private sector matters.

Table 2: Basic Models of Public-Private Partnership

	Governmental Financial Support	Expansion	Inclusion	Excellence
Basic infrastructure model	No saving possible. Support goes up.	Unlikely	Likely	Uncertain.
Outsourcing model, case of a full scholarship	To remain the same. It can decline with a reduction in wastage	Likely if support does not fall	Likely if govt support remains the same.	Uncertain.
Reverse outsourcing model	May decline.	Possible.	Possible	Uncertain.
Equity and hybrid model	Saving possible	It depends	It depends	Uncertain.

Source: Adapted from Grout and Stevens, 2003: "The Assessment: Financing and Managing Public Services", *Oxford Review of Economic Policy*, 19(2), 215-34.

Unfair Practices

If the private party has the inclination to resort to unfair practices, the private party would make additional profit, albeit illegally. One way would be to artificially escalate cost and siphon out the amount (Chattopadhyay, 2012). The other way would be to recover more from the students or charge more for non-core services. If unethical practices creep in, the very foundation for arguing in favour of increased private participation is shaken.

Let c_b be the escalated cost, c' be the new level of cost lower than the earlier level where $c = c' + c_b$. So a change in the composition of c opens up a new avenue for illegal siphoning out of surplus as c_b adds to the regular v. Similarly, let p_b be the extra amount fleeced in addition to the regular fees, p and p_b adds to the v again where $p' = p + p_b$ where p' is the actual cost borne by the students and p_b is the additional payment made by the students off the account. Grants g will not fall as long as,

$$g = (c' + c_b) - p + v$$

So, there is no change in total cost as a cut in c to c' accommodates a rise in c_b while the additional cost recovery imposed on the students is merely a transfer from the students to the private parties without there being not much of a change.

Actual surplus $v' = (v + c_b + p_b)$

So, the new level of profit would be $(v + c_b + p_b)$, a sum of officially approved return, v, illegally siphoned out of the cost of delivery but shown in the official accounts and illegally extracted from the students such as fines and not shown in the official accounts p_b. Even if v is zero, the private party can make a profit, albeit illegally. While one type of corruption is curbed like absenteeism of the teachers with the roping in of the private party, other forms of corruption may resurface which could contribute to illegal profit making by the private providers. The ability of the private providers to achieve efficiency in resource use has to be accepted with a pinch of salt because it would have all the ingredients to border on indulging in unfair practices leading to a compromise with quality.

Can Private Financing Deliver Quality Education?

To understand the fuller implications of PPP, we need to probe whether the very argument that the private sector would be efficient in the use of resources and would deliver quality is tenable or not. Efficiency in the use of resources in the parlance of economic theory in the context of education is not so well-defined. We need to recognize that investment in education is treated as a not-for-profit activity and hence the optimization of the objective function which is often profit for the firms is not readily applicable. Even if the private sector is allowed to achieve efficiency, we can think of as minimization of cost given revenue or maximization of revenue given cost. The pursuit of both the objectives in education has serious implications.

In economic theory, it is assumed that there exist a well-defined technical relationship between the inputs and the output. Apart from the fact that a university is essentially a multi-product firm, and the delivery is determined by the objective as stated in the constitution of the university, we need to focus on the inputs. In general, the inapplicability of the educational production function is well recognized in the literature (Majumdar, 1983; Chattopadhyay, 2012) in contrast to arguments for its applicability (Lumsden, 1974). The major problem with the input is the wide variation in the quality of inputs along with the costs associated with the varying quality. For example, while assuming all the teachers are capable of teaching and supervision, depending on the designations of the teachers, the costs may vary widely. How to blend the various levels of teachers can be an issue for the private party keen to have some control over the costs. Similarly, it is true for infrastructure facilities. Therefore, in view of the wide variation in the quality of inputs, there would be a tendency to compromise with the quality of education. The problems are of two kinds. One, there is no hard and fast rule of combining the inputs to produce and deliver. Two, the inputs are of varied quality and in general, quality depends on the quality of inputs and better the quality, costlier are the inputs. This is like arguing that a well-defined production function does not exist for a higher education institute (Majumdar, 1983; Chattopadhyay, 2012). This also explains why the unbridled growth in the private sector has not delivered quality education (Chattopadhyay, ibid.).

In addition to this, the source of dilemma the government faces with the decision to rope in the private sector to expand the higher education sector. Why should the private sector other than the trusts and charitable organizations invest in higher education which is not meant for business and maximization of profit is not allowed? As per the recent provisions, since profit making is now being explicitly encouraged overtly or covertly, costs of education are sure to rise. Further, since the quality inputs are costly and they are the prerequisites for the delivery of quality education, any attempt to minimize costs would lead to a compromise with the quality. Efficiency in resource use is misleading in the context of the delivery of education. However, there is wastage in the use of resources in the government sector in many different ways. It is expected and argued that a private institute would minimize wastage of resources. The character of the private sector and its objectives are of crucial importance in this regard.

Corporate Governance and the Idea of a University

When the running of the institute is being managed by the private sector, the governance structure is more likely to be of a new public management type. Even if we accept that there could be gains in the use of resources, what implications would this type of corporate governance have for quality? The concept of quality in higher education is contestable and no unambiguous conceptualization of excellence can be put forth. However, we need to grapple with the concept and chalk out what could be the possible implications of governance on the university as a liberal space for liberal education. After all, education is not just like any other commodity and the rationale advanced for PPP in the physical infrastructure sector are not really applicable for education and for an educational institute. Quality cannot purely be measured by quantification of research output. Mere installation of managerial practices is not a guarantee either for quality output. Production of quality output is very sensitive to the culture, norms and values and the practices that take place.

There are a few questions we would like to raise which have implications for the university as an institute of higher learning. In running the university, though it is theoretically argued that the private and the public would work together for pursuing the same aspiration, the question is can they become equal partners? (Tilak, 2014). Is there any hierarchy in the decision-making and where would the centre of power be located? How would the negotiation take place? Do the private sector representatives have adequate knowledge and sensitivity towards what education is and what does a university stand for? These questions are important because formulation of PPPs has been based on the rationale of reshaping the bureaucracy and its practices within a corporate-techno-managerial framework (Mukhopadhyay, 2010).

What implications private participation would have for research is a critical issue because after all, a university is essentially for knowledge generation and knowledge dissemination. If the university remains deeply engaged in the day-to-day running of the institutions by focusing on recovering of cost to defray the expenses, can it focus on the long-term challenges faced by the society and dedication of resources for fundamental research (Goswami 2010)? The implementation of NPM would severely affect the academic freedom and autonomy and it would go to the extent of affecting the collegiality as a competitive environment is engineered through governance reform (Christensen, 2011; Smeenk, et al., 2009). The value of education imparted by inculcating citizenship is in all likelihood to be compromised (Das and Chattopadhyay, 2014).

Concluding Remarks

This paper sought to examine and anticipate the possible ramifications of different models proposed by the government to implement PPP for education and saving of public resources. The paper sought to highlight the trade-off involved in most of the PPP arrangements. Though the private sector engagement may lead to efficiency gains and improvement in quality, a fall in grants can lead to a compromise with quality and access issue. The concept of efficiency gains and improvement in quality remain contestable concepts because of the specific nature of education and an educational institute. The choice of models should not only be guided by pragmatism and acceptance of offer and regulations by the private sector but also the realization of these objectives. Because if PPP models have undesirable implications for higher education as well as for the university as an institution, we should pause and examine the models closely. PPP is a weasel word for privatization. Tilak (2014) argues that PPP is tantamount to private enrichment leading to public pauperization. The paper argues that the stated positives of PPP like efficiency gains and delivery of quality education are not really tenable in the context of education. In particular, the realization of efficiency gains in the delivery of quality education is not conceptually tenable and even if there is a gain in efficiency, it can come at a high cost. Even the corporate style governance reform can curb academic freedom, lead to shrinkage of the liberal space within the university though it may increase research output. The nature of research and knowledge generation would change, and in the process, it would lead to weakening the linkage between university and society but strengthening possibly the university and the economy relationship albeit from a narrow perspective.

Notes

1. Nearly 88 per cent of the funds required for expansion of higher education during the Eleventh FYP were to be generated through PPP (Tilak, 2012).
2. Around 26 per cent of the relevant age group.

References

Ball, S.J. and Youdell, D. (2008). Hidden Privatisation in Public Education. Brussels, Belgium: Education International. Retrieved from download.ei-ie.org/docs/IRISDocuments/ Research%20Website%20Documents/2009-00034-01-E.pdf

Chattopadhyay, S. (2009). 'The Market in Higher Education: Concern for Equity and Quality', *The Economic and Political Weekly*, July 18, pp. 53-61.

Chattopadhyay, S. (2012). *Education and Economics; Disciplinary Evolution and Policy Discourse*, Oxford University Press, New Delhi.

Christensen, Tom (2011). University Governance Reform: Potential Problems of More Autonomy?, *High Educ*, 62: 503-517.

Das, D.N. and S. Chattopadhyay (2014). API: Straight-jacketing Higher Education Reform, *The Economic and Political Weekly*, December 13.

Goswami, Amlanjyoti (2013). Higher Education Law and Privately Funded University Education in India: Towards a Vision, in *India Infrastructure Report*, IDFC Foundation, Routledge, New Delhi.

Government of India (2004). *Report of the PPP Sub-group on Social Sector*, Planning Commission, November 2004.

Government of India, Consolidated Working Group Report of the Department of Higher Education for Twelfth Five Year Plan on Higher Education, Technical Education and Private Sector Participation Including PPP in Higher Education, Ministry of Human Resource Development.

Government of India (2011). *Expert Committee's Report on Public-Private Partnership in Higher Education*, March 2011, University Grants Commission MHRD.

Lumsden, Keith G. (ed.) (1974). *Efficiency in Universities: The La Paz Papers*, Amsterdam, London: Elsevier Scientific Publishing Company.

Majumdar, Tapas, (1983). *Investments in Education and Social Choice*, Cambridge: Cambridge University Press.

Marginson, Simon (2007). 'Five Somersaults in Enschede: Rethinking Public/Private in Higher Education for the Global Era' in J. Enders and B. Jongbloed (eds.), *Public-Private Dynamics in Higher Education: Expectations, Developments and Outcomes*, New Brunswick, USA: Transcript, Transaction Publishers.

Mukhopadhyay, R. (2010). 'PPPs in Delivery of Elementary Education: Present Imperfect, Future Alternatives', in Ramesh, G. et al., (2010) *Public-Private Partnerships*, Routledge, Taylor and Francis Group, New Delhi.

Neema, Sudhanshu (2012). *A Case Against Public-Private Partnership in Higher Education in India*, CCS Working Paper No. 264, Researching Reality Internship, Centre for Civil Society.

Patrinos, H.A., Barrera, Osorio F. and Guaqueta, J. (2009). The Role and Impact of Public-Private Partnerships in Education, Washington D.C.: World Bank.

Ramesh, G., V. Nagadevara, G. Naik, A.B. Suraj (eds.) (2010). *Public-Private Partnerships*, Routledge, New Delhi.

Robertson, S.L. and A. Verger (2012). Governing Education Through Public Private Partnerships' in Susan L. Robertson, Karen Mundy, Antoni Verger, Francine Menashy (eds.), *Public Private Partnerships in Education: New Actors and Modes of Governance in a Globalizing World*, Edward Elgar.

Smeenk, S. et al. (2009). Managerialism, Organizational Commitment, and Quality of Job Performances Among European University Employees, *Res High Educ*, 50: 589-607.

Tilak, J.B.G. (2012). Higher Education Policy in India in Transition, *The Economic and Political Weekly*, March 36-40, pp. 36-40.

Tilak, J.B.G. (2014). Private Higher Education in India, *Economic and Political Weekly*, October 4, pp. 32-38.

Verger, Antoni, Clara Fontdevila, Arián Zancajo (2016). *The Privatization of Education: A Political Economy of Global Education Reform*, Teachers College Columbia University and Educational International International, Teachers College Press, New York.

Verger, Antoni and Mauro Moschetti (2017). *Public-Private Partnerships as an Education Policy Approach: Multiple Meanings, Risks and Challenges*, Education Research and Foresight Working Paper (19), February, UNESCO.

Winston, Gordon C. (1999). 'Subsidies, Hierarchy and Peers: The Awkward Economics of Higher Education', *The Journal of Economic Perspectives*, Vol. 13, No. 1 (Winter) 13-36.

14

Welfarism to Neoliberalism: State of Higher Education in India

G. Haragopal and G. Sudarshanam

Introduction

Seventy years ago, in the wake of the freedom struggle, the terms of discourse on liberalization of higher education, at least in nations like India, would have been cast in a liberal democratic, if not in a socialist tone. Those were not only the days of hope and promise but were also the days of soaring idealism. The nations which went through the freedom struggle were not only aspiring for freedom but were simultaneously engaged in discovering the scope and content of those freedoms. In the wake of those movements, it was thought and believed that generation and distribution of knowledge ought to be located in the public domain. Right to knowledge was considered not only cardinal to educational philosophy of newly emerging nations but its realization also was a collective responsibility. This thinking underwent such a drastic and dramatic shift over the decades that it has come to be believed by a section of Indians that there are no alternatives to liberalization, privatization and globalization. Education in general and higher education more specifically, became the victim of this almost irreversible process.

I

A critical look at the shifting of the thrust of education policies resonate the shift in the overall policy and development direction of Indian social economic and political changes. This is a society with its hierarchical social structure what Dr. Ambedkar characterized as graded inequalities, which blatantly denied access to education to a large mass of people. Although Christian missionaries opened opportunities during the colonial period, it was a decimal percentage. It was Mahatma Phule and Savitribai Phule particularly the latter who fought for girls' education much against the upper caste upper class opposition. Gandhi, Tagore and Dr. Ambedkar added philosophical and sociological dimensions. Universal access to education took concrete shape during the freedom struggle when the freedom fighters pleaded for it and that turned into one of the aspirations of the struggle.

The Constituent Assembly in spite of Dr. Ambedkar's plea, preferred to include education in part IV of the Constitution not part III. This was one of the faults of the Constitution. In 1948, the Government of India, when the Constitution was being drafted, announced Dr. S. Radhakrishnan commission; one of the fruitful outcomes of this commission was the establishment of the autonomous University Grants Commission implying that the primary role of the government is to provide grants and leave the higher education for self-governance.

It was in 1964 that a full-fledged Commission on Education was appointed, popularly known as the Kothari Commission. This was the time when gradually unrest was brewing in society as the economy was growing very slowly and the fruits of development were not trickling down. The Commission in response to the growing unrest made very important and far-reaching recommendations. This included common school through neighbourhood in school education and expansion of opportunities in higher education for which they recommended investment of 6 per cent GDP. Common school was thought to be an antidote to a hierarchical and unequal society. The Commission held that education is the conscience of a nation and further stated that it should respond to social needs and not wants. This is a significant observation. The Commission also recommended the mother tongue as a medium of instruction which is yet another of its significant features. This democratic character of its recommendations was a response to the rising aspirations of the masses and youth born during the post-independence period. It is a sad reflection that neither the common schools were opened for universal access nor 6 per cent of GDP was committed.

After 1964, it took another two decades for announcement of a new education policy in 1985. The policy was publicly debated for almost two years. It had a clear imprint of the global influence as by then the Indian economy was gradually being integrated with global capital. The policy came into effect in 1992 by which time the integration of capital was getting accentuated. The policy, unlike the Kothari Commission did not commit to the common school. It brought in duality in education and gradual opening to the private sector.

During the twenty-first century the emphasis completely shifted. The market forces became very assertive in nexus with the global and corporate capital. The Manmohan Singh government which was totally committed to structural adjustment appointed the Knowledge Commission with Sam Pitroda who was cut off from the Indian realities, as Chairman and P.M. Bhargava a renowned scientist as Vice-Chairman. The working of the Commission was totally ad hoc and Pitroda started sending dispatches in bits and pieces. Disillusioned, socially committed Bhargava resigned from the Commission. Pitroda was very enthusiastic to push the Indian education system into a techno managerial framework. In one of the seminars organized by the University of Hyderabad, this author confronted him with the question how he defined knowledge? His answer was increasing production and enhancing consumption. This is the complete negation of the spirit of the Kothari Commission. This market fundamentalism started shaping education policies. Pitroda in collaboration with Kapil Sibal started pushing through his agenda. It was during this regime that six bills relating to education were introduced as a part of structural adjustment. There was considerable criticism and opposition to these bills. In spite of the determined effort, Kapil Sibal could not push through the bills.

II

Three Arguments for Liberalization and Privatization of Education and Their Validity

The entire debate in favour of liberalization of higher education is deriving its succour from three main arguments; (one) Governments do not have enough resources; (two) Liberalization leads to not only higher resources for education but also greater initiative and dynamism in the educational system; and (three) the state cannot be the right type of agency and should not be the only agency responsible for higher education. These arguments need closer scrutiny as all of them have serious implications for a discussion on emerging trends and organizational dimensions of higher education particularly in India.

The argument that the resources are limited is least tenable. For, the governments never directly generate the resources on their own. All the governments run their affairs from the social surplus. How the governments mop up this surplus and for what purposes this surplus are used depends solely on the philosophy and ideology of the men and women in power. The governments, which are committed to development and change of the society, take upon themselves the task of mobilizing and also allocating the resources to social sectors in such a way that the vulnerable sections do not suffer from serious deprivation of opportunities for their development. If the commitment of the government is far deeper, then it progressively transfers resources from the privileged and propertied classes to the poor and deprived. In an economy, where there are affluent families which are willing to educate their children through prohibitive capitation fees, the complaint of lack of resources carries no weight. Given the context, one can always ask a question. What prevents the government from tapping this social surplus for a long-term social purpose? This only indicates that under the pretext of resource scarcity, the government is abdicating its egalitarian vision and working for preservation of the existing iniquitous and unjust graded socio-economic order.

The second argument that the market can provide more resources and bring in greater initiative and dynamism is related closely to the first argument. The market, it is true, has more resources and it also knows its needs better. But the point is whether the market is aware of societal needs and would use its resources for the larger benefit of the society or for maximization of private gains. Market forces would, no doubt, gear the entire system to the profit needs of the investor. It is difficult to find industrialists or moneyed people willing to finance fundamental research which will not help them in making any immediate gain. In other words, would anyone come forward to finance research on the theory of relativity or Newton's work on gravitation or Marx's laborious work on laws of capital accumulation or theory of alienation? This question needs very serious debate in the context of imposition of intellectual property rights. The situation calls for pursuits in basic research in higher education. But the R and D is being left to the private sector, which is primarily interested in applied and not fundamental research. This is nothing but leaving the finest human minds to the mercy of the marker forces.

Another argument relates to the suitability of the state system—organizationally or otherwise—for management of higher education. This question is raised both on the operational and also ideological grounds. In fact, it is the dominant market ideology that is giving rise to serious doubts about suitability of the organizational system of the state for higher education. The question under debate, however, is not the organizational model per se. It is questioning the very ideological and philosophical foundations of the state system itself. It is this approach that is hitting the autonomy of publicly funded universities.

Changing Pattern of University Autonomy

Indian Universities, particularly those which are under the jurisdiction of the state and central governments, enjoyed some autonomy in the 1950s and early part of the 60s. The Vice-Chancellors were autonomous individuals fired with vision and imagination. They commanded respect of the society. This situation started changing as the quality of the Indian politics deteriorated. By the late 60s there were attempts to tamper with the university system. In the mid-60s, the Vice-Chancellor of Osmania University had challenged the power and intervention of the state government leading to a legal and administrative battle. He won in this battle with full support of students and faculty. But notwithstanding such battles, later this drift continued to a point that today a small bureaucrat from the Ministry of Education—state or central—can interfere with the university administration. The important decision-making bodies of the university have literally been robbed of autonomy and initiative of the universities and adversely affected their unique personality. The university community, including the Vice-Chancellors, are in no way less responsible for what has happened to the entire university system. This led to surrender of universities to the state resulting in serious erosion of the system. The market forces finally succeeded in using the state for promoting privatization and commercialization of education.

Expansion of Universities and Political Exigencies

The universities expanded and proliferated not to meet the growing demands of the society at large, but to meet the political exigencies. The academic world did not resist this unhealthy trend. The reckless expansion was supported in the name of greater access to higher education or democratization of the structure of opportunities. This expansion was not properly planned, the social needs were not properly assessed. Learning was not geared to the local needs, nor was there an attempt to step up the local skills and upgradation of people's technologies. Thus, the symbiotic relation between the society and universities got lost. Consequently, the social support structure, which is so essential to the very survival and autonomous functioning of the system got eroded. Universities, which do not command social support have to depend on the self-seeking political elite who invariably use the system to their political advantage.

Role of the Academic Community

The academic community within the university never fully realized nor appreciated the value of academic freedom. There are several reasons for such a behavioural mode; the middle class in India is not a product of the natural industrial production process. It is largely a creation of the colonial masters as a part of manipulation of power. The nature of capital being crony, it will not need creative and fearless intellectual class.

The organizational culture of the institutions of higher learning, notwithstanding the autonomy, got terribly bureaucratized. Bureaucratization is a part of the power centred culture. Thus, we see that in the industrially developed societies, the power systems seek to benefit from production culture, but in the developing countries the power systems influence the production system. While between power systems and production systems a line can be drawn, but in the case of 'knowledge industry', particularly in the developing economies, one does not know what type of culture can sustain and stimulate pursuits of higher learning. The desirable principles have not yet been discerned. In the absence of it, the university started imitating and imbibing the culture of power. Power is antithetical to creativity and innovative capacity. The stereotypes have been generated. Having seriously suffered on this count, the system instead of searching for better alternatives became victim of its own power-centric culture. This logic led to the forceful argument that only privatization of higher education is the right answer to the present crisis. This calls for a detailed analysis of suitable democratic organizational modes and their intrinsic potential.

Existing Models in the Private Sector

What are the organizational models in the private sector? Have they done well in those areas where they were allowed free space to operate? This requires to be examined in detail. The myth of efficiency of the private sector has been created by the press and propaganda. In fact, in the 1960s and early 70s nationalization or greater state regulation was considered to be the remedy for all the ailments of the private sector. Now the reverse seems to be the case. The private sector in India is equally inefficient. In the wake of massive liberalization, this point missed the attention of many people. Efficiency is essentially a character of a given socio-political system. That is precisely the reason why the slogans of privatization got bracketed with globalization. The pressure for privatization came more from the global powers than the internal demand. It should be pointed out that the Indian private sector had never forcefully demanded liberalization. It is a product of neoliberalism in collaboration with feudal ideology. This in turn resulted in crony capitalism. This could be seen in the very prestigious institutions.

III

Semi-Capitalist Road: Implications for Education

The capitalist development in India, unlike European capitalism was subjected to the pulls and pressures of colonialism which was a constraint on the development of full-fledged capitalist development. The feudal relations, particularly in the agrarian system was another constraint. Consequently the values of liberalism associated with capitalist development are largely missing. The freedom struggle at best was anti-colonial but not anti-feudal. Independent India compromised with the feudal structure. This has come to be characterized as semi-feudal. The universities or several such institutions have not grown into their full stature. Initially after independence, there was some life in them but gradually that promise did not last long.

Nature of IITs and IIMs and Orientation of Their Products

This overall nature of under developed liberal values got fully reflected in the education system in general and higher education in particular. For instance, the so-called centres of excellence—IITs and IIMs—have some foreign collaboration or the other. Their products are in demand either in the international market or in the corporate world. The ambition of any person joining these institutions is to leave this country. Visas and green cards shape their dreams of life. This lack of nationalistic outlook and commitment and concern for millions of fellow suffering people characterize the nature of so-called merit and excellence in higher education. Privatization and globalization are both a cause and consequence of this process. The trends in the expansion of higher education in the public domain in the last four decades were never in question. It is only in the recent past that this craze for privatization has grown. This needs some analysis.

Ground Realities and the Initiation of Private Universities Bill

During the post-independence period, higher education in India has been growing much faster than school education. Compared to primary enrolment, enrolment in higher education rose more than twice in proportionate terms. The number of universities increased from 30 in 1950-51 to 177 in 1990-91. By the 1990s with the expansion of neoliberal ideology, there were about 220 universities or university level institutions. The number of colleges rose from 750 in 1950-51 to 7121 in 1990-91. Similarly, there is a rapid rise in the student enrolment and the number of teachers. Colleges absorb 80 per cent of students in undergraduate courses in Arts, Sciences, Commerce and Education. There are government colleges and private-aided colleges, all depending on government finances, funds and grants-in-aid. After the 90s, in the last three decades the expansion was phenomenal and the stimulus was the private capital.

De-Emphasis on Higher Education and Lesser Budget Allocations by the State and Central Governments

Since the declaration of the National Education Policy, 1986, there is de-emphasis on higher education. Both the National Policy on Education and the 'Programme of Action' emphasized on restricting proliferation of higher educational institutions and encouraging higher education to raise its own finances. The National Policy proposed establishment of State Councils of Higher Education to check unplanned growth of higher education. These councils which were to protect the interests of universities and plead on behalf of universities and colleges, turned out to be more the agents of the government to pressurize the universities on behalf of the government agenda. Due to gradual withdrawal from higher education the plan allocations have declined. The allocation to higher education within the education budget was 20.89 per cent in the Sixth Plan, 17.6 per cent in the Seventh Plan and it came down to 11.2 per cent in the Eight Plan. This trend commenced under UPA Government and continued under the NDA Government too. The planning process has been abandoned by the NDA Government with the abolition of the Planning Commission. It was replaced by NITI Aayog which is fully committed to neoliberalism. In the name of economic crisis and primacy of liberalization and privatization there is a significant shift in the recent past from state-supported higher education to self-financing system. Universities are incurring huge deficits because of decreasing financial support from the government. They are also forced to raise the loans from other sources. This is the trend almost in all the states of India irrespective of the party in power.

Growing Demand and the Phenomenon of 'Capitation Fee'

As the demand for higher education, particularly technical education, kept growing most of the demand was met by establishment of private colleges through what is known as 'capitation fee'. Students studying in these colleges have to pay 15 to 20 times more fee than what they pay the government institutions. Further to overcome the crisis, the government had announced that all donations to educational institutions by individuals or corporate bodies would be 100 per cent tax free. Secondly, universities and colleges should raise some resources on their own and such money would not be adjusted against the grant-in-aid given to them with increase in the tuition fee or introducing job-oriented courses with a different fee structure or going for correspondence courses. Sometimes it is leading to indiscriminate opening of new courses without being able to maintain quality. Often the fee charged by a university correspondence course is so high that even a middle class student cannot afford. This kind of programme is seen as a profit-making activity rather than providing quality education.

IV

Private Universities Bill: Neoliberal Era

Since the demand for higher education is growing the government came out with yet another Private Universities Bill (Establishment and Regulations Bill, 1995). It provides for establishment and incorporation of self-financing universities and for regulating their functioning. The Bill was introduced in the Rajya Sabha in its last session. It says that such universities can play a subsidiary but supportive role to the endeavours of state-run universities in the tertiary education sector. They could not push it through as, there was still some resistance in the system.

According to the Bill, a private university shall have a Board of Governors, a Board of Management and an Academic Council. The Board of Governors would consist, apart from the Chancellor and the Vice-Chancellor, of three persons nominated by the sponsoring body, one representative each of central and state governments where it is located and one academician nominated by the University Grants Commission (UGC). The Chancellor will be the Chairman of the Board of Governors. The Board of Governors will be the supreme governing body of the university. It will approve the budget, review the decisions of other university authorities and lay down broad policies of the university.

The Bill says that the university established under this Act shall have no power to affiliate a college or institution with it and shall not have more than one campus. It further says that every university shall within three years of an establishment obtain accreditation from a nominated body of persons by the UGC and shall review such accreditations at an interval of every five years thereafter.

Nature of Funding of Private Universities

A critical examination of the Bill shows that the government has decided to gradually leave the responsibility of higher education to private enterprise. The private enterprise does not come forward unless there is profit in it. The Bill says that the sponsoring body should create an Endowment Fund of Rs. 10 crore. Unless there is a possibility of gain why should they invest such a large amount? The logic suggests that such universities will offer courses which will only ensure increasing incomes. This is also evident from the fact that the Bill provides for differential fee rates for Non-Resident Indians and foreign students.

The Bill clearly says that the private university is not entitled for any grant from any government or authority. This forces the private institutions to collect high rates of fees from students. It is clear from the Bill that in the matter of appointing the university authorities like Chancellor and Vice-Chancellor and creation of bodies like Board of Governors, Board of Management and Academic Council, the private sponsoring body has a greater say. This will weaken the social regulation and give arbitrary freedom to decide about the amount of fees to be collected from the students. Thus, in the Bill, excepting the provision for weaker sections, there is no mention of the social responsibilities and growing needs of the nation.

This entire thrust of the New Economic Policy triggered by neo-liberal economic reforms is bringing into the debate the whole question of control in higher education. If the control of organization shifts to agencies located outside India or private agencies, how are we going to have anything called manpower planning? The universities in the private sector would start technology or electronics-based institutes or New School of Economics either to meet the growing demands of NRIs for cheaper manpower or to meet the philosophical and ideological demands of the New Economic World order.

This is also a context which will give rise to commencement of universities by religious organizations or Babas or religious cults. The fundamentalists may also get a hold over a part of the system. They would not only perpetuate feudal ideology but repress the younger minds in the name of discipline. Such institutions would not contribute to the knowledge or pushing the frontiers of knowledge forward. They would only contribute to growing authoritarianism and fascist culture.

The fact that two businessmen were asked to suggest educational reforms and later Sam Pitroda a great champion of neoliberalism to head the knowledge commission bears ample testimony of the government's enthusiasm for privatization. From Kothari to Sam Pitroda further indicates the paradox of higher education in India.

Educational Reforms: Birla Ambani Report and the Knowledge Commission

Ambani-Birla Report (Government of India, 2000): That the government asked Ambani and Birla to recommend and advise on education was total submission to the market and corporate forces. They emphasized more on competition and merit than social needs and equitable society. To create a competitive knowledge-based society seems to be the vision of the report. It visualized the market as a destination for affordable high quality education and need for participation of non-resident Indians in educational programmes on a voluntary basis. A mix of state-supported education with private initiative and user pay strategy in higher education is the guiding principle of the report. The students are to be supported by a loan scheme. Shifting from scholarship, which is a matter of right, to loans which is an obligation curtails the freedom of the students and gets them tied up to the system. It recommended the government to progressively reduce the funding for universities. Universities should take the path of self-sufficiency through higher fees, donations and linkages with the corporate sector. The report recommended establishment of private universities in the areas of science, technology and management and encourage industry-university partnership. It further recommended that the government should allow foreign direct investment in education. The report also recommended banning any form of political activity on the university campus and other educational institutions.

The crux of the report is to recommend larger commercialization and corporatization of education. The recommendations did get reflected in the later developments in the field of education.

National Knowledge Commission (NKC) 2006-09: The NKC constituted by the Prime Minister Manmohan Singh in 2005, focused on different aspects of education. It recommended increasing GER in higher education to 15 per cent and above by 2015. In addition to increasing public spending, it recommended diversifying the courses of financing to encourage private participation, philanthropic contribution and industry linkages.

To bring about the expansion NKC has suggested the creation of 1,500 universities by 2015. It also recommended setting up of an Independent Regulatory Authority for Higher Education (IRAHE) which would accord degree granting power to universities. To ensure quality, NKC has called for frequent revision of curricula by universities, introduction of credit system, enhancing reliance on internal assessment, encouraging research and reforming governance of institutions. It felt the need for restructuring of the system of affiliated undergraduate colleges, need for creating community colleges to provide general education as well as employment-oriented education. It also recommended use of ICT and production of quality content of open educational resources.

The Commission drew the attention to the crisis in higher education and recommended establishment of fifty national universities, enable private bodies or charitable trusts to participate in higher education. In this regard the Commission strongly favoured privatization of higher education and growth of private and foreign universities and reduced role of the state (J.B.G. Tilak, *E.P.W.* Vol. 42, No. 08, 2009).

Educational Reform Bills 2010: Second Term of the UPA Regime

The then Union Minister for Human Resource Development, Kapil Sibal introduced important Bills in parliament to bring major reforms in higher education. This was the second time that the Congress Party got elected. It wrongly presumed that their neoliberal reforms got the popular mandate. The following were the bills.

(a) The Foreign Educational Institutions (Regulation of Entry and Operation) Bill seeks to allow the entry and operation of foreign universities in the country. The major provisions of the Bill are conditions like Rs. 50 crore as corpus fund to be deposited by the aspiring institution to be allowed to operate. Each institute has to be registered with the UGC or any regulatory body. Provision of the Section 25 of the Companies Act will be applicable to foreign universities under which they cannot take profit back but will have to plough back the money for further expansion of the institutions here.

(b) Another bill introduced related to Prohibition of Unfair Practices in Technical and Medical Educational Institutions and consider such practices as criminal or civil offences depending on the nature of crime.

(c) The Educational Tribunal Bill provides for the setting up of tribunals to settle all types of disputes including any type of malpractices or harassment of students. This takes away the jurisdiction of judiciary. Tribunalization is one way of evading constitutional mandate.

(d) The National Accreditation Regulatory Authority for Higher Educational Institutions Bill.

(e) Copyrights Bill which also suffered from several drawbacks.

(f) The Higher Education and Research Bill introduced in 2011 sought to establish the National Commission for Higher Education and Research, replacing the existing UGC, AICTE and NCTE.

(g) Kapil Sibal blamed the opposition parties for stalling the bills.

Private Universities Acts: Different States, Different Norms: The Present NDA Regime

The state governments to give a big push to India's higher education keeping in line with the national trends, have been encouraging setting up of private universities. India is now has 330 private universities; the number is expected to reach 500 by 2023. One of the basic provisions for establishing a private university is the possession of land by the sponsoring body. The requirement varies from 100 acres in Tamil Nadu to 50 acres in UP and 30 acres in Rajasthan. The cost of acquisition of land is a major problem. Having invested vast sum of money, they have no option except to commercialize higher education.

Added to this, the Tamil Nadu mandated a permanent endowment fund of Rs. 50 crores. It is clearly stated that private universities are not entitled for any state fund. They have freedom to decide on the utilization of the endowment fund. The policy does not insist on affirmative needs. At present many private educational institutions do not grant reservations to Scheduled Castes, Scheduled Tribes and OBCs since it is not specifically mandated by the policy architecture. The final culmination of this process could specifically be seen in the National Education Policy 2020, pushed hard by the BJP regime. The government did not even follow the normal democratic procedures in formulating it. They started implementing it on a war footing.

V

National Education Policy (NEP) 2020

The New National Education Policy 2020 apart from the other recommendations, paved the way for foreign universities to set up campuses in India. The new National Education Policy (NEP) states that the world's top 100 universities will be "facilitated" to operate in the country through a new law. A major criticism of allowing foreign universities to operate in India was that they would raise the cost of education through higher tuition fees and poaching of faculty from public universities and put it out of the reach for a large section of the population.

The policy says that "A legislative framework facilitating such entry (of foreign universities) will be put in place, and such universities will be given special dispensation regarding regulatory governance and norms on par with other autonomous institutions of India". (*Indian Express,* July 30, 2020, accessed on January 11, 2021)

NEP 2020 would greatly increase the private participation in education, ignore the county's pluralistic traditions and wide social and economic inequalities. The neoliberal agenda of designing a profit-oriented system that serves corporate interests, strongly favoured privatization of higher education and growth of private and foreign universities and reduced the role of the state (cover story, *Frontline*, August 15-20, 2020)

Constitutional Values:

The overall policy has not been formulated in the light of the vision of the Constitution of India. Anticipating such a danger the framers of the Constitution provided for part four of the Constitution with an emphasis on social justice making it fundamental for the governance of the nation. The political and economic context now has transformed to such an extent that a reference to socialism, secularism and even social justice has come to be considered as blasphemy. In a multi-religious and highly diverse society the nation does need certain normative standards which help the polity to negotiate with the heterogeneous groups. If curriculum of education excludes a secular thrust then the nation is not preparing the younger generations for social harmony and appreciation of varied lifestyles.

Market Driven Approach

The thrust of the policy is more skill driven than preparing educated and enlightened citizenry. Imparting skills starts at a young age right from Class 8. The emphasis on vocational education is lopsided and a clear departure from the earlier emphasis on exposing the young minds to general education till Class 10. A society, more so the market, does require skills but the skilled should simultaneously be sufficiently educated. The dichotomy between education and skill reinforces the mental manual labour divide. The policy clearly emphasizes a greater role for the market forces. The policy emphatically advocates "substantial investment in a strong, vibrant public education as well as the encouragement and facilitation of true philanthropic private and community participation". Philanthropy in the context of neoliberalism is mere rhetoric. Earlier, the Tatas and Birlas did invest their own resources without any profit motive. In contrast Ambani is supposedly starting a university which has been provided Rs. 1,000 crores by the government. The present policy does mention "no profit institutions" but in the same breath brings in collaboration between private and public institutions. It does permit charging of fees but does not provide for regulation of fees. It also recommends loughing back of the profit into the education sector. This opens up a channel for building educational empires with huge real estate properties.

Ignoring Social Justice Concerns

This policy document at no point uses the caste nomenclature. It scrupulously avoids reference to caste except somewhere mentioning it in brackets. Instead of caste, it uses 'social category'. The problem in India is that the disadvantage starts with initial endowments and in fact with the birth. Several policy measures in the past used the caste criterion for enforcing equity and dropping it is not accepting the reality of caste. For instance, the affirmative action at this point of time is caste-based and rightly so. This document brings in the merit criterion for even the marginalized categories. Consequently, the present policy shifts the total focus from what is claimed to be as a matter of right by virtue of the disadvantage of birth. It is somewhat puzzling that while the Mandal Commission led to unprecedented turmoil, leading to a widespread discussion all over India and movement and counter movement, the present policy did not yet provoke any reaction from the marginalized caste groups.

Internationalization of Education

The policy welcomes foreign universities although it qualifies it by the term prestigious universities. Assuming that they are invited for stimulating competition, what have we done with our own universities right from the UPA days? Kapil Sibal tried very hard to push through six major and crucial bills including the foreign universities bill. These bills find a place in the present so-called national education policy. For instance, the four-year degree course was attempted to be introduced and to start with it was experimented in Delhi University which led to utter confusion and militant response against it. It was one of the reasons for the defeat of the Congress Party in the Delhi Assembly elections. The Bharatiya Janata Party when it came to power withdrew the order and restored the three-year degree course.

The present document brings back the four year degree course in the form of a recommendation to introduce 5+3+3+4. The four-year degree is being pushed to bring the Indian graduate on par with the American students. One could raise the question that if in India graduation is of three years, why the American student should spend four years and why should we copy the American system? This is perhaps because admission to postgraduation of an Indian student with three years degree and American student with four years will create endemic problems. It is precisely for this reason the National Education Policy was compelled to introduce a four-year degree course in India. Otherwise, four year graduation was never discussed at any point of time in India. A more basic question could be why a political dispensation which talks of 'atmanirbharata' and ultra-nationalism should bring in foreign universities on to the Indian soil. As the political economy context has changed, this is one more indicator and consequence of India's development being drawn into the vortex of global capital. The policy creates an irresolvable contradiction between the thrust on traditionalization and indigenization at one level and globalization and corporatization of the economy at the other.

VI

Summing Up

The entire thrust of the New Education Policy triggered by neo-liberal economic reforms is bringing into the debate the whole question of control in higher education. If the control of educational organization shifts to agencies located outside India or private agencies, how are we going to have anything called manpower planning? The universities in the private sector prefer technology or electronics-based institutes or New School of Economics to meet the growing demands of NRIs for cheaper manpower and to meet the philosophical and ideological demands of the New Economic World order.

The other side of higher education in the public domain which is expected to meet the growing needs of society is continuously starved of funds. Public universities are being coerced to raise their own resources. The private sector industrial or corporate agencies may come forward to finance them through consultancy. This would not only push the public institutions towards commercial ethos, but the entire teaching faculty members would get disoriented. The relation between the teacher and the taught, instead of "guru shishya parampara" will be that of seller and consumer. It is likely that the status and stature of the academics in times to come may be determined by the brand name of his car, palace type of villa, and bank balance than one's own contribution to enlargement of horizons of knowledge. The liberal arts, humanities, and social sciences, which are not commercially oriented, may be continued in an ornamental way. The private universities may introduce commercially viable courses such as hotel management, fashion technology, tourism as a substitute to courses in social sciences. And if there is no resistance, to this move, courses in social sciences may even be abandoned.

The universities, which are already in deep crisis, will get into deeper crisis for want of resources, talent and seriousness of purpose. They may be even asked to manage without teachers, without journals, and without infrastructure. Thanks to the pandemic, online education is gradually replacing the existing system where the teacher-taught relation which has been eye-to-eye, personal and passionately interactive would be missing. The entire university site may gradually turn into an archaeological monument. The younger generation may become increasingly purposeless in the absence of inspiring role models. This would provide the pretext for greater state control giving rise to greater hierarchical and authoritarian structures which are basically antithetical, to the learning and enquiry.

This is also a context which will give rise to setting up commencement of universities by religious and fundamentalist organizations which would contribute to growing authoritarianism and fascist culture.

The organizational system that develops in the wake of privatization of higher education, in no way, can be called upon to be socially accountable. Education should integrate an individual but not let loose him on the society. A society which refuses to educate its younger generation through public funding loses its moral grip over the individual. This will create doctors, who would not mind stealing kidneys for the black market, young bridegrooms thirsty for prohibitive dowries, engineers constructing trembling bridges, IAS officers making money out of public power and professors producing theories, if not ideologies, for the private sector. Can a nation survive with a manpower which is devoid of moral strength? Thus, the crisis in higher education caused by liberalization and privatization is not only material and organizational, but also moral.

People's Resistance: A public policy which has taken a unilinear approach can be contained, if not reversed, only through people's resistance. This is also true of privatization of higher education. There have been several student struggles and expressions of teachers' opposition to the policy. As the movements were gradually picking up, it was in 2009 that an organization "All India Forum for Right to Education" came into being in an all India conference held at Osmania University, Hyderabad. The main architect of the movement was a well-known educationist, who with a vision carried a lifelong resistance for the cause of public education, particularly common school through neighbourhood schools. Soon several prominent educationists expressed solidarity and joined as a part of the Advisory Board. The movement spread and today there are committees in twenty-two states of India each trying to mobilize the public pressure. The movement has built momentum and its voice is heard with respect. The forum presents an alternative vision of higher education and keeps carrying the debate and making all the effort to reach the masses. The historical need of the hour is to build a broad based mass movement. We only hope that the masses of India gradually understand the dangers of privatization of education and would succeed in turning the tide and ensure that educational opportunities become equal, free, accessible and create an environment which will be conducive to and enable every person to realize his or her full potential and contribute to the civilizational process of democratizing and humanizing the Indian society and its people.

15

Privatization *is* Capitalism: Making Sense of the Educational Disaster in India

Ravi Kumar

Privatization and Accessibility Amidst Riches and Poverty

Privatization is more than transformation of an aspect of our existence into a commodity with exchange-value. It is about fundamentally altering the way we live, we think and we behave. The power it possesses in absence of a powerful alternative narrative destroys any imagination of life outside of capitalism. It proposes its own farcical idea of freedom of choice, an illusory possibility that every human being can be a billionaire and a new common sense that cannot imagine a free healthcare or education or social security. In other words, privatization ushers in a new regime that establishes accumulation of wealth by a few at the cost of the majority as the only truth of our life. In these times of capitalism the state has become as ruthless and callous as the private capital because of the similarities in their understanding of the world and people inhabiting it. There cannot be any other explanation to the mercurial accumulation of wealth by Indian corporate houses on one hand, and the utter refusal of the state to ensure employment, education and health to the vast mass of its citizens. The crisis in education and health during the Corona pandemic has already shown the conditions under which the vast mass of population lives (Kumar, 2020; *Hindustan Times*, 2020).

Privatization of education, an oft repeated term, seldom draws attention to the workings of capital thereby once again getting reduced to the idea of education as autonomous and separate from the system. This, among other things, is also a methodological fallacy because it ignores the workings of parts in a dialectical relationship with the whole. By this disjunction it fragments the capitalist system and its workings and never permits identification of the real force behind the whole process. This also gets translated into the curricular and pedagogic practices preparing servile citizens. The academics who have always wished to delink education from the larger socio-economic processes have no doubt looked at questions of education in relation to short-term and immediate realities. A student is educated without any imagination of how the system that governs them actually looks like. Many of those who have been critiques of what is happening to education in terms of privatization, etc., have never tried to locate it as part of the politics of capital. So, if the World Bank wants to give loans to India to have new initiatives in school education it is critiqued merely as encouraging privatization of education and not as how it is happening in connivance with the state and private capital and this policy decision feeds into the designs of capital furthering an exploitative system. Hence, efforts to understand the historical trajectory of World Bank politics as part of how capital thinks and operates in educational reforms is important, which has been done in a certain way by some (Sadgopal, 2001, 2006, 2013; Kumar, et al., 2001) but not by most. This paper tries to make sense of how privatization of education can be understood.

Generally, privatization of education is primarily referred to in terms of the handing over of state-run institutions to private players, if not completely then in parts such as service delivery in different forms. The idea, it has been argued, is to reduce the financial and administrative burden on the state as well as to enhance 'efficiency' of the existing state-run institutions. Verger et al., tried to conclude that there are six paths that the privatization process takes:

> (a) privatization as a deeply ideological and structural state reform; (b) scaling up privatization through school choice reforms; (c) privatization in social democratic welfare states; (d) historical public-private partnerships in education systems with a tradition of religious schooling; (e) privatization through the emergence and expansion of low-fee private schools in low-income countries and (f) privatization through catastrophe. (Verger, et al., 2017, p. 2)

Privatization, above all, needs to be looked at as an idea that is intrinsic to the rule of capital and it operates through the mechanics of accumulation. What appears as welfarism is nothing but an appearance of a system which acquires that form temporarily due to its own crisis or due to its incapacity to take over the big market. In contemporary times it fosters a new imagination that overrides what we feel in actuality. The pain, anger, angst and anxiety created by the tyranny of capital passes into oblivion as it constructs a new, illusory reality of consumption, false possibilities and web of identitarian deceit. This form of privatization, therefore, needs to be understood in its essence as social relations and not only as ownership of educational or health institutions.

It is interesting to read how growth in wealth gets reported as if one is watching a football match where players (corporates) are dribbling past other players (corporates) with the ball (power to do anything) to reach a goal, which in this case is endless accumulation of wealth at the cost of immiserization of the larger population. In July 2020 the *Economic Times* (2020) reported that

> For years, the world's five richest people comprised a little-changed group dominated by Americans, a European or two and, occasionally, a Mexican.
>
> That changed this week. India's Mukesh Ambani overtook Steve Ballmer on Thursday to become the fifth-wealthiest person on the planet with with a net worth of $77.4 billion...
>
> Ambani cracked the group of the 10 richest people just last month. Two weeks ago, he surpassed Warren Buffett, now ranked No. 6. He overtook Elon Musk and Google co-founders Sergey Brin and Larry Page days later... While Ambani's rise has been remarkable, Amazon.com Inc. founder Jeff Bezos's fortune has surged the most this year, adding $64 billion.

The growing inequality in India and across the world has been evident and, in fact, that is no longer a concern for the state or its aligning actors in society and polity. Oxfam reported in January 2019 that "the wealth of the world's billionaires increased $900 billion in the last year, which is $ 2.5 billion a day" (Oxfam, 2019). In February 2019 it reported the acuteness of Indian inequality:

> The top 10% of the Indian population holds 77.4% of the total national wealth.
>
> Just the top 1% holds 51.53% of the national wealth.
>
> The total wealth of Indian billionaires is higher than the total Union Budget of India for the fiscal year 2018-19 which was ta INR 24422 billion.
>
> The bottom 60%, the majority of the population, own merely 4.8% of the national wealth.

> Wealth of the top 9 billionaires = bottom 50% of the population.
>
> In the last 12 months, the wealth of the top 1% increased by 39%, whereas wealth of the bottom 50% increased by a dismal 3% (Samuel, 2019).

When inequality is so sharp and is sharpening every day how does it help people when states decide to opt for wholesale privatization? In the Indian context, there is the tendency to sell whatever the state manages and runs to private capital—from airports, mining, trains, petroleum companies, airlines, insurances, etc. There is also a simultaneous effort to transform the way the state works—through having new work ethics, hiring practices, subcontracting, evaluations of workers (to punish the workers in the name of rewarding them). Whatever is difficult to sell, such as state-run universities, colleges and schools, the effort is to subcontract them or force them to become profit-making enterprises. So, the state plays with concepts and, for instance, shows, that there is an increase in allocation for education but in reality the 'additional' amount provided to higher education institutions is in the form of loans. In 2018 the Indian government said that the amount of Rs. 10,000 crore was given annually to the centrally-funded higher education institutions for developing their infrastructure and came up with a new model called Revitalising Infrastructure and Systems in Education (RISE), through which the centrally-funded institutions could borrow up to Rs 1,00,000 crore in the next four years. This was termed as a huge jump in funding of higher education institutions. The then Minister of Human Resource Development congratulated the Prime Minister "for this innovative funding pattern to fast forward #HE infrastructure development" (*India Today*, 2019). After the Minister said that "the substantial allocation will help India compete at the world stage" an official of his ministry emphasized that this funding pattern was needed because many public institutions were not using the funds allocated in a proper manner. The official went on to say that "There was also a need to bring in private players in the higher education system so that the system can get a boost, and that wherever there is a robust higher education system, it has survived because of the participation of both public and private players. It was high time India moved to this system" (Sharma, 2018).

The catch in this whole process was that it was presented as if there is an increase in the state's commitment towards the public education system but in reality it is to squeeze their funding and compel them to take recourse to 'fund mobilization' and 'resource mobilization', which has its own logic of fee increase, making institutions subservient to the needs of market and kill any critical thinking and education. The idea was, to begin with, to hurl the education institutions in the whirlpool of the market with all its vagaries and destructive power. It was no innocence when the Minister said that "It's a lot like taking a housing loan. You take the money to build a home and, once its ready, you can keep repaying the money over several years" (Chopra, 2018). We know individuals and families have to face hardships to repay their loans. It can even lead them to commit suicide[1]. This catch was revealed when IIT Bombay was unable to pay back its loan. A news report in 2019 (Sahoo, 2019) mentioned their crisis as follows:

> A cash-strapped Indian Institute of Technology-Bombay (IIT-B) paid Rs. 41.5 crore to the Higher Education Financing Agency (HEFA), a joint venture of the central government and Canara Bank, in the academic year 2018-19. According to the annual report of the institute, despite an annual fund deficit of Rs. 82 crore, the institute had to repay a loan sought from HEFA, further crippling its finances.
>
> The institute has diverted funds from its income towards repaying the loan...*HT* had reported that faculty members were asked to bring in sponsors as well as to offer renaming of infrastructure after alumni in exchange for donations.

The underlying argument given by the state for all such measures is dearth of resources, which is not a valid reason given the amount of wealth that is accumulated by a few in the country as shown above and the way economic resources are owned by individuals, corporates and even political organizations today in India. This money could be used to provide education to each and every individual irrespective of their economic conditions. The design is, rather, to take away whatever possible from the control of the state and hand it over to the private. By taking away education from the realm of the state[2] and handing it over to the private does not merely imply making it accessible to a few who can afford it as a commodity but also changing the nature of that commodity itself. By doing this it brings in place a completely new system which does not believe in alternative imaginations, education as a fundamental right, educational workers as an exploited lot, etc.

Private schools existed even prior to the arrival of the 'neoliberal order'. However, it was not the hegemonic system. The domain of education was considered as a non-private entity and that is why the non-state players were primarily philanthropic organizations (at least on paper and in eyes of the law) running schools and colleges. The phase of privatization that had its seeds in the early 1980s policies of the Indian state and which are fully realized from the 1990s onwards have been different. It has been an unabashed pursuit of profiteering and to ensure that the march of private capital continued unhindered it has built its own pedagogical and curricular structures apart from possessing characteristics like any commodity-producing site.

Rikowski, using a host of research material, points out some of the major things that privatization would do: It will lead to undermining

> standards of teaching, learning and educational outcomes...reduction in teachers' pay... and working conditions will be worsened... classroom assistants and support staff are more liable to be sacked... planning (locally, regionally and nationally) is more difficult...trade union representation is at risk... curriculum and pedagogy become more standardised (to save costs) and less inspiring for students... public service values are corroded... corruption is more likely... equity and equality are compromised and discrimination more common... and segregation (by race and ethnicity in particular) increase with privatization in education... (Rikowski, 2019, p. 359).

Ball, on the other hand looks at privatization "as complex and multi-faceted and inter-related" wherein "they can be understood in relation to the development of a set of complex relationships between: (1) organizational changes in public sector institutions (recalibration); (2) new state forms and modalities (governance, networks and performance management); and (3) the privatization of the state itself and the interests of capital (public services as a profit opportunity and 'effective' public service provision)" (Ball, 2009, pp. 83-84).

Contemporary capitalism fundamentally reduces educational training to that of training the labour power as per the requirements of capital. After all, each and every individual is reduced to a wage worker, out in the open market selling his or her labour power. Remember, what Marx said in the *Communist Manifesto* (Marx and Engels, 2008, p. 37) about the bourgeoisie:

> It has resolved personal worth into exchange value, and in place of the numberless indefeasible chartered freedoms, has set up that single, unconscionable freedom—Free Trade. In one word, for exploitation, veiled by religious and political illusions, it has substituted naked, shameless, direct, brutal exploitation.
>
> The bourgeoisie has stripped of its halo every occupation hitherto honoured and looked up to with reverent awe. It has converted the

> physician, the lawyer, the priest, the poet, the man of science, into its paid wage-labourers.

Capitalism brings within in its ambit each and every dimension of our lives, our profession, our creativity and imagination. Human beings across professions are turned into wage workers willing to sell their labour power. When privatization of education takes place it impacts this commodity enormously. Rikowski argues that "The politics of educational (or any other form of) privatization is about making profits, which in turn is based on the capitalization of educational institutions and services; education becoming capital. It is about capitalist development in education" (2019, p. 362). The neoliberal capitalism tries to achieve this by "siphoning off state revenue and turning it into profit" (Rikowski, 2019, p. 361). These are achieved by the state (as representative of capital) and the capital itself through a historically well laid out design, which may appear as moments of educational policy change or as momentary scholarship but when seen in historicity the pieces of puzzle fall in place aiming at achieving one singular aim—a class politics of education that seeks to commodify education and make it part of the circuit of capital as any other commodity. What we are witnessing right now is nothing more than the aggressive nature of capital as Kumar (2012: 1) points out:

> Capitalism is about the perpetual destruction of human creativity and bringing into the ambit of capital circulation every possible aspect of our life, and neoliberalism represents the most callous and aggressive form of this capital-on-offensive. It takes the labour-capital conflict to a new phase where the consensual politics of the ruling class, combined with its mantra of everything is possible to achieve, goes hand in hand with the project of homogenizing our very mode of living and thinking.

Privatization has not only impacted the access to education, it has changed the very way in which the education system should work. The aim of capitalism is to transform the mind of people. This can be seen clearly in the way the education system is always a point of tussle in India between the different political forces. While the commitment of the right-wing politics has been unwavering in this the others have been quite weak. However, at the end of the day these education policies while transforming the minds of people—making them sectarian, homophobic, anti-women, Islamophobic and anti-egalitarianism—never challenges the rule of capital. In fact, the current phase has been amply clear in demonstrating how conservatism and neoliberalism can co-exist. One of the ways it has done this is by attacking the content of what is to be taught and how it is to be taught. As Dave Hill remarks: "Like poets, teachers are potentially dangerous. But poets are fewer and reading poetry is voluntary. Schooling is not" (Hill, 2001, p. 135). Hence, it constantly aims at transforming the education system to suit its politics. There is always an attempt at moulding teachers and students through changes in policy. It has happened in the context of Britain, which is also true for different other contexts. He says that "Government 'reforms' of initial teacher education (ITE) are an attempt to control and 'mould' new teachers and student teachers, to prepare them for what the government sees as the task of the economic, ideological, and cultural (re-)production of future generations of labour power, cohorts of workers, citizens" (2001, p. 135). It is important therefore, for the state, to 'train' teachers rather than 'educating' them. 'Educating' is a subversive act, which takes away the instrumentalizing elements, whereas 'training' instrumentalizes. If teacher education as a method locates future teachers within the dialectics of theory and practice or within the dialectics of socio-economic realties of the children and the theorization of those realities it has the possibility of becoming a transformative agency. This is precisely the reason why a school-going child is not taught poetry of Nagarjun in Hindi or Avtar Singh Pash in Punjabi. These poems transgress the barriers imposed by instrumentalization and they would connect the socio-economic and political reality of the student to the classroom education.

Private capital, furthermore, wants this to become a reality. Hence, it has a detailed plan for how to manage, train and punish the teachers and it follows from the capitalist plan for education. Hill argues that

> World capital has three plans for education. There is a *Capitalist Plan for Education* (what it requires education to do—produce labour power with the skills and ideologically compliant attitudes to develop a workforce from which surplus value can be extracted). There is a *Capitalist Plan in Education* (how it plans to make 'big bucks'/money/profits out of education). There is also (third type) the *Capitalist Plan for Education* Corporations Globally (Hill, 2007, p. 204).

In the British context, Hill (2007, p. 213) looked at how the change in nomenclature from 'teacher education' to 'teacher training' indicates towards a new understanding of education, as desired by the corporate capital. It has "detheorized" and "sanitized" the teacher education. The restructuring between 1984-97 "emphasized school-basing and the development of practical skills. It abjured theory per se as well as critical reflection and its attendant social justice underpinnings". There has been reduction of time spent on discussing issues of 'race', gender, sexuality, special needs and social class among others. The shift that is being forced is towards assessment and learning outcomes, which essentially detheorizes and instrumentalizes the education system. It aims at producing labour-power suitable for the labour market. Employability in simple terms would mean whether a graduate coming out of the university system can be absorbed in the labour market or not. This absorption would depend not only on the skills required by the market but also on how much is the requirement of such skilled-workers. Hence, the sole focus on unemployability is a misnomer and cannot be used as an excuse to push learning outcomes and assessment of students but it has to do with the nature of institutions, educational infrastructure available and the demand in the market. In other words, this would amount to making education subservient to the demands of the capitalist market and shut down the social sciences as has been done at many places and not teach courses such as philosophy, sociology or English literature.

This has seldom figured in the debates pushed by the state, private capital and some parts of 'civil society' about unemployability of university graduates. Nobody tries to link the growing unemployability, emergence of different kinds of work (short-term, ad hoc, casualized and precarious) with the nature of the economy which thrives on creating precarity to optimise surplus accumulation for private capital. Should a question not be asked as to why did private educational institutions shut down in order to understand the much efficacy of such institutions when the state run institutions have been shown as lacking any quality?

> At least 179 professional colleges, including engineering colleges and business schools, shut down in India in academic year 2020-21, amid a tough employment environment, falling demand, and restrictions on the mobility of students because of the covid-19 pandemic… Other than closures, 134 more institutions did not seek approval for fresh batches in 2020, highlighting the disruption in the higher education sector (Nanda, 2020).

If the above instance is attributed to the Corona pandemic then one is mistaken because this has been a recurrent crisis. "In a decision taken by the government, more than 300 private engineering colleges would be reportedly asked to stop functioning from the 2018-19 academic session" (*Financial Express*, 2017). A survey by the corporate research body FICCI-

Ernst and Young "found that only 25 per cent of the Indian professionals are considered "employable" by multinationals and the difficulty of employers in India to fill job vacancies has increased to 67 per cent in 2011 compared with 16 per cent in last year" (Pandey, 2011). The *India Skills Report 2019* puts employability at 47 per cent and the engineers being more employable than the MBA (2019, p. 14). This is not at all about bad education system as ministers tend to portray but more about the whimsical dance of private capital and its inabilities and abilities of job creation of a permanent nature at different moments. Unemployment is an innate characteristic of capitalism. This report demonstrates how the state institutions and different forms of corporate organizations work together to generate particular types of researches and generate debates. *India Skills Report* is jointly brought out by UNDP, All India Council of Technical Education, Association of Indian Universities, Confederation of Indian Industry, Wheebox and PeopleStrong. It writes proudly that «the past five years in the India›s Talent market could be termed as the most defining ones. The move towards the work of the future has changed the job market landscape. Now when we talk about «jobs» it is no longer limited to permanent jobs. With entrepreneurship and gig economy picking pace, there is an entirely new ecosystem of jobs ready» (Wheebox, et al., 2019, p. 14). We know that the celebration of the gig economy[3] also implies, as of now, complete subversion of the labour laws that sought protection of employees. De Stefano outlines in his ILO paper certain fears that this new economy entails. He argues that "the strong links of the gig-economy with broader trends in labour markets such as casualization of work, demutualization of risks and informalization of the formal economy should not be overlooked, to designate comprehensive solutions to labour problems in modern and future labour markets" (2016, p. 21).

Development Agencies as Representatives of Capital: Hoping Against Hope

In June 2020 while the world was battling Covid-19 and children were missing out on schools because the idea of public education could never be part of the post-independent Indian state, the World Bank approved $500 million to improve the quality of education in India for the STARS (Strengthening Teaching-Learning and Results for States Programme) project. There were "appeals" to the Indian government to withdraw from the project because it would open gates for privatization. While making these appeals or by analysing the impact of this World Bank project it has been pointed out how it will not only ensure further destruction of the public education system but is also in contravention to the constitutional rights of people. Some have argued that the Fundamental Right of Right to Education will be violated while others have pointed out that it will gradually nullify all the affirmative provisions made for the socially and economically marginalized communities. Hence, to oppose this project is also about saving the sanctity of the Constitution. Strategically speaking, contesting the massive privatization of private and public domains may require invocation of welfarism but it will be wrong to imagine going back to it because (1) it entails remaining within the rule of capital (a backward shift from the harsher form to softer form) forgetting that the contemporary forms of aggression, exploitation and overall precarity have come about because of conditions created by the so-called welfarist phase of Indian capitalism; (2) it believes that the Constitution as a legal document is outside the larger social relations within which it is actually embedded and which gives it a shape; (3) it establishes that there is no alternative to capitalism.

A general unsaid consensus has been built over a period of time which accepts intervention of the World Bank in Indian education policy. This becomes clear when academics write a letter to the World Bank and suggest ways to make the project more democratic, participatory and avoid conflation of "all forms of non-state actors into a single category". It also misreads the International Finance Corporation's decision to freeze investment in for-profit education by assuming that the freeze is for-private service delivery (which might be a possibility under the STARS project) when it is rather a freezing of "investments in K-12 private, fee-charging schools" (and not government schools). This project is meant for non-profit government schools, which would hire in ‹services› of non-state actors hence, the commitment of IFC remains to freezing while the process of privatization is also ushered in. More than this catch and difference in interpretation the surprise is that everyone is accepting that the World Bank should play a role in improving Indian education. In fact, an education activist was quoted as saying that the "Government of India and World Bank should aim to create an Aatmanirbhar (self-reliant), empowered equitable and innovative public education system" (*ToI*, 2020). This is also somehow inbuilt into the critiques (of the project), which seek to suggest that the World Bank should have worked in a particular way.

Academics wanted the World Bank management and the Government of India "in consultation with the state governments" to refocus the project. They do not mind non-state actors but "If non-state actors are to be involved, ensure state regulatory capacity to enforce compliance with adequate legal provisions and increase transparency as preconditions for any involvement" (Counterview, 2020). No doubt they talk about strengthening the DIETs, etc., and enhance capacity of the state but will this work with the participation of the bank and without changing the orientation of the state itself, which has been on a path for decades now to orient the education system in the interests of capital. While making this appeal what is forgotten is that in order to build capacity under contemporary capitalism the only structure left to fall back on is the private sector. The public sector has been reduced to rubble and there is hardly anything left which will provide ICT capacity building, rebuild DIETs to their original purpose. Without being far away one can look at the universities or higher education in general, which is supposed to be linked to this whole process of capacity building. It survives on ad hoc, temporary and guest faculties today. One after other departments are run through labour of this precarious teaching community. Hence, a suggestion of this kind must take into cognizance the fact of overhauling the entire teaching-learning system and not work in 'scheme' mode, which has been the history of the World Bank in India and the Indian state. It never showed its commitment to building a strong public education system.

Analysts have pointed out how "giving a larger role to non-state actors and by increasing the use of technology" is not the way to capacity building of state institutions. It has been argued that the participation of "frontline bureaucracy" is important in this whole process of improving governance because they can address the local issues and through decentralization be part of decision-making. "Outsourcing to non-state partners not just takes away discretion from state actors but also a sense of accountability and ownership towards their job." If capacity building has to be done greater attention needs to paid to the dilapidated institutions such as DIET (District Institutes of Education and Training). Hiring for vacant positions in bureaucracy as well as teaching cadre needs to be undertaken but none of these issues are addressed by the STARS project. The Project's emphasis on learning outcomes has been criticized on the grounds that it is important to first understand why it is low and it cannot be improved simply by service delivery. Critiques have targeted Prime Minister Modi's slogan of atmanirbhar (self-reliance) on the grounds that the schools, DIETS and BRCs and CRCs need to develop their own capability rather than ask someone do their job. They have also asked the World Bank to "learn from its past mistakes and use evidence, often generated by its own research arms, to formulate projects" (Bhatty and Haus, 2020). In fact, if it is about invoking the memory then it is not only about the World Bank but also the Indian state. It is amply clear that despite so many schemes the education system is in a mess. The problem does not lie with the memory. It lies with the intent. States and institutions like the World Bank have extremely sharp memories. They are not invoked or used because they are not meant to be. The problem, rather, lies with the fact it is in the nature of the state to conceive development through this prism. It is in the nature of capital itself to define and redefine categories of 'development', 'growth' and 'progress' in ways that suits its requirements of sustained accumulation. Both, the international financial institutions as well as the states, have been on the same page regarding this because they are not outside the circuit of capital. Hence, it will be fallacious to even expect them to go the other way and ensure that the public education is fully funded by the state, with the best of infrastructures, etc.

Scholars had shown how the World Bank and IMF were instrumental in destroying the education system in India by replacing "the regular formal schools with low-quality, low-budget parallel streams of primary education for the educationally deprived children, two-thirds of whom are girls" (Sadgopal, 2003). Kumar, et al., also traces the history of how the "quantitative and qualitative crisis" in education were resolved by the Jomtien goals through "the slogans of 'education for all' and 'lifelong learning' opportunities" (Kumar, et al., 2001, p. 561). "In India, in the 1980s and early 1990s, the Bihar Education Project, the Lok Jumbish Programme, Rajasthan, and the Andhra Pradesh Primary Education Programme, ushered in with the help of UNICEF, SIDA, and ODA, represented the 'Education For All' ethos" and India initiated "its relationship with the World Bank in Primary Education through the Uttar Pradesh Basic Education Programme" (Ibid.). The 1991 economic crisis provided the opportunity for the Structural Adjustment Programmes to set in completely and thus came the World Bank funded DPEP. Kumar using Susan George explains that SAP "is a policy support to trade and culture of the US and a large number of Western European countries". The aim of this policy was to make "the governments of developing countries more open to aid, loans, and policy 'advice' from the developed, and creating a general ambience of international cooperation within an unequal nation state system" (Ibid., p. 561). Hence, the World Bank's support to DPEP was nothing about benevolence and emerging out of deep anguish at the site of uneducated and hungry children. Kumar makes it amply clear that "DPEP is a part of the 'Social Safety Net' offered to World Bank borrowers as a short-term protection against the social and systemic turmoil caused by the structural adjustment process" (Ibid.).

The World Bank is known to have fostered a love for privatization of education. There is abundance of literature of how they changed the education system through their structural adjustment programmes, which is part of the larger plan to destroy the public entitlements. An organization of academics from Africa has pointed out that "although the state is the immediate perpetrator, the ultimate responsibility for many violations of academic rights on the African campuses is borne by international financial institutions and, more specifically, by the policy "adopted by Washington and the European Union in the 1980s, that calls for the virtual recolonization of Africa's educational systems". It qualified that "the attack on the universities is part of a broader attack on the place of Africa in the International Division of Labour, on the value of African workers, and on the capacity of Africans to achieve self-determination, the still unrealized goal of the anti-colonial struggle" (Federici, et al., 2000, p. xiii). And this should not be seen as an isolated attack on public education system but "rather, it is part of a concerted attack on all public entitlements and workers' rights..." (Ibid., xiv).

Unless it is understood that the states are working in connivance with international institutions and private capital it is difficult to understand the logic of privatization that is taking place in India. There has been a strong debate historically in India, which has tried to establish the inefficacy of the public education system under one pretext or the other—unionization of teachers destroyed the education system, that the teacher salaries in government schools is too much and that "research suggests that the size of teacher salaries has no significant association with student achievement but that other forms of educational expenditure do" (Kingdon and Muzammil, 2008, p. 21). International organizations such as UNICEF have argued that "public-private partnerships (PPPs) with non-state providers can take many forms and the goal often is the same—expanding quality education for all while reducing costs" (LaRocque and Lee, 2011, p. ix). One form of generic call for privatization has been part of state agenda ever since it started talking in terms of lack of resources. The debate on privatization has moved around the inability of the state to bear the financial burden to efficiencies of the state run educational system. It was in the National Policy 1986 (Government of India, 1992, p. 35) that the Indian state said:

> Resources, to the extent possible, will be raised by mobilizing donations, asking the beneficiary communities to maintain school buildings and supplies of some consumables, raising fees at the higher levels of education and effecting some savings by the efficient use of facilities. Institutions involved with research and the development of technical and scientific manpower should also mobilize some funds by levying a cess or charge on the user agencies, including government departments, and entrepreneurs. All these measures will be taken not only to reduce the burden on state resources but also for creating a greater sense of responsibility within the educational system.

This has stayed with the Indian state, which has consistently argued that the involvement of private players is essential for the education system to run well. The Twelfth Five Year Plan, which could not be implemented, was committed to privatization. It said in its school education section that

> private providers (including NGOs and non-profits) can play an important role in elementary education. Their legitimate role in expanding elementary education needs to be recognized and a flexible approach needs to be adopted to encourage them to invest in the sector. The current licensing and regulatory restrictions in the sector could be eased and a single window approach should be adopted so that the process of opening new schools by private providers is streamlined (GoI, 2013, p. 64).

It was equally committed towards private capital in secondary education. It argued that the state governments "ease entry barriers with dismantling of multiple licensing systems and procedures" and "revisit norms including requirement of land for setting up institutions". It suggested that "the role of the private sector in secondary schooling can be further strengthened through right policies, proper regulation, innovative public—private partnerships and a variety of demand-side financing measures..." (GoI, 2013, p. 73). In the higher education sector it suggested re-examination of 'not-for-profit' criteria "for pragmatic considerations so as to allow the entry of for-profit institutions in select areas where acute shortages persist" (GoI, 2013, p. 100). The Action Plan of the Niti Aayog (the replacement of the Planning Commission) wants to "explore and pilot other bolder experiments by interested states. These could include education vouchers and local government led purchasing of schooling services. Public-Private Partnership (PPP) models could also be explored where the private sector adopts government schools while being publicly funded on a per child basis" (NITI Aayog, 2017, p. 133). It wants to move a few universities "immediately...out from the regulatory system" (NITI Aayog, 2017, p. 134) and let education turn into a full-fledged free market. This was not the first time that privatization was being vocalized. The National Knowledge Commission in its report of "robust public private partnerships" in vocational education and training and recommended that in the field of higher education apart from increasing public spending the state needed to diversify "the sources of financing to encourage private participation, philanthropic contributions and industry linkages" (GoI, 2009, p. 14). It suggested that the public universities should use their land for generating finances and the "fees should meet at least 20 per cent of the total expenditure in universities" (GoI, 2009, p. 62). The Knowledge Commission had a different set of members who suggested these measures. They included Sam Pitroda, Ashok Ganguly, P. Balram, Jayati Ghosh, Deepak Nayyar, Nandan Nilekani, Amitabh Matoo and Sujatha Ramdorai. These are only a few examples of how despite different political parties and different sets of intellectuals thought along similar lines when it came to privatizing education. Some might have wanted it to be masked with a 'human face,' while others would have advocated it brazenly but at the end it was about handing over parts and gradually the entire education system (as far as it generates profit) to the private capital.

The falsity of opposition to privatization emerges when activists and scholars begin appealing to the state and international institutions to not privatize. This is problematic because it (1) assigns the possibility of 'goodness' to these institutions which act as agencies of private capital; and (2) it establishes the illusion that things can be fine even within capitalism. More recently, the opposition to the World Bank STARS project as well as the New Education Policy has been handled this way. Appeals have been made to the Government of India (as the government of the people and as a democratic institution) as well as the World Bank to delete the privatization elements from their respective documents. Why this appeal when, as shown above, historically these institutions have been championing the cause of privatization? Such appeals rather tend to legitimize these institutions.

Kumar (2019) shows how researches have defended the appointment of contractual, low-paid teachers, and argued against relatively higher salaries of government teachers. It has also been argued that low-fee paying schools are more effective when it comes to learning outcomes and they are more affordable as well. Kingdon (2017) says that "...even very poor daily wagers" in UP "can access private schooling". However, they do acknowledge that the infrastructure in such schools is not very good but it nonetheless does not impact educational outcome. Their argument is that "when a high proportion of the well-funded government schools themselves cannot comply with the infrastructure norms of the Right to Education (RTE) Act 2009, how can private schools do so (without public subsidy), since the majority of them run on a small fraction of the unit cost of government schools?" (Kingdon, 2017, p. 23). It is within this framework that there has been opposition from such scholars to the Right to Education Act as impeding the contribution of such schools by imposing norms and conditions for schools. When parents are willingly sending their children to such schools why should the state interfere is the implicit argument when Tooley (2017, p. 46) says that "our conclusion is that there is substantial ongoing research that shows parental demand for low-cost private schools appears to be a reflection of their superior educational quality compared to government schools." Even other reports such as the one published by DFID argues along lines of how teaching in private schools tends to be better. The 'Headline finding' of the report says that:

> Teaching in private schools tends to be better—in terms of more teacher presence and teaching activity, and teaching approaches that are more likely to lead to improved outcomes—than in state schools. Some evidence supports the explanation that this is due to increased accountability of teachers to employers in private schools. However, much of the evidence reviewed also indicates that private school teachers are often less formally qualified, have low salaries and weak job security; such conditions might in part explain the greater teacher effort in private schools" (Day, et al., 2014, p. 19).

The report does point to, but not highlight sufficiently, the shortcomings in such schools—ranging from exploitation of teachers, dignity of labour to the absence of required infrastructure. However, the ultimate argument that can be made furthering these arguments is that if there are so many good things at a lower expenditure the government schools should be shut down and instead the state can pay subsidies to these private schools and save money for something that is more important, which is being demanded now. This would also lessen the financial burden on the state and what more can be expected of a government sloganeering of *Minimum Government and Maximum Governance.*

Privatization, Commodification and Social Relations—Towards a Conclusion

When an institution is controlled by private capital, services are handed over to them or gradually the larger parts of social and economic life are managed by them (obviously for a price). This is also about how social relations are framed in a society. At an obvious level it appears as inequality in access to education but deep under that obvious is the socio-economic formation of a society where the idea is that there are vast masses of people who are forced to sell their labour-power to survive to a minuscule population who buy that labour power.

It is within this relationship of buying and selling that the centrality of *commodity* having exchange-value appears. Educational institutions play an important role in this process. In other words, educational institutions that produce this commodity called labour power need to be seen as any other institution producing any other commodity—the only difference being the nature of this commodity (Kumar and Paul, 2016; Rikowski, 2019). However, as Rikowski puts it "the privatization of labour-power production is invariably ignored". The privatization of educational institutions impacts "the pedagogical activities, processes and forms involved in labour-power production" as they are also privatized (Rikowski, 2019, p. 357).

The trajectory of public education in India in post-independent times has been one of non-committal of the Indian state towards its citizens. It began with not including education as a fundamental right and culminated with gradual destruction of whatever forms of public education existed. The government school system is huge in absolute numbers (though still quite insufficient) but it is designed to be a system for the underprivileged class, gender, caste and religion. The schooling system is a segmented system along lines of the segmented labour market, which might foster the illusion of upward mobility for a few exceptions but not for the masses. Commodities, to be sold have to create a niche for themselves and so do the educational institutions today. The schools, colleges and universities appear as brands, as commodities to be sold, to not only customers seeking training to be more effective (saleable) labour-power but also to the workers employed within those institutions. Hence, one finds the tendency of teacher-workers shifting places where they get a better price for selling their labour-power and there are also instances where institutions want some of them because they are brands that may attract more customers. This intertwining of commodification, cultural dimensions of our life under capitalism and our voluntary immersion into the whole process, reminding us of what Adorno said in reference to the culture industry:

> ...although the culture industry undeniably speculates on the conscious and unconscious state of the millions towards which it is directed, the masses are not primary, but secondary, they are an object of calculation; an appendage of the machinery. The customer is not king, as the culture industry would have us believe, not its subject but its subject but its object... Neither is it a question of primary concern for the masses, nor of the techniques of communication as such, but of the spirit which suffocates them, their master's voice. The culture industry misuses its concern for the masses in order to duplicate, reinforce and strengthen their mentality, which it presumes is given and unchangeable (Adorno, 2001, p. 99).

Privatization of education takes control over curriculum and pedagogy and these mutilations are always aimed at ensuring that the commodity of labour-power that is churned out of what Marx called "a sausage factory" (Marx, 1982, p. 644) is subservient to the masters. The street fights taking place inside India's university campuses are, in a certain sense, indicative of the complete control that the private capital with the help of the state wants over these institutions. The emphasis on teacher management laid down by the Twelfth Five Year Plan, World Bank projects, consistent government documents as well as academic researches are merely one of the instances of how capital wants to transform educational institutions into more and more sausage factories. Hence, it is the conflict of labour and capital that lies at the heart of what to teach and how to teach. It is this relationship which determines what form education takes and if privatization as an evil has to be contested it has to be contested through this understanding rather than the superficiality of merely not allowing certain parts to be outsourced because the logic of capital would destroy the 'public', the 'commons' and convert them into private like it is doing with each and every aspect of lives without our realization and with us celebrating it often like parents of private schools getting angry about why their children are not taught more than one and a half hours per day. Rather, we ensure that the system sustains, flourishes and continues its unabated oppressiveness at our cost. It is our self-oppression that ensures that privatization works—we vilified the state run services—from schools to electricity supply—and sought refuge under the umbrella of private capital not knowing that it 'costs' to avail facilities and we lose control over it. One has to purchase everything and when there is unequal purchasing power education cannot be bought by the majority. It also becomes undemocratic in terms of control and management as people lose their right to say what they want and how they want it to run. Ultimately, one is compelled to buy education—different kinds for people with different purchasing power.

Notes

1. One can see as an example some of the following news items: https://www.indiatoday.in/india/story/unable-to-repay-loans-two-farmers-commit-suicide-in-up-1607230-2019-10-08; https://www.thehindu.com/news/cities/Delhi/loan-of-8-lakh-costs-man-his-life/article28714747.ece; https://timesofindia.indiatimes.com/city/surat/unable-to-pay-emi-diamond-worker-commits-suicide-in-amroli/articleshow/71729244.cms
2. I would like to make a distinction between the state and the public. The state represents the interests of the ruling class in different ways depending on the balance of forces and the immanent form it takes across history. The public, on the other hand, is the contested domain of warring classes and communities. It plays a role in formation of the state depending on who wins the battles and it also occasionally keeps the state in check depending on the material conditions and political exigencies confronting the state at that particular moment. In this sense it is always better to have a publicly controlled education system rather than a state-owned education. However, in context of this paper, the debate is about who should control, manage and run educational institutions—the private capital or the state, which gets constituted through the participation of people through elections in a liberal bourgeois democratic system.
3. "The gig-economy is usually understood to include chiefly two forms of work: "crowdwork" and "work on-demand via apps"... The first term is usually referred to working activities that imply completing a series of tasks through online platforms... Typically, these platforms put in contact an indefinite number of organizations and individuals through the internet, potentially allowing connecting clients and workers on a global basis. "Work on-demand via apps", instead, is a form of work in which the execution of traditional working activities such as transport, cleaning and running errands, but also forms of clerical work, is channelled through apps managed by firms that also intervene in setting minimum quality standards of service and in the selection and management of the workforce..." (De Stefano, 2016, p. 1).

References

Ball, Stephen J. (2009). 'Privatising Education, Privatising Education Policy, Privatising Educational Research: Network Governance and the 'Competition State', *Journal of Education Policy*, Vol. 24, Issue 1, pp. 83-99.

Bhatty, Kiran and Haus, Martin (June 29, 2020). 'The World Bank's STARS Project Needs an Overhaul', *The Hindu*, available at https://www.thehindu.com/opinion/the-stars-project-needs-an-overhaul/article31947675.ece (accessed on July 10, 2020).

Chopra, Ritika (February 2, 2018) 'Union Budget 2018, Education: Loans to Replace Infra Grants to IITs and IIMs', *Indian Express*, available at https://indianexpress.com/article/business/budget/union-budget-2018-arun-jaitley-education-loans-to-replace-infra-grants-to-iits-and-iims-5048413/ (Accessed on April 10, 2019).

Counterview (June 22, 2020). 'World Bank 'Fails to Provide' Safeguards for Engagement of Private Sector in Education', available at https://www.counterview.net/2020/06/world-bank-fails-to-provide-safeguards.html (accessed on June 25, 2020).

Day, Ashley L., Mcloughlin, C., Aslam, M., Engel, J., Wales, J., Rawal, S., Batley, R., Kingdon, G., Nicolai, S. and Rose, P. (2014). The Role and Impact of Private Schools in Developing Countries: A Rigorous Review of the Evidence. Final Report. *Education Rigorous Literature Review*. Department for International Development.

De Stefano, Valerio (2016). 'The Rise of the "Just-in-Time Workforce": On-Demand Work, Crowdwork and Labour Protection in the "Gig-Economy"', *Conditions of Work and Employment of Work and Employment Series No. 71*, ILO: Geneva.

Economic Times (July 25, 2020). 'Mukesh Ambani is World's Fifth-Richest Person with $77 Billion Fortune', available at https://economictimes.indiatimes.com/news/company/corporate-trends/mukesh-ambani-is-worlds-fifth-richest-person-with-77-billion-fortune/articleshow/77161724.cms (Accessed on July 26, 2020)

Federici, Silvia, Caffentzis, George and Alidou, Ousseina (eds.) (2000). *A Thousand Flowers: Social Struggles Against Structural Adjustment in African Universities*, African World Press, Inc.: New Jersey.

Financial Express (December 2, 2017). 'AICTE to Shut Down 300 Engineering Colleges in India? Check if Your Institution is in Danger Too!', available at https://www.financialexpress.com/education-2/aicte-to-shut-down-300-

engineering-colleges-in-india-check-if-your-institution-is-in-danger-too/957417/ (Accessed on January 15, 2018).

Government of India (GoI) (2013). *Twelfth Five Year Plan (2012-17), Social Sectors*, Vol. III, Planning Commission, Sage Publications: New Delhi.

Government of India (GoI) (2009). *National Knowledge Commission: Report to the Nation 2006-09*, Government of India: New Delhi.

Government of India (GoI) (1992). 'National Policy on Education (with modifications undertaken in 1992)', available at http://www.ncert.nic.in/oth_anoun/npe86.pdf (Accessed on May 18, 2020).

Hill, Dave (2001). 'State Theory and the Neo-Liberal Reconstruction of Schooling and Teacher Education: A Structuralist Neo-Marxist Critique of Post-modernist, Quasi-Postmodernist, and Culturalist Neo-Marxist Theory', *British Journal of Sociology of Education*, Vol. 22, No. 1, 135-155.

Hill, Dave (2007). 'Critical Teacher Education, New Labour, and the Global Project of Neoliberal Capital', *Policy Futures in Education*, Vol. 5, No. 2, pp. 204-225.

India Today (January 11, 2019) 'Rs. 5310 Crore Approved by HEFA for 10 Higher Education Institutions and 44 New KVs, Says Prakash Javadekar', available at https://www.indiatoday.in/education-today/news/story/rs-5310-crore-approved-by-hefa-for-higher-education-says-javadekar-html-1428512-2019-01-11 (Accessed on May 10, 2019).

Kingdon, Geeta Gandhi (2017). 'The Emptying of Public Schools and Growth of Private Schools in India' in *Report on Budget Private Schools in India*, Centre for Civil Society, New Delhi, pp. 12-31.

Kingdon, Geeta and Muzammil, Mood (September, 2008). *A Political Economy of Education in India: The Case of Uttar Pradesh*, Oxford Policy Institute, available at http://ceid.educ.cam.ac.uk/publications/OPI_KingdonMuzammil20081.pdf (Accessed on October 23, 2018).

Kumar, Ravi (2019).' When the Idea of a Second Grade Education for the Marginalized Becomes the Dominant Discourse: Context, Policy, and Practice of Neoliberal Capitalism', in Saltman, Kenneth J. and Alexander J. Means (eds.), *The Wiley Handbook of Global Educational Reform*, Wiley Blackwell: New Jersey.

Kumar, Ravi (July 10, 2020). 'Pandemic, Migration and the Education Crisis: How Capitalism Aggravated It', *Newsclick*, available at https://www.newsclick.in/Pandemic-Migration-Education-Crisis-Capitalism-Aggravated (Accessed on July 11, 2020).

Kumar, Ravi and Paul, Rama (2016). 'Slaying the Monster Called Capital: Teacher-Worker's Potential and Revolutionary Politics', *Knowledge Cultures*, Vol. 4, Issue 6, pp. 272-290.

Kumar, Ravi (2012). 'Neoliberal Education and Imagining Strategies of Resistance: An Introduction', in Ravi Kumar (ed.), *Education and the Reproduction of Capital: Neoliberal Knowledge and Counterstrategies*, New York: Palgrave Macmillan.

Kumar, Krishna, Priyam, Manish and Saxena, Sadhna (February 17, 2001). 'Looking Beyond the Smokescreen DPEP and Primary Education in India', *Economic and Political Weekly*, pp. 560-568.

LaRocque, Norman and Lee, Sena (2011). *Non-State Providers and Public-Private Partnerships in Education for the Poor*, ADB and UNICEF: Bangkok.

Marx, Karl and Engels, Frederich (2008). *The Communist Manifesto*, Pluto Press: London.

Marx, Karl (1982). *Capital: A Critique of Political Economy*, translated by Ben Fawkes, Penguin Books: Middlesex.

Nanda, Prashant K. (July 28, 2020). '179 Professional Colleges Wind Up Amid Uncertainty', *Live Mint*, available at https://www.livemint.com/news/india/amid-pandemic-pain-179-colleges-including-engineering-b-schools-shut-shop-a-9-year-high-11595853839404.html (Accessed on July 19, 2020).

Niti Aayog (2017). *Three Year Action Agenda 2017-18 to 2019-20*, Niti Aayog, Government of India: New Delhi.

Oxfam (January 2019). 'Public Good or Private Wealth', available at https://www.oxfamindia.org/sites/default/files/2019-02/Report.pdf (Accessed on May 10, 2020).

Pandey, Vineeta (September 16, 2011). 'India Has the Most Unemployable Population: Report', available at https://www.dnaindia.com/india/report-india-has-the-most-unemployable-population-report-1587604 (Accessed on May 10, 2018).

Rikowski, Glenn (2019). 'Privatisation: Education and Commodity Forms', in Derek R. Ford (ed.), *Keywords in Radical Philosophy and Education: Common Concepts for Contemporary Movements*, Brill: Leiden, pp. 356-374.

Sadgopal, Anil (November 22-December 5, 2003). Education for Too Few, *Frontline*, Vol. 20, Issue 24, available at https://www.educationforallinindia.com/anilsadgopalnew.htm (Accessed on June 12, 2020).

Sadgopal, Anil (December 22, 2001). 'Political Economy of the Ninety-Third Amendment Bill', *Mainstream*, pp. 43-50.

Sadgopal, Anil (2006). 'Dilution, Distortion and Diversion: A Post-Jomtien Reflection on the Education Policy', in Kumar, Ravi (ed.), *The Crisis of Elementary Education in India*, Sage Publications: New Delhi, pp. 92-136.

Sadgopal, Anil (July-August 2013). 'FYUP: Hidden Agenda of Dismantling India's Higher Education', *Social Scientist*, Vol. 41, No. 7/8, pp. 5-18.

Sahoo, Priyanka (December 30, 2019). 'Cash-Starved IIT-B Repays Centre's 41.5-Crore Loan', *Hindustan Times*, available at https://www.hindustantimes.com/mumbai-news/cash-starved-iit-b-repays-centre-s-41-5-crore-loan/story-RrQ7SLkhUupAAUytCoWfSP.html (Accessed on January 22, 2020)

Samuel, Vineet John (February 7, 2019). 'What is Inequality?'. *Oxfam India*, available at https://www.oxfamindia.org/blog/what-inequality (accessed on May 10, 2020).

Sharma, Kritika (July 4, 2018). 'To Reform Education, Modi Government Makes Institutions Accountable for Their Funds', available at https://theprint.in/india/governance/to-reform-education-modi-govt-makes-institutions-accountable-for-their-funds/78823/ (Accessed on June 29, 2020).

ToI (June 21, 2020). 'Academicians Urge World Bank to Postpone Loan to MHRD for STARS Project', available at https://timesofindia.indiatimes.com/home/education/news/academicians-urge-world-bank-to-postpone-loan-to-mhrd-for-stars-project/articleshow/76494419.cms (Accessed on June 25, 2020).

ToI (July 27, 2017). 'Hand Over Schools, Colleges, Jails to Private Sector: Amitabh Kant', available at https://timesofindia.indiatimes.com/india/hand-over-schools-colleges-jails-to-private-sector-amitabh-kant/articleshow/59782227.cms (Accessed on January 12, 2018).

Verger, Antoni, Fontdevila, Clara and Zancajo, Adrián (2017). 'Multiple Paths Towards Education Privatization in a Globalizing World: a Cultural Political Economy Review', *Journal of Education Policy*, Vol. 32, Issue 6, pp. 1-32.

Wheebox, People Strong, UNDP, AICTE, CII, AIU (2019). *India Skills Report 2019*, Wheebox: Gurgaon.

Contributors

Prabhat Patnaik is currently Professor Emeritus after his retirement as Professor and Sukhamoy Chakravarty Chair at the Centre for Economic Studies and Planning, Jawaharlal Nehru University, New Delhi. He was the executive head of planning board in the state of Kerala. Author of several books, he has been honoured by various academic associations and holding several visiting professorships. He currently edits the monthly journal *Social Scientist*. He is known particularly for the advocacy measures to directly improve the lives of the poor.

Syeda Hameed was Member, Planning Commission, New Delhi from 2010-2014 and Chancellor of Maulana Azad National Urdu University, Hyderabad. She has authored many books and sits on the boards of several academic organisations. She is a founding member of several of rights and education groups including the Muslim Women's Forum and is at the forefront of many development issues concerning Minorities, Dalits, Adivasis, Women and Children.

Kuldeep Mathur retired as Professor of Political Science at the Jawaharlal Nehru University and was earlier concurrent professor at the Centre for the Study of Law and Governance in the same university. He was also Director of the National Institute of Educational Planning and Administration. His research interests encompass Public Policy Processes, Plans and Implementation, Bureaucracy Administration and Decentralisation and has published several books.

Jyotsna Jha has been Director of the Centre for Budget and Policy Studies (CBPS), Bengaluru since 2011. With a PhD in Economics from Jawaharlal Nehru University, her research primarily focuses on Education and Gender. Before her association with CBPS, she worked as an advisor of Education at the Commonwealth Secretariat, London for five years.

Ashok Pankaj is currently Professor at the Council for Social Development, New Delhi. His area of specialisation includes law and political economy with focus on public policies, institutions of governance and development. He has directed/co-directed several research and evaluation projects sponsored by the Government of India and UN agencies.

Poornima M. is an Assistant Professor at the Council for Social Development, New Delhi, with more than 10 years of research experience in the areas of education, gender studies and local governance. She holds a PhD on Educational Reforms from the Centre for the Study of Law and Governance, JNU. She has recently co-edited a volume for Routledge on *India's Social Sectors and SDGs: Problems and Prospects.*

Anjela Taneja is an activist who leads the work on education, health and inequality at Oxfam India in Delhi. She is one of the founder members of the Right to Education Forum, India's largest network, and coordinates the Fight Inequality Alliance in India.

D. Narasimha Reddy was formerly Professor of Economics at the University of Hyderabad, and late Sankaran Chair Professor, National Institute of Rural Development, Hyderabad. His areas of specialization include Labour Economics, Agrarian Studies and Political Economy of Development.

Kiran Bhatty is a senior fellow at the Centre for Policy Research, New Delhi. She works mainly on governance issues in elementary education through action research and policy. She had drafted Guidelines for Social Audits of Right to Education Act for the National Commission for Protection of Child Rights and the Ministry of Human Resource Development.

Nilay Ranjan, Head, Corporate Social Responsibility and Sustainability at Vodafone Idea Limited, Mumbai, has 20 years of experience working with the Government, United Nations, NGOs and social organizations in India on projects relating to sustainable development, education, employment, community-level planning and health. In his last assignment, he was UNDP's Rural Development Expert for the MGNREGA project based in New Delhi.

Poonam Batra is Professor of Education, Central Institute of Education, University of Delhi. She has published internationally and domestically in areas of public policy in education, elementary education curriculum and pedagogy, developmental and educational psychology and gender studies. She has had a long association with the Eklavya Elementary and Social Science Programmes in Madhya Pradesh.

L. Reddeppa is a former Professor, Council for Social Development, Southern Regional Center, Hyderabad. His areas of research include small industry and self-employment, agriculture and allied activities, school education, and the development of vulnerable groups.

Jandhyala B.G. Tilak is former Professor and Vice-Chancellor, National University for Educational Planning and Administration. He is the ICSSR National Fellow and currently Distinguished Professor, Council for Social Development, New Delhi.

Saumen Chattopadhyay is Professor School/Special Centre, Zakir Husain Centre for Educational Studies, Jawaharlal Nehru University, New Delhi. His areas of interest/specialisation include Economics of Education with special focus on education policy, governance and financing of education and public finance with focus on tax evasion and black money.

G. Haragopal is visiting Professor, National Law University, Bengaluru and formerly Professor of Political Science and Dean of School of Social Sciences, University of Hyderabad.

G. Sudarshanam, former Professor and Head, Department of Political Science, University of Hyderabad, is presently ICSSR Senior Fellow, Centre for Economic and Social Studies, Hyderabad.

Ravi Kumar is Professor in the Department of Sociology, South Asian University, New Delhi and is an Associate Editor of *Society and Culture in South Asia* (Sage) and co-edits the book series on 'Social Movements, Dissent and Transformative Action' (Routledge, Delhi).